OXFORD POLITICAL THEORY

Series Editors: Will Kymlicka, David Miller and Alan Ryan

# DEMOCRATIC AUTONOMY

# OXFORD POLITICAL THEORY

Oxford Political Theory presents the best new work in contemporary political theory. It is intended to be broad in scope, including original contributions to political philosophy, and also work in applied political theory. The series will contain works of outstanding quality with no restriction as to approach or subject matter.

OTHER TITLES IN THIS SERIES

*Justice as Impartiality*
Brian Barry

*Real Freedom from All: What (if anything) Can Justify Capitalism?*
Philippe Van Parijs

*Justificatory Liberalism: An Essay on Metaphysics and Political Theory*
Gerald F. Gaus

*The Politics of Presence: Democracy and Group Representation*
Anne Phillips

*On Nationality*
David Miller

*Multicultural Citizenship: A Liberal Theory of Minority Rights*
Will Kymlicka

*Creating Citizens: Political Education and Liberal Democracy*
Eamonn Callan

*Civic Virtues: Rights, Citizenship, and Republican Liberalism*
Richard Dagger

*Inclusion and Democracy*
Iris Marion Young

*Republicanism: A Theory of Freedom and Government*
Philip Pettit

# DEMOCRATIC AUTONOMY

## Public Reasoning about the Ends of Policy

HENRY S. RICHARDSON

OXFORD
UNIVERSITY PRESS

2002

# OXFORD
UNIVERSITY PRESS

Oxford   New York
Auckland   Bangkok   Buenos Aires   Cape Town   Chennai
Dar es Salaam   Delhi   Hong Kong   Istanbul   Karachi   Kolkata
Kuala Lumpur   Madrid   Melbourne   Mexico City   Mumbai   Nairobi
São Paulo   Shanghai   Singapore   Taipei   Tokyo   Toronto

and an associated company in Berlin

Copyright © 2002 by Oxford University Press, Inc.

Published by Oxford University Press, Inc.
198 Madison Avenue, New York, New York 10016

www.oup.com

Oxford is a registered trademark of Oxford University Press

Library of Congress Cataloging-in-Publication Data
Richardson, Henry S.
Democratic autonomy : public reasoning about the ends of policy /
by Henry S. Richardson.
p. cm—(Oxford political theory)
Includes bibliographical references.
ISBN 0-19-515090-2
1. Democracy.   2. Representative government and representation.
I. Title.   II. Series.
JC423.R485   2002
320'.6—dc21      2002020123

1 3 5 7 9 8 6 4 2

Printed in the United States of America
on acid-free paper

*For Mary*

# PREFACE

This project had its origin two decades ago in my dissatisfaction with instrumental techniques of policy analysis. Although I have never considered them invalid or useless, I was convinced that the most important deliberative work for democracies to undertake—in administrative agencies as well as in informal public fora—requires noninstrumental deliberation. To act wisely, intelligently, and democratically, we must reason together about our aims—about the final ends for the sake of which we pursue policies of any kind. In this book, I undertake to explain how we may do so.

Given the essentially constructive aims of this book, I must pass quickly over traditions of political thought and rational choice that are the subjects of entire literatures. Among my opponents, public choice theorists, game theorists, cost-benefit analysts, risk analysts, and decision theorists more generally will find me questioning some of their fundamental presuppositions, attacking their preferred conceptual primitives, and moving on to develop a constructive alternative rather than engaging with their views in detail. Among my friends and fellow travelers, many—including those who have worked on distributive justice, constitutionalism, toleration, administrative law reform, and the epistemic merits of different voting procedures—will again find that while I touch on these issues, I do not treat them in depth.

The compensation for this absence of specialized engagement will be that I integrate a compelling account of how we can deliberate about the ends of policy with a clear statement of why it is important, in a democracy, that we do so. The account of reasoning about final ends presented here builds on that defended in my first book, *Practical Reasoning about Final Ends* (Cambridge, England: Cambridge University Press, 1994), which focused on individual deliberation. While I recast many of its principal arguments here, the interested reader is referred to that book for a fuller response to philosophical arguments against the possibility of deliberating about final ends. The account of democracy I put forward here does not aim at novelty.

Rather, it aims to articulate and weave together the republican, liberal, populist, and rationalist strands of our commitment to democracy. Only once we understand how these elements coherently fit together can we rightly see both how we might structure democratic reasoning about the ends of policy and why this reasoning matters in the first place.

While this book is about processes of collaborative reasoning, it has grown up in a traditionally solitary fashion. That does not mean, however, that I have not received lots of help. I am greatly indebted to several anonymous referees. David Estlund, as one of the readers for Oxford University Press, provided detailed, constructive, and far-reaching comments. His writings on deliberative democracy have guided me in many places, and I have learned much from him in seminar settings as well. Matthew D. Adler, James Bohman, Gerald M. Mara, Cheryl J. Misak, and Mark C. Murphy each provided helpful written comments on extensive stretches of the manuscript. In addition, I have received valuable help from Bruce Ackerman, Tom L. Beauchamp, George Brenkert, Wayne Davis, David Dyzenhaus, Rainer Forst, Jody Freeman, Samuel Freeman, Stefan Gosepath, Amy Gutmann, Frances Kamm, Douglas MacLean, Betsy Postow, William Rehg, Gopal Sreenivasan, Raimo Tuomela, LeRoy Walters, Stephen M. Young, the members of two graduate seminars in deliberative democracy, and audiences at Bowling Green State University, Georgetown University, the Gesellschaft für Analytische Philosophie, St. Louis University, the University of Chicago, the University of Toronto, and the Prague Social Theory Workshop of 1995. I have received insightful advice from Dedi Felman of Oxford University Press and resourceful research assistance from Matthew McAdam. My initial work on this book was supported by a Research Fellowship from the Alexander von Humboldt Foundation, which allowed me to spend a stimulating year working with Axel Honneth in Berlin. A Senior Faculty Fellowship and two Mellon Summer grants from Georgetown University and, in 1999–2000, a Fellowship for University Teachers from the National Endowment for the Humanities allowed me to complete the penultimate draft. I am most grateful for all this support and assistance.

Small portions of this book have appeared previously. Chapter 9 is based on "The Stupidity of the Cost-Benefit Standard," *Journal of Legal Studies* 29 (2000): 135–67. Portions of chapter 12 draw on "Democratic Intentions." in *Deliberative Democracy*, edited by James Bohman and William Rehg (Cambridge: MIT Press, 1997): 349–82. I am grateful to the University of Chicago Press and to MIT Press for permission to reuse this material.

I regret that my father, Elliot L. Richardson, a consummate bureaucrat and a passionate believer in reasoned rule by the people, did not live to see this project completed. Had he been able to see its pages, he could have helped curb its academic indulgences. Both he and my mother, Anne F. Richardson, who chaired a national literacy organization, exemplified for

me what it is to be concretely committed to the public good. When I aban-
doned my professional preparation for public service, long ago, in order to
take up philosophy, my parents wanted to be reassured of only one thing:
that I still intended to serve the public good. I had to confess that such was
not my aim, for I sought instead to understand the notion of the public
good and how we might reason about it. Perhaps, though, promoting
greater clarity on these matters would be a contribution to the public good,
after all.

Such direct experience as I have had of collaborative reasoning has come
in two much smaller contexts. Ever since I arrived at Georgetown University's Philosophy Department in 1986, it has always been a remarkably
collegial group. Although I argue against unanimity criteria in the body of
this work, that is not because of any negative feelings about the remarkable
abilities of my department chair, Wayne Davis, to generate unanimity on a
reasonable basis (even though he did once ask me to explain why I had
insisted on being the lone dissenter on a particular vote). I am grateful to
my colleagues and to the department for providing a philosophically stimulating yet peaceful environment in which to work.

When I have not been totally immersed in writing this book, I have been
most actively and regularly engaged in collaborative reasoning with my
wife, Mary E. Challinor (and now also with our wonderfully thoughtful
children, Benjamin and Hope). Through this process, I have learned three
important things. The first is that it is a mistake to present one's spouse
with game-theoretic matrices to model spousal choices. The second is that—
as I argue on general grounds hereafter—collaborative reasoning depends
on some level of shared substantive commitment and caring. The third is
that mutual love really helps the reasoning go well, and helps patch things
up when it does not. This lesson is unfortunately of little use in politics,
but it is why I dedicate this book to Mary.

# CONTENTS

1. INTRODUCTION                                             3

PART ONE: WHY PUBLIC REASONING?

2. FREEDOM AND LEGITIMACY                                  23
3. THREE CONCEPTIONS OF NONARBITRARINESS                   37
4. THE CASE FOR A QUALIFIED POPULISM                       56
5. DEMOCRATIC RULE MUST BE REASONED                        73
6. EQUALITY IN A DELIBERATIVE DEMOCRACY                    85

PART TWO: THE NATURE OF PUBLIC REASONING

7. TYPES OF PRACTICAL REASONING                            97
8. THE NAIVETÉ OF AGENCY INSTRUMENTALISM                  114
9. THE STUPIDITY OF THE COST-BENEFIT STANDARD             119
10. TRUTH AND DELEGATED DELIBERATION                      130
11. DEEP COMPROMISE                                       143
12. FORGING JOINT INTENTIONS AND SHARED ENDS              162

PART THREE: INSTITUTING PUBLIC REASONING

13. THE PUBLIC                                            179
14. REPRESENTATIVE GOVERNMENT                             193
15. MAJORITY RULE AS A CLOSURE DEVICE                     203
16. DEMOCRATIC RULEMAKING                                 214

17. THE DEMOCRATIC TREATMENT OF RISK     231
18. CONCLUSION     242
    NOTES     253
    BIBLIOGRAPHY     293
    INDEX     305

# DEMOCRATIC AUTONOMY

# CHAPTER 1

## Introduction

Democracy is everywhere triumphant, yet no one truly believes in its existence. In all parts of the world, the trappings of democracy abound, yet nowhere is it credible to believe that the people rule. Because it possessed a popularly elected legislature, the Soviet Union in its heyday proclaimed itself a democracy. Rightly, no one believed that claim. Today, while the leading nations of the world can with somewhat more justice claim to be democracies—affording freedom, as most of them do, for multiple political parties in addition to popularly elected legislatures—still the claim that the people rule rings hollow. A politician all too often seems a member of an alien breed, not "one of us." Instead of ruling ourselves, it is thought, we are ruled by politicians, bureaucrats, and the special interests that hold the politicians and bureaucrats captive. Conversely, those suspicious of officials sometimes suppose that as long as "we" control them, perhaps by being able to "vote the bastards out," that is all we can hope for from democracy.[1] Yet, as I will show, there is serious question as to who "we" are in that formulation. "We" are certainly not to be identified with the majority in a given election.

However one conceptualizes democracy, it is plain that bureaucracy poses a threat to it. The policy-making power held by officials in the large and complicated administrative agencies that are relied on by all modern states—and by both provincial and transnational governments—is difficult to control in practice and to reconcile with our democratic ideals. Given how much discretionary decision-making power rests in executive agencies, it is everywhere a serious question whether we as citizens are subject to the kind of domination that consists in being vulnerable to the arbitrary power of others.[2]

The reasons for the existence of discretionary administrative power are various. Sometimes the discretionary power falls to bureaucrats because of a considered legislative judgment that matters of a certain kind are better left to experts at some remove from the fray of democratic politics. Central bankers making monetary policy and military officials devising procedures for peace-keeping forces fall into this category. In other cases, the discretionary power seems to arise from de facto agency expertise that simply makes itself heard. This naturally happens when the legislature has given an agency custody over something. A national park service develops expertise about the parks it administers; a small business administration develops expertise about policy pertaining to small businesses; and because these agencies possess such expertise, they gain deference for their use of discretionary power. (While I will often have recourse to examples from the United States, having less familiarity with other governments, the phenomena that concern me are, of course, found everywhere.) In a third kind of case, legislatures turn over to agencies issues they find too difficult to settle themselves. This often happens in devising social benefit programs and in regulating the environment. Note that these are all potentially *good* reasons for the existence of administrative discretion, monetary and military policy might *need* to be insulated from partisan politics; custody over public goods might generate *appropriate* claims to expertise; and the difficulty of working out compromises in detail in the legislature might *justify* leaving the details to be settled by some relevant agency. Yet these reasons all point as well to powerful empirical forces that have made the delegation of power to administrative agencies a central fact of all modern governments. I will examine the normative weight of these reasons in due course. For now, the point is just that for these and other reasons, discretionary administrative power is an apparently permanent feature of modern governments, including purportedly democratic ones.

We must worry whether the broad discretionary power that resides in administrative hands will be used arbitrarily. When it is, then administrative power gives rise to an illegitimate kind of domination, independently of whether the legislature is democratically controlled. This kind of nondemocratic domination plainly coexists with a democratically elected legislature when that legislature lacks effective legal tools to control what the administrative agencies do. For such a case, we need not travel as far as the world of Franz Kafka, in which officials act on the basis of no discernible public rules whatsoever. Instead, bureaucrats may indeed rule by means of general policies that are well promulgated but beyond the influence of the democratically elected legislature. Then, too, their influence will be arbitrary in the relevant sense: arbitrary not because, like the rulings of K.'s judge in *The Trial*, their shape and rationale are utterly mysterious but because they do not bear an appropriate connection to "the welfare and world-view of the public."[3] This kind of arbitrary and antidemocratic bureaucratic domination, existing alongside a veneer of democratic institutions, is no mere fiction. Consider the following description of Peru in 1990. "Peru is considered a democracy because it elects a president and a parliament. In the five years after an election, though, the executive branch has been known to make 134,000 rules and decrees with no accountability to the congress or the public. After elections, no ongoing relationship exists between those who make decisions and those who live under them,"[4] Where such a description holds true, domination of the citizens by the officials makes a mockery of democracy.

"That is indeed a problem in emerging democracies," those of you who reside in the advanced or established democracies (whichever those are) may be thinking, "but we have well-developed legal mechanisms for assuring that administrative discretion is kept within bounds. These are sufficient to assure that bureaucratic power is exercised neither mysteriously, as in Kafka's world, nor arbitrarily with respect to the views of the citizens, but in a way that respects the will of the democratic legislature. These mechanisms take different forms: In the United States, they are largely statutory. In particular, the Administrative Procedures Act of 1946 details public notice and comment procedures through which must pass almost all administrative policies that apply directly to the public (as opposed to the government's own actions in implementing monetary policy or directing its soldiers) and that have the force of law (unlike informal directives). In Germany, the federal constitution steps in, requiring that any administrative rules have a definite and substantive basis in the legislation that authorizes them.* In these various ways, the rule of law keeps the exercise of administrative discretion within bounds—specifically within the bounds set by the legislative will."

This response, which views the problem of administrative discretion as a serious threat only in "emerging" democracies that have not fully established the rule of law, is overly smug. It is true that legal devices of the kinds mentioned—rulemaking procedures that openly invite the public to comment and requirements that legislation be relatively definite—mark a true advance over unconstrained agency rulemaking, just as agency rulemaking of any kind marks a true advance over Kafkaesque caprice. Yet these procedural devices do not suffice to exclude the arbitrary exercise of governmental power. To illustrate just how much scope for agency discretion is left, even within the use of such legal devices, I will describe a pair of cases from U.S. social policy.[5]

---

* While a vaguer provision of the U.S. Constitution vesting "legislative" power solely in the Congress (art. 1, sec. 1) had been taken to prohibit delegation of "legislative" power, the so-called "non-delegation doctrine" has been largely vitiated by recent Supreme Court decisions. See David Epstein and Sharyn O'Halloran *Delegating Powers: A Transaction Cost Politics Approach to Policy Making under Separate Powers* (Cambridge, England: Cambridge University Press, 1999), 19–20.

In 1972, the U.S. Congress was debating the Supplemental Security Income (SSI) proposal, which was aimed at helping poor people who are elderly, blind, or disabled.[6] As originally formulated, the bill applied only to adults. While the bill was in committee, a senior official in one of the federal human welfare agencies inserted the following twenty-six-word parenthesis into the 697-page bill: "(or, in the case of a child under the age of 18, if he suffers from any medically determinable physical or mental impairment of comparable severity)." The official who inserted these words has since acknowledged that he kept this brief and cryptic in the hopes that it would get through the Congress without much notice. It did. Although the House version of the bill contained the provision and the Senate version did not, the provision was in the end retained without any serious debate or any discussion of the additional cost involved in extending SSI benefits to children. As of 1991, the costs of extending disability payments to children ran to over $3 billion a year.

It is astonishing that such a large-scale program could have been established without any serious democratic discussion. Even more surprising is the fact that, because of inherent differences between adults and children, the twenty-six-word addition left almost completely undetermined what should count as a "disability" in a child. Since the act defined adult disability largely in terms of inability to "engage in any substantial gainful activity," its explicit standards were hardly applicable to children. It was left to the agencies to determine what would count as "disability" in a child.[7]

The Administrative Procedures Act requires that such agency determinations themselves take the form of promulgated law. Accordingly, in the area of disability payments, as well as in more classical domains of "regulation," federal agencies must write "regulations" that set out how they plan to interpret and administer the laws. After giving the public ninety days to comment on the proposed regulations, often in the forum of a hearing run by the rule-writing agency, these regulations become law and are published in the Code of Federal Regulations (C.F.R.). In the case of SSI payments for children with disabilities, it required forty thousand words in the C.F.R. to give some determinacy to the twenty-six little words that had been slipped into the statute and slid through Congress. A major new program had been enacted without any democratic deliberation and took determinate shape only because of the work of unelected regulation-writers in the executive agencies.

The worry that I am raising has little to do with taking sides on an issue such as this: It is a structural issue going to the heart of democratic legitimacy. By 1996, sufficient reaction had developed against the program's size and its alleged susceptibility to abuse that Congress tightened the standards of disability. At that point, advocates for children and the disabled credibly complained that the new rules written to implement the new legislation were even more restrictive than what these laws called for.[8]

Although the degree of legislative thoughtlessness, unexpected expense, and statutory indeterminacy in this case are extreme, none of these phenomena are rare. Famous instances in the United States have arisen in the context of the Clean Air Act amendments and occupational safety regulations. An additional dramatic U.S. example—one to which I will recur—concerns the case of vague statutes passed by Congress in the last few decades demanding that localities make "special efforts" to make transportation available to the disabled. The statutes did not define what was meant by "special efforts," leaving it to the agencies and the courts to attempt to sort this out. The statutes did not define "making transportation available," either, throwing the agencies into a major political controversy about whether to insist on adapting existing means of mass transportation to make them accessible to the disabled or instead to opt for providing specially tailored means of transportation that were potentially more cost-effective at "providing transportation."

Cases such as these illustrate the distance between formally assuring that agencies comply with the rule of law and with the directives of a democratic legislature and really making sure that they do not exercise arbitrary power, power that does not appropriately track the interests, views, or will of the citizens. Since these cases arose in a legal context that required fidelity to statutory law and public promulgation of agency policies, they represent instances of apparent arbitrariness that these means failed to prevent. Agency and executive discretion directly invited by the legislature (as in monetary and military policy) or otherwise unconstrained by the process of public rulemaking is in all the more danger of being arbitrary. This book will concentrate on cases in which rulemaking occurs; but we must keep in mind that these may just be the easiest cases of administrative discretion to bring under democratic control.

My purpose in focusing on these dramatic cases of administrative discretion is not to lament its existence or to call for its removal but simply to focus attention upon it. Although I will be arguing that statutes ought to meet minimal constraints against vagueness, these will not rule out broad delegations of power to the agencies. A book dealing more with the substance of policy in some jurisdiction or other might well focus on the question whether it allowed for too much, or too little, delegation to administrative agencies.[9] Here, my point is a broader one: Some considerable administrative discretion is not only inevitable but also (for republican reasons) to be welcomed. Democratic theory, therefore, must face up to this fact by considering how bureaucratic domination can be avoided and whether this sort of discretion is compatible with rule by the people.

Which exercises of administrative discretion one takes to be heinous abuses of public power will depend on one's political position. Where administrative power is as unconstrained as it had been in Peru, democracy can be wholly subverted by military or economic elites, resulting in crimes of all kinds against the weak. Even under the protection of procedures of public notice and comment, however, administrative rulemaking is easily hijacked by powerful interests.[10] The threat of bureaucratic domination, then, is a major political problem. It also poses a serious difficulty for normative political theory, for it unsettles our understanding of democracy. This theoretical problem is also a political one, however, for insofar as we remain hazy about what the ideal of democracy requires of us, we will also remain ill prepared to protect and defend it.

## A Relatively New Focus for Democratic Theory

Concern about bureaucratic domination undermining democracy is a newer worry than those chestnuts of democratic theory, the tyranny of the majority and the antimajoritarian power of a constitutional court such as the U.S. Supreme Court. This is not to say that the first is a wholly novel concern. The last century saw tremendous growth in the social welfare, regulatory, and military bureaucracies in many parts of the world. There has been ample time for the worry to be articulated.[11] Yet it remains the case that democratic theory has not fully assimilated the import of this newer challenge.

Before setting out to address the problem posed by the threat of bureaucratic domination, I should indicate in a preliminary way how I see my approach to this newer question relating to the older issues of majority tyranny and countermajoritarian courts. While some of what I now have to say will depend on points developed more fully in later chapters, this discussion will at least situate my task in relation to these more traditional difficulties. I will suggest that fully recognizing the threat that bureaucratic domination poses to democracy tends to blunt the force of the two more traditional concerns. Nonetheless, the difficulties they raise are real and important.

The worry about countermajoritarian courts presumes that the majority ought to rule. Presumably, in a modern state, it will do so via an elected legislature. When constitutional courts invalidate laws passed by democratic assemblies, therefore, they appear to be going against the expressed will of the people. How can that be just?

Traditional answers to this question have come from liberal and republican directions. According to the liberal response, individuals have fundamental rights and liberties that are often threatened by governmental action.

A central function of constitutions is to protect those rights and liberties from infringement by majorities, especially shifting and opportunistic ones. But is judicial review, which potentially invalidates majority-enacted laws, a necessary or even an especially effective means of protecting such rights? This is an empirical question and is open to debate.[12] Some attribute a recent tendency to give an affirmative a priori answer to liberals' satisfaction with the U.S. Supreme Court under Earl Warren.[13] Whatever the right answer to this set of empirical questions may be, however, we may certainly recognize that if judicial review is, in fact, an essential means of protecting important individual rights, then it is probably just even though it does constrain democratic majorities.

A second traditional defense of judicial review focuses less on individual rights and more on the danger that unconstrained power, in anyone's hands, poses to individual freedom: This is the republican strand. On a republican view, absolute monarchy is objectionable first and foremost because it lodges unconstrained and arbitrary power in one individual who stands entirely above the law. Limited monarchy is slightly better but still leaves too much opportunity for the monarch to dominate his or her subjects. Yet, as Locke observed, it would be irrational to reject an arbitrary, unconstrained monarchy in favor of an arbitrary, unconstrained assembly.[14] From the republican point of view, then, judicial review represents less a bulwark for the protection of certain listed rights than a means of dispersing power and hence checking the concentration of arbitrary power in anyone's hands.[15] For the republican, avoiding majority tyranny or domination is a compelling reason for instituting a strong judiciary.

Bringing the worry about bureaucratic domination into the center of the picture shifts the perspective dramatically. When the bureaucratic apparatus takes the foreground, we cannot escape seeing that "ruling" any sizable polity—whether that of a monarch or a legislative assembly—is something not effectively done without the cooperation of a broad array of officials, including both administrators and judges. As Max Weber noted, bureaucratic organization seems to have been essential to the stability of the irrigation-based empire of the ancient Mesopotamians and that of the more trade-based Egyptians—a mode of organization facilitated by lines of communication along canal and river.[16] While rule can be carried out by structures that are less regular and hierarchical than the bureaucracies Weber analyzed, it cannot be effective without the cooperation of many, via procedures that are somehow institutionalized. In building their case against absolute monarchy, seventeenth- and eighteenth-century republicans understandably understated the degree to which the monarchs could rule without depending on ministries and courts, on administrative and judicial bureaucracies. Hence the polemics of these early republicans may accidentally have encouraged the thought that democratic control could step into the place of the monarch and itself become absolute or total. To refocus on administrative discretion, however, is to notice that, in any large jurisdiction, no one's effective power is absolute.[17] Even a ministry handed specific directives to implement can still sit on its hands.

More generally, focusing on the issue of administrative discretion brings out the fact that what we are concerned with, in normative political theory, is how the effective law of some jurisdiction is being made.[18] The reason our normative concern takes this form and not simply that of an inquiry into how power is centrally exercised somewhere or other is that we subscribe to the general ideal of the rule of law. This ideal (explored more fully in chapter 16) implies that the legitimate exercise of any governmental power works via laws that are regular, are general, and afford a basis for predictability. Hence we may set aside as obviously illegitimate the possibility of rulers or their officials operating wholly without rules and think about what is required to make effective law legitimately. As soon as the question is thus posed, it immediately becomes obvious that an institutionalized system of elaborating and interpreting the laws is a necessary part of bringing them to bear on citizens' lives in a legitimate way.

From this perspective, both administrative agencies and a judiciary are necessary handmaidens to the legislature's power, as well as potential traitors to it. Indeed, bureaucracy and the rule of law are partially reciprocal ideas. Bureaucracy provides a natural means of implementing the rule of law as opposed to rule via the nobility, while a regular legal system seems necessary to instituting bureaucratic authority. Because of this link, modern bureaucracies historically arose in support of large-scale democracy. As Weber succinctly put it,

> bureaucracy inevitably accompanies modern *mass democracy* in contrast to the democratic self-government of small homogeneous units. This results from the characteristic principle of bureaucracy: the abstract regularity of the execution of authority, which is a result of the demand for "equality before the law" in the personal and functional sense—hence, of the horror of "privilege" and the principled rejection of doing business "from case to case."[19]

For this reason, reliance on administrative officials and on the courts appears to be a necessary means to the legitimate exercise of power, most especially democratic power.

Reinforcing this shift of perspective is a corollary of an effective system of law, namely its settled jurisdiction. Once we are talking about what it takes to make effective law, we must ask what we take the scope of its potential jurisdiction to be. In federal systems, such as the United States, Germany, Mexico, Switzerland, or the European Community, characterizing jurisdictional boundaries and overlaps is a complicated matter. As time goes by, national boundaries have been diminishing in importance as jurisdictional barriers. Incidentally, while the U.S. national government provides my most frequent model in this work, all that I really suppose is that we are talking about the democratic governance of some settled jurisdiction or other, be that subnational, national, or international. I leave it to others to work out how best to elaborate the issues and views about democratic reasoning set forward here for cases in which jurisdictions stably overlap or dynamically undergo fissure or merger.

Returning to the countermajoritarian difficulty, the new perspective that results from focusing on the threat of bureaucratic domination suggests that the problem is often ill posed. In general terms, a constitution is a fundamental law, explicit or implicit, that settles basic issues of jurisdiction and articulates the structures wherein law can be made, elaborated, and implemented. So understood, a constitution is a precondition of the effective rule of law and thereby of a legitimate large-scale democracy. When it invalidates legislatively enacted laws that it uncorruptly takes to offend against the constitution, thus understood—say because the law oversteps the authority or jurisdiction granted to the government or to its legislative branch—the judiciary is thus engaged in maintaining the integrity of the system whose democracy is in question. This is not to say that one should not be worried about the potentially antidemocratic power of constitutional courts, especially those empowered to nullify democratic legislation; but it is to point out that constitutional courts are an essential, if two-edged, tool of democracy. Accordingly, constitutional constraint of a legislative assembly's decision-making is less external to democracy than the traditional concern with the countermajoritarian difficulty supposes.

You may object that the protection of individual rights, as in the U.S. Bill of Rights, reflects a quite different kind of consideration than do the constitutional provisions allocating powers to the national government and to its legislative, executive, and judicial branches. That is correct, and highlights the importance of the liberal response to the countermajoritarian difficulty. Indeed, I believe that there are deep truths in both the liberal and the republican responses to the difficulty. What I seek to show in part I, however, is that the liberal's and the republican's fundamental ideals are not opposed to those of democracy, as these responses make it seem. To the contrary, I will argue, liberal and republican ideals instead stand behind our commitment to democracy and shape its very meaning. In invoking those ideals, therefore, one is not so much revealing the limitations of democracy as articulating its meaning more deeply.

In saying this, I am implying that it is a mistake to identify democracy with a simple idea of majoritarianism. That this is an error can be seen by examining the traditional worry about tyranny of the majority. Of the many forms this protean worry takes, I am more interested in that expressed in the context of institutional design by James Madison than in the broader cultural diagnosis offered by Alexis de Tocqueville. I will first discuss Madison's classical formulation of the problem and then turn to its revival in the so-called public choice theory of James Buchanan.

Madison framed *Federalist* 10 around the danger under popular governments, that "the public good is disregarded in the conflict of rival parties, and that measures are too often decided, not according to the rules of justice and the rights of the minor party, but by the superior force of an interested and overbearing majority."[20] Notice several aspects of Madison's formulation. First, he here sounds both the concern about arbitrary power not appropriately linked to the public good that I have identified as republican and the concern for individual rights that I have identified as liberal. Second, he speaks of the public good as an apt object of potential knowledge, as something that can be either taken account of or ignored, and as an object conceptually distinct from the sum or aggregate of the good of individuals. In so doing, he introduces into his account of democracy a rationalist strand that I will retain and to which I will return in chapter 5. Finally, he thinks of the problem of majority tyranny in conjunction with a more general problem that preoccupied the Federalists, that of unruly, interested factions.

Since I have already treated the liberal and republican themes in discussing the countermajoritarian difficulty, I can be even briefer with them here. The shift in perspective that arises from thinking about administrative discretion and hence about the bureaucratic-*cum*-judicial apparatus necessary to give effective force to laws in a good-sized democracy, works a similar effect here. The principal institutional solution to the problem of potential majority tyranny put forward by Madison and the Federalists involved the dispersal and division of power. If democracy is thought of naively, perhaps on the model of the Athenian city-state, such devices can seem alien to it. If instead we think realistically about what is required to give effect to law in modern democratic states, this "dispersal" will, in general, seem simply a necessary concomitant of viable democracy. Yes, a system of checks and balances provides a safeguard against the exercise of arbitrary power by any one branch of government and so serves a distinctively republican aim; but we must understand this fact against the background of the inevitability of dispersed power. In the example of Peru in the 1990s, it is apparent how easy it is for such dispersal of power to be carried so far that the will of a democratic legislature is largely stymied by overly independent agencies. Much harder to imagine is that a legislature could rule without at least de facto dependence on agencies and the courts. What the Federalists pioneered was not the use of dispersed power but the argument to the effect that the dispersal of power helps prevent democratic majorities from themselves becoming agents of domination.

The second principal plank in Madison's response to the danger of over-bearing majorities and unruly factions involves an even more stunning re-evaluation. I refer to his treatment of the issue of size.[21] Prior to Madison, democracy had been thought of mainly on the model of the ancient city-states that enjoyed popular rule. On this ancient conception, face-to-face discussion and direct democratic rule was the norm. Understanding de-mocracy along these lines as a government in the hands of the majority of the people, Rousseau was no promoter of it and held that it was even pos-sible only in "a very small State, where the people can readily be got to-gether and where each citizen can with ease know all the rest."[22] Size thus loomed as an obstacle and a problem for promoters of democracy. Madi-son's reversal arose from his insight that size can provide a natural basis for mitigating the danger of disruptive factions. Thus, the second plank of his solution to the problem of majority tyranny was that a large society may depend on "comprehending [within it] so many separate descriptions of citizens as will render an unjust combination of a majority of the whole very improbable, if not impracticable."[23] Plainly enough, the larger the so-ciety is, the more applicable will be this approach to minimizing the poten-tially deleterious influence of factional interests.

The soundness of Madison's response to the worry about arbitrary or tyrannical majorities depends crucially on his cognitivist and not reductively individualist conception of the public good. If we ask how multiplication of factions will help mitigate the danger of factionalism, on the basis he proposes, the answer must have something to do with the contrast he has in mind between proposals in the public interest and those that merely serve the private interests of some faction. Where a lot of factions jockey for advantage, their attempts to secure private gain will to some extent cancel out, leaving standing the influence of something else, namely discussion oriented toward the public good.

The problem of majority tyranny looms larger in views that recognize no such cognitive object as the public good, as something independent of an aggregation of individuals' goods. An influential example of such a view is the public choice theory championed by James Buchanan and given its first full articulation in his 1962, book written with Gordon Tullock, *The Calculus of Consent.* Buchanan and Tullock eschew "the grail-like search for some 'public interest' apart from, and independent of, the separate in-terests of the individual participants in social choice," intending instead to confine their normative basis to what follows from facts about the welfare of individuals. In order to avoid implicitly falling back into an "organic" conception of the public good or otherwise smuggling in what they would consider illicit normative assumptions about how to compare individuals' welfare, they do not countenance adding it up across individuals (as the

utilitarian standard of "the greatest good of the greatest number" demands).
Furthermore, they limit themselves to the least controversial standard that
remains once interpersonal comparability of individual utility or welfare is
given up, namely the standard of unanimity and what follows from it.[24] On
such a basis, Buchanan and Tullock constructed "an intellectual attack on
majoritarianism and majority rule ... along with a defense of republican
systems in which majorities are constrained."[25] Within their spare normative
framework, the danger of majority tyranny takes a particularly stark form.
When "public goods" in the economists' technical sense are at stake—shared
goods such as clean air and effective national defense, goods that it is not
possible to exclude anyone from enjoying—it is possible for majorities to
join together and place the burdens of financing such programs on minorities (such as the wealthy, victims of progressive taxation). When goods that
can flow to some and not to others are at stake, the danger is even more
dramatic. Majorities can combine to devote public resources to goods that
only they care about, be that maintaining hiking trails, promoting fine arts,
or building roads to certain remote areas, and place the burden of paying
for these programs either evenly on everyone (including those who do not
care about the goods in question) or again, as before, solely on the minority,
which does not care. Under either scenario, as Buchanan insists, the outcome is objectionably "discriminatory."[26]

As has already emerged in my discussion of Madison's concern with the
tyranny of the majority, republican devices such as the dispersion and separation of powers are needed; and my discussion of the danger of administrative domination strongly suggests that republicanism of this sort is not
foreign to democracy. Yet the public choice school, under Buchanan's leadership, has shifted away from an embrace of Madisonian republicanism
and—oddly enough—toward a view that has more in common with the
abstractly philosophical core of Rousseau's doctrine of the general will. Dispersal of power is insufficient to avoid the kind of exploitation of minorities
that Buchanan is concerned with, for public choice theorists emphasize that
administrative agencies, too, are subject to controlling influence by the dominant forces in society. They engage in a kind of jockeying for material
advantage—"rent-seeking behavior"—that the majority can control via its
superior aggregate command of resources.† Accordingly, Buchanan now
rests more weight on an insistence, à la Rousseau and via Friedrich Hayek,
that laws meet a strong standard of generality.

---

† Countering this concern from within the public choice framework, Geoffrey Brennan
and Alan Hamlin, *Democratic Devices and Desires* (Cambridge, England: Cambridge University Press, 2000), observe that the seeking of advantage or "rent" is thought to turn out all
right in the market.

The proper principle for politics is that of generalization or generality. This standard is met when political actions apply to all persons independently of membership in a dominant coalition or an effective interest group. The generality principle is violated to the extent that political action is overtly discriminatory in the sense that the effects, positive or negative, depend on personalized identification.[27]

Although sometimes described as a possible constitutional constraint, this generality principle is clearly framed more along the lines of a philosophical principle than as a concrete suggestion for institutional design. In chapter 3, I will argue that the generality principle cannot do the work that Buchanan invokes it for, that of eliminating what he calls "discrimination."

Here it is worth noting that the individualist assumptions of the public choice framework have been modified to generate a powerful way of reinforcing Madison's conclusion that size is a friend of democracy. Assumptions about individual rationality such as those from which Buchanan begins make it puzzling why it is that individuals should bother to vote at all. The problem arises not because the individualism carries with it a further assumption of self-centeredness or lack of caring about social issues but rather because a rational individual, seeking to promote the satisfaction of his or her interests, which may or may not include social concerns, will realize that his or her single vote is so unlikely to tip the balance of an election that it is not worth making the trip to the polling place. Hence it becomes a puzzle why so many people vote. To explain the phenomenon and provide a richer account of human rationality as a basis for a normative theory of politics, Geoffrey Brennan and Loren Lomasky have suggested, we need to see voting behavior not as a way of attempting to secure an outcome but as a kind of behavior that expresses one's value commitments.[28] This richer account of human motivation offers an empirically and normatively attractive approach. It is empirically attractive because it can explain voting behavior, and it is normatively attractive because it makes a place for value commitments that we hold dear and that are otherwise apt to be ignored by individualist models—though Brennan is careful not to romanticize the idea of expressing value commitments, noting that these can be racist, reactionary, or otherwise nasty.[29] In broad outline, I agree that voting should be understood along expressivist lines, and I will develop a kind of expressivist account in chapter 12. Here, the point is just that expressive voting *depends* on the large size of the electorate. It is only when the electorate is large that instrumental concerns will rationally recede and allow expressive voting to come to the fore. As the size of a voting body decreases—approaching, say, the size of a typical legislative assembly—instrumentally or strategically motivated voting starts again to become rational and may displace expressive voting. Hence getting citizens to vote on the basis of their conception of the public good may actually require a large polity.

From the perspective introduced by focusing on the problem of administrative discretion, then, traditional discussions of judicial review and tyranny of the majority can be seen to introduce valuable concerns but in a way that rather oddly proceeds as if we were not talking about the governance of large-scale societies. Both of these debates grapple with appropriately relating the ideal of democracy to valid republican concerns about the arbitrary use of power and liberal concerns about the protection of fundamental rights and freedoms. These concerns provide a sound basis for accepting the republican device of the separation of powers and the liberal device of constitutionalism. Perhaps still carrying the stamp of their origin in eighteenth-century polemics against monarchy, however, these issues are typically framed in a way that tends to abstract from the facts from which the problem of bureaucratic domination begins: (1) that legitimate rule is a matter of making law effective in some jurisdiction or other; (2) that a constitution, implicit or explicit, is necessary to giving shape to any process of making law; (3) that a bureaucratic apparatus is required in order to elaborate and implement the law in any large-scale society, democratic or not; and (4) that power to shape the law is thus inevitably dispersed over some relatively complex set of institutions. From these facts it follows that the traditional concerns with judicial review and majority tyranny are often overstated. Constraint by some constitutional system is inevitable, as is some check on majority decision flowing from the dispersal of power. From the same facts it also follows that the problem of administrative discretion, taken broadly as the problem of reconciling the discretionary power of the parts of this apparatus not directly subject to democratic control, inevitably arises for any large-scale democracy.

In this era of globalization, to call for a return to no government except that by small city-states and rural communes would be to spit into the wind. As Weber noted, possibilities for centralized control follow lines of potential communication; and broadband connections now link us all. Compelling reasons of coordination combine with irresistible temptations for exercising control to make it inevitable that these possibilities will be exploited. Politics being the art of the possible, normative political theory appropriately takes on board such basic facts about the possibilities for political organization. Our utopias must at least be realistic, as Rawls puts it.[30]

There remains a more realistic way to obtain the benefits of the scale of a Vermont or an Uttar Pradesh, small in relation to their nations. This would be to decentralize power and authority to the smaller units within a federal system. Within limits, and with respect to certain issues, that is certainly a good idea. Again, though, since I am abstracting altogether from questions of federalism—having no new insights to offer on the subject— I leave it to others to articulate the case for decentralization within a federal system.

# The Structure of the Argument

This discussion of the problems of judicial review and tyranny of the majority has proceeded as if we knew what democracy requires; and in a sense, we do. Pointing out the scale of modern democracies and the inevitable scope of their administrative apparatus, however, has an unsettling effect. Older conceptions of democracy often did presuppose a small electorate and abstract from questions of administration. Accordingly, if we wish to face the problem posed by the threat of bureaucratic domination, we will have work to do in restating the ideal of democracy appropriately.

In this book, I will begin by developing an interpretation of the ideal of democracy, one suited to addressing the problem of potential bureaucratic domination. My overall aim is to develop a normative solution to this problem, a conception of public reasoning that, if it served to orient democratic policy-making, would reconcile administrative discretion with democratic control in such a way as to prevent bureaucratic power from being exercised arbitrarily.

Whether the solution I offer is an effective or attractive one depends, of course, on just how we interpret the demands of the democratic ideal. On some interpretations, democracy sets a fairly low bar. For example, some would hold that bureaucratic power is nonarbitrary and compatible with democracy just so long as the elected legislature has a chance to review agency decisions and does not object to them.[31] As I will argue, this position underestimates what democracy requires of us. To a considerable extent, then, as I elaborate for my own conception of democracy, I shall be making my own constructive task more difficult. Yet there is no gain in solving a problem simply by redefining difficulties away.

How best to interpret the ideal of democracy is an endlessly contestable question. Indeed, that it should be regarded as endlessly contestable will follow from my conclusions (in chapter 10) about how democratic reasoning ought to be understood. Still, it matters to my argument to establish a certain conception of democracy, one that unifies the liberal and republican elements that I endorsed in the previous section with populist and rationalist strands. As I see it, our ideal of democracy commits us to reasoning together, within the institutions of a liberal republic, about what we ought to do in such a way that it is plausible to say that we, the people, rule ourselves (the last is the populist demand). To be sure, it does not matter to my argument that each of these elements—republican, liberal, populist, and rationalist—be counted as constituents of the democratic ideal, so long as they are elements to which we are or ought to be committed. Still, I will argue that each ought importantly to influence how we understand what democracy requires. So as not to have to use the compound adjective "republican-liberal-populist-rationalist" every time I refer to my favored interpretation of democracy, I will instead call it the "democratic autonomy" interpretation or "democracy as democratic autonomy."[32]

The most distinctive feature of this conception of democratic autonomy is that it holds that we must reason together in order to rule ourselves. I will make the case in part I for understanding democracy this way. In part II I will then characterize, in general terms, how it is that we may reason together. In part III I pursue questions about how the resulting conception of democratic reasoning can be instituted in structures of representative government employing majority rule. Turning (still in part III) to the role of administrative agencies in institutionalizing democratic reasoning is what will finally make it possible to describe what would prevent bureaucratic domination.

My argument in part I for conceiving of democracy as democratic autonomy will have two main aspects, a value-based one and a reconstructive one. I will need, first, to bolster the importance of each of the elements—republican, liberal, populist, and rationalist—on which this conception of democracy draws by articulating the values on which each of these elements rests. This task I will accomplish in various ways, depending on the element involved. (In the case of the liberal and republican strands, I have already described some preliminary reasons for taking them seriously.) Second, I argue that each element is plausibly taken to have a home within the best interpretation of the ideal of democracy. That aspect of the argument is carried out largely by reconstructing the reasons why legitimate government must be democratic. It will turn out that each of the elements is necessary to making sense of why it is that we suppose that democracy is normatively required. Those readers (if any there be) who do not antecedently believe that governments ought to be democratic will thus be largely unmoved by that part of the argument. Still, it is my hope that even those readers may be somewhat moved by the independent support offered for the republican, liberal, populist, and rationalist ideas that, put together, make a strong case for democracy. Taking the two aspects of the argument together, my aim is to build support in both directions, providing justification for democratic autonomy by showing how it supports, and is supported by, these component ideas and the values underlying them.

The resulting conception of democracy as uniting republican, liberal, populist, and rationalist strands describes it as a mode of collectively reasoned self-rule. Reasoned self-rule—or self-rule responsive to the reasons one takes there to be—is autonomy, at least in one important sense of that protean term.[33] Collectively reasoned self-rule via democratic procedures is democratic autonomy. Hence the label "democracy as democratic autonomy."

In part II I develop an account of the type of collective reasoning required for democracy, understand as democratic autonomy, to flourish. My thesis is that democratic reasoning must be regarded primarily as truly collective reasoning about public ends, the ends of policy. It is truly collective in that it involves multiple citizens attempting to forge joint intentions that will determine institutional decisions. In the course of this collective reasoning, the participants need to be open to revising their ends on the basis of reasons. In some cases, new collective ends will be settled upon by this reasoning.

In chapter 7 I will lay out the basic distinction between instrumental reasoning and noninstrumental reasoning and recapitulate the argument I have given elsewhere for the general conclusion that we can reason about even final ends, sought for their own sakes.[34] This possibility is fundamental to the constructive conception of democracy I am offering. To reinforce this point, note the way that skepticism about collective reasoning often presumes that one cannot modify ends via reasoning. Buchanan and Tullock's classical work in public choice theory, for instance, rejects the notion of collective reasoning at the outset. While this is of course in keeping with their individualistic approach, their reasons for doing so also reflect their assumption that all practical reasoning is instrumental. They see only two possibilities for collective reasoning: It may either be the reasoning of some mysteriously organic political subject, from that subject's ends, or else it may proceed from ends that are presumed, by the political theorist, either to be held in common or to be objectively important.[35] The first possibility, they suggest—and I agree—wields and encourages a dangerous metaphysical fiction. The second possibility, they assert—and I agree—leaves "little room for the recognition that different individuals and groups seek different things through the political process."[36] Rejecting the possible uses they see for the idea of collective ends, they reject altogether any talk of the ends of policy. Crucially, though, if collective, noninstrumental reasoning is possible, then these two possibilities are not exhaustive. The important third possibility is that, reasoning with one another, we can *work out* or *settle upon* ends to seek in common. This we can do, I will argue, even if we start with quite divergent views.

My account in part II of democratic reasoning both ratchets up what is required by the rationalist strand of my interpretation of democracy and provides the key to the solution of the problem of bureaucratic domination. My principal task in part III is to explain how noninstrumental, democratic reasoning can be distributed across the legislative and administrative institutions of representative government in such a way as to satisfy the populist requirement that the people rule. Carrying out this task requires explaining how representative government is compatible with rule by the people and why the use of majority rule is not inimical to their ruling by reasoning with one another. In part III I will also have to explain the possibility of collective rational reflection, which depends on the existence of a public—

an informal institution not to be taken for granted. Once the pieces are in place, the example of risk regulation will show how collective, noninstrumental reasoning can cope with policy issues that have long been considered the province of technical, instrumental modes of analysis.

While the problem of bureaucratic domination provides a pressing motive and a salutory discipline for this reexamination of democracy, developing a compelling account of democratic reasoning is an equally important aim of this work. Theories of deliberative democracy have recently been popular. They call for us to reason with one another. Insufficient attention has yet to be paid, however, to the modes of reasoning that must be involved.[37] This book aims to rectify that neglect. In order to do so, it must first reconstruct the case for democracy in order to have a clear understanding of why it is that we must rule by reasoning with one another.

# PART I

# WHY PUBLIC REASONING?

# CHAPTER 2

# Freedom and Legitimacy

To examine the conditions of legitimate rule, we must consider the conditions of legitimate lawmaking. Presumably, lawmaking must be democratic; but I will need, over the course of the coming chapters, to articulate what conception of democracy follows from the basic normative demands we would make on politics. Only when we have firmly in view what is required of legitimate democratic government can we adequately address the challenge posed by the threat of bureaucratic domination.

We should begin by asking why political rule must meet the burden of legitimacy. The fundamental reason is that government impinges on individual freedom. In the present chapter, I will look at this question two ways. First, I will consider the basic issue of impingement and the kind of burden of legitimation it imposes. Considering the question from this point of view will suggest a basic case for democracy. Next, I will look further at a specifically republican interpretation of freedom, which points up the general significance of the danger of domination.

## The Burden of Legitimation

Government action comes under a burden of legitimation because it impinges on freedom. It does so in two ways. The liberal is rightly concerned about government action because it can undercut or violate fundamental rights. The republican is rightly concerned about government action because it can put us under new duties and may do so arbitrarily. Because of these threats to freedom, government decisions need to meet strong requirements of legitimation.

When a local shop puts shirts on sale for half price, that does not enhance my freedom. When an airline cancels a cheap fare to Orlando, that does not diminish my freedom. We interact with other persons and institutions all the time, and they shift our incentive and opportunities, both on purpose and unintentionally, all the time. Although the result is that we are faced with a different set of feasible options from what we otherwise would have had—sometimes greater, sometimes smaller, and sometimes incomparable in size—still, such simple shifts in everyday interaction do not, as such, enhance or limit our freedom. While the examples seem trivial, the underlying point is not. These cases point up the difficulty of building a useful interpretation of freedom on the basis of an overly simple notion of noninterference. It would extend the term beyond usefulness to regard individuals' freedom as shifting in extent with every change in the set of options available to them.

Freedom is implicated when changes in options significantly impinge on what individuals are permitted or required to do. Hence freedom starts off as a normative notion. For convenience of exposition, I will divide freedom into two aspects, corresponding to the republican and liberal strands of political theory mentioned in the introduction.

One way that the actions of others can seriously impinge on what one is permitted to do is that they can do things that either support or undercut one's rights. Consider a shopping mall that is the main gathering place for a suburban town's people. If the shopping mall operator bans leafleting within the mall, that impinges on the right to free speech of the people there. Because this restriction impinges on a fundamental liberal right, we may say that it undercuts freedom. Again, if a private hospital makes space available for an ecumenical chapel, that action enhances the freedom of religion of its patients. Because this enhancement supports a fundamental liberal right, we may say that it enhances freedom. Specifying liberal freedoms thus depends on specifying a list or theory of fundamental rights.

The second way that the actions of others can impinge on what one is permitted to do is that they can put one under—or release one from—duties.* Not all such actions are of the relevant kind. Someone who does me a great favor puts me under a duty of gratitude but does not obviously thereby diminish my freedom. An intention to put one under a duty seems to be a necessary aspect of affecting freedom in this way. More important for my purposes, an intention to do so is not enough. A stranger who walks up to me on the street and says, "You are hereby obligated to pay me a thousand dollars" is merely being ridiculous. If an intention to put someone under a new duty (or to release someone from a duty) is necessary, but not

---

* While it sounds, to my ear, somewhat more natural to say that one is "put under an obligation" or "obligated" than to say that one is "put under a duty," it is common among philosophers to limit the term "obligation" to duties that are voluntarily entered into; and that is emphatically not what I am discussing. That said, I will not always avoid the cognates of "obligation."

sufficient, to impinging on their freedom in this second way, what else is required?

Thinking of the case of government, we see that actions can impinge on freedom in this second way even if they do not, in fact, succeed in imposing a new duty on someone. Precisely how this can happen depends on the nature of the relationship between law and morality, a question I have no ambition to try to settle or even to clarify here. Thus, suppose that one holds a "natural law" position according to which the law cannot diverge from morality. That by itself does not entail that no new duties can be imposed. Indeed, Aquinas's classic statement of the relation between the natural law and the civil law assumes that different civil regimes will specify the natural law differently, filling out the bare bones of natural duty with compatible, but more specific, elaborations of legal duty.[1] But the natural law theorist holds that legislation that is contrary to morality, or to the natural law, makes no true law. Still, the legislation may purport to make law and hence purport to lay a duty on the citizens. On a positivist understanding of the relation between law and morality, things will look different. If, as a positivist holds, law and morality are not essentially linked, then valid law can depart from morality; even so, lawmakers can fail to put citizens under legal obligation. For instance, prior to and independent of any court's ruling, we might want to say that an obviously unconstitutional law does not actually impose any legal duty on citizens. Still, again, the lawmakers are purporting to put citizens under new duties by enacting the legislation. On either understanding, an invalid law can limit freedom. A law that is invalid because (on the natural law conception) it violates fundamental human rights or because (on a positivist conception) it violates basic constitutional provisions is clearly no less threat to freedom just because it is invalid.

What impinges on freedom in the second way, then, are actions that seriously purport to put individuals under new duties. Actions can seriously purport to do so only when they are actions of a general kind that normally does succeed in putting people under new duties. In addition, of course, the idea of purporting to put someone under a duty picks up the requirement of intention, for one cannot unintentionally purport to do something.

Governments' enactments with some color of legitimacy seriously purport to put individuals under new duties. A tyrannical government may so obviously lack legality or so obviously violate morality that it cannot seriously purport to generate duties. Such an unjust government will presumably impinge on freedom in the first way, by undercutting and violating individuals' fundamental rights. A government that meets basic requirements of legality and justice, however, will make a serious claim to generating new duties with its enactments. Hence the governments that I am concerned with—those democracies that are candidates for legitimate governments—will also impinge on freedom in the second way.

Placing its citizens under new (legal) duties is an essential role of governments. We want government to impinge on freedom by putting us under duties we would not otherwise have. We need government (1) to coordinate our actions (on the roadways or the internet); (2) to resolve certain collective-action problems (in controlling arms races or environmental degradation), and (3) to enable us to achieve certain ends together that we cannot feasibly achieve through private action (exploring outer space or catching and punishing violent criminals). In each of these modes, our government, when it acts legitimately, or as a form of authority, typically puts us under duties that would not otherwise apply to us.[2] The explanation of this possibility is different for each of the three roles of government just mentioned: (1) coordination problems often involve a kind of indeterminacy that leaves room for settling matters conventionally (as when a nation adopts a standard electric socket); (2) collective-action problems often involve a standoff in which the collective imposition of a duty is necessary to avoiding a bad result for each; and (3) the achievement of joint projects requires settling joint aims in ways that (as I will argue in chapter 12) can give rise to new duties and obligations. In each of these three ways, government can put us under duties. It typically does so—and generally ought to do so—by means of the law (on which more in chapter 14). I do not mean to imply that all that government does is to impose duties; but it is this feature of government that directly restricts individuals' freedom of action, understood normatively.

In sum, governments are under a special burden of legitimacy because they impinge on freedom in two different ways. First, government actions run the risk of undercutting and violating fundamental individual rights. Second, government actions often seriously purport to put individuals under new duties. Further, these categories are not entirely independent: While it is possible for governments to undercut fundamental rights by offering differential incentives, say by offering tax breaks only to observant Christians, many of the most worrisome violations of individual rights occur when governments impose requirements on citizens. On account of both these ways that government impinges on freedom, then, and on account of their intersection, government actions must meet a strong burden of legitimacy.†

---

† Of course, it is not only governments that can impinge on freedoms in these ways. Corporations and other institutions can violate individual rights, for example by discriminating; and they can also seriously purport to put individuals, such as their employees, under new duties. Compare the case of a department putting a student under a duty to pass a language exam, in Christine M. Korsgaard *The Sources of Normativity* (Cambridge, England: Cambridge University Press, 1996), 26.

This conclusion is important to my case for democracy as democratic autonomy in two ways. First, in conjunction with some simple liberal premises, it directly gives rise to what we might call "the basic case" for democracy. In this way, it sets us on the road of uncovering the value commitments involved in an attachment to democracy. Second, it provides an initial orientation to the republican concern with domination. Each of these ways of following up on the importance to democracy of freedom draw on the thought that power ought not to be employed arbitrarily. I turn first to the basic case for democracy, which builds directly from this requirement that power not be arbitrarily used to impose duties on citizens.

## The Basic Case for Democracy

The ideas, here, are simple and familiar, and I can be brief. My aim in this section is to sketch a basic argument for democracy that, though it will ultimately prove to be incomplete, will uncover some of what legitimate democracy requires and why. The argument invokes two values: freedom (of the two types distinguished in the last section) and equality (of a kind fundamental to conceptions of liberal democracy).

Because of the two ways that government action impinges on freedom, governments stand under a burden to justify or legitimate their actions. To justify or legitimate anything requires offering reasons in favor of it. Government action without any reasons in support of it is arbitrary in an elemental sense, epitomized by the arbitrariness of K.'s judge in *The Trial*. While the following chapter is devoted to honing a more precise interpretation of arbitrariness particularly suited to filling out the republican idea of domination, this elemental sense of arbitrary action is common currency among a wide range of views. The burden of legitimation entails that governments must not act in an elementally arbitrary way but must instead offer reasons for their actions. That government decisions must be made on the basis of reasons is the first premise of the basic case for democracy. Since both the liberal and republican aspects of freedom that are impinged on are individualistic—pertaining, respectively, to the rights and the duties of individuals—an appropriate set of legitimating reasons must be addressed to, or must pertain to, the individuals impinged on.

The second premise of the basic case is a premise of equality that constrains what can count as an appropriate set of legitimating reasons. As with arbitrariness, political equality has both elemental and richer meanings. Chapter 6 is devoted to giving an interpretation of the requirements of political equality that fits the theory of democracy I will be developing. The basic case for democracy depends only on an elemental interpretation of equality.

The elemental ideal of political equality requires that, in developing reasons to impose one set of duties or laws rather than another, government must be structured so as to give equal consideration, or "equal concern and respect," to each citizen.[3] While it is of course disputed how the requirement of equal concern and respect ought positively to be interpreted, that there is such a requirement is common ground among almost all contemporary political theorists.[4] In chapter 4 I turn to its positive implications. For the basic case, its negative implications suffice. These are clear. The elemental negative requirement of treating citizens with equal concern and respect implies that citizens of no class may be treated as making an inherently weaker claim on justification than citizens of any other class.

Together, these simple ideals of freedom and equality rule out some of the most significant historical alternatives to democracy. Aristocracy privileges one class of citizens over others, allowing their interests to count for more in the justification of governmental decisions. Monarchy, as historically realized, perpetrated the same injustice in a more extreme form. The basic case for democracy, then, is a case for democracy as opposed to aristocracy or monarchy. It holds that only democratic government is legitimate because only democracy appropriately institutionalizes the equal consideration of each citizen in the process of generating new duties through the establishment of laws.

Thus far, then, it is apparent that because government impinges on freedom by threatening to undercut or violate basic rights and liberties and by putting individuals under new duties, its actions face a special burden of legitimation. This means that its actions must be based on reasons. The independent ideal of elemental equality demands that in the process of developing those reasons, individuals be treated with equal concern and respect. Aristocracies and monarchies fail this requirement, while democracies can satisfy it. This basic case for democracy, though, characterizes democracy only sketchily. To begin to uncover the kind of argument that supports democracy as we know it, it is necessary to turn to a specifically republican interpretation of the value of freedom or liberty.

## Freedom as Nondomination

One reason that democratic theory has not progressed far with the problem of bureaucratic domination is that, in the view of many individualist thinkers, the ideal of freedom opposes only governmental interference. On their view, freedom calls mainly for reducing the size of the public sector. Because government regulations interfere with the scope of individual freedom, a primary political desideratum, they would say, is to reduce the scope of governmental regulation. Thus cast as an enemy to all governmental action, the idea of freedom is of little use in addressing the question of what would be required in order for governmental regulation to meet the requirements of democratic legitimacy. My aim in this section is to criticize this naive interpretation of freedom as freedom from interference and to offer support for a different interpretation of freedom as nondomination. The latter has been put forward by Philip Pettit in his masterful revival of republican ideas.[5]

Too much recent political theory, Pettit complains, has been ruled by Isaiah Berlin's dichotomy between negative and positive liberty.[6] This dichotomy, Pettit points out, not only leaves out the idea of freedom as nondomination but also indicates how to construct it. Negative liberty, on Berlin's classic formulation, is the absence of interference, while positive liberty is the presence of self-mastery. Latent in this contrast is at least one other interpretation of freedom or liberty, for the contrast between negative and positive liberty involves two logically independent distinctions: that between absence and presence and that between mastery and interference. The missing republican interpretation that Pettit supports involves the absence of mastery or domination: freedom as nondomination.[7]

Because "interference and domination are different evils," Pettit notes, "non-interference and non-domination are different ideals."[8] The idea of domination is linked to that of mastership. The case of master and slave provides a paradigm. As bad as slavery is, however, it need not involve active interference:

> I may be the slave of another . . . without actually being interfered with in any of my choices. It may just happen that my master is of a kindly and non-interfering disposition. Or it may just happen that I am cunning or fawning enough to be able to get away with doing whatever I like. I suffer domination to the extent that I have a master; I enjoy non-interference to the extent that that master fails to interfere.[9]

Conversely, interference can occur in the absence of domination. Importantly, as the republican tradition stresses, this can be the case with government; but first consider a nonpolitical case. Suppose that you have asked your friend to promise to hide your keys rather than let you drive home drunk. When the situation that you had feared comes to pass and your friend prevents you from driving, your friend has interfered with you, but—because of the conditions under which the friend does so—the friend does not exercise mastery over you. So interference can occur without mastery, just as mastery can be present without any active interference. Berlin's dichotomy contained both notions but considered mastery only on the positive side, in the case of self-mastery. Mastery by others, though, or domination, is a better focus for a theory of political freedom.

To show why, I will first review some of the deficiencies of negative liberty as a political ideal. Taken as an organizing ideal for political theory, it tends to be either crude or unjustifiably one-sided.

The ideal of negative liberty is crude when it supposes that the idea of interference can be made out without presupposing a rich set of political values. Such was the tendency of Herbert Spencer's social Darwinism, which conceived of "natural" liberty as a condition marked by absence of interference by the government.[10] Concrete cases reveal the artificiality of the picture of an uninterfered-with condition. Pettit offers two cases of acts of omission: "Consider the pharmacist who without good reason refuses to sell an urgently required medicine, or the judge who spitefully refuses to make available an established sentencing option involving community service instead of prison. Such figures should almost certainly count as interfering with those whom they hurt."[11] In an excess of charity, Pettit remarks that these sorts of case reveal how "context fixes the baseline" by reference to which we count an action as an interference. That is true, but it understates the normative weakness of the ideal of noninterference. What these cases really exemplify is how much the distinction between interference and noninterference depends on one's prior and independent ideas about who is entitled to what. This kind of normative judgment is what makes the pharmacist who withholds urgently needed medicine seem closer to the landowner who refuses to allow the shipwreck to take shelter on his land than to the corporate executive who refuses to give a poor person a job. Or consider a case of encountering a stranger in an elevator. You can see that he is on his way to a job interview, and you can also see the gob of mayonnaise on his tie. Whether telling him about it would count as interfering with him depends not just on facts about how doing so would affect the options open to him (if you tell him, he can no longer proceed in blithe ignorance of the blob) but also on a normative issue, namely whether, say, basic respect for him as a fellow human being requires filling him in.[12] In a similar fashion, whether government prohibition of sweatshop labor counts as interference depends on whether such labor conditions violate human rights.

This last link to the marketplace will lead many to countercharge that it is I who am being too crude. Government interference is to be judged against the backdrop of market interactions, and the market is a voluntary system.

Well, no, not in the relevant sense. *Once* a basic system of property rights is in place, *once* lines between free contracts and duress have been established, *once* a system for adjudicating and settling disputes about property and contract is in place, and *once* a fiscal system for paying for that system of adjudication has been established, *then* the market can be regarded as a voluntary system.‡ Each of these steps, however, involves and depends on controversial decisions about the shape of rights. Property law and contract law have no natural, undisputable content but instead reflect multiple compromises between the rights and interests of individuals and corporations, rich and poor, and so on.[13] This is the deep point in Rawls's insistence on taking "the basic structure of society"—that set of institutions that determines how, through voluntary interactions, basic rights and liberties, goods and advantages, will be distributed in society—as "the primary subject of justice."[14] Only against the background of a structure of legal institutions specifying rules of property, contract, and so on can market interactions go on; and if those background rules are themselves unjust, we can hardly expect the market interactions that go on within them to be just. From the vantage of the question of "interference," the point is that there is no market without government playing a pervasive role in settling such matters.[15]

The crudeness that pervades the political theory of negative liberty is tied, as Pettit notes, to its rejection of the traditional republican distinction between liberty and licentiousness.[16] According to this distinction, the concept of liberty is internally delimited by prior normative constraints—of natural law, natural right, or what-have-you. Licentiousness is not. Licentiousness is crimped when murder, or wanton imposition of contracts of adhesion by an agent with vastly superior bargaining power, or the uncompensated seizure of property from indigenous inhabitants is prohibited. By contrast, liberty of the kind the traditional republican is concerned to protect is not reduced by any of these prohibitions because one was never permitted to murder, exact agreements under duress, or seize property to begin with.§

In addition to being crude, political theory based on negative liberty is often one-sided. It is one-sided when it concerns itself only with interferences by government, ignoring the myriad ways that powerful individuals, institutions, and corporations can interfere with people. According to such views, the government interferes, while the economy is a zone of free interchange.

Suppose we fix an appropriate normative baseline against which to judge when someone has been interfered with. Plainly, whatever reasonable back-

---

‡ I have been concentrating on the concept of interference; but as the issue of defining duress in contract law suggests, parallel problems arise in attempting to proceed as if the concept of coercion could do the heavy lifting in political theory without leaning on an independent understanding of rights or obligations.

§ What is crude in the theory of negative liberty is not its taking licentiousness to be a form of liberty but its assumption that, as such, it ought to be protected. As Gopal Sreenivasan argues in "A Proliferation of Liberties," *Philosophy and Phenomenological Research* 63 (2001): 229–37, such matters ought not be settled by claims to monopolize the concept of liberty.

ground we fix, it will turn out to be true that one can be interfered with by kidnappers as well as tax collectors, domineering bosses as well as peremptory regulators. Of these three, the kidnappers are the ones who most clearly impose an interference in which their victims are not voluntarily complicit. As to work and taxes, some workers, such as migrant farm workers, may have as little effective choice whether to accept employment as citizens in general have whether to pay taxes in a democratic regime. In both contexts, just because one has voluntarily entered into a regime—of work or of taxation—does not mean that one has consented to whatever those in power within that regime decide to impose on one. In neither context does the bare possibility of exit—of quitting or emigrating—mean that one is not interfered with by a boss who decides to demand overtime work at regular pay or a political leader who ventures into war without public support. Interferers also include the principal who orders that students be searched on the way into school and the parent who demands that the children stay home to mow the lawn.

A balanced development of the ideal of noninterference would need to recognize that individuals can interfere with each other and that all sorts of institutions—including schools, churches, and employers—can interfere with individuals. Government has no monopoly on the power of interference. Why, then, is the theory of negative liberty so often developed in a one-sided way that focuses predominantly on government interference? One answer may be that many trust their schools, churches, and employers more than they trust government. Whether one should trust government is in part a function of whether that government is a democracy that is of, for, and by the people. What it takes to have a democracy that truly lives up to this demand is the subject of this book.

More fundamentally, a balanced development of the ideal of freedom as noninterference is unlikely because it would be so theoretically unmanageable. It would have to address questions such as whether encouraging a certain type of neighborhood input into land-use decisions unduly enhances the ability of existing homeowners to block development projects, or whether giving patients the right to sue health maintenance organizations for the consequences of nontreatment yields more interference by disgruntled patients in the policies of the organization) than the interference it prevents (by the organization in the health-care choices of its clients). A balanced conception of liberty as noninterference, which kept in view the many ways individuals, groups, and institutions can interfere, would thus be intractable.

Because not all cases of interference are cases of domination, the republican view need not get caught up in the tangles I have just glanced at. Yet, as I have noted, the republican conception of freedom as nondomination cannot be classed as more permissive than the theory of freedom as noninterference, for there are also cases of domination that are not cases of interference, such as that of the kindly slavemaster or the hoodwinked one. The republican interpretation of liberty provides a better normative starting-point for political theory than does the negative interpretation.

It is time to look more carefully at what "domination" means. Since I started out from the threat of bureaucratic domination, this question is a fundamental one for this book as a whole and not just for its account of republican freedom. I adopt the main lines of Pettit's account—agreeing that to dominate is to have the capacity to exercise power arbitrarily. I depart from him only in characterizing the relevant kind of power along the normative lines explored at the outset of the chapter rather than simply as a capacity to interfere in a negative or damaging way.

One who dominates has the capacity to exercise arbitrary power. The slavemaster, whether kindly and hoodwinked or nasty and keen, has the capacity to exercise arbitrary power over the slave. In employing the analogy to slavery, the early republicans meant to point up the degree to which monarchs were able to exercise arbitrary power, unconstrained by any concern for the public good. Someone who is dominated has no effective means of resisting arbitrary impositions, should they occur. Even if they occur only seldom, domination exists where some can exercise arbitrary power. A dominator will not need to flex his muscles continually if the dominated become, in the words of the eighteenth-century republican Richard Price, "like cattle inured to the yoke . . . driven on in one track, afraid of speaking or even thinking on the most interesting points, looking up continually to a poor creature who is their master, their powers fettered, and some of the noblest springs of action in human nature rendered useless within them."[17] Domination may become so thorough, in other words, as to make the actual use of the whip only rarely necessary. Thus, the great complaint of the American colonists against King George III was not so much that he constantly exercised his power against them as that he had the power to do so arbitrarily. Pettit paraphrases Joseph Priestley, who agitated against England's power to tax the colonists.

> It is proof of the unfreedom of the Americans, as he puts it, that the Parliament of Great Britain could arbitrarily tax them for their last penny, even though it now only taxes them for one penny and even though, he might have added, it is unlikely ever to try and tax them for their last penny. The mere fact of being exposed to such a capacity on the part of others, the mere fact of being dominated in this way, meant for Priestley that the Americans were unfree.[18]

In this case, we do not have oxen trudging along, uncomplaining of the yoke; there is domination so long as there is the real threat of arbitrary subjugation.

We can now integrate this conception of freedom from domination with the more general account of freedom with which this chapter began. In looking at why it is that governments stand under a special burden of legitimation, we saw that it is largely because they impinge on freedom in two ways: They threaten fundamental rights and liberties of the sort that the liberal is concerned with, and they impose new duties on us, in a way that republicans have traditionally been concerned with. Or, more precisely, as shown, they purport to impose duties on us. If we take another look at paradigmatic cases of domination—that of master over slave, king and parliament over the colonies, or a Victorian father over his household—we will see that these are all situations in which the dominators acted under a claim to authority. The slavemaster, the colonizing power, and the Victorian father all purported to be able to put the persons they dominated under new duties and to do so on an arbitrary basis.¶ This purported exercise of normative power—the power to modify the rights and duties of others—is, I suggest, essential to the idea of domination.[19]

Neglecting this point, Pettit concedes too much conceptual primacy to the idea of freedom as noninterference by suggesting that the capacity to dominate can be defined as the capacity arbitrarily to interfere.[20] To see that this definition is overly broad, think of the case of the kidnappers. They have a capacity arbitrarily to interfere with people's lives. Partly because they do so under no color of right, no claim of authority, however, we do not say that kidnappers dominate their potential victims, who might include all of us. Pettit's nonnormative definition of domination also loses contact with the way he initially located freedom as nondomination as a third possibility in addition to the negative and positive forms of liberty distinguished by Berlin. As Pettit himself points out, Berlin's schema introduces the idea of mastery on the positive side, in the guise of self-mastery. Self-mastery cannot be understood, however, as the capacity to interfere with oneself. Rather, self-mastery is a matter of developing the capacity to put oneself under obligations. Although it is quite mysterious how this works, or whether this works, in the self-oriented case, that is not the point. What returning to the case of self-mastery shows is that mastery, or domination, is a normatively richer notion than the idea of a capacity to interfere. Domination is the capacity to make people's lives or situations worse by arbitrarily imposing duties on them, or by arbitrarily purporting to impose duties on them.

---

¶ That the slavemaster claims to put the slave under a duty to obey this or that command is part of the reason that the relation between master and slave gives rise, as Hegel famously argued, to a dialectic: for a being subject to duties cannot be consistently conceived as being as deprived of rights as a slave is thought to be.

With this relatively minor amendment to Pettit's definition of domination taken as read, I would now like to recapitulate three important points he makes about the political theory that flows from the republican ideal of freedom as nondomination.

First, as is the case with interference, the potential sources of domination are highly various and are not limited to the government. They are connected, as Pettit observes, with a wide range of kinds of resource that can be unequally held, including "financial clout, political authority, social connections, communal standing, informational access, ideological position, cultural legitimation, and the like."[21] A firm with great financial clout may be able to dictate terms of cooperation to its employees or clients, imposing contractual obligations, or purported ones, at will. Social connections and communal standing can give people standing to dictate, or to purport to dictate, what may or may not be done on the tennis court or in the boardroom. One-sidedness of informational access can give those with the advantage the ability arbitrarily to lay down what is to be considered a safe standard for disposing of nuclear waste or an appropriate way to design a web browser. And the cultural legitimacy of priests, imams, and shamans can allow them unchecked power to shape the duties the believers take themselves to be under. Just as it is not only governments that purport to put people under duties, it is not only governments that can have the power to do so arbitrarily. Still, we must take the case of potential government domination especially seriously.

Second, a contemporary republicanism will want to take a more inclusive and egalitarian view of who it is who must not be dominated than did the seventeenth- and eighteenth-century versions. We are no longer concerned only with white male property-holders but with all who are subject to a jurisdiction's laws.** In the seventeenth and eighteenth centuries, as Pettit notes, nascent egalitarianism had enough of a toehold that some of republicanism's critics thought they could reduce the view to absurdity by showing that it implied "that women too must legislate for themselves."[22] His conjecture is that this potential radicalism, as archaic sensibilities perceived it, was one of the reasons that the republican view lost influence within political theory. However that may be, we now should want to embrace, with Pettit, a form of republicanism that vigorously affirms that neither man nor woman, householder nor domestic servant, landowner nor migrant laborer ought to be subject to domination.

Third, the republican conception of freedom as nondomination allows for the possibility that government does not dominate. Government does

---

** Not that we face no doubts along these lines; consider the plight of resident aliens.

interfere, and it does so by imposing duties, or purporting to do so; but if it is adequately checked and constrained, it will not be able to do so arbitrarily. To achieve that constraint is the principal reason the republicans developed and promoted such devices as the dispersal of lawmaking powers. This possibility that a legitimate government does not dominate dovetails with the traditional republican notion of liberty that is distinct from licentiousness. Pettit quotes Blackstone: "Laws, when prudently framed, are by no means subversive but rather introductive of liberty; for (as Mr Locke has well observed) where there is no law there is no freedom."[23] What is crucial to nondomination is that power not be arbitrarily exercised. An effective system of laws is a necessary condition for the exclusion of arbitrary power.

But what does it mean to say that governmental power must not be arbitrarily exercised? Are democratic institutions merely the most effective means to blocking arbitrary government power, or are they necessary constituents of nonarbitrary government? Are the modes of contesting power afforded by periodic elections and a free press merely heuristic devices for determining whether state interference is arbitrary, or are they also conceptually necessary aspects of defining nonarbitrary power? To these questions I now turn.

# CHAPTER 3

# Three Conceptions of Nonarbitrariness

The ideal of freedom, as I have explained, gives rise to two powerful arguments against the arbitrary use of power, placing government under a burden of legitimation. Meeting this burden requires that government actions be based on reasons. In conjunction with the elemental ideal of treating persons with equal concern and respect, this basic rationality requirement in turn gives rise to a basic case for democracy. In addition, compatibly, the republican ideal of freedom from domination further demands that the government not have the *capacity* to exercise power arbitrarily.

In light of these arguments, how should we understand the idea of nonarbitrariness? The basic case suggests a minimal interpretation. The use of government power—in particular power that purports to put citizens under duties—must be nonarbitrary at least in the sense that it rests on reasons. The republican ideal clearly demands more than this. Slaveholders and tyrants often have their reasons for what they do, after all. How, then, should we understand the kind of nonarbitrariness to which the basic case and the ideal of domination commit us? How we assess the threat of bureaucratic domination will hinge on our answer to this question.

In this chapter, I will consider three ways of interpreting the republican demand for nonarbitrariness: an objectivist way, a welfarist way, and a liberal way. (The welfarist version itself has three variants that are important to discuss as they introduce themes that I will pursue throughout.) Although these three main variants do not exhaust the conceptual possibilities, they are influential interpretations that seem compatible with other democratic themes. I shall argue for the superiority of the liberal interpretation, concluding that liberalism should enter into the ideal of democracy at this point. Liberal ideas are needed to help give an appropriate rendering of the idea of nonarbitrary power. A liberal conception of democratic politics as a set of procedures that respects the freedom and equality of citizens is a necessary support, I shall claim, to an adequate understanding of nonarbitrary power.

Each of these three conceptions of nonarbitrary power is also a conception of the role that the public good must play in politics. That is indeed what we should be looking for here, at least if we seek to be guided by traditional forms of republican theory. The antimonarchical republicans, from John Locke to Tom Paine, were concerned that the unchecked power of the monarch meant that his or her actions might have no connection to the public good. Pettit quotes Paine: "It means arbitrary power in an individual person; in the exercise of which, *himself*, and not the *res-publica*, is the object."[1] In more modern language—language that, taken loosely, expresses a thought common to all three of the conceptions of nonarbitrariness I will look at—Pettit restates Paine's idea as follows: "What is required for nonarbitrary state power . . . is that the power be exercised in a way that tracks, not the power-holder's welfare or world-view, but rather the welfare and world-view of the public."[2]

The three conceptions of nonarbitrary power differently model the way the public good constrains political power. On an objectivist understanding, the public good is thought of as a determinate object, like Paine's *res-publica*: Political power is nonarbitrary so long as it is adequately constrained—by procedures of contestation and deliberation or in any other way—so as to come out to *that* result. On a welfarist understanding of nonarbitrary power, the political theorist does not think of the public good as having a settled content, but it does have a settled form. It consists in the aggregation of individuals' goods. Political power, on this approach, is adequately constrained if it must base itself, in some appropriate way, on the good of each. Which ways are appropriate (I shall consider three) will depend, of course, not just on the precise nature of individual welfare but also on whether the welfare levels of different individuals are held to be interpersonally comparable. Finally, on the liberal understanding of nonarbitrary power that I favor, the public good is not thought of as having a fully determinate form or content independent of the actual conduct of democratic politics. Rather, on this third view, it takes some considerable time for democratic politics to *fashion* "the welfare and worldview of the public." What is needed to prevent power from being arbitrary, on this third view, is not the idea of the public good, in either its determinate form or content, but rather a set of fair procedures, the shape of which is supported by independent, liberal ideals of respecting citizens as free and equal.

Before turning to the comparative merits of these three conceptions of nonarbitrary power, let me make two things clear about the liberal conception. First, although it implicitly holds that neither the form nor the content of the public good is an adequate basis for interpreting nonarbitrariness, it does *not* entail noncognitivism or skepticism about the public good. Accordingly, while I argue for a liberal interpretation of nonarbitrariness, I also affirm the existence of a conceptual object, the public good, toward which democratic deliberation is oriented. This will be a central point of chapter 10. It is just that the existence of such an object and hence of true and false claims about what, politically, ought to be done does not entail that the idea of the public good provides an adequate basis for elucidating what is meant by arbitrary power. Second, although the liberal conception does not take the bare idea of the public good to provide sufficient structure to give an adequate account of nonarbitrariness in the use of political power, that is not because the liberal conception is or means to be neutral as among conceptions of the good. I say this because it was popular during the 1980s to describe liberalism as being neutral about the good, taking its stand on the supposedly distinct territory of justice or the right.[3] I believe that it is always a mistake to think of liberalism in this way.[4] Whether or not I am right about that as a general matter, I am certain that the appeal to liberalism that I make in this chapter is not neutral about the good; rather, it takes a stand on the distinctive importance to politics of the good of fair cooperation among free and equal citizens.[5] This is a distinctively liberal good, one not carried along by the concept of the public good—not, at least, unless one presupposes the particular sort of specification given to the idea of a public in chapter 13.

As I compare alternative conceptions of nonarbitrary power in this chapter, then, I will be looking at versions that are increasingly committal as to the content of the public good. The objectivist conception lets the public good be whatever it may be and finds the desired constraint of power in whatever procedures are involved in discovering and pursuing it. The welfarist conception assumes that the public good has an individualist structure and utilizes that assumption to generate specific criteria of arbitrariness. The liberal conception invokes a still more specific assumption about the public good to generate an even richer conception of the procedures that must be followed for power not to be arbitrarily used. Once we have seen the reasons to prefer a liberal conception, we face a further issue as to whether to understand the liberal constraints hypothetically or not.

## The Objectivist Conception of Nonarbitrary Power

The objectivist conception of nonarbitrary power takes up in a literal-minded way Tom Paine's talk about the public *res*, or object, and Pettit's talk about "tracking."[6] To philosophical ears, at least, "tracking" has a strongly epistemic ring. As reliable virtues of scientific inquiry are ones that let inquiry track, or be guided by, scientific truth, so reliable virtues of political inquiry will let it track, or be guided by, the public good.

A word about the term "the public good." I use it, here, because it anticipates features specific to my own account without stacking the deck against either the objectivist or the welfarist conceptions of nonarbitrary power. The term provides a convenient way of summing up the conception of final ends toward which political action is aimed and which is invoked in addressing questions about what we should do through our political institutions. The public good is the normative aim of collective action, helping articulate and determine what it is that we ought to do. Unlike the phrase "the common good," however, "the public good" does not carry with it the specifically welfarist idea that the public good is to be understood in terms of a sum or overlap or coincidence across the individual goods of each citizen. "The public good" denotes the ends of collective, political action without laying down any particular restriction about the relation of these collective or institutional ends to individual well-being. What is required is that there be a distinction between politics and life as a whole and that the political institutions that define the relevant collectivity give a central place to the institution of a public, a notion to which I will give a specifically liberal interpretation in chapter 13 but that for now can be left relatively vague. Since the idea of the public good is the idea of an object that is potentially one that we can know, I will need to distinguish, in some contexts, between the actual and the apparent public good. The actual public good—or the public good, for short—comprises those significant final ends that in fact ought to regulate political action. A *conception of the public good* I will understand as a view about how public action *should* be regulated.

The public good—the actual public good—is thus by definition an object worth tracking. On an objectivist interpretation, power is nonarbitrarily used so long as it issues from some decision-making process that fairly reliably tracks the truth about what we ought to do. As an interpretation of republican ideas, this objectivist notion is close to being a nonstarter; but discussing it here will both introduce questions of political epistemology that will be central later on and clarify, by contrast, what the other interpretations of nonarbitrary power are.

How could the political process track the public good? The answer, obviously, depends on what the content of the public good is. If achieving the public good is, above all, maximizing economic growth, then a political process may do best that leaves market forces almost entirely unchecked, including in the ways they influence the political process. If, by contrast—as the general ideal of freedom as nondomination might suggest—eliminating the oppression of the weak and poor is a more central element of the public good, then the processes that track it will look more populist.* In yet an-

---

* Note, though, that for contexts of nonpolitical domination, as well, we would need an interpretation of "nonarbitrary."

other direction, if the public good consisted principally in the promotion of the noblest and best facets of human nature, then the processes that best tracked this good might turn out to be quite elitist.

The fatal objection to an objectivist interpretation of arbitrary power is that it excludes from counting as domination what should be counted as one of its primary cases, namely domination on the basis of superior knowledge and information. Whatever the content of the public good may be, we may suppose—absent liberal justificational restrictions—that there are some who are relatively expert in discerning it. One way to track the public good with reasonable reliability, then, is to turn political decisions over to these experts or wise persons. If we accept an objectivist interpretation of what "nonarbitrary power" *means*, then we could not count such Platonic guardians as dominating us. Intuitively, however, I think that we would: They would be dominating us precisely in virtue of their superior knowledge and information about the public good.

These considerations about Platonic guardians reveal that the republican ideal of freedom as nondomination is hardly compatible with every possible interpretation of the public good. If, as supposed, the guardians are truly reliable in tracking the public good, then their not abdicating is good evidence that they should not abdicate and hence are not acting arbitrarily, in objectivist terms. Our intuitive rejection of the suggestion that they would not be dominating us is therefore an implicit rejection of the hypothetical: We think that it cannot be compatible with the public good for political rule to be handed over to elite guardians. In accepting the republican ideal of freedom as nondomination, therefore, it seems that we are thereby delimiting what we would count as an acceptable interpretation of the public good. As an empirical matter, we doubt that there are any real experts in discerning what the overall public good is; but our doubts about this can hardly flow from the idea of the public good itself, which well fulfills the role of a potential object of wisdom. Rather, they stem, as I shall ultimately suggest, from our liberal political commitments.

To pick up on this kind of delimitation of the public good, we will need at least to move beyond the objectivist interpretation of nonarbitrary power. Whatever it is that delimits the interpretation of the public good, it is something besides the very idea of the public good, itself.† The welfarist and liberal interpretations of nonarbitrariness build in two different accounts of what that something might be.

---

† I am using the term "public" in a loose sense here, without the specific implications attributed to it in chapter 13.

## Welfarist Interpretations of Nonarbitrary Power

According to welfarist interpretations, political power is not exercised arbitrarily so long as it tracks, or is appropriately constrained to consider, the welfare of each individual who is subject to it. These interpretations pick up on the antimonarchical strain of republicanism. The monarch thinks only of his or her own welfare, whereas the government of a republic ought to keep in mind everyone's.

So how can the political process track everyone's welfare? It turns out that there are various answers, depending on what it means to track everyone's welfare. There are three main families of views. On utilitarian views, to track everyone's welfare is to track the sum or average of their welfare, an approach that typically assumes that individual welfare levels are interpersonally comparable. On unanimity interpretations, to track everyone's welfare is accept only those government actions that literally promote each person's welfare or preference-satisfaction. On Rousseauean or generality views, to track everyone's welfare is to consider only those aspects of each person's views or preferences that meet a test of generality.

While each of these different ways of thinking about what it means to track everyone's welfare is subject to problems peculiar to it, I should note at the outset that each is also theoretically subject to the worry about expert domination raised in the previous section. Whatever promoting everyone's welfare might mean, it is conceivable (I do not say "likely") that there could be trustworthy experts in how to do so to whom government decision-making could be delegated. And again, contrary to the present suggestion about how to define "nonarbitrary power," we might feel that such experts dominated.

Wholly apart from this possibility of welfarist guardianship, a utilitarian interpretation of nonarbitrary power clearly will not do. Notoriously, an evenhanded promotion of total or average welfare is quite compatible, within known laws of psychology and economics, with severely exploiting and even enslaving the few for the benefit of the many. In overall assessments of utilitarianism as a moral theory, it has become fashionable to spurn consideration of such purported counterexamples as being too far-fetched, too unlikely to occur in the ordinary run of things.[7] Yet such a response ignores historical instances in which the oppression of the relatively few in fact seems to have led to greater social welfare in the aggregate. Consider, for instance, how the suppression of Native American land claims has allowed the U.S. economy to grow apace, unfettered by doubts about property titles. Of course, nothing about the U.S. government of a century ago, say, ever reliably even took any account of Native Americans' interests; but if it had done so in a utilitarian way, it could still have endorsed policies as callous as the ones in fact taken, for the Native Americans were relatively few and the economic benefits to the many were enormous. My concern, in any case, is not with moral theory but with the proper interpretation of the notion of nonarbitrary power as it occurs within the ideal of nondomination. Because the Native Americans clearly suffered domination within the U.S. political system and because a responsible utilitarian calculation could have allowed for that domination, we should not countenance a utilitarian interpretation of nonarbitrary power.

With this sort of case in mind, we are naturally thrown from the utilitarian version of welfarism into the arms of a unanimity interpretation. As public choice theory would have it, unanimity establishes a normatively privileged benchmark against which the potentially "discriminatory" depradations of democratic majorities are to be judged.[8] The particular version of a unanimity requirement that inspired James Buchanan, the founder of public choice theory, was that developed by Knut Wicksell in the end of the nineteenth century.[9] Rawls expounds Wicksell's unanimity criterion as follows.

> [It] means that no public expenditures are voted upon unless at the same time the means of covering their costs are agreed upon, if not unanimously, then approximately so. A motion proposing a new public activity is required to contain one or more alternative arrangements for sharing the costs. Wicksell's idea is that if the public good is an efficient use of social resources, there must be some scheme for distributing the extra taxes among different kinds of taxpayers that will gain unanimous approval. If no such proposal exists, the suggested expenditure is wasteful and should not be undertaken.[10]

The idea seems compelling; and on a simple welfarist basis, it is. If the benefits of the proposal are not, in the aggregate, sufficient to outweigh the aggregate costs of funding the notion under *any* possible way of distributing those tax burdens, then, it may appear, the measure should not be adopted.[11]

The appearance is deceiving. Any decision procedure that requires more than a simple majority to pass affirmative proposals is biased in favor of the status quo (for further discussion, see chapter 15). We must ask both what seems to be lending a color of legitimacy to this bias in the case of Wicksell's criterion and what its consequences might be. Clearly enough, the normative basis of the status quo bias in public choice theory is the kind of one-sidedness to which, as shown in the previous chapter, the conception of freedom as noninterference is prone. The criterion places the burden of proof on government interferences with the status quo. After all, it does not simultaneously require unanimity in favor of defeating a motion. If we overcome this one-sidedness and recognize that individuals interfere with individuals all the time, and firms with firms, and firms with individuals, we will no longer be so sure that government proposals should meet a unanimity requirement. If, further, we accept—as I have argued we should—the republican theory of freedom as nondomination, then we will be alive to the possibility that government power should be used to counter private domination and to do so in a way that cannot command unanimous support.

The Wicksell criterion is appropriate only once such major problems with the status quo have been taken care of. The potential need to use government power to counter private domination is just a special case of the kind of consideration that should hold the Wicksell criterion in abeyance. Rawls qualifiedly endorses the criterion—but only for judging government programs that are *not* required by justice and only on the strongly idealizing assumption that the status quo already meets the fundamental requirements of social justice. Where there is widespread private domination of individuals, there is a serious problem of social justice. And where there is a serious problem of injustice, we must not employ a unanimity requirement that gives an effective veto to the beneficiaries of injustice. Nor is injustice the only serious normative defect that a status quo can suffer. Justice is at best "the first virtue of social institutions," not the only one.[12] A social status quo can also suffer, for example, from widespread economic imprudence, as seen in a heedless accumulation of debt and frenzied chase after speculative gain or an irresponsible approach to the maintenance of environmental quality and fragile ecosystems.‡ Widespread social vices of these kinds, too, must be fixed before the occupiers of the status quo are given effective veto power over changes. This need for remedial social virtues—the pressing necessity of redressing injustice, protecting the environment, calming bellicosity, and so on—is a deep reason why politics calls for mutual compromise rather than unanimity.[13]

These wholly reasonable provisos mean that the Wicksell unanimity criterion cannot be an acceptable rendering of nonarbitrary power in our actual situation. The same would hold true *a fortiori* of any stronger unanimity criterion that did not hypothesize an optimal rearrangement of each proposal's tax burden. Thus, similar objections would apply to a literal-minded invocation of the Habermasian formula, according to which the aim of democratic deliberation is to find resolutions that are "equally in the interests of each."[14] That power *would* be nonarbitrarily exercised if it met a unanimity standard in ideal conditions free of injustice and other social vices tells us little, if anything, about what it means, in any realistic situation, to exercise power nonarbitrarily. A normative theory of politics should not idealize as markedly as a theory of justice may. Curing serious social ills

‡ As I mean here to imply, I do not believe that the value of environmental protection can be adequately captured in terms of individual welfare or preference-satisfaction.

being one of the primary tasks of politics, it serves political theory poorly to imagine all serious social ills away.

A third kind of welfarist reading of nonarbitrariness invokes the idea of generality rather than unanimity. This idea harks back to Rousseau's social contract theory. It also has a firm place in the republicanism of the American founders, who feared factionalism and hoped that a reasonable pursuit of the public good might result from a system that offset opposing factionalisms. If—as sometimes in Rousseau's treatment of "the general will"—a factional or particular interest is simply contrasted with a correct view of what ought to be done, then taking up this idea would cycle us back to an objectivist interpretation of nonarbitrary power.[15] We may remain within the family of welfarist interpretations, however, if we think in terms of a generality filter through which individuals' political views or preferences must pass—an idea one can also find in Rousseau.[16] On this sort of approach, a general view or interest is contrasted with a partial or particular one.[17]

A generality constraint is either formal or substantive. If it is merely formal, it is both unobjectionable and a key component in the ideal of the rule of law but cannot generate sufficient constraints on the arbitrary use of power. A substantive generality constraint, by contrast, is both objectionable and far too constraining to yield an acceptable construal of nonarbitrary power.

A formal generality constraint is indeed an essential element of the rule of law.[18] The constraint bears on the form of political proposals, that is, proposed items of legislation. They must be general in the sense that they make no essential reference, explicit or implicit, to particular persons. A classic example of particular legislation violating this requirement is a bill of attainder, which strips the heirs of a particular named offender of their inheritance rights. Bills of attainder are expressly forbidden by the U.S. Constitution; the ban is interpreted as ruling out all punitive cases of particular legislation. Important as this kind of generality is to the rule of law, it is plainly impotent to block the arbitrary and dominating use of power. Laws forbidding Jews to sit in public parks and nonwhites to enter public restrooms meet at least this requirement of the rule of law yet express brutal domination.

A substantive version of a generality requirement, one that rules out all discrimination against particular groups, might be thought of as addressing this weakness of a formal interpretation. Indeed, in the libertarian thought of Friedrich Hayek, a substantive interpretation of generality is described (misleadingly) as arising out of the more formal ideal of the rule of law.[19] Recall from the introduction Buchanan's quite abstract worry about the kind of "discrimination" that majority rule can produce: A majority can get together to pass a measure that benefits them, while imposing the costs on others or at any rate on the citizenry as a whole. One way to block this kind of discrimination is to impose Wicksell's unanimity rule. Another is simply to demand, as Buchanan does in a recent work with Roger Congleton, that no legislation ever differentially benefit citizens. Buchanan and Congleton call this a demand for generality. "The generality norm," they write, "is clearly violated when a collectively financed program is aimed explicitly to offer benefits to some members of the polity to the exclusion of others."[20]

While the exploitation by a majority coalition of its temporary hold on the reins of power is, as already discussed, a serious form of domination, this principle of substantive generality imposes a would-be cure that is worse than the disease.[21] Whereas most of the interpretations of nonarbitrary power that I have examined are too lax, failing to capture certain important forms of domination, this one is, more saliently, too strict, as it would count as domination many governmental actions that should not be so counted. When the majority of representatives in the U.S. Congress enacted a program to benefit disabled children, they may not have known very well what they were doing, but they were not engaged in domination. Programs designed to benefit the disabled, or AIDS sufferers, or disaster victims are all "aimed explicitly to offer benefits to some members of the polity to the exclusion of others" but are not on that account cases of domination. To the contrary, such programs are often key to helping redress domination.

Buchanan and Congleton will object that I here understand majoritarian domination at the wrong level: Such domination occurs, even in passing such politically correct programs as the ones I have just mentioned, when the majority that cares, say, about AIDS sufferers imposes its view on the whole society. In response to this objection, I would repeat that I take their point that majoritarian domination is one form of potentially arbitrary power with which to be concerned; but their generality principle is the wrong instrument with which to get at it. Or, to be fair, it is a correct instrument only under the highly unrealistic assumption, orthodox in the public choice literature, that individuals simply vote for what most benefits them. As already shown, however, Brennan and Lomasky's theory of expressive voting gives a far more realistic rendering of voting behavior, still within an individualist framework. The cases at hand reinforce the explanatory power of the expressive theory. Representatives enact programs to benefit blind children, or tornado victims, or AIDS sufferers, not because they personally will benefit from such programs, nor because the benefited individuals represent powerful voting blocks, but rather because they, the representatives, and so many of their constituents, believe that such people ought to benefit. But to the extent that majorities are formed on the basis of votes that express citizens' or representatives' views about what ought to be done, the generality principle as Buchanan and Congleton articulate it, which rules out differential benefit, is simply the wrong instrument to employ in addressing the danger of majoritarian domination.§ Accordingly, their substantive generality requirement not only rules out many potentially progressive programs that would reduce domination; it also fails to cure the disease of majoritarian domination against which it is addressed.

Although there are other conceivable ways one might try to define the nonarbitrary use of political power, it is time to turn to a definition that seems to work. I have argued that objectivist definitions fail adequately to account for the interpersonal nature of domination, which can be exercised even by well-meaning wise men. Welfarist or individualist definitions, I have argued, have problems that vary with the precise criterion developed: Utilitarian criteria fail to rule out egregious forms of domination in which some benefit at the expense of others; unanimity criteria threaten to entrench forms of domination present in the status quo; and generality criteria either rule out nothing much at all or else exclude much political action that is not only nondominating but also directed against domination. To arrive at a more satisfactory definition of nonarbitrary power, we need to move from those that rely mainly on the content of the public good (the objectivist interpretations) or on its form (the welfarist interpretations) and look instead to the process whereby collective decisions are made.

## A Liberal Interpretation of Nonarbitrary Power

My simple proposal is that political power is nonarbitrarily used when it is constrained to operate within fair procedures that respect persons as free and equals and provide adequate protection for their fundamental rights and liberties. This is obviously a distinctively liberal proposal. It gains support from the distinctive liberal values of promoting fair social cooperation, respecting persons as free and equal citizens, and securing their fundamental rights and liberties. As such, this interpretation of nonarbitrary power makes important assumptions about the content of the public good. In sharp contrast to the objectivist interpretation, it is not compatible with whatever content the public good might turn out to have. If we accept this proposal, therefore, we cannot claim any longer simply to be following

---

§ What would be the proper interpretation of nonarbitrariness for this purpose? A reformulation of the Marxist theory of ideological distortion, generalizing his views about how class interests can distort political views and their expression? That is an avenue I will not pursue.

through on the general idea of the public good; we will also have declared ourselves as liberals. As part of the reconstructive aspect of my argument, however, I also mean to claim that insofar as we are committed to democracy, we are thereby committed to a liberalism of this kind. This step of the argument will be completed only in the following chapter. The prior step is to see how republicanism leads us to liberalism. It does so because only a liberal interpretation of nonarbitrariness, hence of domination, is adequate. The liberal interpretation of nonarbitrariness I have just articulated is, I contend, the only adequate basis for understanding the republican ideal of freedom as nondomination. If I am right, liberal democratic institutions are not merely an effective means—even the only effective means—of promoting freedom as nondomination, and not merely a heuristic device for determining what would be a nonarbitrary use of power, but rather a conceptually necessary constituent of political nondomination.[22]

The whole idea of focusing on procedures or process is sometimes itself taken to be distinctive of liberalism.[23] Before turning to the features of democratic process necessary to the nonarbitrary use of state power, I will defend this proceduralist aspect of my proposal. The necessary place for appropriate procedures can be seen by considering the lessons of a branch of individualist theorizing about the public good that I have not yet considered, namely social choice theory. In drawing this lesson, I will be standing on its head the conventional wisdom about the central result of that tradition, Arrow's impossibility theorem.[24]

Considering Arrovian social choice theory will allow me, at the same time, to address an objection that may linger from my treatment of welfarist interpretations of no nonarbitrariness: the objection that in the previous section I addressed only three among the myriad possible welfarist accounts of the appropriate relation between individuals' preferences or interests and social choice. In this respect, the merit of Arrow's approach is that it addresses all possible such accounts at once.

Taking a broadly welfarist approach, Arrow assumed that any rationally acceptable social choice would be some function of the preferences of the individuals in the society. What function? He proceeded by assembling seemingly unobjectionable conditions that any acceptable social welfare function ought to meet. Sacrificing some niceties to speak colloquially, these are: (P) The social ranking ought to respond to individual preferences in the appropriately positive way fingered by Vilfredo Pareto: If no one prefers alternative $y$ to alternative $x$, then the social ranking ought not to do so, either. (D) No one individual's rankings should, by itself, be taken to dictate the social ranking. Because a welfarist approach seeks to be neutral as to the content of the public good, and speak only to its form, the third condition is that (U) the aggregating function must be able to accept as input any conceivable individual ranking of the alternatives; the domain of individual rankings is taken as being unlimited. Finally, Arrow added a pair of more technical requirements: (C) The social welfare function must generate a complete ranking of alternatives, and (I) its ranking of any given pair of alternatives must be independent of any way the set of alternatives is broadened to include additional options. What Arrow famously proved is that no social welfare function, no welfarist way of mapping from individual preferences to a social ordering, can meet all five of these requirements.

Arrow's impossibility theorem generalized the kind of result that was independently familiar from the so-called voting paradox, which Amartya Sen economically presents as follows.

> Consider three individuals 1, 2 and 3, and three alternatives $x$, $y$, and $z$. Let individual 1 prefer $x$ to $y$, and $y$ to $z$, and individual 2 prefer $y$ to $z$, and $z$ to $x$, and individual 3 prefer $z$ to $x$ and $x$ to $y$. It is easily checked out that $x$ can defeat $y$ by two votes to one, $y$ can defeat $z$ by the same margin, so that transitivity [a logical prerequisite of any social ordering] requires that $x$ should defeat $z$ in a vote too. But, in fact, $z$ defeats $x$ by two votes to one. Thus, the method of majority decision leads to inconsistencies.[25]

This possibility of cyclical social preferences reveals a logical defect in defining the will of the people in terms of majority rule or any other social choice function; but far worse, as William H. Riker and others have emphasized, is that it opens majoritarian procedures up to possibilities of manipulation. As can be seen from this schematic example, everything depends on the order in which the pairwise votes are taken. Agenda-setting thus becomes an unavoidable issue for democracies and democratic theory.[26] The sort of instability and manipulability of pure majority rule that the voting paradox reveals stands behind public choice theory's suspicion of majoritarianism.

What Arrow's impossibility theorem shows, though, is that it is not only majority rule that is subject to this sort of danger. Any conceivable social choice function that is supposed to be able to map from any set of individual preferences to a social ordering will be subject to this kind of instability and manipulability. The vast literature on voting procedures tends to confirm this conclusion.[27]

Confining ourselves to the conceptual level for the moment, the orthodox reaction to Arrow's impossibility theorem takes it to undercut the very idea of the public good or the public interest. This response is typified by Riker. Together with the voting paradox, he wrote, Arrow's theorem "forces us to doubt that the content of 'social welfare' or the 'public interest' can ever be discovered by amalgamating individual value judgments." Given the robustness of the welfarist assumption of normative individualism, this in turn "even leads us to suspect that no such thing as 'the public interest' exists, aside from the subjective (and hence dubious) claims of self-proclaimed saviors."[28]

This common move to skepticism about the public good is unwarranted.[29] What the negative results of the social choice tradition tend to show, I suggest, is not that individualist assumptions force us to give up the idea of the public good but rather that these individualist assumptions cannot operate in an institutional vacuum. The reason that no mathematical function can adequately capture, in full generality, an appropriate relation between individual preferences and social choice is that social choice procedures can adequately operate only against the backdrop of fair procedures of agenda selection, debate, and discussion. These are the sorts of procedure that the liberal has the ambition to describe, although not on the basis of abstract axioms; instead, the liberal democrat describes procedures allowing fair opportunities for citizen participation that have evolved against the backdrop of established individual rights. Within the context of fair procedures that treat citizens as free and equal, the idea of the public good can play an essential role.[30] By adopting a liberal conception of concrete political processes, we may grant what is correct in the individualist assumptions of social choice theory—namely that political decision ought generally to depend on the views of the citizens, and in the right direction—without taking the unwarranted further step of holding that the people cannot be wrong about what ought to be done. There are, as already discussed, standards external to any actual process of decision, including a unanimous one.

To respond in this unorthodox way to Arrow's impossibility theorem is not simply to express a Luddite distaste for abstract, logical models. Rather, it is to point out a distinctive way in which, in any process of legitimate political choice, condition (U) is violated.[31] It is violated because no legitimate set of political procedures can be normatively neutral. Commitment to liberal procedures, as I have noted, reflects a commitment to the fundamental good of fair cooperation among free and equal citizens. To demand that political procedures of agenda formation, debate, and discussion be consonant with this deep liberal value, however, is to impose significant practical restrictions on the otherwise logically unlimited scope of possible individual preference rankings. The preferences of would-be dictators who would achieve power by shouting down everyone else are frustrated by fair procedures of debate and discussion; and those who would abrogate fundamental rights and liberties will not find that their views easily get on the agenda.[32]

I do not claim that Arrow's impossibility theorem backhandedly proves that liberalism is correct. There are other ways of escaping his conditions—including, of course, other ways of restricting the domain of potential preferences.[33] Recourse to liberal procedures, however, provides an attractive way of reconciling what is attractive in the individualist assumptions of welfarism—an insistence on the importance of the preferences and welfare of each individual—with the elemental values of freedom and equality that build the basic case for democracy—in the first place. While majority rule has a central place within democracy—a place I describe and defend in chapter 15—its democratic virtues are best seen not by considering it as a social choice function but instead by viewing it as one part of a broader set of procedures that respect citizens as free and equal while protecting their fundamental rights and liberties. Liberalism can thus serve to protect the objectivist idea of the public good from the potentially erosive influence of welfarist individualism.

In so doing, liberalism can help synthesize what is best about objectivism with what is best about welfarism. The liberal proposal, again, is that political power is nonarbitrarily used when it is constrained to operate within a set of fair procedures that respects persons as free and equals and provides adequate protection for their fundamental rights and liberties. Understood as taking a stand—albeit a partial and schematic one—on the content of the public good, this liberal proposal retains an objectivist's concern with the truth about what we ought to do. Further, because of its insistence on the status of individuals as free and equal, it will certainly accord importance to the preferences and welfare of individuals. The proposal simply insists that the objectivist's insight that the public good serves to orient democratic deliberation and the welfarist's insight about the responsiveness of the public good to individuals' views need to be supplemented and constrained by a liberal's recognition of the necessary value and role of institutions of fair debate and discussion and constrained by a protection of fundamental rights and liberties.

The resulting substantive or committal account of the public good grounds an adequate rendering of the republican notion of nonarbitrary power. Its insistence on fair procedures that recognize a role for individuals as free and equal discussants captures the interpersonal requirements of nondomination that are potentially ignored by ojectivist interpretations. Even benevolent guardians, as noted, may dominate if they do not consult with those whom they rule. Liberal procedures will provide for consultation. Giving constitutive importance to individual rights will shield against the kind of domination that unconstrained utilitarian aggregation can allow, while fair procedures of discussion will encourage forms of reasonable compromise that will prevent a welfarist concern for the good of each citizen from so tying the political process in knots that domination present in the status quo is left unredressed. (Reasonable compromise is the subject of chapter 11.) And while liberal procedures cannot wholly rule out majoritarian domination, requirements of giving fair hearing to the views of each and respecting the fundamental rights of each can help keep it at bay. I do not claim that the resulting interpretation of nonarbitrary power can count as a sufficient definition of it. Surely it is conceivable that some forms of political domination might not be captured by this interpretation. What I do claim, though, is that the liberal interpretation represents what seems the soundest way, and perhaps the only viable way, to work out for politics the republican ideal of freedom as nondomination.

To recapitulate that ideal, as thus interpreted, it is this: The political process ought to be arranged so that individuals are not subject to arbitrary power, by which we centrally mean uses of power that do not flow from, and are not subject to being constrained by, a fair process of discussion in which individuals are treated as free and equal citizens and their fundamental rights and liberties are protected. The resulting view, a liberal republicanism, is hardly novel. John Locke was a liberal republican, subject to the limitations common to his era pertaining to the set of people he considered citizens. A more inclusive liberal republicanism is well represented in our day by such thinkers as Frank Michelman and Cass Sunstein.[34]

## Rejecting Hypothetical Acceptance

One may ask why it is that we should accept an interpretation of nonarbitrary power that refers to actual procedures, as opposed to hypothetical ones. Why not appeal to more general liberal ideas about legitimacy, such as the very idea of reasons that no one can reasonably reject, or reasons that everyone can accept? This idea is popular in theories of deliberative democracy.[35] It may also influence Pettit's own preferred understanding of "nonarbitrary." "Not only ought government to be orientated toward the satisfaction of people's common, recognizable interests," he writes; "those are the only factors that it ought to take its ultimate guidance from."[36] A hypothetical standard arises when he in turn glosses "common interests."

> A certain good will represent a common interest of a population . . . just so far as cooperatively avowable considerations support its collective provision. What are cooperatively avowable considerations? They are considerations such that were the population holding discussions about what it ought to cooperate in collectively providing, then they could not be dismissed as irrelevant.[37]

Hence, Pettit builds a standard of hypothetical acceptability, of a certain sort, into his criterion for licit reasons for government action. Perhaps he also takes it to give a working definition of nonarbitrariness.

Although this seminal idea of reasons acceptable to each (or not rejectable as irrelevant by any)[38] is of great importance in theories of justification, there are two reasons to reject it in an account of nonarbitrary power.

First, notice that the liberal interpretation I have given of the republican ideal stands at an intermediate position in regard to vagueness or specificity. My interpretation remains vague insofar as it does not detail what should count as a fair process of debate and discussion among free and equal citizens or what should be counted among their fundamental rights and liberties. The latter work I leave largely to other political theorists, such as Rawls, while the former topic I undertake to say more about in chapter 6. For the purposes of glossing the republican ideal, however, it seems fully appropriate to leave such details unsettled at this point. To move in the other direction, however, from the liberal ideal of fair constitutional procedures to the underlying ideals of justification, would be to accept an account of nonarbitrary power that is unnecessarily vague.

Let me illustrate this point by reference to the idea of reasons that all can accept. While this notion can doubtless do *some* work within liberal arguments for fair constitutional procedures, it is far too vague to do much all by itself.[39] What constitutes a reason that one cannot accept? Not one that generates a contingent conflict with other reasons one accepts, for we can and do accept conflicting reasons all the time; for example, we can accept that we have reason to hold the line against budget deficits as well as reason to do more for indigent seniors, all the while knowing that, in our contingent circumstances, we cannot achieve both of these aims. Ruling out reasons on that basis would rule out most of the practical reasons we have. If conflicts of some other kind are to be the basis on which reasons are ruled unacceptable, then it seems that we need to locate a nonconflicting core of each individual's commitments, with which a conflict can signal unacceptability. Given the wide range of individual's core commitments in a pluralist society, almost any proposed reason is likely to conflict with someone's, again leaving the public forum depleted of reasons. Prolifers cannot accept, on this basis, arguments that deny that the fetus is a person; prochoice advocates cannot accept arguments that assert it. Little is left as a possible basis for conceiving of nonarbitrary decision. One might seek to avoid this result with a recursive maneuver, holding that the core commitments must themselves be ones that everyone can accept; but then one would need a different basis for trying to understand the "can accept" at that level.

These casuistical questions proceed as if finding reasons that all can accept were a constraint on ordinary participants in political debate. These sorts of difficulty do not bear directly on the hypothetical participants in a liberal social contract, who may well be prevented by a "veil of ignorance" from knowing what their personal core commitments are. Within contractarian arguments aimed at generating or justifying fundamental principles, the abstract ideal of reasons acceptable to each does indeed have an important role, one that the abstract framework of those arguments enables the theorist precisely to define. For everyday politics, however, it seems more effective and forthright to refer directly to the kinds of fair procedure that those contractarian arguments aim to support.

Still, one might say that a nonarbitary use of power is a use that would be accepted by suitably motivated and constrained parties in a hypothetical choice situation. There is a second reason for resisting this kind of liberal formulation, however—one that goes to its hypothetical character. In common with the objectivist interpretations of nonarbitrary power, one that was built around a hypothetical social contract leaves out the essentially interpersonal aspect of nondomination. Just as well-meaning guardians dominate if they do not in any way consult the people they rule, so too would those who ruled in such a way that hypothetical discussants could accept (or would not reject). Thus, there are two possibilities: If the social contract requires fair procedures of debate and discussion in which individuals are actually treated as free and equal, then while they will not be dominated by rule that adheres to the social contract's procedural requirements, it would be more direct to build those requirements directly into the interpretation of nonarbitrariness. If the social contract does not require such procedures, however, but sometimes allows exercises of power that flout such consultative processes, then it will countenance domination.

The defender of the hypothetical standard might here object to this line of argument by analogy to the issue of paternalism. Imagine a nongovernmental authority, such as one's parents, that continually makes unilateral decisions for one about whether one should ride a bicycle to work or when one should be allowed to date and under what conditions. If the paternalist authority is moved by nothing other than a correct (or even reasonable) conception of what is in one's best interests, then, it might be argued, that authority is not exercising domination, for its power is not being used arbitrarily and instead tracks ones interests.

The parallel fails in the political case, however, for reasons brought out most dramatically by my discussion of Arrow's theorem. The notion of "our best interests" or "tracking the interests of each" is, as shown in my discussion of the welfarist interpretations, a deeply contested and problematic one. The abstract liberal ideal of seeking reasons that are acceptable to each (or not rejectable as irrelevant by any) remains too vague to grapple with the tension between unanimity and decisiveness that this discussion brought out. Hence acting in accordance with that idea is not relevantly similar to the idea, in the case of paternalistic treatment of an individual, of promoting that person's interests.

The liberal idea of fair consultative procedures does help give a more definite rendering of the idea of "tracking the welfare and worldview of the public." It resolves these conceptual difficulties by having recourse back to the fundamental values of freedom and equality that make the basic case for democracy. Accordingly, a liberal conception of fair procedures, appropriately constrained by fundamental rights and liberties, is not merely a useful means for assuring that political decision tracks the public good nor yet a helpful heuristic for ascertaining its content but is rather an essential element of the very idea of the public good.[40]

# CHAPTER 4

# The Case for a Qualified Populism

I have argued that a legitimate government must be democratic, republican, and liberal. It must be of the people—that is, democratic as opposed to aristocratic or monarchical, according equal consideration to each in its processes of decision. It must be republican, dispersing and checking power so as to prevent domination. And for its procedures really to achieve the republican aim of preventing domination, which exists where power may be arbitrarily exercised, it must be for the people, in the sense that its procedures must respect the fundamental rights and liberties of each and treat each as a free and equal citizen. This account of a liberal-republican democracy thus begins to exhibit some flesh on its bones. It at least gives a theoretical context for my question about bureaucratic domination. Yet there are important dimensions still missing. These characterizations of how the political process ought to treat citizens are, indeed, fine as far as they go. What needs to be added is not any further qualification of how *it* must treat *us* but rather a proper recognition, suitably free of mystification, exaggeration, or romanticization, that we *are* it: that democratic government is rule by the people.[1] Hence, we need to broach the theme of populism, which will bring us, finally, to the value of autonomy.

Whereas the combination of republican and liberal ideas that I have advocated has a long and flourishing history, both contemporary republican theorists and contemporary liberal theorists have sharply criticized the populist ideal of rule by the people. From the liberal direction, Riker's book, *Liberalism against Populism*, portrays populism as a mask for coercion and majoritarian domination. Riker, as noted, took Arrovian social choice theory to cast doubt on the idea of the public good, which, according to populist ideas, is supposed to provide the focus or aim of the popular will. Believing that there is no proper object of the will of the people only endlessly varied ways to configure and constrain processes of majority decision, Riker emphasized the importance of ensuring that governments abide by liberal constraints. If Riker is right, the populist idea of the will of the people is a dangerous chimera.

Republican resistance to populist ideas is typified by Pettit.[2] As noted in chapter 2, he initially locates the ideal of freedom as nondomination on our conceptual maps by contrasting it with both (negative) freedom from interference and (positive) freedom as self-mastery. The ideal of collective autonomy or self-mastery is one that, he explains, he ignores:

> In arguing for the attractions of freedom as non-domination, I shall be comparing it exclusively with the negative ideal of non-interference, not with the positive ideal of self-mastery. If positive freedom is interpreted in populist fashion as democratic participation, then this neglect will scarcely need explanation: such a participatory ideal is not feasible in the modern world, and in any case the prospect of each being subject to the will of all is scarcely attractive.[3]

Thus, whether as dangerous and chimerical or merely as infeasible and unattractive, the idea of rule by the people, or democratic autonomy, currently stands under a cloud.

My aim in this chapter is to rehabilitate and defend the populist ideal in the face of these criticisms. It would be too bad to give up on it, for, as I shall argue, it is part and parcel of our commitment to democracy. I will allow Riker's definition of populism to be definitive: "In the populist (Rousseauistic) view, voting is a method for citizens to participate directly in making law, which is then the will of the people."[4]

The four major criticisms of populism, to restate them more analytically, are the following: First, it is *dangerous*, inviting the rationalization of all sorts of oppression on the specious Rousseauvian grounds that the general will is infallible and that obedience to it is liberty. Second, it is *unattractive*, bearing no significant attraction over and above that of the liberal-republican version of democracy I have so far presented. Third, it is *chimerical*, invoking a notion of the public good or the will of the people that is incoherent or in principle impossible to instantiate. And fourth, it is *unfeasible*, there being no way sufficiently to involve the people in decision-making in a modern government for the result to count as reflecting their will.

In responding to these criticisms, I will sometimes be engaged in direct rebuttal. Sometimes, however, what is called for will instead be a more nuanced account of what populism is or entails. While I will stick by populism as Riker defines it, I will introduce distinctions and qualifications that, many of the critics would say, materially alter the view. If they do, that is fine with me; my aim is not to contradict the critics but, as I say, to rehabilitate the populist ideal of rule by the people. A first step in this rehabilitation will be to cut the ideal of popular self-rule loose from some of its supposed "Rousseauistic" implications.

## Popular Rule Ensures Neither Freedom Nor Rectitude

Jean-Jacques Rousseau is due both credit as a progenitor of the populist ideal of collective self-rule and blame for claiming so much for that ideal as to make it appear positively dangerous. It is doubtful that Rousseau himself can count as a populist. As noted, he was not even an advocate of democracy, which he sharply distinguished from republican government. Still, his resonant idea of the general will inspired much populist thought and is considered by many to provide the philosophical foundation of populism. In order to rebut the charge of dangerousness, we must separate what is useful in Rousseau's legacy from the rhetorical excesses that are not. In light of the preceding chapter's criticism of the generality constraint inspired by the idea of the general will, I am not sure that any of Rousseau carries over into my own version of populism.[5]

The worst danger in populism, according to its critics, is that it holds that the will of the people can do no wrong. If this were true, this could be for one of two reasons: (1) because obedience to the will of the people is perfect freedom or (2) because the will of the people is infallible, always settling correctly on what ought to be done. If we bracket Rousseau's aversion to democracy and therefore read "the will of the people" for "the general will," we will find both of these claims in his *Social Contract*. There he writes that because "obedience to a law we prescribe to ourselves is liberty," the social contract whereby people enter into a civil condition "tacitly includes the undertaking . . . that whoever refuses to obey the general will shall be compelled to do so by the whole body. This means nothing less than that he will be forced to be free."[6] What could be more sinister? If we again bracket Rousseau's differentiation between the will of the people and the general will,[7] we also find him making frightening claims about the infallibility of the popular will.[8] What clearer invitation could there be for majoritarian tyranny than to claim that the majority is always right and that, besides, obedience to the will of the majority is perfect freedom?

So far, Rousseau. Fans of his may be able to generate interpretations that show that he did not really mean to make claims so radical or that other things he says mitigate the impact of these dangerous claims.[9] Not wanting to get caught up in irrelevant issues of textual interpretation, I will take a simpler tack. To rebut the charge of dangerousness, it suffices for the populist to disavow the additional Rousseauvian claims that make for trouble.[10]

Populism, to repeat, is the view that voting is a method for citizens to participate in making law and that the law thus made is the will of the people. There is nothing in this idea that implies either that satisfying the populist idea assures freedom or that the people cannot be mistaken about what ought to be done. Hence the short answer to the charge of dangerousness is that this charge wrongly tars all of populism with the Rousseauvian brush. While some of Rousseau's ideas may have helped rationalize the

Reign of Terror, those ideas can simply be separated off from populism and jettisoned.

Somewhat longer answers to the charge of dangerousness derive from embedding populism within the liberal-republican theory that I have developed so far. Consider freedom first.

What I have shown is that freedom is a complex and multifaceted ideal and that among the facets important for political theory are (1) the basic idea that one should not be placed under new duties without good reason and (2) the republican idea that one should be free of domination. Whatever else one might want additionally to say about positive freedom, it will remain true that these two aspects of freedom are important to assessing the legitimacy of any government. Hence even if obedience to the will of the people were counted, per the Rousseauvian claim that I have rejected, as a case of positive freedom or self-mastery, it could not count as perfect or entire freedom, for it hardly guarantees elemental and republican freedom. Even if it were freedom in the one respect, it might well fail to count as overall freedom.

Even this response does not go far enough, however; for we have strong, principled reasons for rejecting the thought that obeying popular rule makes one free in any sense. The reason is that this claim illicitly purports to draw a conclusion about all individuals from a form of self-mastery that is inherently collective. (I analyze the collective aspect of the popular will in chapter 12.) Popular rule is a way that we rule ourselves. As such, it may fairly be taken to ground a sense in which *we* are free. When the American colonists secured popular self-rule after the Revolutionary War, they not only became free from domination by Great Britain but arguably also became their own masters. This kind of claim about the freedom conferred by populist self-mastery applies only at the collective level, however, and does not factor down to the individual level.[11] In going over the pitfalls of the utilitarian, unanimity-based, and generality interpretations of welfarism in the preceding chapter, I showed just how difficult it is to move between the individual and collective levels. Hence even if rule by the people does involve a kind of collective freedom as self-mastery, this does not entail the dangerous Rousseauvian claim that each citizen experiences or enjoys a kind of freedom whenever he or she obeys the law.

Partly as a reminder to avoid this dangerous Rousseauvian trap, I speak of "democratic autonomy" rather than of "freedom as collective self-mastery." Since the term "autonomy," with the etymological meaning of "self-rule," was originally applied by the ancient Greeks to city-states free of foreign domination, there is, I hope, a firmer basis for understanding "autonomy" in an essentially collective and institutional sense.

In short, the populist simply need not claim that obedience to the will of the people is a kind of freedom. A populist who, like me, also recognizes the importance of liberal and republican ideals will have strong reason not to make this claim, for the existence of other important aspects of freedom makes it at best seriously misleading, while the conceptual gap between collective self-rule and the wills of individuals makes it almost surely false.

There is no more reason for a populist to accept the second dangerous claim traceable to Rousseau, the claim that the will of the people cannot be mistaken. The short response, again, is simply that this further claim is not entailed by populism, as I have defined it. And again, there are strong reasons why a populist who means to build on the kind of liberal-republican basis I have set out should not accept this further claim. As far as I can make out, those who would foist this further claim on populism do so either simply because it rings of Rousseau or because they cannot see what the normative significance of the will of the people is, unless it were infallible. I will try to enlighten them.

I will start with a more basic negative claim about the normative significance of the will of the people: That something is willed by the people cannot constitute a fundamental reason for doing it. Reasons are an important category in politics. The burden of legitimation under which all government stands requires that its actions be based on reasons. But the category of will does not mark out an appropriate place to look for reasons. We know this from the individual case. If my children ask me why they cannot go to a certain movie, I may answer by saying, simply, "because I say so." So to answer is to assert my authority without offering any reason. If I instead say, "because that is my will," I have done no differently. Attempting to bootstrap a decision or a willing into a reason fares no better in the first-personal case. If I am trying to decide whether to go see that movie myself, I cannot rationally decide to go *because* I so will it: That would be to put the smoke before the fire. The same is true in the political case, where, as the populist would have it, we are trying to decide what we ought to do.* We can give ourselves no good reason to do something by deciding to do it. It follows from this that there can be no good reason to expect the will of the people to constitute, in this kind of bootstrapping way, an independent reason—let alone a conclusive one—for doing what is willed.

If the will of the people cannot even give an independent reason for our doing something, then it can hardly be infallible about what we ought to do. But what, then, is the normative significance of the will of the people? Critics of populism seem to have seen only two possibilities: Either democratic procedures constitute the will of the people, which then stands as an independent and infallible normative touchstone, or else democratic pro-

---

* Although using the phrase "what we ought to do," as distinct from the simpler phrase "what to do," anticipates later chapters, it will not hurt to start getting used to it now.

cedures are means for attempting to discover the will of the people, in which case, given the voting paradox, their reliability is seriously questionable, as different detailed procedures and different configurations of the agenda will yield quite different portraits of the people's will. The significance of these technically derived worries has been debated.[12] Whatever their importance, however, the will of the people is not properly regarded as an object to be discovered. The reason why not, ironically enough, is expressed by Riker himself.

In the last chapter, we saw that Riker took Arrow's impossibility theorem to cast suspicion on the very idea of the public good. "Not so fast," was my response; "it casts doubt on the idea that the individualist assumptions of welfarism can suffice to limn a conception of the public good independently of a liberal conception of a fair political process; but it does not impugn the very idea of the public good." By the same token, we must admit that, granted the individualist assumptions, again, Arrow's work undercuts the idea that the will of the people exists latently in the set of citizens' wills, only needing the political process to discover it or make it manifest. It cannot simply exist latently in the wills of all individual citizens, because there is no acceptable function that could generate it from those wills *in abstracto*, specifically, in abstraction from an actual, fair political process.

So the normative importance of the will of the people lies neither in its infallibility nor in its being the object that democratic deliberation ought to discover. Terminology can help us from falling into either of these mistaken views. The appropriate object of democratic deliberation. I have suggested, is not the will of the people but the public good. "The will" is ambiguous between the faculty of choice and something it has chosen: The will of the people, in the second sense, emerges from the exercise of the people's will, in the first. (I will mainly confine myself to the second, emergent sense, on account of the dangers of mystification and hypostatization that go along with speaking of the people's will in the first sense: Our faculty or capacity for collective choice is embodied or spread out, in fact, across a wide variety of institutionalized settings.) This differentiation between the will of the people and the public good is suggested by Aristotle's philosophy of action, according to which the object of choice is the good or the apparent good.[13]

If, with the help of this terminology, we keep at bay any tendency to elevate the will of the people to a normative importance it does not deserve, we will have done much to domesticate it. In supporting the populist ideal of the will of the people, I am neither casting obedience to it as a proxy for freedom nor holding it out to be infallible. But I have not yet tried to say what the normative significance of the will of the people is. To do so will be to address the charge of unattractiveness.

## Popular Will and Individual Autonomy

In the previous chapter, I promised that I would argue that the liberal commitment to fair procedures of collective decision that treat individuals as free and equal and respect their fundamental rights and liberties is part of our commitment to democracy. I now seek to undertake this reconstructive step. In doing so, I will enrich the description of liberalism somewhat further by adding the idea that the procedures of decision must be ones in which we respect individuals as autonomous persons. That government ought to consist in rule by the people is entailed by the liberal ideal of respecting persons as free and equal autonomous beings—an ideal without which, I will argue, one is not really committed to democracy.

The idea that individuals ought to be treated as free and equal autonomous persons is, indeed, a fundamental liberal ideal. It traces, of course, to Kant. To be treated as autonomous here means to be treated as being capable of making up one's own mind on a rational basis. One of the great obstacles to political process in his own day, Kant thought, was that individuals lacked sufficient confidence in their own rational capacities to be willing to think on their own; they needed to free themselves from their "self-incurred minority"—the legacy of centuries of ecclesiastical and aristocratic domination—and "to dare to make use of [their] own understanding!"[14] Nowadays, of course, our situation is different. Those who participate in radio call-in shows seldom seem to lack for confidence in their views. Their stance more often resembles that of President George W. Bush, who said in response to protests, "I know what I believe. I will continue to articulate what I believe, and . . . I believe what I believe is right." What may need greater stress today is the part of the ideal of autonomy that refers to deciding "on a rational basis," which carries with it a recognition of one's fallibility.† Kant thought that, despite their timidity and reticence, individuals ought to be regarded as being capable of rationally making up their own minds about what ought to be done. We think that, despite their forwardness and lack of self-restraint, individuals ought to be regarded as being capable of rationally making up their own minds about what ought to be done. At least, the political process ought to so regard citizens.

This liberal ideal of individual autonomy underlies our objections to guardianship and explains why guardianship must count as nondemocratic. In the previous chapter, I argued that rule by benevolent guardians, even guardians who took each individual's welfare into account, would count as

---

† We also need to be encouraged, both via education and via our political institutions, to reason with one another—the topic of the following chapter. Chapter 10 explores the link between reasoning and a recognition of fallibility.

a form of domination. Precisely because there is no noncontroversial formula or function for translating the welfare of each into the public good, I argued, nonarbitrary public power requires fair procedures that treat people as free and equal and actually consult them about what ought to be done. It follows that one who has accepted republicanism has reason to embrace liberalism. This conceptual link between republicanism and liberalism helps explain why rule by benevolent guardians cannot count as an acceptable form of government. A process that fails actually to consult individuals' views in a fair way fails to treat them as free and equal autonomous beings.

The liberal demand that the political process treat individuals as autonomous persons immediately gives rise to three subsidiary requirements: (1) that the political process publicly address each citizen as someone capable of joining in public discussion; (2) that the political process solicit the participation of each citizen as a potential agent of political decision; and (3) that the political process treat individuals as "self-originating sources of claims," people whose claims "carry weight on their own."[15] To be sure, the requirements of publicity and participation, at least, might simply stand on their own, and they might be also provided with additional rationales— as republican means of avoiding governmental domination, for instance. I believe, however, that the general commitment to treating people as autonomous has independent plausibility and helps establish the importance of these three requirements. Together, the first two requirements—those of publicly addressing citizens as autonomous beings and engaging their agency—imply that democratic government should be a form of rule by the people. (I come to the importance of the third requirement in chapter 10.) In particular, the requirement that the political process solicit the engagement of each citizen as a potential agent of political decision demands a greater possibility for continuing involvement than a permanent and wholesale delegation to guardians would allow.[16] The only realistic way to engage citizens as autonomous agents in the political process is to invite them to vote and express their opinions in public discussion. The real attraction of populism, therefore, is that it is a necessary aspect of politically respecting individual autonomy.

The value of autonomy is here seen to do real work in building the argument for democracy. To confirm this, I will briefly describe two possible forms of governance that arguably respect the elemental freedom and equality that go into making the basic case for democracy but that we should not, I think, count as democratic. First, suppose rule were delegated not to a special class of guardians but to an impersonal, utilitarian want-collation machine. This machine would gather information from people about which options would satisfy their wants, preferences, or interests, and to what degree, and then would calculate which option will yield the greatest sum (or average) level of satisfaction of the relevant kind. Ridiculously unrealistic? Yes; and also inimical to the employment of practical intelligence, as I will argue in chapter 9. Yet while delegated rule by a want-collation machine is unrealistic and pragmatically unacceptable, its *conceivability* points up a gap in the argument so far developed for democracy. To locate that gap, consider a second possible means of impersonally securing impartiality. Suppose that rule were delegated on an entirely random basis—for example, by randomly selecting a dictator for the day (or year, or whatever).[17] The selected person would not use any discretion in ruling; rather, which collective decision should be taken would simply be read off from the dictator's previously known preference ranking.

My point is that neither rule by the want-collation machine nor rule by random selection of a dictator for a day should be counted as legitimately democratic. Adding republican opportunities for people to contest the machine's or the dictator's determinations and liberal protections of individual rights and liberties would not suffice to convert either form of rule into a democracy. If you join me in thinking that democracy requires more involvement by the people than either of these rather far-out possibilities would allow, then you accept in some form the populist notion that rule by the people is an essential feature of democracy. Hence reconstructing our grounds for insisting that only democratic rule is legitimate will unearth the importance of respecting individuals as free and equal autonomous beings.

Stepping back, one can see how the various strands of the democratic ideal support each other. Working in a value-based direction, I have argued that democratic legitimation is important because government impinges on freedom but that a proper recognition of freedom also requires incorporating the republican value of nondomination. Understanding the latter value requires one to draw on a liberal understanding of fair procedures. And a deeper view of the liberal ideal in turn leads one to recognize that democracy must be rule by the people. Working in the opposite, reconstructive direction, I have shown how each of the values these arguments draw on—elemental freedom, equality, and respect for citizens as free and equal autonomous beings—is important to explaining why it is that we take democracy to be normatively superior to alternative forms of government. Freedom and equality combine, as in the basic case, to show democracy superior to monarchy and aristocracy. The liberal ideal of autonomous citizens is needed to show why, in addition, the impersonal rule of a want-collation machine or a dictator for a day device would be illegitimate even if it were feasible.

Perhaps, though, by putting together so many values that legitimate democratic rule must serve, I have described an impossible ideal. Is it possible for democratic government to count as rule by the people? Is it possible for liberal-republican democratic government also to be populist? In the remainder of this chapter, I will address at a general level questions about populism's incoherence and its unfeasibility. Of course, insofar as questions about the feasibility of rule by the people are motivated by worries about administrative discretion and bureaucratic domination, it will take me the rest of the book to answer them. Much of that later discussion would be wasted, however, if, as some of its critics charge, the populist idea of the will of the people is a chimera.

## What Is the People's Will?

In this section, I will consider three forms of the charge that the idea of the will of the people is incoherent or illusory. The first two pertain to the very existence of the will of the people, while the third pertains to the possibility of our knowing it.

The most elementary objection to the idea of the will of the people is that the people is a collective entity and collective entities cannot have wills. Now, I agree that there are serious dangers in hypostatizing the people. We must be leery of Rousseau's metaphors of "the body politic." The reason for not thinking in these terms, however, is that doing so is dangerous, not that collectives cannot decide what to do. A pair of people can decide what movie to attend, and a government can decide whether to declare war. There has been a prejudice against collective states in the philosophy of mind. Recent work, however, has overcome this prejudice and has made considerable headway in explicating collective states of mind in ways that do not invoke spooky "selves" that have four ears, or two hundred million ears, apiece.[18] So yes, the people is a collective, and yes, it can have a will.

The second reason critics have thought the idea of the will of the people was incoherent, or at least suspect, is the one that, as I have mentioned, Riker articulated. If, as Arrow showed, there is no acceptable function from individual wills to a collective will, then how can a collective will be taken to exist? And I have already given the answer: Even if Arrow's impossibility theorem and the instability of majority rule casts doubt on the idea of a will of the people that exists in abstraction from any actual, fair procedures, that is not what we are looking for.[19] Instead, we are looking for the will of the people that concretely emerges from such procedures.[20]

As I have argued in this chapter, the normative importance for democracy of the idea of the will of the people is not that it is an object to be discovered. Rather, the requirement that the political process respect the autonomy of citizens demands that the process invite them to take a role in deciding, together, what ought to be done. What they then decide is their will. This role for the will of the people does not demand that it exist as an object independent of procedures that treat individuals as free and equal. Rather, it demands only that the political process be constructed so that what emerges from it can fairly be counted as constituting the people's will.[21] At this point, this demand remains quite vaguely formulated. I have shown that rule by a want-collation machine and by a randomly selected dictator for a day would not count as constituting the will of the people, for these methods do not adequately engage citizens as autonomous participants. What must be involved for the political decisions of a modern state to count as constituting the will of the people is something that I must address, hereafter. Bureaucratic structures pose a difficult challenge to the populist hope; but I aim to show how this challenge may be surmounted.

A third objection to the very idea of the will of the people also mistakes its role in democratic theory. One might think that the point of saying that democratic procedures constitute the will of the people is to put one in a position of going on to say that, from that point onward or downward, and until the people change their minds, this will must be obeyed. If that is what one thinks, then, the objection runs, the idea is chimerical because such processes cannot be read—and not just because no text can be read for univocal meaning but rather for reasons particular to this sort of process. The point is familiar from the rocky grounds of "legislative intent," a legal category that shows up in the judicial review and implementation of statutes. When a decision issues from a collective agent, the variety of reasons taken seriously by its various participants will mean that there is no straightforward or indisputable way of reading the collective intention off of the collective action.

In response, I would concede that the objection is essentially correct in its pessimistic conclusions about reading underlying collective intention off of collective decisions, but I would assert that this point does not undercut the normative importance of the idea of the popular will. This importance, to repeat, is that governmental procedures must be so set up that they can count as forming a public will. It does not matter, for this purpose, whether anyone can "read" that will. What matters is that individuals are respected as autonomous and equal participants in the process of decision. For this to succeed, what the government decides to do must indeed count as expressing the will of the people; but to say that is just to refer to the overt or obvious level of description—say, to the statute that the court is trying to implement when it squints to discern "legislative intent" more sharply. It is not at all to imply that the will or intentions of the people will be available to resolve disputed questions about what it is, exactly, that the government has done.

So all that is necessary is that individuals participate sufficiently in the political process for them to count as deciding, together, what ought to be done. But this is exactly what the critics of populism say is unfeasible. To answering this last criticism I now turn.

## Distributed Popular Sovereignty

If the idea of the will of the people implied that the people must decide everything or that they must decide everything within their purview at one time or in a single, unified forum, then it would indeed be an infeasible ideal. In this section, I undertake an initial defense of populism's feasibility by explaining that it carries neither the first, radical implication nor the second, monistic one. The first point can be made quite briefly. After addressing the second, I will offer some constructive remarks about what populism does require.

The radical interpretation of populism comes to ruin on what I have called the constitution—that set of stable legal arrangements that establishes the processes of governmental decision. In demanding that the people decide everything, the radical populist insists that even the constitution must have been established by an act of popular will. Yet, as already discussed, the will of the people cannot coherently be conceived as existing apart from some set of procedures within which the people arrive at their decisions.[22] For one thing, the constitution will need to clarify who the people are by defining a jurisdiction and indicating who is to be counted as a citizen. It follows that if the constitution is to issue from the will of the people, there must be some set of procedures from which it issues. But then, as Frank Michelman argues in a searching and poignant essay, the radical populist who wanted even "the most fundamental laws" to issue from the will of the people will want *those* procedures to issue from the will of the people, as well.[23] The radical populist thus lands in a vicious regress, in a futile search for a fair way to determine the will of the people via legally instituted democratic procedures themselves instituted by the will of the people. There is no way to do that.

The autonomy-based rationale for populism does not generate this radical demand. If one were proceeding into democracy with the will of the people as one's sole guiding idea, then one would, indeed, naturally land in the radical's impasse; but the idea does not stand on its own. Rather, it is a corollary of the liberal ideal of respecting persons as free and equal autonomous beings. There is no reason to think that so respecting persons necessarily leads in a radical populist's direction. Consider the implications of respect for autonomy in an entirely different setting, clinical medicine. While it is debated what precisely is entailed by a proper respect for patients' autonomy, no one thinks that it requires giving them total control over every detail of the medical procedures they undergo. In addition, the reference to rationality that is built into the idea of autonomy suggests another kind of limit: Even in the individual case, it seems, there are certain normative presuppositions of acting autonomously.[24] In the case of populism, the political system's respect for everyone's autonomy must take into account what sorts of uses of autonomy are necessarily incompatible with a like use of autonomy by others.[25] More particularly, as I have suggested, the ideal of autonomy stands at the core of a richer and more complex liberalism, which articulates some of the needed limits in the form of fundamental rights and liberties and basic constraints on fair process. Stemming, as it does, from such liberal roots, an autonomy-based populism will naturally adapt itself to these liberal limits. The rationale I have provided for populism does not license understanding it radically.

Monistic views about forming the popular will accept the necessity of prior constitutional structure but demand, within such a structure, that there be one place where the popular will is formulated. I draw the term "monism" from Bruce Ackerman's insightful writings on constitutional law.[26] Ackerman's arguments against monism will force us to adopt a more sophisticated conception of how the will of the people can be embodied in political procedures.

With his eyes on American constitutional history, Ackerman seeks to vindicate the ideal of rule by the people, as articulated in that context by Madison and Lincoln. Most thinking about these issues, he claims, has been hampered by the assumptions of the view he labels monism, which has two defining tenets. First, all significant acts of lawmaking must be viewed as acts of the people, and second, for this to be the case, some one institution in the government must possess a legitimate claim to speak for the people. Generally taking the elected legislature to speak for the people, monists typically succumb to a view of representation according to which the part validly stands for the whole. "All is lost," Ackerman warns, "if we are captured by this naive synecdoche. If we mistake Congress for the People Assembled, and give it supreme power, it will act in a way that belies its populist rhetoric."[27] The idea of representation will enlighten us, he suggests, only if we see how the Federalists used it to deconstruct the monists' hope. By establishing a system of government in which each of many parts (the House, the Senate, and the president, especially) represent the people in different ways and guises, the Federalists attempted to hold all naive synecdoche at bay.

Ackerman himself favors instead a "dualist" account of populism, the two assumptions of which contrast with those of monism.[28] According to dualism, there is no governmental institution that can claim to speak for the people: "No institution of normal politics can be allowed to transsubstantiate itself into the People of the United States."[29] Correspondingly, dualism limits its hopes for rule by the people. The second defining tenet of dualism is that "decisions by the People occur rarely, and under special circumstances."[30] This is Ackerman's famous theory of "constitutional moments": the rare occasions on which the people speak. The people are involved only in making "higher," or constitutional, law and then only at epochal moments when the constitution is remade.

And why should we believe that the people are involved even then? In making his case, via a historical examination of three periods of constitutional revision in U.S. history, Ackerman subtly shifts the terms of assessment. Instead of structural features ("naive synechdoche") that might underwrite the claims of some body to speak for the people, whatever that body says, Ackerman provides a set of features that apply to what some body of people *has said*: to the changes they have proposed. Roughly: if some proposed constitutional change is accepted as legitimate by the institutions it unsettled, gains support, is ratified (as by the process of constitutional amendment), and sees its legalistic opposition melt away, then it becomes hard to deny that it represents the will of the people.[31] If the people do not object via the existing institutions subject to this reform, in the states and their legislatures, or by organizing legal opposition, then how can they be said to object at all?

As valuable as this account may be for understanding U.S. constitutional history, it does not provide us with a usable understanding of the will of the people for purposes of democratic theory. We need to understand what it is about the institutions of democracy—whether of any actual democracy or of a reformed democracy that we might attain—that licenses the claim that they instantiate rule by the people. If this claim is to be made good by any regime's institutions, it must be a claim that can be supported *ex ante*, on the basis of general features of those institutions, rather than depending on an *ex post* analysis of how a particular set of that institution's decisions have fared with the people. Particular reforms instituted by dictators and absolute monarchs can also turn out to be quite popular, can be accepted as legitimate and generate no significant opposition. Such popular acceptance of particular reforms may even lend such reforms a temporary legitimacy. They do not, however, indicate why we should think that they emerged from a process that adequately engaged individuals' autonomy.

Furthermore, as I argued in rejecting rule by a want-collation machine or a dictator for a day, rule by the people demands more ongoing engagement of citizens' autonomy than Ackerman's dualism can account for. Since it is the day-to-day operations of government whereby we are ruled—whereby we impose new duties on ourselves—it is in the day-to-day operations of government, if they are to be legitimate, that the will of the people must express itself. A second reason that Ackerman's dualism is unsatisfactory as a tool of democratic theory, then, is that it gives up on describing how the day-to-day operations of democratic government can reflect the will of the people.

Accordingly, we need to find a third alternative to monism and dualism. The foregoing arguments for populist democracy imply that we should remain committed to one of monism's two assumptions, that all significant acts of lawmaking must be acts of the people. (In part III, I will carry this thought beyond the level of legislative creation of statutes and look at the

administrative rulemaking that importantly specifies and carries out the statutes.) The plank of monism that must go, therefore, is the assumption that
there must be one institution of government that validly speaks for the
people, be that an elected legislature, a popularly elected president, or a
supreme court that guards the founding revolutionary spirit. As Ackerman
rightly says, "there can be no hope of capturing, in some simple snapshot,
what the citizenry really think about an issue."[32] This does not imply, however—as he takes it to—that we must give up on the idea that the ordinary
lawmaking operations of government instantiate rule by the people. Instead,
what we need to do is to try to understand how rule by the people is
distributed among government institutions, which extend from elections
through legislative debate and voting to administrative elaboration, all
within the context of an informal public sphere that enables and encourages
free political discussion.

In short, the populist idea of the will of the people has a complex and
symbiotic relationship to the idea of a constitution. As radical populists fail
adequately to realize, it requires a constitutional structure for a will of the
people to exist at all. Monists take this point but then unrealistically imagine
that the will of the people will emanate from some focal point within that
structure. Since an adequate engagement of citizens' autonomy does demand
that the will of the people be expressed in day-to-day lawmaking, we must
therefore look for a way in which the formation of the popular will can be
distributed across various parts of a constitutional structure. Thus we arrive
at the idea of institutionally distributed systems for forming the will of the
people—"institutionally distributed popular sovereignty," for short.‡

Although Ackerman's theory of "constitutional moments" does not describe a sufficient place for the will of the people, it does suggest an important general feature of autonomy, which in turn may be invoked to
comfort the disappointed radical populist. It is not possible for the will of
the people to construct itself from the ground up without relying on decision procedures that are provisionally used to get going. As Ackerman
reminds us, though, it is possible to amend a constitution piece by piece.
We cannot start from scratch, but we can stand back enough to reflect on,
and potentially revise, any aspect of our procedures.[33] This possibility of
reflective revision, rather than a history of reflective creation, is what
grounds our constitutional autonomy.

This point about the possibility of constitutional amendment must be
taken to supplement a distributed account of day-to-day popular rule rather
than to supplant it. Noticing the importance of the kind of *possibility* of
reflective revision that shows up in the amendment process, Pettit—as

---

‡ As the context should make clear, I use the term "distributed popular sovereignty" as
an abbreviation for "a distributed system of popular will formation."

noted, a critic of populism—suggests that such possibility is enough for collective self-rule:

> By analogy [to the individual case], the self-ruling demos or people may . . . often run on automatic pilot, allowing public decision-making to materialize under more or less unexamined routines. What makes them self-ruling or democratic is the fact that they are not exposed willy-nilly to that pattern of decision-making: they are able to contest decisions at will and, if the contestation establishes a mismatch with their relevant interests or opinions, able to force an amendment.[34]

Yet while the possibility of reflective revision is crucial to autonomy or self-rule, whether individual or collective, it is not sufficient for it.[35] This is in part because historical forces shape and mold present selves. Past oppression can so distort what it is that a person would decide on reflection that the mere possibility of reflecting cannot produce autonomy. The possibility of reflecting on how to amend the structure of Saudi rule would not suffice to bring the citizens of the Saudi kingdom any significant measure of popular rule. It is not that Pettit thinks otherwise but rather that he here underrates the importance of the happy history of the democratic republics he is discussing.

In politics, there are two additional reasons that autonomy cannot be reduced to the mere possibility for reflection and contestation. One is that, as I have argued, a proper political respect for individual autonomy requires actually involving individuals in the course of forging political decisions. That they could be involved is not enough. Perhaps Pettit would object that this first reason begs the question against his more minimal interpretation of "self-rule." A second reason, however, confirms and reinforces the first. When individuals run on "automatic pilot," they may indeed be acting autonomously—unless, of course, they have been oppressively socialized to go on the way they are. When public decision-making emerges from "more or less unexamined routines," however, something importantly different is going on, namely: the people are being ruled by *someone else*. Whether one is making one's own decisions or is simply under the sway of another is always an issue pertinent to autonomy, individual or otherwise.[36] I began my examination of democratic autonomy with the concern about whether bureaucrats rule us. We should not blind ourselves to that danger by putting the day-to-day routines of administrators on a par with the habits of an autonomous individual. Of course, the capacity for popular rule will not always be fully realized; but we will not even be able to discern the capacity unless we look for a form of self-rule that is more proactive than after-the-fact contestation.

Democratic self-rule depends on a happy constitutional history; but it depends on actual history in another way, as well. An individual can make up his or her own mind in a moment. Given that the formation of the people's will in a democracy must be regarded as being distributed across an entire constitutional structure, a people cannot do so. Rather, successful democratic self-rule will depend on the proper alignment of the various stages of the process, from public discussion and voting to debate and voting in an assembly, due ratification (if needed) by a chief executive, refinement and implementation by administrative agencies, and reflective public acceptance in the end. Rule by the people demands far more than the bare possibility that each of these stages come into adequate alignment: It requires that they generally do so, and for nonaccidental reasons.

I can now summarize my defense of populism. The political ideal of populism, or the idea that the law ought to express the will of the people, who actively participate in its formation by voting and otherwise, rests on the liberal ideal that the political process ought to respect citizens as free and equal autonomous persons. Once we see that this is the basis of populism, we can easily separate it from the dangerous claims of infallibility and freedom-constituting obedience. We can also describe the point of the idea of the people's will without either casting it as an object to be discovered or as a key to resolving disputed questions in the interpretation of law. The point is simply that the political process must be so structured that it adequately respects the autonomy of individual citizens; if the process is so structured, we may regard the decisions that emerge as reflecting the will of the people. Securing the active participation of autonomous citizens in political decision would be impossible if it had to extend back to the constitution's historical origins or if it had to find adequate expression at a single moment within the political process. By contrast, a popular will formation that is distributed across the constitutional structure does seem feasible. Part III will describe a realistic set of conditions for realizing distributed popular sovereignty.

I have arrived at a conception of liberal-republican-populist democracy, one that is, in Lincoln's deathless phrase, "government of the people, by the people, and for the people." Before I can revert to the abbreviating label "democratic autonomy," I need to add one more qualifying adjective: "rationalist." We need to understand why we must rule ourselves by reasoning together.

# CHAPTER 5

# Democratic Rule Must Be Reasoned

I have not yet integrated the idea of deliberative democracy into my account. This idea is currently popular and is taken by some simply to be obviously attractive. Others, reacting perhaps to the idea's very popularity, deny its attractions. On both sides, there is vagueness and equivocation about what "deliberative democracy" means. In part to avoid these confusions, I start instead with the term "reasoning."[1] Those who engage in practical reasoning about what ought to be done are engaged in deliberation in a core or paradigm sense. I will argue that citizens in a democracy must rule by reasoning with one another. Collective self-rule thus must be reasoned. Hence, if you will, democracy must be strongly deliberative.

The aims of this chapter will emerge more clearly if a limitation of the recent deliberative democracy movement is recognized, one that arises from aspects of that movement's polemical context and from weaknesses in its philosophical development. Two features of the movement's polemical context have tended to limit its vision. Some recent proponents of deliberative democracy have concentrated on opposing the sort of preference-aggregation approach shared, in various forms, by the public choice and social choice schools. Against these powerful intellectual constructs, advocates of deliberative democracy have insisted that a crucial function of democratic dialogue is to *change* preferences.[2] Sometimes it is persuasive argument that does it, as in the case of Patrick Henry's speech to the Virginia Assembly in 1775.[3] Sometimes information is what does the trick; for instance, widespread publicity about endangered species has surely led people who otherwise would not even have heard about them to care about preserving them. Sometimes these two effects are mixed together: U.S. Senators who had not heard about the Arctic National Wildlife Refuge before the 2000 presidential campaign probably soon afterwards formed some view about whether drilling for oil should be allowed there. This point about preference change is a powerful one; I will build on it in chapter 11.

Other proponents of deliberative democracy, influenced by the German critical theory tradition, contrast their approach more prominently with the narrowness of instrumental (end-means) reasoning, which they associate with a top-down, authoritarian system of control.[4] Instrumental rationality is the natural key in which bureaucratic domination is played. If a Bismarck or a Mussolini can centrally control the setting of ends and can discipline bureaucracies to conform to a narrow mode of end-means reasoning, then this domination can be almost total. Critical theorists insist that to block such dangers of organized domination, governmental processes must be open to discursive contestation that substitutes a more open-ended form of communication for the narrow, top-down mode that instrumentalist conceptions of reasoning encourage.

The principal weakness in the theory of deliberative democracy, to date, is that it has not developed a convincing account of how the open-ended, preference- and end-changing discussion in which we are supposed to engage together can count as a form of *reasoning*. The main reason why not, as I see it, is that the task has not been squarely faced of describing how public reasoning can be noninstrumental—how it can extend to the ends of policy and not just concern the selection of means. To insist that public debate will change preferences or ends is to insist that it has a noninstrumental *effect* but does not explain how one gets there by reasoning. That discussion should be open-ended and "communicative" is certainly an attractive idea but again does not tell us how public reasoning can extend to ends.[5]

To rectify this weakness, the following chapter sets out a conception of noninstrumental reasoning, reasoning that extends to establishing new ends (and thus, *a fortiori* new preferences). It will take the remainder of this book to explain how reasoning about the ends of policy can be public. In the meantime, however, one should notice how this philosophical weakness has combined with the polemical focus of many deliberative democrats to leave their flank unprotected against a forgotten foe, the liberal proceduralist. Let me explain.

The liberal strand of democracy, as it entered my argument in chapter 3, centers around the importance of fair procedures of decision that treat individuals as free and equal—and, I added, autonomous. Some of those who advocate deliberative democracy are not fully satisfied with liberal procedures as they currently exist. Especially those writers inspired by the critical theory tradition would like to see reforms that more truly realize equality by empowering the weak and unsettling the status quo. There is indeed a lot that needs to be done in that direction. In the United States, one might start with campaign finance reform. To emphasize the need for such reform, however, is not to jettison the idea of fair procedures that treat individuals as free and equal but to beef it up.[6] But now comes the liberal proceduralist, who says: "Yes, people need to get together and talk; and as you deliberative democrats all agree, they need to do so within fair procedures that treat people as free and equal. Liberal principles of free discussion and public debate will assure plenty of talking. So really, when you come down to it, that is *all* that is required.\* Any further insistence on deliberation or on people reasoning together is misdirected." Insofar as it lacks a clear vision of the nature and importance of democratic reasoning, the deliberative democracy movement lacks a sufficiently clear and forceful answer to the liberal proceduralist.[7]

To be sure, looked at from the opposite angle, liberal proceduralism, too, is weak insofar as it fails to incorporate a clear conception of democratic reasoning. This weakness shows up clearly in the domain of administrative decision-making, where there often seems to be plenty of communication. A liberal proceduralist will emphasize the value of notice-and-comment constraints on rulemaking, for instance. In 1983, taking a more proactive approach, the then administrator of the U.S. Environmental Protection Agency (EPA), William Ruckelshaus, went out into the Pacific Northwest to conduct public discussions about proposed regulations to implement the Clean Air Act.[8] These would have threatened the operation of a plant run by the American Smelting and Refining Company (Asarco), a major local employer and emitter of arsenic near Tacoma, Washington. The EPA ran public hearings and workshops. In the course of these, many locals not only expressed their views but refined and changed them. Consensus, however, did not emerge; if anything, the differences between those who were most concerned about their jobs and those who were worried about air quality were sharpened. Collecting public comments and soliciting public discussion is a good thing, but the question that begs to be addressed and is not satisfactorily answered by the liberal proceduralist is: "And once heard, what then?"[9] Because consensus cannot be often expected in politics, a democrat must go beyond establishing procedures for eliciting citizen input and specify modes of reasoning whereby that input may be translated into a public decision. Unless a conception of public reasoning takes over where the procedures for gathering input leave off, we will rightly suspect that the procedures are simply window dressing—that the bureaucrats patiently listen to the input and then do what they want.

In fact, I believe that such cynicism is not called for—not because liberal procedures are more powerfully constraining than the cynic recognized but because honorable officials like Ruckelshaus often do engage in a legitimate and serious form of public reasoning that takes over where such procedural

---

\* A liberal-republican proceduralist can add in procedures for contesting governmental decisions, affording still more opportunity for discussion.

input leaves off. Accordingly, I do not take my task to be that of peddling a radical new invention, a hitherto untried mode of public reasoning, but rather to be articulating and providing a philosophical defense for a mode of reasoning that our best public servants actually use.

Postponing the task of fully unfolding the nature of this democratic reasoning, this chapter takes up the challenge of explaining why citizens ought to rule by reasoning with one another. It will examine two potential rationales: an epistemic one, which seems rather shaky, and a moral one, which provides a firmer basis. Before examining why citizens ought to reason with one another, however, I should be clear about what I take that to mean.

## The Nature of Reasoning in General

What ultimately distinguishes a truly deliberative conception of democracy from one, such as the liberal proceduralist's, that merely emphasizes the importance of properly structured talk is an orientation to truth.[10] Reasoning in general is oriented to truth in the relevant way.

We can arrive at this idea of reason's truth-orientation via a brief consideration of the fact that reasoning sifts reasons and arguments. Thus, a noncontroversial mark of reasoning, as opposed to entirely intuitive or unconscious modes of thinking, is that it is potentially discursive.[11] It treats of considerations and of inferences that can in principle be made publicly explicit. In sifting them, reasoning is not neutral about their merits. Reasoning is also to be distinguished from musing and fantasizing, or writing fiction. Reasoning is thinking that sifts discursively expressible reasons and arguments either in order to ascertain the truth of certain propositions or to derive new true propositions from ones that are initially believed to be true.[12]

Practical reasoning, reasoning about what to do, is similarly oriented to the truth. People who reason practically are trying to figure out what they ought to do. Not what they morally or politically ought to do but simply what they ought to do.[13] One can decide what to do in a way that does not count as reasoning. For instance, one can flip a coin. If "deliberating" just meant "deciding what to do," then deliberation would not be oriented to the truth. It might simply concern what to do and not what one ought to do. "Deliberation" in a truer sense, however—that which is needed to make deliberative democracy a view distinct from liberal proceduralism—will count as practical reasoning, reasoning that is oriented to figuring out the truth about what ought to be done. As we might more colloquially say, practical reasoning aims to figure out what really ought to be done.

So the question is, why ought democratic discussion be a process of reasoning oriented to figuring out what really ought to be done?

## The Fragility of the Argument from Reliability

One possible reason why people ought to reason with one another in fair processes of political decision is that they will thereby be led to decisions that better approximate what actually ought to be done than if they did not. To make this argument is to take truth-orientation to provide not only the defining mark of democratic deliberation but also its primary rationale.[14] While I am attracted to this claim and would be happy if democratic reasoning could be defended on the basis of its reliability, I am not fully persuaded.

It is surely true that encouraging deliberation has some epistemic benefits. Intuitively, we might come up with three. (1) Public deliberation, Aristotle suggested, is akin to a public feast or a potluck dinner to which each invitee contributes a different dish; each participant contributes a unique perspective, helping to make up for the one-sidedness of each.[15] (2) In a large republic, as Madison hoped, encouraging public discussion can also help cancel out the various partialities of factions, generating a more impartial basis for decision. (3) Finally, deliberation can help assure that policy is formed on a measured basis and not in thoughtless reaction to the passions of the moment.

At this level of armchair theorizing—which is where we are stuck so long as the truth about what ought to be done remains deeply disputed—each of these benefits can be and has been questioned. (1) Given the incommensurability of worldviews present in contemporary publics, there is reason to fear that multiplying perspectives will simply foster confusion and paralysis. We already see such paralysis in debates about abortion. It is not clear how adding in more perspectives will help resolve such an impasse, and it is easy to imagine how it might make things worse. (2) As to faction, even if we accept that Madison was essentially correct about how to quell the instability due to faction, we might wonder whether so doing contributes to the epistemic reliability of the political process. As Marx pointed out, public deliberation is pervasively subject to distortion as participants seek to mask their narrow interests in language appealing to universalizable reasons.[16] In addition, the community may share prejudices to which public deliberation is forced to pander.[17] Hence the pressure on factions to present their views in a publicly palatable way may harm reliability as much as it helps it. (3) Finally, we know from experience that policies formed after long discussion are not always moderate in their nature or their grounds.

The McCarthy era of anticommunist demagoguery typifies how political discussion can become dominated by bullying rhetoric and manipulative public relations techniques.[18] Further, it is not even generally true that deliberate action taken "in a cool hour" is more reliable than immediate, emotionally generated action.[19]

Each of these problems might be addressed by strengthening other virtues of the political process and its participants. Thus, the confusion and paralysis that potentially flows from multiplying perspectives might be reduced by disseminating techniques for accommodating "difference."[20] Dangers of ideological distortion and pandering to prejudice would be lessened if society were more just and less marked by power imbalances or invidious discrimination. And demagogic misuse of rhetoric might be dampened by more effective republican devices for contesting its bullying use. Each of these virtues is to be encouraged, and each has its place within the account of democracy I have been developing.

Although an idealizing approach could, in a hopeful mood, rest the importance of democratic reasoning on its epistemic merits—on its comparative reliability at yielding correct decisions—I am uncomfortable resting this important conclusion on so rickety a support. Accordingly, I turn to a more straightforward and secure normative argument, which builds on the value of autonomy—a value the importance of which I have already defended.

## Respecting One Another's Autonomy

That citizens in a democracy must rule by reasoning with one another follows from the previous chapter's argument for populism. Here is the argument in a nutshell: In that chapter, I argued that because the political process ought to respect citizens as free and equal autonomous persons, democratic government ought to be a form of rule by the people. Hence, I argued, we must take seriously the idea that we rule ourselves. If it is we who are ruling ourselves, I must now add, then it is we who ought to respect each other's autonomy. It is each of us, as citizens, who owe to each other the duty of taking account of the reasons and arguments that each offers in the political process.[21]

The populist point, that we should be ruling ourselves in a democracy, is essential to this argument. The idea of respecting one another's autonomy, taken by itself, will not carry us to the conclusion that we ought to reason with one another. In other contexts, and on other assumptions, it would instead imply that we ought to leave one another alone. This is one aspect of a parent's delicate struggle with teenaged children: As a parent, one probably wants to encourage young adults' nascent autonomy, their growing

sense of personal responsibility and their increasing ability to make decisions on their own. Pulling in the other direction are fears about bad things
that they can do or suffer. Clearly, though, respect for their autonomy, in
that context, argues for giving them leeway to make their own, independent
decisions without parental oversight or interference.

In politics, this concern to make room for individuality and independence
certainly does not disappear. To the contrary, it undergirds the liberal's insistence on protecting fundamental freedoms. One reason that we do not
want government making too many decisions for us is that, within limits,
we tend to believe in individuals' ability to make their own decisions.† As
shown in chapter 2, because government impinges on the freedom of autonomous individuals, it stands under a burden of legitimation.

The freedom, rights, and liberties of individuals that the liberal and republican strands of democracy emphasize also carry individual responsibil-
ities with them. One cannot consistently insist on the importance of individual autonomy as the basis for populist democracy and then turn around
and suggest that individuals are not severally responsible for doing their
part in democratic self-rule. The duty to respect one another's autonomy
in the political process, therefore, is one that cannot be fully satisfied by us
jointly unless each of us individually plays his or her part. How democratic
decision-making gets articulated into stages involving institutionalized joint
agents, such as a legislature, is the topic of part III. Looking at the process
more abstractly, it is clear that each citizen has a role to play and a responsibility to fulfill as a voter and as a discussant.

Supposing, then, that there is a government that is impinging on individual freedom, exercising some legitimate functions (including that of securing
the rule of law, without which freedom as nondomination is impossible),
we ask: What does a proper respect for individual autonomy require of
citizens as they participate in democratic processes? Should citizens struggle,
like some parents of teenagers, to stifle their critical comments and even
constructive suggestions and strive for a mutual independence of political
judgment?

Conceivably, a radical believer in majority rule would think that mutual
respect for each other's autonomy does call for refraining from arguing with
one another. Imagine someone who comes to be persuaded of the epistemic
virtues of majority rule on the basis of Condorcet's jury theorem.[22] When
the choices are binary, one of the two choices will be correct (or will represent a true conception of what we ought to do) and the other will not
be.[23] If there are many voters; if they are, on average, better than random

---

† We may also believe that, as John Stuart Mill argued in *On Liberty*, individuality is a
good thing.

at selecting the correct alternative; and if their decisions are statistically independent of one another, then the jury theorem says that majority rule will pick the correct choice a very high proportion of the time. Now clearly, in any actual democratic process, statistical independence among the voters' opinions is violated all the time. People do not form their political views in isolation but in ways that are systematically influenced by others. Nonetheless, someone inspired by the jury theorem might press for doing whatever can be done to ensure that people do not influence one another's political views.[24] Hence, they might hold, the ideally fair and reliable democratic process would be one in which people simply vote, without talking to one another at all.

Plainly enough, this ground for suppressing mutual discussion is crazy. It reveals a hankering to reduce democracy to an impersonal decision rule—in this case, majority rule—whereas it cannot but be rule by people. To be reminded of the impossibility of the reduction, just ask: Who is it who frames the items for the agenda? Who is it who will put forward a concrete proposal about how to make transportation systems accessible to the disabled or about the circumstances in which clients of health maintenance organizations will be allowed to sue for nonprovision of medical services? Such proposals cannot be put together by majority rule. Often it is bureaucrats and lobbyists who frame such proposals. Since we do not want to be ruled by lobbyists and bureaucrats, however, we must find a way to integrate the framing of proposals (and their elaboration once adopted) within the democratic process by which we rule ourselves. The only good way to do so is by discussing with each other the merits of the various possibilities.

In short, the suggestion that mutual respect for each other's autonomy requires standing back and letting citizens exercise their right to vote fails to take seriously the populist idea that democracy is a form of government in which we must rule ourselves. We must frame alternatives and make decisions. In doing so, there is a lot of deliberative work to do.

As we attempt to frame alternatives and make decisions, a due respect for each other's autonomy does require that we give reasons for the proposals we favor and that we attend, as best we can, to the reasons and arguments that each person offers.‡

These reasons and arguments will be of many kinds; there will be no dearth. Specifically, as I have shown, having accepted the liberal ideal of respecting persons' autonomy in politics, we have also taken on board the

---

‡ I will address in chapter 6 the way in which the ideal of political equality intersects with the requirement of attending to the reasons that individuals offer in democratic deliberation.

corollary idea that individuals are to be regarded as self-originating sources of claims. This means that the mere fact that someone prefers a proposal provides us with some reason—of course, a potentially defeasible reason—to adopt it.[25] I mention this point here only to cement the claim that reasons and arguments to consider will not be lacking. Citizens in any reasonably well-functioning democracy are of course able to offer far more sophisticated arguments for and against political proposals, as well.

Furthermore, just as the government's respect for individual autonomy requires that it offer reasons and arguments publicly, so too our respect for each other's autonomy requires that we frame our reasons and arguments in such a way that others may be reasonably expected to recognize them as reasons and arguments. Systematically so to conduct oneself in politics is to exercise the virtue of public reasonableness. It is here, at the level of characterizing a necessary virtue of democratic citizenship, and not, as I argued in chapter 3, at the level of stating a criterion of nonarbitrariness in the use of power, that the idea of "reasons and arguments that all can accept" is concretely useful to democratic theory. In describing a virtue, we can tolerate a level of vagueness that we could not in formulating a foundational criterion.

For the purposes of my argument, all that matters is that addressing arguments and reasons to one's fellow citizens and attending to the reasons and arguments they offer is a requirement of mutual respect in a democracy. This vague conclusion will be enough to establish (via one more step, in the next section) that democratic rule must be reasoned. Yet since it is currently hotly debated just how to characterize this virtue of "public reasoning" in conditions of pluralism, I must say a little more about it.[26] (I shall have more to say about deep compromise, another approach to pluralistic conflict, in chapter 11.)

Start out with simple cases, not involving pluralism. Given the understanding of citizens as self-originating sources of claims, "because it would benefit the residents of Tacoma" should count as a reason in favor of a proposal. Sometimes, however, this kind of appeal to individual interest or preference carries with it another consideration sufficient to defeat it. "Because it would benefit the multibillionaires who got rich on internet companies" is not, on its face, a good reason for anything—not because billionaires are not due consideration but because, as we are apt to believe, they already enjoy benefits beyond what justice would allow. Hence, unlike the invocation of benefit to Tacoma, benefiting billionaires is not a consideration that others may be reasonably expected to recognize as a reason in favor of any proposal.

The cases at the focus of recent debates about the contours of the virtue of public reasonableness are the much harder ones involving religious and cultural pluralism. In illustrating their account of the democratic virtue of offering reasons that others can accept, Amy Gutmann and Dennis Thompson instance a case in which Christian fundamentalists in Hawkins County, Tennessee, objected to certain school textbooks in part because they mentioned "belief in the dignity and worth of human beings." The fundamentalists apparently found such sentiments "incompatible with true religious faith."[27] Given the importance that the fundamentalists attach to religion, they thus have a powerful basis for rejecting the liberal demand to offer reasons and arguments that all can accept, for they deny the value of individual autonomy on which that demand rests. Correspondingly, liberals have a powerful basis for rejecting the fundamentalists' conception of true religious faith.

Several comments about such cases: First, it seems fatuous to forbid individuals to cite reasons or make arguments that are based on their personal religious or moral views or to hold them vicious for so doing. What seems instead more reasonable is to demand that they *also* be willing to offer reasons and arguments that others can reasonably be expected to recognize as reasons and arguments.[28] Second, one must admit that, on certain issues, such as whether or not to allow the cited textbook to be taught in Hawkins County, one will not find reasons or arguments that everyone can reasonably be expected antecedently to recognize as reasons and arguments and that settle the issue one way or another.§ At such points, duly constrained by a liberal protection of fundamental freedoms—always relevant when fundamental religious convictions are at stake—recourse to majority rule is most helpful. Third, however, a liberal should not on that account conclude that the exigencies of the virtue of public reasonableness there run out. Since the virtue is grounded on the ideal of respecting persons as autonomous, one should try not to give up on people. One should explore, for instance, whether there is any wiggle room in the fundamentalists' conception of religious faith that might allow in something like the value of human dignity. As Gutmann and Thompson write, the backup virtue is that of doing one's part to keep open the possibility of mutual respect:

> This is a distinctively deliberative kind of character. It is the character of individuals who are morally committed, self-reflective about their commitments, discerning of the difference between respectable and merely tolerable differences of opinion, and open to the possibility of changing their minds or modifying their positions at some time in the future if they confront unanswerable objections to their present point of view.[29]

§ That other, peripheral reasons, such as comparative textbook cost, could be invoked as tie-breakers seems irrelevant.

Hence citizens in a democracy, who should abide by the virtue of public reasonableness, should maintain the hope that reasons and arguments addressable to all can be found to settle any issue, while not letting this hope lead them to compromise the rights of individuals or the integrity of the liberal-democratic state.

The strand of democracy that I have called "rationalist" thus picks up on a powerful current in recent political theory. Within a system in which we rule ourselves, a due respect for the autonomy of our fellow citizens does indeed require that we be willing to offer one another reasons and arguments and to attend to the ones that others offer. Does that mean that we must reason together? The final step to democratic rationalism is truly a short one, but it is worth making explicit.

## From Reasons to Reasoning

If we ought to rule ourselves by deciding what to do, and if, in the process, we ought to offer one another reasons and arguments that bear on the alternatives under consideration or help us in framing them, then it follows from the definition of "reasoning" I have offered that we ought to rule ourselves by reasoning with one another.

"Reasoning," I suggested, is "thinking that sifts discursively expressible reasons and arguments either in order to ascertain the truth of certain propositions or to derive new true propositions from ones that are initially believed to be true." What, exactly, is this "sifting"? I have not yet attempted to say; but we all have some idea of what is meant. We take the reasons and arguments into account. When, via our constitutionally instituted processes of democratic decision, we determine what we ought to do, the virtue of public reasonableness entails that we ought, in the relevant sense, to be sifting the reasons and arguments that have been offered.¶ That is what deliberative democracy is all about.

In sum, the liberal ideal of individual autonomy that underlies democracy in general and populist democracy more particularly also requires that democracy have a rationalist aspect. Respecting each other's autonomy as we rule ourselves requires that we reason with one another.

---

¶ Whether it is *possible* for us to orient ourselves to figuring out what we ought to do, and hence to orient ourselves to a truth-bearing proposition, depends, as I shall argue in chapter 10, on the existence of a minimal level of substantive moral agreement that qualifies the level of pluralism that democratic deliberation can encompass.

## Democracy as Democratic Autonomy

With all of the qualifying adjectives now in place—"republican," "liberal," "populist," and "rationalist"—I have arrived, as promised, at the conception of democracy as democratic autonomy. I showed that the conception of freedom that underlies the basic case for democracy and generates the burden of legitimating government in the first place also undergirds the republican ideal of freedom as nondomination. Incorporating this republican ideal is also necessary to making full sense of the problem that orients this work, namely the worry about bureaucratic domination. Pressing more deeply, I showed that the component republican idea of the "nonarbitrary" exercise of power must be interpreted along lines that refer to the liberal ideal of fair procedures that respect individuals as free and equal persons. A deeper look at that liberal ideal in turn revealed that at its core lies the value of respecting persons as free and equal autonomous beings. From this richer liberalism, a qualified and sensible commitment to populism, or rule by the people, flows. And from the same source, as I have now shown, comes the conclusion that the people ought to rule by reasoning with each other. Reasoned self-rule is autonomy; reasoned political self-rule is democratic autonomy; and democratic autonomy that both protects people from domination by dispersing power and providing opportunities for contesting it and employs fair decision procedures that protect fundamental rights and liberties is democracy as democratic autonomy.

In developing the case for democracy as democratic autonomy, it was necessary to examine at some length the interpretations of freedom and autonomy that underwrite this ideal. Although the ideal of political equality is of equal importance as a basis of democracy, I have left it uninterpreted so far, as its contribution to the claim that only democratic government is legitimate is relatively obvious. As I proceed to explore further how citizens may address one another as equals and how a deliberative political process can treat them as equals, however, I will need a more detailed description of political equality.

# CHAPTER 6

---

# Equality in a Deliberative Democracy

The emphasis that a deliberative theory of democracy, such as democracy as democratic autonomy, lays on citizens' reasoning with one another stands in some tension with the basic democratic ideal of equality. While each person can be given just one vote, people plainly differ in their reasoning and persuasive abilities. A theory of democratic reasoning must take account of this fact and must address the problem of political inequality that it raises. Thomas Christiano puts the point well: The quantitative equality secured by the principle of "one person, one vote"—whether in the electorate or the legislature—does not suffice; the process of democratic deliberation must also satisfy the requirements of "qualitative equality," which assure a fair or an equal chance of influencing debate, both within the legislature and the agencies and in the public domain more broadly.[1]

In this chapter I will give an account of the kind of qualitative equality that democratic procedures ought to afford. While the quantitative principle of "one person, one vote" is just as important, it is less problematic. There are issues that arise about how to interpret that principle as well, and some of these come up in my discussion in chapter 14 of systems of election.[2] Here, however, I will concentrate on qualitative equality. Threats to qualitative democratic equality can come from inequalities of power, of resources, or of persuasive ability. I will begin by concentrating on the first two sources of difficulty, reserving for later a discussion of persuasion and persuasive abilities. The first step will be to survey some of the difficulties facing any effort to spell out a principle of qualitative equality for democratic politics.

## Some Difficulties

It is very difficult to specify sensibly what qualitative democratic equality requires. I will suggest that we not try to specify this requirement directly but instead content ourselves with spelling out indirect, institutional measures that promote this vague aim or concern. The direct approaches to interpreting qualitative political equality of which I am aware fall prey either to a romantic idealization of politics or a false presumption of precision.

Discussions of deliberative or qualitative political equality inspired by Habermas have tended to illustrate the first, idealizing mode. We must assume that inequalities of power and resources will continue to exist and will make themselves felt in actual processes of democratic deliberation. Habermas's development of the ideal of communicative rationality, however, sometimes leads him to idealize inequalities of power away; and some of those influenced by his work have transposed his ideal directly to politics with this idealization intact.[3] According to this ideal, "the structure of communication rules out all external and internal coercion other than the force of the better argument and thereby also neutralizes all motives other than that of the cooperative search for truth."[4] Given our orienting commitment to democratic equality, we might indeed wish "that the existing distribution of power and resources does not shape [individuals'] chances to contribute at any stage of the deliberative process."[5] Whatever the merits of these formulae might be in helping us imagine or describe an ideal justificational stance, they are not useful in setting out conditions that any actual democracy must meet; for no actual democracy can meet this kind of condition. The very freedoms that, as I argued in the previous chapter, are necessary to nurture the existence of a public will also leave latitude for some individuals or groups to gain more influence than others over the effective channels of communication. Hence invariance with respect to the distributions of power and resources represents a wholly unrealistic interpretation of qualitative democratic equality.

Recognizing this, James Bohman's account of qualitative political equality takes a somewhat more realistic tack. "In order to be applicable to actual public deliberation," Bohman writes, "Habermas's ideal conditions must be recast. This is the task of a theory of deliberative equality; and the best definition for the purposes of deliberative arrangements is related to requisite capacities. Perhaps the most important form of communicative equality of opportunity is the capacity to initiate public debate on a theme or a topic."[6] If we keep focused on equality and assume that inequalities of power, wealth, and persuasive ability will persist, then we will have to admit that Bohman's definition remains quite idealized. It will also be seen to suffer from the second sort of problem, that of illusory precision. We have no meaningful way to measure individuals' capacity to initiate public debate on a theme or topic. And what topic? Taken as a definition of equality, Bohman's statement makes it sound as if deliberative equality is defined only relative to some topic or other. With respect, say, to the rights of the disabled, citizens do or do not enjoy deliberative equality. But why should we not expect that disabled citizens have greater capacity to initiate public debate on that topic than do other citizens? Perhaps, rather, the idea is that each citizen should equally have the capacity to initiate debate on *some* set of issues. Which issues? If we say, "on important ones," we bump up against the facts of pluralism, which block a shared social ranking of issues as more or less important. If we say, "on the ones important to him or her," then we have to face up to the implications of the fact that some citizens—the flat-earthers, the creationists, the atheists, the socialists, or the Nazis, as the case may be—may have views that are so despised by the great majority of citizens or so antithetical to the constitution that they will not have much capacity to initiate debate on the issues that they care about. This being unavoidable, we cannot assure an equal capacity for citizens to initiate public debate on issues important to them.

To be sure, concern with citizens' capacities to initiate debate becomes immediately more plausible and workable if we shift from a standard of equality to the idea of a minimum threshold. That, in effect, is what Bohman does. Despite his apparent definition of "communicative equality," he shifts his efforts to the defense of a "threshold of political inclusion," developing an insightful account of "political poverty."[7] This move, in turn, leads naturally to the sort of indirect approach to deliberative equality that I mean to defend here; but before coming to that, I will glance at one other direct approach, which defines deliberative equality in terms of views rather than opportunities to initiate debate.

This other direct way of directly attempting to spell out the content of deliberative equality also runs into trouble. Along these lines, Christiano proposes that qualitative equality in democratic deliberation demands that each "view" be given an equal hearing: "Resources for social discussion ought to be allocated to each view, not to each person." Subsequently, he qualifies this position, noting that the existence of different arguments for a given view need to be taken into account: "If John and Jane have different arguments in support of *A* and Joel has one argument for *B*, then both John and Jane ought to have a chance to give their arguments, which may mean that more will be said for *A* than for *B*."[8] The problem with this proposal is again not unrealizability but illusory precision. We have no good way of counting views or arguments. People we know how to count; but political positions shade into one another with all degrees and types of vagueness, and the arguments for them multiply wildly in their expression. Given the facts of pluralism, which deny the possibility of picking out a stance of encyclopedic authority for some state philosopher to employ in counting up the arguments that the people offer for their political views, this unruly variety cannot be even roughly counted. In this context, any suggestion that we might apportion resources or time to views or arguments is meaningless, as we lack the conceptual means to implement it.

## Backgrounding Qualitative Equality

To admit that we cannot give a precise gloss of deliberative or qualitative political equality is not to concede that it does not matter; rather, it is to suggest that we take a different tack in working out the practical implications of this ideal, to which we clearly ought to remain committed. Although each of the proposals I have canvassed about how to interpret qualitative democratic equality is unworkable, we may discern in each of them an important concern that needs to be addressed. First, inequalities in power and resources ought not be allowed unduly to distort the process of public political reflection. Second, political institutions ought to be arranged so as to protect against political poverty. Finally, each person ought to have a meaningful chance to air his or her political views and arguments.

I suggest that the appropriate way to address these concerns is not by pursuing the futile enterprise of providing a more exact interpretation of equality than these circumstances allow but is instead by developing an account of the institutions needed to preserve the background justice of democratic deliberation.[9] This is to develop an account of the constraints on the basic structures and processes of political deliberation such that, if they are fulfilled, we can be confident that the concerns of qualitative political equality are met. I will mention four conditions that help us fill out a conception of the background justice that addresses the vague concern with qualitative democratic equality. Each of these conditions has an independent normative basis, but each would also help provide a kind of qualitative equality.

The first condition of background justice is the constitutional protection of equal political liberties. These include the freedoms of speech and assembly and the freedom "to take part in public affairs and to influence by constitutional means the course of legislation."[10] These freedoms represent a first condition of background justice that must be met if the ideal of qualitative democratic equality is to be achieved. These freedoms are to be equal freedoms in the formal sense: Each citizen is to enjoy the same freedoms of speech, assembly, and political participation.

The second condition of background justice is the equality of citizens before the law, more generally, which I have already described. This implies that the set of fundamental constitutional rights afforded to each citizen is the same, irrespective of birth, class, or status. This holds true, for instance, of the constitutional protections of freedom of speech and association, which are afforded to all. No one has a claim to stand above the law, nor may statutes single out any particular person for punishment or preferment.

The third condition of background justice is the implementation of effective measures designed to mitigate the tendency for economic power to concentrate in the hands of the few. Many tools may be adapted to this purpose, including antitrust regulation, a progressive income tax, and in-heritance taxes—just to mention ones that have been employed in the United States. Property ownership should be sufficiently dispersed that it is not easy for anyone to buy the vote or the political participation of another or to overwhelm their voices in a public sphere in which access to privately owned channels of communication is sold in the open market.[11] In recent campaigning in Peru, for example, rallies of the then incumbent presidential candidate Alberto Fujimori were apparently filled out with women who were faced with a forced choice. As cooks in roadside restau-rants, food was their normal form of compensation, no cash wage being provided. Fujimori's political party apparently had sufficient sway over the restaurant owners to offer these women the following alternative: Attend the rally or go without your food. While that means of pressuring them ought to be and surely was illegal, it is also true that the background justice needed for qualitative democratic equality should see to it that each citizen enjoys a secure, decent minimum of subsistence and hence is not so easily prey to being influenced by the more powerful. More positively put, the basic institutions of society should be arranged so as to support the capa-bility of each citizen to engage meaningfully in democratic deliberation.[12] Part of this needed support is economic, but education and the social basis of self-respect are also elements important to sustaining citizens' sense that they have something to contribute to public discussion. Unless minimal conditions of this kind are met, as Rawls puts it, citizens will not enjoy the "fair value" of their political liberties.[13] I do not pretend to have provided clear standards for how much should be done to protect the fair value of the political liberties by addressing distributive justice; but in some such way the laws of the society must counteract the tendency for economic power to concentrate in the hands of a few and must help secure a decent minimum for each.

The fourth and final background condition for qualitative democratic equality is that the process of democratic debate and decision must itself be structured so as to allow each person a fair chance to participate and to counteract to a degree the potential influence of disparities in economic and political power. Without having a specific jurisdiction's institutions in mind, it is difficult to start to specify the kinds of regulation that are required to achieve these aims. Consider the public debate surrounding the election of legislators or a chief executive. In the United States, for instance, it seems clear that attempts to regulate the influence of money in election campaigns have not succeeded. Those with a lot of money to spend have found ways around the per capita cap on campaign contributions. More effective reg-ulation is needed to prevent undue distortion of qualitative equality by unequally distributed economic power. Within legislatures, steps need to be taken to ensure that the use of majority rule does not silence those in the minority. The devices of a loyal opposition, as in parliamentary systems, or of minority committee staffs, as in the U.S. Congress, help guard against this danger, as do rules of debate that allocate time evenly to members of each party. At the stage of administrative rulemaking, it is important that public hearings on proposed rules be advertised in a way that makes them known to citizens not represented by well-funded lobbying organizations.

It is obvious that each of these conditions of background justice needs more definite specification even to stand as an adequate theory of qualitative equality in politics. I hope at least to have said enough to make it plausible that these conditions of political liberty, equality before the law, distributive justice, and procedural fairness provide a good indirect way of getting at the concern with qualitative or deliberative equality. They indicate in a general way what must be done if public deliberation is to live up to the ideal of equality embedded in our commitment to democracy.

The inequalities I have been concerned with in this section are those of power and economic resources. The general idea of deliberative fairness also raises the question about how to think about inequalities in persuasive ability.

## Persuasive Rhetoric as a Tool of Democratic Reasoning

Persuasive rhetoric is the art of employing language so as to bring about changes in one's audience's practical commitments, especially by making appeal to their emotions. Concern about the place of persuasive rhetoric's interference with qualitative political equality might center on its persuasiveness or its artfulness. (I postpone discussion of the role of emotions in democratic deliberation to chapter 13.) I shall take up these two features in turn.

Mutual persuasion is essential to democratic politics: This much follows from the previous chapter's conclusion that we must respect one another's autonomy by being willing to reason with one another about what we ought to do. More specifically—to anticipate a point to be developed in chapter 11—democratic deliberation essentially depends on our willingness to reason toward deep compromises, in which individuals modify their ends in response to and on account of considerations that have been put forward by others. Hence the mode of reasoning involved in politics intrinsically involves an openness to changing one's practical commitments. To bring about that result is the aim of persuasive rhetoric. As I shall argue at more length in chapter 13, this aim of changing individuals' practical commitments does not imply that rhetoric interferes with reasoning's truth-orientation. Indeed, far from conflicting with an orientation to truth—as philosophers from Plato to Habermas have intimated—this mutual openness to persuasion is part of what is involved in the political orientation to truth.[14]

The central ways that rhetoric can go wrong all result from faults independent of its persuasive aim. Rhetoric will go wrong if the condition of mutuality just mentioned is not met. This might be because the speaker is not open to being potentially persuaded by what the others say but is simply throwing out arguments in an unprincipled or cynical effort to persuade the others and thereby gain advantage. Political rhetoric so misused often gives itself away by the inconsistencies that show up as those deploying it say one thing to one audience and something contradictory to another. Of course, democratic deliberation neither demands that all speakers argue from abstract and general principles nor precludes developing a public consensus by speaking differently to different potential coalition members.[15] What matters is an openness to mutual persuasion that supports the mutual orientation to truth. When we see participants in political debate being willing to craft contradictory arguments for different audiences, we rightly begin to doubt that they are engaged in a sincere effort to determine what we ought to do.

Another way the mutuality condition can fail is for the speaker to regard the audience as incapable of joining in the collective search for truth. "I am committed to the political truth, but *they* are not worthy of joining me in a search for it; hence, my only job is to whip up their enthusiasm in favor of the views I regard as true." This is the abuse of rhetoric common among ideologically committed demagogues, among whom Hitler stands out.[16] The problems in these cases are not problems with persuasive rhetoric, as such; rather, they are failures of sincerity and open-mindedness.

We may conclude, then, that the persuasive aspect of political rhetoric as such is not a problem. What of its artfulness? While the worry about unequal persuasive abilities is theoretically compelling, it is not clear that it remains a serious practical problem if the conditions of openness and background justice are met. Consider the issue at two different levels, that of office-holders and candidates and that of ordinary citizens.

Among office-holders, it is just not clear any more what outstanding persuasive ability comes to. Ciceronian rhetoric is no longer prized, even in Britain's House of Commons or the U.S. Senate. Al Gore was widely assumed to have better persuasive abilities than George W. Bush—certainly Gore was a better debater, in a narrow sense—yet the widespread perception was that Gore lost most of his debates with Bush in part *because* of his confidence in his superior ability to persuade. Here can be seen a tendency of mass politics at work about which we would rightly feel ambivalent: Where democratic habits have taken strong hold, as they have in the United States, any claim to superior understanding will tend to be looked on with derision. This attitude will surely undercut the quality of democratic deliberation, which is a bad thing.[17] Yet it will also attenuate the ability of individuals to capitalize on any superiority in persuasive ability that they may in fact possess. In response to this halfway comforting thought, it will be objected that it misdescribes persuasive abilities: Under the mass-society conditions described, they are to be found not in a classical orator's inflated rhetoric or in a policy wonk's mastery of detail but in Ronald Reagan's ability to deliver humble platitudes with an actor's manufactured sincerity or in Jane Fonda's ability to clothe her words in an aura of celebrity. Well, perhaps so; but now we approach the platitudinous conclusion that whatever works works. However frustrating it is when telegenic pablum prevails over serious substance, it is surely not correct to label this problem as one of inequality. To be sure, the unequal flow of wealth into the coffers of candidates and political parties, which may pay for packaging the purveyors of political pablum, does need to be rectified and regulated; but, again, that is a problem of background justice rather than a new problem posed by inequality in persuasive abilities.

If we think, instead, about ordinary citizens, what becomes immediately apparent is the tremendous variety of deliberative fora in a modern democracy. Citizens can air their views and arguments at town meetings and public hearings, at coffee shops, on radio call-in shows and the Internet, in association newsletters and pamphlets, and on and on. This diversity of fora represents one of the best ways of diffusing and mitigating the impact of the fact that individuals do vary in their persuasive abilities. Society should protect freedom of association and expression so that such a variety of fora can flourish. If it does, then there is a reasonable hope that each citizen who cares will find a forum in which he or she can be persuasive. Undoubtedly, there is more that modern states can and ought to do to promote a parallel variety in the ways in which they directly receive input from citizens. I describe one important possibility in chapter 16. A further possibility that may be particularly useful in giving a persuasive voice to those otherwise unheard is for officials to organize a forum, not around a predefined issue, such as whether to allow logging in a given national forest or to site a halfway house in a given location, but rather around listening to people's life stories so that their perspectives might indirectly inform policy-making.[18] Such fora would help put on the public agenda issues that might not otherwise surface.

In sum, I suggest that democracy meet concerns with deliberative equality by combining two complementary approaches: by promoting the conditions of background justice, so that inequalities of wealth and economic power do not readily translate into political advantage, and by protecting and promoting the proliferation of a variety of political fora. Only such an indirect approach to assuring deliberative equality seems compatible with individual freedom.[19] An approach that went beyond the indirect, background approaches to protecting deliberative equality might first specify precise, enforceable principles of qualitative equality and then enact them the way our electoral laws enact "one person one vote." Never mind exactly how. Suppose that the temporary result were that everyone would have equal influence on democratic deliberation. Then suppose that the Spice Girls decide to get involved in a political cause, and many individuals voluntarily decide to give some credence to their political statements, perhaps because they were already fans of theirs. This shift would probably destroy the deliberative equality so painstakingly achieved by legislation. Celebrities can and do gain disproportionate political influence in this way; but there seems to be no way to prevent this happening short of taking extreme measures to curtail individual freedom of speech and expression. Hence it seems that we ought to rely on background justice and on a healthy variety of fora—rather than on direct regulation—in order to protect deliberative equality.

This account of the conditions supporting deliberative equality rounds out my discussion of the main component ideals of democracy. Before turning to concrete questions about how to institute democracy as democratic autonomy, I must first explore different ways to conceive of the modes of reasoning that must be involved. These modes of reasoning will be needed to help structure and distribute the formation of the public will—for, as I showed in chapter 4, we cannot realistically regard the public will as being formed at one place or in one step.

# PART II

# THE NATURE OF PUBLIC REASONING

# CHAPTER 7

## Types of Practical Reasoning

Returning to the issue of "making transportation systems accessible" to the disabled—how should that be done? As policy problems go, this one is relatively small in scale. It presupposes that we have decided, in some more general way, that the disabled deserve special governmental measures designed to benefit them. In a scheme of statutory provisions that aim to do so, those that regulate access to transportation play but a small part. Such statutes generally also define "disability," indicate who is authorized to determine whether someone is disabled, set out remedies against discrimination, lay down requirements on employers and schools, and much more. The question of how to make transportation systems accessible to the disabled arises against this sort of backdrop.

It has arisen in many different jurisdictions of all different sizes. In the 1980s, the city of Munich worked out an innovative timetable information system for its public transport with an eye to advising the disabled how to minimize awkward transfers.[1] In 1992, Canada mandated that its national transportation system be made accessible to the disabled.[2] The Swedish government, which early mandated uniform accessibility standards for common carriers, was apparently one of the first governments to be concerned with how easily the disabled could switch from one mode of transport to another on a long-distance journey.[3] The European Union, for its part, has developed hortatory guidelines aimed at promoting "flexibility" and "seamlessness" in the travel of the disabled.[4]

As a relatively small-scale policy question, this one about making transportation systems accessible to the disabled is the sort of issue that is typically handed over to administrators. As a question that is now beginning to be addressed all over the world, it is not one of merely parochial interest. Drawing on an insightful case study by Robert A. Katzmann, I will use the issue to illustrate the importantly different modes of reasoning available to us as we make such policy.[5]

In 1970, Mario Biaggi, a freshman U.S. congressman from the Bronx, had become impressed with the plight of the disabled. He needed an issue; and "[he] and his staff were impressed with a study showing that most people at some time in their lives suffer some disability, however temporary, which makes mobility difficult."[6] During debate about the Urban Mass Transit Act (UMTA) of 1970, Biaggi introduced an amendment on the floor of the House of Representatives—"the Biaggi Amendment"—that declared that "elderly and handicapped persons" had the same "right" to use mass transportation as anyone else and that "special efforts" must be made to design systems of transportation to make them accessible to such persons. This amendment became law as section 16(a) of the UMTA, and as such affected the distribution of federal dollars subsidizing local transportation systems.

The Biaggi Amendment sparked a lengthy policy debate about what sort of special efforts ought to be made. Stylizing the debate somewhat, we may characterize it as pitting against each other two competing interpretations of access. Understandably concerned about the potential costs of this vague statutory provision, the officials in the Department of Transportation who were charged with administering the UMTA, as well as representatives of localities and of business purveying mass-transit vehicles, initially argued for providing transportation to the disabled in the most efficient manner. Rather than always spending huge amounts of money to retrofit existing buses, subways, and so on, this argument ran, the statute should be interpreted so as to allow special, targeted services for the disabled, such as vans available on call, when doing so is more cost-effective.[7] Although advocates for the elderly tended to like the idea of door-to-door van service, advocates of the disabled eventually coalesced around the competing, "mainstreaming" approach, which required that the existing modes of transportation available to those without disability be modified so as to make them accessible, without concern about cost-effectiveness. Disabled persons should be able to use ordinary modes of transportation.

We all know how the debate came out. In the United States the Americans with Disabilities Act of 1990 solidified legislative backing of the second, mainstreaming approach. But putting ourselves in the shoes of citizens and policy-makers in 1970—how should this sort of issue be decided? In particular, given that we ought to be making decisions by reasoning with each other, what sorts of reasoning are available to us in settling such issues?

Simplifying somewhat, and suppressing some ambiguities that will arise later, the available modes of reasoning may be divided into three types, two purportedly instrumental and one not:*

---

* I ignore strategic reasoning not because it is unimportant but because it is not a way that we might reason together. Rather, game theory and other accounts of strategic reasoning analyze reason's role in noncooperative situations. I will come to bargaining in chapter 11.

1. End-means reasoning, which starts from a given end and determines the best means to it
2. The weighing of pros and cons, or costs and benefits, to determine which action optimally achieves the many objectives that matter
3. Reasoning about ends, which revises the working conception of which ends matter

At the level of policy-making I am talking about, each of these three types of reasoning corresponds to a distinct model of how to curb bureaucratic domination and achieve the ideals of deliberative democracy, as follows.

(M1)   *Agency instrumentalism:* Significant lawmaking and democratic deliberation is to be confined to legislatures, while bureaucratic domination is to be curbed by limiting administrators to following the strictures of narrowly end-means rationality.

(M2)   *Cost-benefit analysis as policy standard:* While the public is not able to settle all significant policy questions through the legislature, their views can sufficiently be taken into account on all questions that legislatures do not settle and can thereby sufficiently curb bureaucratic domination, if subordinate policy decisions are made on the basis of a cost-benefit standard.

(M3)   *Public reasoning about ends:* In order to operate in a sufficiently flexible and intelligent way, whether in the legislature or in the agencies, public reasoning must extend to ends; ways must be found to ensure that agency reasoning can count as that of the public.

Each of these models depends on holding forth the corresponding mode of reasoning as one that policy-makers ought to follow. Whether and how such a normative demand could be enforced or implemented is, of course, an important question; but first I will have to examine whether any of these three models would, in fact, adequately address bureaucratic domination and sufficiently allow for public reasoning. After criticizing the first model in chapter 8 and the second in chapter 9, I will go on to elaborate and defend the third over the remainder of the book, returning to the context of the administrative agencies in chapter 16.

Before coming to my criticism of agency instrumentalism, however, I must clarify the distinctions among the three modes of reasoning that underlie the three models. These distinctions rest on the categories of end and means, which are largely forgotten in recent theorizing about practical reason. If invoked at all, they are often misused. We need to be clear about these notions and how they differ from the alternative, catchall primitive preferred by economists and decision theorists, the preference ranking. I must, in addition, defend the possibility of reasoning about ends. This I have done at length elsewhere.[8] Here I summarize key parts of the argument.

## End and Means

We deliberate in terms of ends and means. We start with some goals at least vaguely in view, and we figure out how to attain them. Once we have figured out what we ought to do and, indeed, have ranked the available alternatives, then, if our preferences obey certain constraints of formal rationality such as transitivity, we will have a preference ranking, or at least a partial one. But the category of preferences is not one that is useful to us in first-person deliberation.† *Making transportation systems accessible to the disabled* is the end that the Biaggi Amendment most obviously put on the policy table, and *requiring localities to retrofit existing modes of transportation* is a candidate means to that end. We cannot settle on which means to pursue *by* ranking the alternative means, however; rather, we have to do our deliberative work in order to rank the alternative means. Since I am exploring alternative possible accounts of first-person-plural deliberation, I stick with the categories of end and means.

A final end is something we pursue for its own sake. Not all ends or aims of action, and not all goals that orient deliberation, are final ends. Some are simply what Dewey called "ends in view": aims whose status as final or not is fluid or unsettled and subject to shifting with shifting contexts of deliberation.[9] In legislative hearings on military spending, *maintaining an effective capacity for rapid response to crises* may be the end in view and alternative weapons may be among the means we consider; but in broader discussions of foreign policy, *maintaining peace and a stable system of international law* may be the end in view and having an effective rapid-response capability an available means. In distinguishing instrumental from noninstrumental reasoning, what matters is the category of a final end. Instrumentalists hold that reasoning can only proceed from final ends and cannot establish them.

As categories available introspectively within deliberation, the ideas of end and means are naturally psychologically richer than the notion of a preference ranking, which originated in economics.[10] As an empirical science aiming to predict human behavior from the outside, economics has had an understandable tendency to eschew notions as psychologically messy as "end" and "means." I do not mean to draw any judgment, here, about this use of preference rankings in economics.[11] I simply want to be sure that the significance of my shift in categories is remarked.

The notion of a final end involves forms of counterfactual commitment and normative judgment that are not involved in the idea of a preference. In good Aristotelian fashion, we can define the relevant notions by reference

---

† Except, of course, when we are deliberating about whether to modify our preferences, say by enrolling in Alcoholics Anonymous.

to the more fundamental idea of pursuing something for something's sake.[12] A final end is something we pursue for its own sake, while something is pursued as a means to something else if it is pursued for the sake of that other thing. As the example of shifting contexts for considering rapid-response forces suggests, it is also coherent to say that we pursue something *both* for its own sake *and* for the sake of something else. When we pursue *x* for the sake of *y*, two related claims are true of us: (1) we would pursue (or choose) *x* even if *y* were the only good we expected to come of it; and (2) we judge it appropriate or acceptable to regulate the manner and extent of our pursuit of *x* by reference to *y*.[13] The first of these clauses articulates our counterfactual commitment, while the second expresses a normative judgment. If I decide to pursue a writing project for the sake of clearing up my thoughts about some difficult subject, then it follows both that (1) I would pursue it even if that clarification were all that I expected out of the effort and (2) I find it appropriate to regulate how much time I spend on the project and the ways I research and write it by reference to what will best contribute to my own clarity of understanding.

The element of normative judgment involved in the idea of pursuing something for something's sake is important to explaining why it is that the relation tends toward ordering our ends. If we seek to have an effective rapid-response force in order to be better able to preserve peace and international law, then it does not make sense to say that we also seek peace and stable international law in order to have an effective rapid-response force. The notion of pursuing something for the sake of something else suggests an antisymmetry.[14] Why? Why does it not make sense, if having such a force is so wonderful that, in some contexts, it counts for us as a final end? The aspect of normative judgment helps answer this question, for it makes clear that pursuing something for the sake of something else involves deciding not only that something is worth pursuing, in some absolute sense, but also that it appropriately regulates how and in what ways the first item is to be pursued. We think it is appropriate to configure and equip a rapid-response force on the basis of considerations about the likely threats to peace and international law; and we do not think that it is appropriate to qualify and prioritize our quest for peace and international law on the basis of what would give our rapid-response forces the best workout in the field. That would be a kind of perversion of our values. Limits on symmetry of pursuing one thing for the sake of another thus derive from the natural antisymmetry of the normative self-regulation of action. This tendency to order the object of pursuit in a hierarchy need not be thought of as a feature of "things in themselves"; it is equally understandable as a feature of how we attempt to bring order to our concerns.

I should note that taking the notion of a final end to be our central primitive hardly limits the possible content of our practical thinking. I have said nothing about the nature of the objects of pursuit, beyond what is implied by their being pursuable in action. *That the integrity of international law be maintained and respected* can count as a final end, as can any other commitment of principle.‡ Even the attitude of respect for persons can be fit within the framework: To respect persons (as autonomous beings or otherwise) is to be committed to treat them in certain ways and not in others and to take this commitment to be quite fundamentally regulative of one's conduct.[15] Talk of final ends in no way limits us to a simple pursuit of determinate "goods" or metaphysically basic "states of affairs." It is not "teleological" in any narrow sense of the term.[16]

I can now define "final end" and "means" more precisely by reference to this analysis of pursuing $x$ for the sake of $y$. A final end, as we think of it intuitively, is something we pursue for its own sake. This is just the case in which $x$ equals $y$. Hence something is a final end for us just in case (1) we would pursue it even if nothing else were thereby attained and (2) we find it appropriate to let this pursuit be self-regulating. All other cases are cases of pursuing something as a means, in a broad sense. We pursue something, $x$, as a means to something else, $y$, in the broad sense, just in case (1) we would pursue $x$ even if $y$ were the only good thereby attained and (2) we find it appropriate to let consideration of $y$ regulate our pursuit of $x$. When we pursue $x$ as a means to $y$, this obviously entails that we believe that pursuing $x$ is a way to attain $y$. Note that, on these definitions, we can pursue something both as a final end and as a means to something else. Hence lowering unemployment can be something we pursue for its own sake (because we believe that working is an intrinsically worthwhile activity) and for the sake of promoting health.

And what if it be said that we also promote health in order to enable people to work? Rather than falsifying the antisymmetry of pursuit, what this possibility shows is that we are under some pressure to try to formulate an ultimate end, something that is sought for its own sake and *only* for its own sake. That is, we are led to try to articulate a conception of human flourishing in which we sort out the relative place of health and work.[17] The pursuit of a such an ultimate end—the human good or, in the case of our democratic deliberations, the public good—need not be regulated by reference to anything else. Although we are thus under some rational pressure to try to formulate such a conception of an ultimate end, we seldom get very far with this task. Accordingly, we do not often deliberate with an ultimate end directly in view.[18]

---

‡ If the noun phrase seems awkward within the framework of pursuing one thing for the sake of another, it can always be preceded by "seeing to it" or "doing what we can to ensure."

With these categories—end-in-view, means, final end, and ultimate end—now defined, I turn to the three types of reasoning mentioned earlier, which are distinguished from one another on the basis of these categories.

## End-Means Reasoning, Broad and Narrow

The simplest form of instrumental reasoning is devoted to settling on a way to attain a single, given end. Narrow end-means reasoning seeks to settle on causal means to achieving that end, while broad end-means reasoning asks after a way to achieve that end that might simply be a more refined description of the end.

A striking and important fact about even narrow end-means reasoning is that it resists formal characterization. There has been no lack of attempts.[19] Aristotle was perhaps either carried away by the success of his logic of propositions, or else has been misunderstood by us in the same vein, when he wrote about a "practical syllogism," in which the first or major premise states the end, the second or minor premise notes the available means, and the conclusion either is or designates the action to be taken.[20] Yet inferences do not flow through practical syllogisms with the inexorability that characterizes theoretical (or ordinary, or "real") syllogisms. There are three nested reasons why not. First, we typically are satisfied with sufficient means to our ends and are seldom in a position of having to accept a means as strictly necessary. Here is one of Aristotle's best-known examples of broad end-means reasoning:

> I need a covering,
> a coat is a covering:
> I need a coat. (*Movement of Animals* 701a17–18)

While this example does well capture a common kind of practical reasoning, there is clearly no necessity to using a coat as one's covering. The same is true of narrow end-means reasoning: If we aim to lower carbon-dioxide emissions, there are obviously many causal means to choose from, none of which is necessary to achieving the goal. A second reason that practical reasoning resists formalization flows directly from the first: Since there are typically a number of alternative means that would be sufficient, we must (as Aristotle again says) select "the easiest and best."[21] There is obviously no simple formula, however, for determining which means is easiest and best. The case of making transportation available to the disabled is a case in point. Even when working from a single, fixed end, we must exercise creativity and imagination to generate options and to reflect about their relative merits.[22] A third reason why practical reasoning cannot be formalized arises from the second: If instrumental reasoning seeks the easiest and best means to given ends, sometimes it bumps up against the fact that all available means are either too hard or not good enough. Sometimes, in other words, consideration of the available means reasonably leads us to give up on our pursuit of the end from which we began deliberating. If the only available covering was poison ivy, I, for one, would feel justified in going naked.§

While end-means reasoning is not formalizable, it is absolutely familiar. That it is not formalizable should not lead us to doubt that it is a mode of reasoning. Rather, we should resist conceptions of reason that demand formalizability. The notion of formalizability played no part in the definition and explication of "reasoning" offered in chapter 5.

The distinction between narrow and broad end-means reasoning will be important for the purpose of distinguishing different approaches to democracy and the problem of bureaucratic domination. Narrow end-means reasoning, to repeat, is confined to selecting causal means to a given end. The notion of a causal means is a familiar one, on which cause precedes effect and does not logically entail it. Broad end-means reasoning can extend also to settling on constitutive means, which is either the end itself realized in a certain way or else a part of the realization of the end.[23] A cloak is a kind of covering, not a means of producing one. A world in which laws are publicly promulgated is an aspect of a world in which the rule of law is maintained, not just a causal means to such a world. A constitutive means need not temporally precede the realization of the end and does entail at least the partial achievement of the end.

In broad end-means reasoning, we often start from ends that are vague and abstract and make them more specific. When we specify an end, we thereby focus on or narrow down to a way of achieving it. It is a matter of narrowing-down if we take the specification to supersede our initial, vaguer formulation (as my liberal interpretation of nondomination replaces the uninterpreted version of the republican ideal of nondomination); it is a matter of focus if we take it to supplement and gloss the more general formulation (as the republican ideal of freedom as nondomination provides an important gloss of one aspect of freedom). Specification, in this sense, may be thought of as a relation between two ends (or norms) and, derivatively, as a process whereby an end (or norm) is made more specific.[24] Specification is important because, whether as individuals or collectively, we often start from ends that are vague and abstract: *to be successful, to combat air-quality degradation, or to make transportation available to the disabled.*

---

§ The availability of poison ivy suggests that hypothermia is not likely to be an underlying concern. The existence of underlying concerns again pushes us in the direction of an ultimate end.

A crucial step in deliberation, often, is to come up with more concrete and specific interpretations of these ends.

This process of specification has an interestingly ambiguous relation to ordinary causal-instrumental reasoning. Obviously, if ends are left too vague, it will not be sensible to launch a causal investigation into how to achieve them. Suppose you are advising someone who has simply told you that they want to be a success. True, you *could* do an empirical study of what the easiest way to attain success of any kind might be; but you would be a better adviser if you first asked your companion a bit more about how he or she would like to understand "success." Hence specifying ends is often an important prerequisite to sensible causal investigation. Yet it is also true that the process of specification will often make significant causal investigation unnecessary. If we begin with a vaguely stated aim of having an effective rapid-response force and then specify that end more fully as a military unit that can move certain numbers of infantry battalions and air and naval squadrons to any place in the globe in two days, then it may become obvious that we just have to have a modernized version of the C-5A transport. Accordingly, specifying the ends can make serious efforts at causal-instrumental investigation effectively unnecessary.

What was the situation in 1970 with the Biaggi Amendment's demand that serious efforts be made to make transportation systems accessible to the disabled? The initial reaction of the staff in the Department of Transportation, as I have mentioned, was to proceed by narrowly instrumental reasoning to find efficient or relatively cost-effective means to that end. Admittedly, the end was vague. For the purposes of doing cost-effectiveness studies, however, a natural interpretation suggested itself: One could compare the costs of various methods of seeing to it that a disabled person could get from point A to point B.

While such patterns of reasoning are common in policy-making, it is at least equally common that we have to face up explicitly to making trade-offs or finding compromises between two or more competing values. I turn now to an instrumentalist way of doing so.

## Weighing Pros and Cons

When we try to balance the reduction of arsenic emissions against the jobs of smelter employees in Tacoma, or the protection of commercial interests against the integrity of other nations' sovereignty, we need something besides simple end-means reasoning. We need some basis for comparing the various harms and benefits, which can be quite different in kind—at least, that is what we need if we are to remain within the confines of instrumental reasoning.

Sometimes the methods of reasoning that we employ in such situations rest heavily on intuition. Benjamin Franklin suggested a marvelously hokey but useful method for dealing with multiple pros and cons: (1) For each pro, try to find a con that is intuitively of the same "weight" or importance. (2) Consider that such matched pairs cancel each other out. (3) Hope that what is left over is a single consideration that indicates which way to go.[25]

Philosophers with more rigorous commitments to systematicity than Franklin's have demanded that there be some substantive *basis* for these comparisons, some overall standard by which to measure or appraise the contributions of the various more specific considerations, for the purposes of arriving at a choice (or overall evaluation).[26] They have insisted that such a basis is necessary if the weighing of pros and cons is to be rational. This is to insist that, when competing considerations are involved, commensurability is a prerequisite of rational choice.[27] This basis for commensuration could be subjective, in the sense of being peculiar to the individual. For instance, an individual might commensurate options on the basis of what promises him or her pleasure. For these philosophers, however, it must be a real basis that allows the choice to be other that merely intuitive.

There are many dispositive reasons for thinking that commensurability of this kind is not generally available. Values are incommensurable, in this sense. One can see this in the phenomenology of tragic conflict. Suppose, in a heightened version of the Asarco case, the EPA had to choose between allowing the continuing emission of poisons that was killing dozens of local residents a year and throwing thousands of people out of work with no prospect of reemployment. In such a case, the administrators would rightly feel deep anxiety about how to choose. Someone who sought to mitigate this sense of tragedy by thinking "Oh, well, it is just a matter of how aggregate life expectancy is affected" would show that they did not really grasp the values of human life and livelihood that were at stake.[28] Further, some values or commitments bear on practical issues via deductive argument and not as reasons pulling for or against a conclusion. If it is wrong to discriminate on the basis of race in a certain way, then that consideration ought to stand as a side-constraint on decision and not simply count as a con to be weighed against pros.[29] In short, the metaphor of "weighing" pros and cons not only misleadingly suggests that there is a dimension that the pointer of the balance tracks but also sometimes wholly fails to be apt. Values are not all commensurable.

In policy circles, however, this is only the beginning of the story, for policy analysis has long been influenced by the use of the economist's preferred primitive, the preference ranking. Neither of my arguments for the incommensurability of values implies that individuals cannot form a preference as among the relevant options. The administrator at the EPA who deeply feels the tragedy of the situation can still form a preference between

closing the plant and not doing so; and someone who takes race discrimination as a side-constraint on policy choice can still form preference about
what to do when that issue is at stake.

The mode of policy reasoning involving a balancing of pros and cons that
I will consider hereafter is that of cost-benefit analysis. Cost-benefit analysis
works with individual preference rankings as its fundamental primitive.
These rankings are either as revealed in the marketplace or as elicited by
surveys. As far as cost-benefit analysis is concerned, the rankings that individuals come up with may or may not be the product of reasoning. They
may or may not reflect deliberation and choice. What matters is just that
individuals can form a preference. Where reasoning enters into the picture,
in cost-benefit analysis, is in its suggestion that one can construct a standard
for governmental decision-making on the basis of this information about
individuals' preferences. Using this information, we can sort and sift proposals for action.

Clearly enough, these modes of balancing pros and cons, like simple end-
means reasoning, remain forms of instrumental reasoning. They do not provide ways of establishing new ends. Not all practical reasoning is instrumental, however.

## Reasoning about Ends

No one was satisfied with the first set of administrative rules that the Department of Transportation (DOT) issued by way of implementing the
Biaggi Amendment. Although DOT had been largely moved by cost-
effectiveness considerations, no one had a clear sense, at the time the rules
were drafted, of what the technological possibilities were. Accordingly, the
rules as issued mainly revealed DOT as trying to keep its options open.[30]
Within a few years, however, DOT was under pressure from both sides—
from local transportation officials and from the disabled—to issue a more
definite set of rules.

In the interim, another piece of legislation had put on the public table a
second end that could not be ignored: that of not discriminating against the
disabled. This was Section 504 of the Rehabilitation Act of 1973, which was
administered by the (then) Department of Health, Education, and Welfare
(HEW). The way that the HEW staff had written the regulations implementing Section 504 gave great prominence to considerations of nondiscrimination when it came to dealing with the disabled. The DOT accordingly came under tremendous pressure to work out its transportation
regulations consistently with the HEW approach. While this pressure might
rationally have been resisted, the HEW regulations also provided a new
way for the advocates for the disabled to express and focus their lobbying.

Mainstreaming should be accepted in the domain of transportation not merely as "the easiest and best" way to provide transportation to the disabled but as an essential mode of avoiding discrimination against the disabled within this domain.

This push in the direction of a mainstreaming approach fell on sympathetic new ears within DOT, those of Martin Convisser, the acting assistant secretary for environment, safety, and consumer affairs, and the department's general counsel, Linda Kamm.[31] Crucially, the intervening years' research into new technologies for giving the disabled access to standard modes of transportation had been sufficiently successful to leave Convisser with a fundamental confidence that something along these lines could be worked out at a cost that would not be too prohibitive. Kamm, for her part, used her ability to control the DOT's internal agenda to ensure that HEW's focus on avoiding discrimination against the disabled remained in the foreground of discussion. The DOT issued a second set of regulations to implement the Biaggi Amendment in 1979, after holding hearings in 1978 to which 870 individuals and organizations supplied comments.[32] This second set of regulations adopted a mainstreaming approach.

What went on in this process of reasoning was that two vague ends, making transportation systems accessible to the disabled and avoiding discrimination against the disabled, were combined in such a way as to give rise to a new end, that of mainstreaming the disabled into existing transportation systems. To confirm that this new end was not latently present in the end of making transportation systems accessible, recall the simple interpretation of the latter end that was taken up in the initial cost-effectiveness analyses, that of enabling the disabled to get from point A to point B.

Considerations of cost were not lost on the DOT or the local officials and transit operators who testified on the proposed regulations, however. In the course of drafting and redrafting them, DOT officials happened upon a phrase specifying the mainstreaming end that provided for considerable leeway as to what, exactly, would be required. Each mode of transportation was to be made accessible "when viewed in its entirely."[33] This meant that the bus system was to be made accessible, the subway system was to be made accessible, and so on. It also implied, by omission, that it might not be necessary to make each and every bus and station entrance accessible. In the end, the regulations spelled out many explicit compromises along those lines.

What we see in the course of this official reasoning is the rational establishment of a new end on the basis of its fit and coherence with other ends and commitments. The end of mainstreaming is not deductively entailed by the ends of nondiscrimination and accessibility but provides a way of making the two cohere well with each other. Adding the specification about making each mode accessible when viewed in its entirely is supported in a similar fashion: It helped to reconcile the abstract aim of mainstreaming with the concern to prevent costs from ballooning. This specification obviously did not emerge from a study of the most cost-effective way to mainstream the disabled into existing modes of transportation, nor could it have; for it bears on how that end is to be understood in the first place.

One way that reasoning can establish new ends, then, is by locating new ones at the intersection of ends to which we are already committed. Instrumentalists may not be impressed by this example, however, for mainstreaming the disabled might seem to them simply a means to the pair of ends, nondiscrimination and accessibility. I do not believe that that is how the public in the United States now treats the aim of mainstreaming. In particular, I have the impression that advocates for the disabled take mainstreaming to be valuable for its own sake (perhaps also as a constituent of nondiscrimination, but that is another issue). They would rightly be insulted at the suggestion that money grants that would allow them to pay for private transportation could adequately substitute for a public requirement of mainstreaming.

To solidify the conclusion that reasoning can establish new ends, however, let me indicate another way in which this can happen. To illustrate it, let me speculate, in a fictional mode, about what may have gone on in Mario Biaggi's mind in 1970 when he proposed his amendment.[34] As already mentioned, as a freshman legislator, he was casting about for some issue that he could make his own. His sole initial aim, let me suppose—perhaps unfairly—was thus opportunistic. He wanted to make a name for himself and enhance his reputation with his constituents, and he thought that identifying himself as the champion of some distinct cause would help him out in this regard. Fortuitously, he and his staff had read about the prevalence of mobility handicaps. It struck them that this is just the sort of issue he needed. Initially, then, as I am reconstructing the story, promoting accessible transportation for the disabled was a means to making the congressman's reputation. But that is only the beginning of the story. Imagine, not unrealistically, that the initial reactions to Biaggi's proposed amendment were predominantly those of alarm. Local transportation providers, including those back home in the Bronx, were horrified and deluged Biaggi's office with letters of protest. Still, Biaggi had read about those disabled people and could not get them out of his mind. With all the fuss about the proposed amendment, it was no longer clear what its impact on his reputation would be, either with his constituents or with the nation at large. If he were to regulate his pursuit of the amendment by reference to his reputation, he would probably do just as well to drop it. But Biaggi was also deeply disgusted, let us suppose, by politicians who cynically used the plight of the poor just to get elected and stay elected. Accordingly, he decided that he could not let his commitment to the disabled be conditioned on its effect on his reputation. Rather, he would pursue it for its own sake.

Whether the actual Biaggi was less initially cynical at the outset or more so at the end I do not know. What matters to us is that this is a mode of reasoning that was available to him. What mode this was bears some reconstruction. Deliberation about how to achieve an initial end, enhancement of reputation, led to the selection of a means to that end, proposing the amendment. Consideration of an independent end, avoiding cynically using the plight of the poor, in turn suggested that it would be unacceptable to regulate his pursuit of the amendment solely by reference to the initial end of enhancing reputation and hence unacceptable to abandon pursuit of the amendment (now taken as shorthand for his pursuit of the cause of the mobility impaired) on that or on any such account. That consideration, together with his having been impressed with the plight of the disabled, instead supported the conclusion that pursuit of the amendment ought not be regulated by any such ulterior consideration.¶ Rather, it should be regarded as standing on its own, or as normatively self-regulating to an extent. This is a revised specification of the initial means (pursuing the amendment) to the initial end (enhancing reputation). So to specify the means, however, is to promote it in status to a final end. What was a mere means is now a final end.

The conclusion that this hypothetical course of thinking was a case of reasoning may again be defended on the grounds that its steps can be discursively shown to enhance the coherence of the set of ends to which, on reflection, the agent remains committed. Instrumentalists who resist the possibility of establishing new ends by reasoning often do so because of a failure to distinguish what we might call "the order of finality" from the order of justification. "The order of finality" is the ordering among our ends usually induced by the antisymmetry of pursuing one thing for the sake of another. In Biaggi's promotion of the pursuit of the amendment, what had been subordinated to the pursuit of reputation in his order of finality is, at the end of the day, no longer so. The order of justification lays out the reasons and arguments that support our conception of the good, including whatever ordering of finality it contains. If the structure of justification had to follow the order of finality, this would be a puzzling move and one that, it would seem, could not be undertaken on a rational basis.

---

¶ The remaining vagueness, here, reflects the fact that promoting the pursuit of the amendment to the status of an ultimate end is here not in question. To take it as a final end is not to imply that considerations of justice or national security, say, would not sometimes override it.

The train of thought that has led philosophers to conflate the order of finality with the order of justification is a familiar one. A chain of increasingly final ends is generated by continually asking "Why?" "Why do you want to get into law school?" "To be able to pursue a career in elective politics." "Why do you want to pursue such a career?" "To exercise my social skills in a way that benefits my fellow citizens." "Why do you want to exercise your social skills at all, let alone in that way?" To the more skeptically minded philosophers who start down this kind of road, the prospect of an endless regress of reasons looms, suggesting that no end is ever rationally established. More confident philosophers who have asserted that there *must* be some end or ends that puts a stop to this regress have often supposed that to accept this solution about the rational basis of practice is to give up on the rational justifiability of the end or ends that stand at the end of the line(s). Alternatively, it is thought, if those most final, or "ultimate," ends are rationally justifiable at all, that must be on a necessary or a priori basis that allows for no deliberation, no rational refashioning by an active, practical intelligence.

It is simply a mistake, however, to suppose that the structure of justification must mimic that revealed by the order of finality. The order of finality has a crucial psychological function: to help us order and regulate our pursuits and to articulate our commitments. How we justify our conception of what we ought to pursue and of what is worth being committed to is a wholly different matter.

As I have argued more at length elsewhere, the most fundamental layer of practical justification is coherence among the commitments to which we adhere on reflection.[35] We can defend our practical commitments, and the changes we make in them, by tracing the lines of mutual support among the ones we consider important. Laying out such lines of mutual support—which is a matter of articulating arguments and explanations—is not the same as invoking a criterion of coherence. Coherence is a complicated and messy idea that will resist being captured in a simple criterion; rather, it is an ideal that itself is open to respecification.[36] The purpose of invoking the idea of coherence is not to point to a ultimate criterion of rationality but rather to remind ourselves that practical justification need not be bound by the order of finality and instead can reach out to fit with more particular or subordinate considerations or to ones that are sideways in the hierarchy of ends. These further considerations, as shown relevant by arguments and explanations that trace relations of fit or of clash, can be the basis for rational revisions in one's conception of one's ends, by addition, subtraction, or reordering.[37]

In short, clear patterns of reasoning exist that allow us to expand our set of final ends by locating new ones at the intersection of old ones and by promoting mere means to the status of a final end. The idea of coherence—or of reaching out in a nonhierarchical way to show connections of mutual support among the commitments to which one remains committed on reflection—explains how this pattern of thinking can count as generating cases of justified changes of mind.**

Remember, as well, that we have not subjected instrumental reasoning to any such pressure to prove itself. Why should end-means reasoning, or the weighing of pros and cons, count as a case of reasoning? Not because it can be formalized or treated as a kind of logic, as I have shown. Instead, the answer will be similar to that just given for noninstrumental reasoning: It follows intelligible patterns of changes in view that can be discursively defended on the basis of mutual fit among the commitments with which one rests on reflection. Indeed, as I will argue shortly, it is difficult for end-means reasoning and reasoning that weighs pros and cons to stick within instrumentalist bounds.

## How Should We Think about Democratic Reasoning?

It is clear from what has already been said that democratic reasoning should extend to ends. In democracies, we need to settle on collective aims, such as making transportation accessible to the disabled, preserving endangered wildlife, stimulating small-business initiatives in inner cities, protecting our sources of oil, and supporting and regulating medical researchers. These broad policy decisions being among the most important ones giving shape to the way we rule ourselves, they are obviously ones that we should try to make by reasoning with each other. Hence legislatures—and also the platform committees of political parties in parliamentary systems in which party discipline plays a large role—ought to be arenas of collective deliberation about ends. So should the public sphere, especially as it intersects or interacts with legislatures and political parties.

How we can reason with one another so as to establish, refine, and revise collective ends is a topic that I will explore further, especially in chapters

---

** One other historically important source of skepticism about practical reasoning extending to new ends concerns the ability of reasoning to reshape motivation. Yet both the transfer of motivation—from nondiscrimination against the disabled and making transportation accessible to them to mainstreaming the disabled into transportation systems—and the refocusing of motivation, in the fictionalized case of Biaggi on the basis of his commitment to avoiding cynically using the plight of the weak, are equally intelligible as the transfer of motivation from covering to cloak. Further, as emphasized in Elijah Millgram, *Practical Induction* (Cambridge: Harvard University Press, 1997), we can learn from experience what is important, as Biaggi began to do when he first read about those with mobility difficulties.

10–12; but reasoning about ends is not the only mode of practical reasoning, and legislatures are not the only democratic institutions that matter. I have also been concerned from the outset about the policy-making that goes on in administrative agencies. In particular, I want to describe how administrative decision-making might be constrained so as to prevent it from counting as arbitrary domination. Here the three models of rational constraint mentioned at the outset of this chapter come into play. Looking critically at (M1)–(M3) will serve as an initial exercise in considering how the labor of our collective, democratic reasoning ought to be divided. It will also support the recognition that our collective reasoning about ends must extend into the administrative agencies.

# CHAPTER 8

# The Naiveté of Agency Instrumentalism

In situating his own approach to democratic deliberation, Habermas describes twin dangers that he seeks to avoid:

> Discourse theory drops all those motifs employed by the *philosophy of consciousness* that lead one either to ascribe the citizens' practice of self-determination to a macrosocial subject or to refer the anonymous rule of law to competing individual subjects. The former approach views the citizenry as a collective actor that reflects the whole and acts for it. In the latter approach, individual actors function as dependent variables in power processes—processes that operate blindly because beyond individual choice there can be at most aggregated, but not consciously formed and executed, collective decisions.[1]

In examining two instrumentalist conceptions for agency reasoning in this chapter and the next, I will show that each falls into one of the traps that Habermas describes. Although (M1), agency instrumentalism, is hardly inspired by Rousseau's metaphors of collective consciousness, it nonetheless turns out to fail to take seriously enough the differences among persons and models governmental reasoning as if the government were a single subject. Model (M2), which takes cost-benefit analysis to be the crucial policy standard, falls instead into the second trap of casting individuals as blind and passive elements in a process of aggregation.

My task, here, is to begin to explore the implications of democracy as democratic autonomy, with its populist and rationalist aspect, for decision-making within administrative agencies. To do so is also, as I have indicated, to begin to think about how to divide the difficult labor of reasoning collectively about such complex matters.

## Agency Instrumentalism's Simple Cut

Accepting the basic aspects requirements of democracy as democratic autonomy, agency instrumentalism proposes to deal with the problem of administrative discretion on the basis of a simple and stark division of labor between the elected legislature and the agencies. The legislature is to set the ends, while the agencies are to be constrained by the norms of end-means reasoning to selecting effective and efficient means to those ends.

Agency instrumentalism reflects some fundamental assumptions about the forms of expertise upon which democracies may safely rely. While both factual and evaluative judgments—issues about causally effective means and alternative ends—can be controversial in politics, it might be thought that scientific experts can sort out the causal issues in a relatively impartial and orderly way, whereas evaluative judgments need to be hammered out in the democratic process. As Herbert Simon put it in his pioneering study of administrative rationality, "democratic institutions find their principal justification as a procedure for the validation of value judgments. There is no 'scientific' or 'expert' way of making such judgments, hence expertise of whatever kind is no qualification for the performance of this function."[2] Guided by this thought (which I will later show to be mistaken), the agency instrumentalist hopes to confine the significant and controversial evaluative decisions to the legislature. In this way, the essential requirements of populist rationalism can be met in the legislature. Bureaucracies, in turn, may be kept in check by a combination of this normative constraint and a variety of republican modes of contestation. Agency instrumentalism thus reconciles administrative discretion to the populist demand that rule reflect the will of the people by reference to the idea that "they who will the end will the means."

Since the historical proponents of views in the neighborhood of agency instrumentalism have not tended to accept the ideal of deliberative democracy, or rationalist populism, it is not clear that anyone has actually held the view I will go on to criticize. Max Weber, as already mentioned, analyzed bureaucracy in terms of instrumental rationality. Politics otherwise, he thought, was prey to an irrational "ethic of ultimate ends."[3] Hence he seems not to have recognized the possibility of rational deliberation about ends at all.[4] A theorist who is more open to democratic deliberation and who has employed a cut between settling ends and selecting means along the lines of agency instrumentalism's is Thomas Christiano, in his recent egalitarian defense of democracy. As Christiano puts it, the core thought is that "those who choose the aims of a society are the ones who hold decision-making authority."[5]

Agency instrumentalism's twin hopes of confining significant and controversial evaluative judgments to the legislature and relying on the agencies to deploy a relatively impartial causal expertise indicates that this model would confine agencies to *narrowly* instrumental reasoning. The agencies are to be limited to selecting causally efficacious and efficient means to the ends indicated by legislation. While these questions will often prove controversial, the hope of this model is that the controversies facing the agencies will revolve around factual questions on which a relatively impartial expertise may be brought to bear.

## Agency Instrumentalism Is Unworkable

The fatal flaw of agency instrumentalism is that it tries to get way too much mileage out of the idea that "they who will the end will the means." This formula does indeed have some limited application to our practical reasoning under certain conditions. The main conditions are two: (1) The end must be relatively clear and definite; and (2) there must not be significant disagreement relevant to selecting certain means as the easiest or best ones in the circumstances. Thus, if we decide to increase potential traffic volume across a given river, and if current bridges obviously cannot be widened, then we may, in effect, have decided to build a new bridge. If we decide to raise short-term interest rates, then we may, in effect, have decided to tighten the money supply. The trouble with building an overall conception of popular rule around this idea, however, is that both of these conditions for the applicability of "they who will the end will the means" generally fail in politics. The ends are frequently, and unavoidably, left vague by legislatures, and we disagree quite pervasively about factors pertaining to selecting means as the best ones. I will go over these two points in turn.

The vagueness present in the Biaggi Amendment or in the extension of the SSI program to children may be extreme, but they represent an endemic and unavoidable feature of policy-making in complex democratic societies. The passage of the Biaggi Amendment evinced a general commitment to the idea that transportation systems ought to be made accessible to the disabled. As already noted, it was not until the second round of rulemaking under the Amendment that it began to be clear what some of the major issues were in implementing it. These issues arose as agency officials and lobbyists for transportation companies and for the disabled began to think about what it might mean to "make transportation systems accessible" to the disabled. That is, the issues began to emerge only in the course of trying to implement a framework of legislation that had been handed over to the agency by the legislature. The central reason why democratic legislatures cannot always avoid passing vague pieces of legislation is that it would vastly overwhelm their deliberative capacities to consider all the ramifications of all the different ways they might draft legislation on a given issue.[6]

To say this is not to condone unnecessary vagueness in legislation. I share the agency instrumentalist's hope that important and controversial evaluative questions be settled in the legislature insofar as that is reasonably possible. To that end, legislatures should strive to avoid vagueness in legislation.[7] The present point, however, is simply that a significant level of vagueness is both practically unavoidable and rationally sensible, given the impossibility of following up on the causal and evaluative implications of every alternative way that a complex piece of legislation might be drafted.

Defenders of agency instrumentalism might here object that instrumental reasoning can perfectly well proceed from an abstract and vague end. If I think otherwise, that may be because I have in mind an overly rigid understanding of how instrumental reasoning must go. Perhaps I have forgotten my own observation that, as Aristotle noticed, instrumental reasoning does not proceed mechanically but instead involves an implicit or explicit judgment about which means are easiest and best.[8] Once this is understood, one will see more scope for instrumental reasoning. For instance, the following would be a simplified reconstruction of some instrumental reasoning by the Reagan administration.*

1. We must above all preserve freedom.
2. Containing the Soviet empire is an important means to preserving freedom.
3. Building an antimissile defense system is a crucial means to containing the Soviet empire.
4. Hence we should build an antimissile defense system.

Surely, the defender of the reach of instrumentalism will point out, there is nothing that makes "providing aid to disabled children" or "making transportation available to the disabled" any more vague than "preserving freedom." If instrumental reasoning can proceed from the last, then it can proceed from the others as well.

It is here that we see the defenders of agency instrumentalism ignoring the differences among people that give rise to the need for democratic deliberation in the first place and instead treating the government as if it were a single, macrosocial subject. Of course an individual can reason in a narrowly instrumental way from vague ends. There is generally no problem with that, because there is generally no problem as to who gets to make the subsidiary normative judgments, which help indicate which means are "easiest and best." In the case of agency reasoning, however, this defense of agency instrumentalism papers over the very problem that this view had been designed to avoid, namely the seepage of controversial evaluative questions into agency decision-making.

The Evil Empire syllogism, for instance, conceals an important division in the electorate's understanding of political ends. Supporters of the Reagan administration interpreted "preserving freedom above all" in such a way as to support this result, despite the tremendous dollar costs and the additional

---

* I am at a loss as to how to update the example in the form of a valid-seeming syllogism.

buildup of the military-industrial complex that would have been involved. Critics of the administration did not interpret "preserving freedom above all" in this way. In the cases of SSI disability payments to children and transportation for the disabled, the fault lines as to the best interpretation of the ends lay closer to the surface, in part because these goals were meant to be relatively operational yet turned out to involve important ambiguities: People were overtly fighting about how to interpret the relevant ends. Even the Evil Empire "syllogism" goes through only on the basis of implicit understandings of freedom, its priority, and what threats to it are important. Single individuals, reasoning instrumentally, rarely articulate fully the understandings of their ends that would support the inferences they carry out. In the case of a single individual, it is at least a plausible default assumption that he or she is of one mind about these matters. When many individuals are involved, however, as in politics, these understandings typically diverge; and when that is the case, it distorts the actual possibilities of joint reasoning to suggest that instrumental reasoning can proceed as if that disagreement about the interpretation of joint ends did not exist.

As this reply highlights, the problem with agency instrumentalism is not a straightforwardly conceptual one. There is nothing *formally* wrong with the suggestion that agency reasoning might be cast as instrumental reasoning that proceeds from legislatively established ends. What is wrong with it, instead, is that, given the unavoidability of significant vagueness in legislation, which in turn rests on a sensible division of deliberative labor between legislatures and agencies, agency instrumentalism cannot achieve its aim of confining significant evaluative controversies to the legislature. The formal possibility of proceeding with end-means reasoning on the simplifying assumption that the government is a single, macrosocial subject masks agency instrumentalism's failure to achieve its normative aim. Once we remember, however, that we are many, and that we differ about how these vague provisions ought to be specified, then we cannot but recognize the naiveté of agency instrumentalism.

# CHAPTER 9

## The Stupidity of the Cost-Benefit Standard

The ends settled on by legislatures being often too vague and abstract to provide sufficient guidance for a noncontroversial form of instrumental reasoning to take over, the natural next move for the instrumentalist is to suggest collecting additional information about individuals' ends in order to help agencies make difficult trade-offs. As I argued in chapter 7, there is no objective basis on which to commensurate the many competing goods and values that matter to us.[1] Reaching out to individuals' preferences about how trade-offs should be dealt with accommodates this fact. By further taking individuals' views into account, such an approach better fulfills the populist ideal than does agency instrumentalism. With collective, legislative agreement about the ends of policy only taking us so far, the hope is to get further—not by attempting to deepen or extend that agreement by means of further collective reasoning but instead by taking direct account of the disagreeing views of individuals, which are what create trouble for agency instrumentalism. Instead of treating the government as a single macrosocial subject with its own set of values, the approach I am now considering attempts to achieve an ersatz populism within the agencies by aggregating individual preferences.

There are various approaches to policy reasoning that take this tack, involving varied ways of conceiving of and gaining access to individuals' practical commitments. By far the most influential of these approaches, however, is cost-benefit analysis. I shall argue that (M2), the model constraining agency reasoning to follow the standard of cost-benefit analysis (CBA), suffers from a severe intellectual defect that, for reasons I shall explain, counts as a form of stupidity. Now, a stupid way of achieving the ideals of democracy as democratic autonomy is perhaps better than none at all. Hence a final judgment on (M2) must await your verdict on my defense of a more robust rationalist populism in the following chapters. If my defense at all succeeds, however, we must judge (M2) to offer a rather poor "second-best" form of policy reasoning.[2]

## Cost-Benefit Analysis as a Normative Standard

The type of policy reasoning I am now considering dominated the first round of rulemaking under the Biaggi Amendment. Concerned about runaway costs, analysts in the Department of Transportation strove to figure out what would be the most cost-effective way to make transportation accessible to the disabled. As far as I know, they never considered the approach that would have been favored by some economists, namely writing checks to the disabled to cover their special transportation costs, as opposed to imposing any mandatory guidelines on localities whatsoever.[3] Mandatory regulations always create what economists call "inefficiencies," costs imposed on individuals that can in principle be recaptured by a more flexible approach. But department officials did try to estimate the costs of alternative ways of enabling disabled people to get from point A to point B, and on those grounds they leaned against retrofitting all existing modes of transportation. Now, they *might* have instead considered the comparative costs of alternative ways of avoiding discrimination against the disabled in transportation systems. What cost-benefit analysis neither includes nor invites the public to participate in, however, is the kind of reasoning whereby "making transportation systems accessible" is specified as "mainstreaming the disabled into existing transportation systems."

In discussing (M2), I take up CBA as a sample method of generating a normative standard for selecting among alternative policies by aggregating information about individuals' preferences. In relation to other approaches to policy reasoning that do this, such as multiattribute decision analysis, CBA is distinguished by its use of a single dimension of aggregation and a monetary index. These two features make CBA normatively more problematic than some of the other methods of aggregation but practically more useful and—whether helpfully or dangerously—rhetorically more powerful. Since my aim is to use CBA as emblematic for a whole class of aggregative approaches, I will not dwell on its particular defects. Instead I will focus on a problem that CBA shares with the other members of this family of instrumentalist approaches that seek to constrain policy choice by reference to information about individuals' revealed preferences. This is the problem, as I will call it, of "stupidity."

The stupidity of using (M2) to fill out an instrumentalist understanding of democratic reasoning is related, it will turn out, to its failings as a contribution to instrumental reasoning. Agency instrumentalism takes an ordinary conception of instrumental reasoning, such as an individual might conduct, and unreasonably projects it onto the governmental stage, thereby riding roughshod over the differences among actual individuals. Model (M2) avoids this problem by incorporating information about individuals' commitments; but the way it does so, it will turn out, leaves no room for intelligent instrumental reasoning.

Let me emphasize that (M2) casts CBA in a special role, one with which not all of CBA's fans would be comfortable. I am viewing it as a sample way of filling out an instrumentalist conception of distributed democratic reasoning. The idea is to maintain the kind of delimiting role for the legislature that was the centerpiece of agency instrumentalism. Hence we may take legislative directives as establishing the ends in view. Once the legislature decides what is to be accomplished, CBA can come in to rank alternative ways of accomplishing that objective on the basis of information about individuals' preferences. This approach can admit, as agency instrumentalism cannot, that the legislative directives are so vague that they often leave important and controversial issues unsettled. Model (M2) aims to settle these remaining issues democratically, or at least in a way compatible with democratic ideals, by recurring to information about what individuals variously prefer. This role for CBA, as a crucial piece in an improved instrumentalist account of democratic reasoning, contrasts with other roles that this economic tool might be called on to play. For instance, CBA might serve as a useful accounting device, one that might perhaps be supplemented by the use of other accounting devices more sensitive to hard-to-quantify considerations involving the environment, justice, or community solidarity. In addition, CBA might play an even more modest role in policy deliberation, simply providing a way to raise red flags about particularly costly options. In each of these modest roles, CBA can be highly useful. Here, however, I am assessing CBA as the central normative component of (M2)'s constraint on agency reasoning. On this model, agency decisions will be adequately related to individuals' views because they will be made on the basis of CBA's preference-aggregating standard.[4]

The fundamental problem with casting CBA or any of its instrumentalist, preference-aggregating relatives in an option-ranking role is not that it cannot provide a way of ranking policies that is grounded in individuals' preferences; the problem is, rather, that this approach to ranking is a stupid one. In using this jarring term "stupid," I have been anticipating the main lines of my argument, which are simple to sketch. As Dewey most clearly recognized, an intelligent approach to practical problems, whether individual or public ones, requires above all a flexible willingness to remake one's aims in light of new information, especially information about costs.[5] But CBA models decision-making in two unconnected steps. First one collects willingness-to-pay information, capturing individuals' preferences as revealed by their economic behavior (or, less standardly, as gathered through surveys). These preferences stand proxy for individuals' ends or aims. Second, one aggregates that information by calculating how much money individuals affected by a project would have to give up or receive to be indifferent with the state they are in absent the project.[6]

In this two-step approach, there is no room for the collective application of what Dewey termed "practical intelligence," which encompasses the ability to reformulate ends and aims in light of what emerges about the costs and benefits of proceeding with a project. Since even intelligent instrumental reasoning will do that, raising this worry does not presume the falsity of instrumentalism. Consider a pair of examples from an exhibit on animal thinking at the National Zoo in Washington, D.C., which contrasts human thinking with that of other animals: a salmon, in order to reproduce, sets out to swim back up the river in which it spawned; finding the river dammed, and unable intelligently to reformulate that "end in view," it dies of exhaustion from its repeated attempts to leap the dam. A human being, in order to get a pizza, sets out to the pizzeria on the corner; finding the pizzeria closed, it intelligently shifts its end-in-view, heading instead to the supermarket for the dough, cheese, and tomato sauce it needs to cook up a pizza at home. It is because it fails to make room even for this kind of basic practical intelligence, despite touting itself as an approach to be favored by those who would use their resources wisely and effectively, that I will be faulting (M2).

I substantiate this charge in two stages. The first will make out a prima facie case for the stupidity of (M2)'s CBA standard by contrasting it with intelligent practical deliberation, as generally described for an individual deliberator. This account of intelligent deliberation will introduce Dewey's understanding of the interdependence, in deliberation, of end and means ("the continuum of end-means"), which will be central to my own constructive account in later chapters.[7] The second stage of my argument critical of (M2) will spell out its lack of intelligence in more detail, elaborating four key uses of intelligence in deliberation and confirming that each of these is unavailable in using the CBA standard.

## The General Case for a Want of Intelligence

The initial case for the stupidity of the standard underlying CBA may be made by contrasting the general nature of intelligent deliberation with the assumptions underlying the theory of the revealed preferences that are the informational basis of CBA.

The first step toward understanding why a model of policy reasoning built around CBA is bound to be wanting in intelligence is to see that its primitive notions do not mesh well with the structure of deliberation, even instrumental deliberation. While this may be a result of stretching CBA to fill a role for which it was not designed, so be it: Whether it can serve as a key element of an instrumentalist understanding of distributed democratic reasoning is the question I am now examining.

To explain the nature of practical intelligence, I will revert to the richer vocabulary of end and means. While I cannot even lucidly present the defects of using cost-benefit analysis as a fundamental normative standard for agency reasoning without shifting to a different vocabulary, I will not thereby be begging the question against this approach. I will shortly return to revealed-preference theory in its own terms.

As I noted in chapter 7, there are three reasons why end-means reasoning cannot be formalized. First, it is only very rarely that circumstances present us with a single necessary and sufficient means to any end. More commonly, if there are any sufficient means, there is a plethora out of which we must choose. Second, we need to exercise some judgment in selecting a sufficient means. We seek the easiest and best means; and there is no noncontroversial formula that will tell us which one that is. Third, it sometimes happens that although sufficient means to our end do exist, none of them is acceptable to us on reflection.

Corresponding to the three reasons that instrumental reasoning cannot be formalized are three indispensable modes in which practical intelligence is exercised. First, since we often face a plethora of potentially sufficient means to our ends, we must be able to refine or specify our characterization of those ends so as to start to narrow down among the potential alternatives. Second, since, as the phrase "easiest and best" indicates, we operate with an irreducible plurality of ends that are always in the background of any choice, we must be able to bring them to bear in some way both in refining the end in view (the one from which we began deliberating) and in assessing alternative means. Third, since we have to accept that some ends in view will turn out not to be reasonably achievable, we have to be able to decide when it is appropriate to abort incipient projects or give up on cherished plans. In suggesting that we have these abilities, I am not making any particularly controversial claim. In particular, each of these three aspects of practical intelligence is compatible with instrumental rationality, as I have defined it.

I have also argued that we have forms of practical intelligence that transcend the limitations of instrumental rationality. For the purposes of showing the stupidity of (M2)'s CBA standard, however, it will suffice that practical intelligence requires the three abilities described in the preceding paragraph: to refine our ends, assess alternative means in light of multiple ends or objectives, and give up on pursuing an end when it seems appropriate to do so. There is no room even for these simple exercises of practical intelligence within (M2)'s model of choice.

Economists, including the proponents of CBA, are not committed by virtue of their theories to any specific theory of preference formation. Preferences might arise any which way, as far as their theories are concerned. This fact may generate the suspicion that while practical intelligence is not accounted for in CBA (or other economic theories of practical reasoning), that is only because it is included in something that these economic theories take as exogenous input, namely the preferences. If that is where practical intelligence comes in, it might be thought, then it need not be included in the account of how it is rational to proceed with the preferences one has. Now, I have already indicated that it is a mistake to think of preferences as being fixed independently of deliberation. The need to refine and possibly to reject ends crucially implies that they must be reformulated as one proceeds. Definitively to shut off this reply, however, which foists concern with practical intelligence off on an exogenous and phantom theory of preference formation, the easiest and best way to proceed is to examine the theory of revealed preference a bit more carefully.

The three necessary modes of practical intelligence raise a problem for the theory of revealed preference that goes by the name of "incomplete thinking." This problem for revealed-preference theory is a third-person or observer's version of the gappiness of instrumental practical reasoning that I have been noting from the deliberator's first-personal perspective. The deliberator needs to exercise practical intelligence in dealing with the gaps resulting from the usual plethora of sufficient means, the multiplicity of standards relevant to sorting among them, and the possibility that it may turn out that no sufficient means to one's end is reasonable. Correspondingly, in trying to infer someone's preferences from their actual, revealed choices, the observer must rely on a host of assumptions about the extent to which, and the ways in which, the individual has dealt with these gaps in linear and explicit assessment. A lecture by Amartya Sen gave the following example:

> I am inclined to believe that the chair on which you are currently sitting in this room was not chosen entirely thoughtlessly, but I am not totally persuaded that you in fact did choose the particular chair you have chosen through a careful calculation of the pros and cons of sitting in each possible chair that was vacant when you came in. Even some important decisions in life seem to be taken on the basis of incomplete thinking about the possible courses of action, and the hypothesis of revealed preference, as a psychological generalization, may not be altogether convincing.[8]

Sen's observations suggest two kinds of difficulty for the theory of revealed preference, one more fundamental and relevant to my argument than the other. The less deep worry has to do with interpreting behavior. As Sen's case makes clear, it is always a dicey business trying to interpret behavior in psychological terms. We must make assumptions about what alternatives were salient for the individual and under which descriptions before we can with any confidence say what preference a given action reveals. But this problem is not unique to the theory of revealed preference; and in any case, that theory's application in CBA can perhaps get around this problem to some extent by relying on statistical data about a group of individuals, letting the relevant factors emerge empirically from econometric analysis.

The more fundamental and relevant problem of incomplete thinking is also the one that follows most straightforwardly from the reasons that practical intelligence must be exercised: Since preferences as revealed at any given time are inevitably the result of incomplete thinking about the pros and cons, they are always liable to being overturned by more complete thinking. Sometimes, indeed, this more complete thinking depends on experience. Perhaps you had not considered the dimension of smell at all when you chose your seat; but as soon as you realize that the person sitting next to you must have had garlic soup for lunch, you may come to regret your choice. "Be careful what you wish for," we are warned; but it is in the nature of human life that our thinking can never be complete enough to be sure to capture all the pros and cons in advance. Sometimes we have actually to try something to see how it goes.[9] At least as often, new kinds of pros and cons occur to us halfway through the process of planning something to which we are already committed. For all these reasons, when we later spurn a choice we had once revealed, it is often not because we are simply fickle—though we are that, too—but because we had not thought our choice through completely.

Modern economists, in employing the idea of revealed preferences, have tried out two contrasting responses to this problem of incomplete thinking. These responses seem to represent the two available moves. The first, natural to those whose enterprise is spinning out ideal conceptions of social choice, has been to assume the problem away. Here Arrow's work on social choice is exemplary. Arrow well recognized that a complete consideration of pros and cons must always take account of the issues of "interdependence of values" that will multiply as dimensions of deliberative assessment multiply. Accordingly, he suggested, we are led in the direction of postulating that "each decision is effectively a choice among total life histories."[10] For the purposes of developing his impossibility theorem, it was perfectly acceptable simply to stipulate that we have available each individual's ordering across total life histories. For the purposes of making public policy, however, the impossibility of generating an acceptable social welfare function is compounded—or, depending on your point of view, made irrelevant—by the fact that individuals' final orderings of this kind, even highly partial ones, are, as a practical matter, simply not available.

This idealizing approach to preferences presupposes that all significant deliberation has been completed prior to their formation. One sign of this is the way that complete thinking, of the kind that Arrow postulates, squeezes out ordinary end-means reasoning.[11] If I prefer mainstreaming to special vans just because mainstreaming is generally a better means of getting the disabled from point A to point B, then my completely-thought-through preferences would cover different packages combining mainstreaming and vans with different levels of transportation service to the disabled, according to the probabilities buried in the "generally," and the end-means aspect of my thinking would thus be factored down to its supposed basis. To be sure, if I prefer the mainstreaming means because it is less discriminatory, then I may care intrinsically about what sort of means is employed to transport the disabled; and if I do, completely-thought-through preferences will not wholly wash out end-means relationships. They will remain because they are items about which I have intrinsic preferences.[12] But my point is only that once one has done this job of completely thinking preferences through, there is no need, any more, for end-means reasoning. Rather, one simply picks the highest ranked of the available alternatives. Again, this line of thought is what pushes the preference theorist in the impractical direction of postulating the availability of rankings of alternative life histories, in the manner of Arrow.

In light of the fact that preference orderings resting on complete thinking are not to be found, however, economists of a more practical bent have argued that we should content ourselves with the preferences as revealed in the marketplace. Supply and demand information, they argue, while not a perfect or definitive basis for getting at individuals' preferences, still tells us more than any other source might. Taking this tack amounts simply to taking the problem of incomplete thinking on board and hoping that one can live with it. Of course, one would have to, if there were not a more intelligent way to think about policy deliberations, but there is, as I will argue in the remainder of this book. Defenders of (M2)'s CBA standard of choice thus face a dilemma: Either they must unrealistically require that preferences reflect complete thinking, in which case their theory will be practically useless, or they must simply try to live with the fact that preferences do not reflect complete thinking, in which case they make no room for practical intelligence. Either way, the approach is doomed to stupidity.

## Types of Practical Intelligence: The Costs of Stupidity

Is failing to make room for practical intelligence all that bad? To argue that it is, I will elaborate four key ways in which (M2)'s CBA standard blocks the use of practical intelligence. In so doing, I aim to reveal how the behaviorist flatness of the idea of revealed preference contrasts with the rational richness of the categories of end and means, which are crucial even to an account of intelligent instrumental deliberation.

The stupidity of handing agency deliberation over to the cost-benefit standard arises from the fact that this standard takes its content from willingness-to-pay information that is empirically fixed and unresponsive to the analyst's conclusions about costs and benefits. My account in chapter 7 of rational deliberation of ends helps provide, by contrast, a picture of what a more intelligent approach to practical deliberation looks like. Recall the kind of specification of ends that was involved in the second round of rulemaking under the Biaggi Amendment: The example helps suggest what goes missing when preferences, and thereby ends, are frozen at the outset. Without by any means attempting to give an exhaustive list of the foregone possibilities, I will highlight three.

1. *Failure to generate new solutions.* We show our intelligence in practical reasoning largely in our ability to adapt our purposes to the means available. Sometimes, as I have shown, this requires giving up on a project entirely. More commonly, we respecify our end in view in some way. If that end in view was rather vague, the new specification may simply add emphasis and refinement that points us in new directions; if it was already specific, we may need to revise it—sometimes by differently specifying a more general end of which our initial end was itself a specification, and sometimes by specifying a more final end for the sake of which our initial end was sought. In any of these ways, we can free ourselves up to seek new and better solutions. For example, *winning the war* may become an end that seems practically unreachable. If we interpret it more restrictively, however, as *winning the war in the sense of establishing a secure boundary between us and the insurgents*, then we will be led in the direction of a negotiated solution. If even that proves too difficult, we may look to what our underlying concerns were and settle for "peace with honor," security of our oil pipelines, or providing a safe exit for those of a threatened ethnicity. Similarly, *finding a cure for cancer* turned out to have been a naively grandiose goal that would, pursued literally, bankrupt the nation; however, *understanding the mechanisms giving rise to the most common cancers so as to develop effective ways of treating them* is an achievable goal. Now, of course, if we imagined CBA being applied only after ends or goals have been completely thought through, then we could simply say that CBA will take account of all of these refined and realistic specifications. Yet stipulating complete thinking is radically unrealistic. The trouble, then, is that since CBA's willingness-to-pay standard must take the ends as fixed from the outset, it lacks a provision for this kind of intelligent reformulation of them.

2. *Failure to resolve conflicts.* Another reason practical intelligence is called for, besides our so often being stymied by circumstances, is that, as I have shown, we have so many mutually incommensurable ends and values. Difficult policy decisions typically involve competing values that are different in kind. As others argue, attempting to resolve these conflicts on a

single, willingness-to-pay scale does violence to our commitments in various ways.[13] While I agree with that, the point I want to emphasize here about these conflicts is a different one: Intelligent deliberation involving competing ends or values will often find ways of respecifying one or all of them so as to relieve their conflict in the case at hand, yielding (*pro tanto*) a more coherent overall set of commitments. For instance, promoting resource conservation conflicts with the goal of economic growth; but it does not conflict (at least not in all the same ways) with the goal of *sustainable* economic growth. Adding that qualification makes for a more coherent package of commitments. Because it makes no place for reformulating ends, (M2) also fails to make room for this kind of useful conflict resolution.

3. *Failure to discriminate among ends.* The idealizing preference theorist may stipulate that preferences based on complete thinking reflect an optimal individuation of alternatives, one that treats options as distinct whenever they reflect discernible advantages or disadvantages. This fine-grained individuation of alternatives thus depends on an ideally fine-grained individuation of desiderata; this, in turn, is pie in the sky. Intelligent deliberation, involving the explicit reformulation of ends, can at least move in the direction of a finer discrimination among the things that we care about. By contrast, CBA employs a fixed individuation of costs and benefits. Of course, if we can think of distinctions that might have eluded us, we can also claim that they would not have. Still, examples of the kinds of discrimination that might well elude us unless we are actively and intelligently engaged in specifying ends in a context of deliberation are: (1) the distinction between a disabled person getting from point A to point B and he or she doing so in a way that conveys no social stigma; (2) the distinction between an innocent person being shot and an innocent person being shot by a member of the police force (distinctions of agency); and (3) the distinction between that aspect of environmental aims that involves protecting wilderness from human encroachments and that aspect that centers instead on protecting the ecological supports of human health and flourishing (distinctions of interpretation within an abstract goal). Intelligent deliberation will be in a position to generate such discriminations in response to features of the circumstances of action; (M2) is not.

This list of failings amply demonstrates the relative stupidity of using a revealed-preference-based standard of public choice. They involve three kinds of intelligent refashioning of ends that are available to ordinary deliberation but foreclosed by any model of decision that takes as its contentful normative basis a given set of revealed-preference information.[14]

Since (M2)'s CBA standard represents a stupid basis for public practical reasoning, filling out an instrumentalist conception of the structure of democratic reasoning by adding CBA as a constraint on agency deliberation about how to fulfill the ends settled by the legislature is not an attractive or reasonable approach. This way of attempting to reconcile agency discretion to democratic populism is an improvement over agency instrumentalism but is still highly problematic.

The defects both of agency instrumentalism and of instrumentalist models built on the idea of revealed preferences strongly suggest that we should try to see how democratic autonomy can be intelligently realized in a noninstrumentalist form that extends to agency decision-making. Before setting out this constructive account, however, I have a further issue to examine, which concerns how a strongly deliberative, or truth-oriented, approach can be compatible with the delegation of decision-making authority, period.

# CHAPTER 10

## Truth and Delegated Deliberation

I have argued that it is naive to think that legislatures can complete the work of settling our collective ends and silly to constrain administrative agencies' resulting discretion by a normative standard that makes no room for the intelligent refashioning of ends. Accordingly, we should think of agency deliberation as in some sense a continuation of the public's and the legislature's broader process of reasoning about what we should do—a process that is not instrumentally confined. This conclusion, in turn, forces us to reconceive the relation between the legislature and the agencies. If it is wrong to think of the legislature as setting the ends and the agencies as determining efficient or cost-effective means to those ends, then how should we think about the division of deliberative labor between the legislature and the agencies? More specifically, how is administrative deference to the legislature's prior decisions compatible with the open-ended and intelligent orientation to truth that a continuation of our collective, noninstrumental deliberation would seem to entail?

Think back, once more, to the 1970s. The Congress has passed the Biaggi Amendment, calling for special efforts to make transportation systems accessible to the disabled. The idea that officials in the Department of Transportation might have confined themselves to figuring out the best causal means to that end I have rejected as naive. I have also rejected the idea of using cost-benefit analysis as the standard of any further decision, on the grounds that an intelligent approach requires flexibility in remaking aims. In fact, the department did employ a flexible and defensible mode of deliberating about ends that extended even beyond the limits of broadly instrumental reasoning. Part of what it did was to specify the aim of making transportation accessible to the handicapped; but as I have shown, it did so on the basis of articulating—with help from HEW and from advocates for the disabled—a new end, that of not discriminating against the disabled. Articulating this end is hardly a way of reasoning instrumentally from the transportation aim, for making transportation accessible to the disabled is a means to avoiding discriminating against them and not the other way around. Now, this intelligent flexibility in specifying aims and in fashioning new aims to guide the implementation of legislative directives is all very nice; but how is it compatible with deference to what the legislature has decided?

In fact, there are two aspects to this last question. One concerns what rational constraint on agency reasoning can possibly reconcile deference to the legislature with intelligent flexibility. My answer, which I will develop in chapter 16, is that the requirement that the agencies work out a specification of the relevant statute allows for an appropriate balance of flexibility and deference (thus, while the nondiscrimination aim was a new, superordinate end, the purpose of articulating it was still to help work out regulations implementing the Biaggi Amendment). Before we get to that issue of normatively constraining bureaucracies to act the way we want them to, however, we must face the second, logically prior aspect of the question of deference, which is how it is that deference to the legislature's decision is conceptually compatible with the idea of flexible, truth-oriented deliberation about the ends of policy. This logically prior question is the one I seek to address in this chapter. It is a question about how to think about delegated deliberation in a noninstrumentalist way.

Perhaps you do not yet consider this a serious question. Perhaps you think that our public deliberation is simply divided into stages, and that is that. To further motivate the question, then, let me explain how it gives rise to a puzzle. In chapter 4, in examining the notion of the will of the people and its importance, I observed that we can give ourselves no good reason to do something simply by deciding to do it. The will cannot bootstrap itself into reason-giving just by deciding. If agency deliberation is simply a continuation of our reasoning about what to do, then why should it give any serious consideration to what the legislature has decided? If it is open-ended and flexible, noninstrumental public deliberation, rather than deliberation that is constrained to move along instrumental lines, then why should it take the legislature's prior decision as shaping its premises? The apparent dilemma is this: Either agency reasoning relapses into an instrumental consideration of the best means to given ends and gives up on an open-ended truth-orientation or it bursts all bounds of constraint and deference and searches, freelance, for the political truth. In the case of the DOT staff, either they operate using standard modes of cost-effectiveness analysis without concerning themselves with deep questions about political truth or they import their own conceptions about what ought to be done for the disabled and leave deference to the legislature's judgment behind. Either truth or the legislature will be the master; there appears to be no in-between.[1]

This issue is not resolved by a showing that the legislature's action is legitimate. As long as it is, the agency officials ought to obey it.[2] They ought to obey, even if they would not have endorsed the legislation themselves. When officials act this way, the principle or commitment on which they act is that of due deference to the legislature's commands: "Whatever the legislature legitimately asks us to do we ought to strive to accomplish. The legislature has legitimately asked us to make transportation accessible to the disabled. Hence we ought to figure out how to do that." What will result is instrumental reasoning constrained by the principle of deference. In contrast, if intelligent reasoning about the ends of policy is to be divided between the legislature and the agencies, it will be necessary for agencies to accept what the legislature has decided—under some description or interpretation—as directly stating a commitment or end. On this alternative approach, the link must go as follows. "Since the legislature has legitimately decided to make transportation accessible to the disabled, that is what we ought to do. We will reason further about what we ought to do, taking this commitment to making transportation accessible on board as the end from which we begin our deliberations." Administrators must be able to take this second attitude to legislative actions if they are to be able to cooperate in an intelligent way in our joint effort to decide what we ought to do.

At issue here is how to think about rationalist populism at the level of agency decision-making. The two contrasting links between legislative and agency reasoning characterized in the preceding paragraph correspond to two different pictures of the limits of populism. On the traditional way of thinking of populism, we formulate our will via public debate and then more definitely in the legislature, and then we hand this decision over to "them"—to the agencies—for refinement and implementation. As I have argued, however, this picture fails to satisfy the normative demands of democracy as democratic autonomy, for controversial decisions about public ends that bear significantly on how we are to be ruled are inevitably handed over to the agencies. Further, (M2)'s ersatz way of bringing the public's preferences back into the process is unintelligent, failing to engage us in further reasoning about what we ought to do. The reason that it is important to find the proper kind of rational continuity between legislative decision and agency reasoning, then, is that we do, after all, need to see if we can credibly conceive of the agencies continuing the process whereby we make up our minds about what we ought to do.

As I have implied, the dilemma of truth and deference is merely apparent. Both truth and the legislature can be masters, *if* we can make out how it is that the legislature's decision can plausibly be taken to affect (the truth about) such matters as whether we ought to make transportation systems accessible to the disabled, subsidies available to artists, or incentives available to small businesses to locate in the inner cities. I believe we can make out how legislative judgments can constitutively affect what we ought to do. Attempting to make this out will have the side-benefit of bringing us to a deeper understanding of the relationship between truth and commitment in practical reasoning. I will make my case in three steps. First, I will go over, in more detail than hitherto, what is involved in truth-orientation in general. Second, I will explain how the truth-orientation of practical reasoning always depends on prior substantive commitments. Finally, I will explain how the prior decisions of the legislature can, after all, offer reasons that should be taken into account in open-ended, noninstrumental reasoning about what we ought to do.

## Orientation to Truth

The idea of truth has three importantly distinct aspects or faces: correspondence with the way things are, coherence with the evidence, and acceptance of fallibility. While philosophers have often puzzled over how these are related to one another and have sometimes controversially emphasized one to the detriment of the others, it is doubtful that any account of truth that wholly ignored one or more of these aspects could count as analyzing our concept of truth. These aspects correspond to the descriptive, commending, and cautionary uses of "true."[3] I will briefly explain each. My aim here is to muster platitudes in an instructive way rather than to break new philosophical ground.

The descriptive use of "true" is the most obvious. To state the truth is to say how it is. Hence a true statement is one that corresponds to the facts. The aspect of correspondence is probably most familiar in a metaphysically ambitious version; but it need not take that form. Metaphysically ambitious correspondence theories of truth attempt to characterize in some way the World, or the set of facts, to which assertions correspond. Having done so, they then need to say something about the relation of correspondence that is supposed to hold between facts and true assertions. Such theories collapse for various reasons, not least of which is the impossibility of giving an appropriately general interpretation of the correspondence relation.[4] Yet the aspect of correspondence is not thereby denied; it lives on in a less metaphysically ambitious version familiar among philosophers and logicians. Here, the leading idea is that of disquotation. Take a sample proposition— say, "We ought to provide transportation assistance to this disabled." The thought is that to assert that this proposition is true is to assert that we ought to provide transportation assistance to the disabled. Truth-conditions for any proposition whatsoever can be stated simply by removing the quotation marks that served to refer to it. Whatever one thinks of such truth-conditions, it is undeniable that the truth-predicate has this disquotational function.[5]

Contrary to what some philosophers have recently claimed, however, the disquotational idea cannot capture the whole of the concept of truth. There is nothing wrong with the disquotational idea as far as it goes, but it cannot by itself explain the normative uses of "true," whether to commend or to caution.

To give an account of "true" that captures its normative force, we need to include something about the way it functions within our practices of giving and accepting reasons, our practices of inquiry. It serves to refer, broadly, to the ways in which our beliefs cohere. The commending use of "true" presumes the importance of these epistemic practices. Against the background of this practice, to say that something is true is to say that one ought to believe it and whatever follows from it.

Shifting wholly over in that direction are coherence-based accounts, broadly understood, which attempt to define or account for the nature of truth wholly by reference, say, to the convergence of an ideal community of inquirers or to an ideal speech situation.[6] Yet it seems intuitively clear that a belief might be agreed to by an ideal community of inquirers, or in an ideal speech situation, and still not be true. Similar doubts arise with *any* nontrivial definition of truth.*

Coherence-based accounts of truth thus fail on account of ignoring the third aspect of the concept of truth, which is the way it serves to remind us of our ever-present fallibility. Even an ideal community of inquirers might be wrong. Marking out potential fallibility is one of the most important functions of discourse involving the word "true." Notoriously, analytic philosophers have had some difficulty accounting for the importance of this little word. To believe a proposition to be true is simply to believe it; to assert a proposition to be true is simply to assert it. Why, then, could we not simplify our language and simply say that we ought to help the disabled, without bothering about whether or not the proposition "We ought to help the disabled" is true or not? To be sure, there are miscellaneous technical reasons why we cannot wholly dispense with the predicate "is true." For one thing, we use it to cover a whole range of statements, as in "Everything Pericles said was true." For another, there are the difficulties exemplified by the liar paradox.[7] Yet revising our understanding of truth in the technical ways required to meet these sorts of logical considerations will leave unaccounted-for the cautionary role for the truth predicate. That role is to provide a way of marking and recognizing our own fallibility, as in: "I see that strong reasons support that conclusion; still, it may not be true."[8] Whereas the correspondence aspect has, in the past, seemed an invitation to metaphysical ambition, this third aspect of truth demands a little modesty.

What the failure of each of these one-sided theories of truth suggests is that a correct understanding of the concept of truth must integrate all three

---

* The qualifier excluding triviality is needed because one can safely gloss "true" as "corresponding to the facts" so long as one is not pressed to interpret this notion of "correspondence."

of these aspects.⁹ On this basis, we can construct an account of what it is to be oriented to truth. To do so, we will need the conception of reasoning laid out in chapter 5 as an intermediary. Reasoning, as I there defined it, is intrinsically truth-oriented, for it is thinking that sifts reasons and arguments—jointly, considerations—that bear on the truth of propositions for the sake of determining whether they are true or not. The preceding account of truth's three aspects simply allows us to elaborate this idea somewhat.

Following the lead of the metaphysically nonambitious account of the correspondence aspect of truth, we may say that reasoning is truth-oriented just in case it aims to be guided by the considerations that there are. Here, I cannot pretend that there is anything as neat as the disquotational relation to capture the idea of there being a reason in favor of some proposition; still, I hope the general idea is plain enough. One whose reasoning is truth-oriented aims to be guided by a true conception of which reasons and arguments bear on the issues under consideration and of how they bear on them (i.e., of what relevance they are). While we thus start with a focus on the correspondence aspect, the others follow close behind. In sketching rational deliberation of ends in chapter 7, I have shown how, in the practical case, such an orientation includes within it both a concern for coherence among one's commitments and an awareness of the fallibility of one's understanding, at any point, of what reasons there are. It is thus that one's conception of ends, or of the principal reasons that ought to guide one's conduct, are rationally subject to reformulation on grounds that pertain to the resulting coherence of one's view. To be oriented to the truth is to seek to be guided by such reasons as there are, recognizing that one's conception of these reasons is always fallible yet always seeking a coherent account of them.

This account of truth-orientation does not aim to be controversial; quite the opposite. My hope is that it seems quite obvious, at least once the three aspects of the concept of truth are recognized. While it is nearly trivial, or lacking in analytic precision, it nonetheless points us toward an important conclusion about the relationship between truth-orientation and commitment.

## The Need for Initial Commitments

In abstract terms, the key implication of the foregoing sketch of truth-orientation is that we cannot reason in a truth-oriented way without having some initial substantive commitments that give a definite shape to the practices or patterns of inference whereby we test the coherence of our beliefs. In politics, if we had no idea whether arbitrary imprisonment were wrong, whether laws ought to be general in form, whether hyperinflation were to be avoided, and whether children should be taught to read, then we would be rather at a loss about what we ought to do. Without some fixed points by reference to which to take our initial bearings, we would be unable to orient our political reasoning toward the truth.

To elaborate this point, I want to return to the difference, alluded to earlier, between two questions that might orient practical thinking: "What shall we do?" and "What should we do?" Democratic deliberation, as I have been describing it, is addressed to questions of the latter sort. My dual thesis here is that questions about what we should do, unlike questions about what we shall do, necessarily call for truth-oriented reasoning and that it takes some initial set of normative commitments to give shape to a question of the latter form.

"What shall we do?" is perhaps the most general or unrestricted practical question for a group. A question of this form can be satisfactorily answered by arbitrarily "picking" or plumping for an option, as opposed to choosing one for some reason or on account of some argument.[10] Accordingly, it would show no misunderstanding of language to answer the question "What shall I do?" in a way that did not involve reasoning. In its openness, this question straddles the deliberative and the merely willful. When the tyrant, acting on whim, declares "Today I shall annex our neighbors to the east," he may be opposed but cannot be rebutted. In contrast, the question "What should we do?" always calls for answers that are candidates for truth or falsity. That is because this question carries sufficient structure to orient inquiry, allowing us to bring reasons to bear, one way or another. In arguing that democracy ought to be deliberative, populist, and rationalist, I have argued that it ought to be oriented by the question "What ought we to do?"

It is crucial at this point to resist a mistaken interpretation of what is implied by the necessity of having some initial commitments to give shape to our practical questions. This mistake would lead us back to instrumentalism and would fail to capture all three aspects of the concept of truth. It is the mistake of building the presuppositions explicitly into the question. We do this when we ask "What ought we do if we are to promote accessible transportation for the disabled?" Such a question draws an answer that remains in the conditional: "If we are to promote accessible transportation for the disabled, then we ought to _____." Of course, questions of this conditional form are susceptible of true and false answers, to which instrumental reasoning may be directed; but given the importance, in a democracy, of reasoning about ends, we should ask whether we are stuck with this conditional form.

One likely chain of reasoning that would lead to the conclusion that we are stuck with this conditional form harkens back to Kant's dichotomy between hypothetical and categorical imperatives. Hypothetical imperatives are "ought" statements of the conditional form just noted, whereas a categorical imperative is an unconditional demand of reason. The only way to get a categorical imperative, Kant argued, is to see it as arising from pure reason, precisely *without* presupposing any substantive normative commitments.[11] But—comes the second link—it is commonly recognized that Kant's attempt to derive a categorical imperative from the structure of pure reason failed: There are no categorical imperatives, in his sense.[12] Hence the conclusion: There are only hypothetical imperatives. There is no way to answer the unrestricted question "What should we do?" and no sensible perspective from which to ask it.

The possibility that Kant missed is that the substantive presuppositions needed to structure a practical question demanding truth-oriented inquiry can lie in the background that gives shape to this inquiry rather than having to be built explicitly into the question. Building the presuppositions into the question limits the reach of the answer. It copes with our fallibility by hedging. "I am not sure if we really ought to help the disabled find transportation, but *if* we should, then this is what we should do." The overlooked alternative is that the presuppositions, instead of delimiting the question, give shape to the practices of inquiry within which it is addressed.

In the case of democratic inquiry, it is above all the commitment to processes of decision that treat individuals as free and equal autonomous persons that gives a definite shape to our inquiries about what we ought to do. There is certainly enough meat in those values of freedom, equality, and autonomy to give coherence considerations some grip. While these fundamental considerations obviously do not exhaust those with which we start, they do provide enough constraint to indicate that some views about what we ought to do are false and others true. Further, the questions we are pursuing are clearly not conditional ones along the lines of hypothetical imperatives; the values presupposed by our commitment to democracy do not entail that we are really asking "What ought we to do if we are to promote the freedom and equality of autonomous persons?" Rather, the presuppositions inform the constitutional structure that enables us to ask what we should do, period.[13]

Having said this much, I must return to the aspect of fallibility. In truth-oriented deliberation about what we ought to do, we must recognize that any of our initial commitments might be shown to need revision. In difficult moral and political cases, when we debate what we should do, we are in fact often drawn into reconsidering quite fundamental commitments, whether constitutional or informal. The substantive commitments presupposed by moral and political questions about what should be done are presupposed in order to get the deliberation started but do not need to remain presupposed in the answer.

This account of what it takes to pursue practical inquiry in a truth-oriented way now suggests a possible avenue for explaining how agency reasoning can serve both the legislature and the truth. It can do so if the legislature's prior action can be rightly regarded as a source of reasons that are properly taken as initial presuppositions of agency reasoning. Yet would it not be bootstrapping to suggest that the legislature's answer to its practical question—its articulation of the people's will—thus becomes a reason bearing on what we should do?

## Normative Fruitfulness

In order to avoid the bootstrapping difficulty, or the incoherence of directly saying "We ought to do this because we have decided to do it," I must return to the deliberation of the legislature and show a plausible way to characterize it as being not only truth-oriented but also able constitutively to affect what is true.

There is no problem in describing a *nondeliberative* democratic procedure as affecting what ought to be done. This account would draw on the liberal ideals that underlie democracy. These imply that the political process ought to respect individuals as autonomous beings. One of the three subsidiary requirements of this broad political ideal, as I mentioned in chapter 4, is that individuals ought to be regarded by the political process as "self-originating sources of claims." That is, in a democracy, what individual citizens think should be done intrinsically matters as a consideration bearing on what ought to be done. To be sure, this kind of consideration can be overridden—and will be easily overridden in a case in which a billionaire seeks a special subsidy—but it is a consideration that bears on what we ought to do. Now suppose a process of democratic discussion that is not strongly deliberative—not truth-oriented. People air their views and attempt to persuade one another. This process will undoubtedly change individuals' views about what ought to be done. Majority procedures of decision will tend to track these changes. Correspondingly, via the principle of respecting individuals as self-originating sources of claims, the democratic process may well affect what ought to be done. There is no great mystery in that.

What is more difficult to see is how this kind of effect can coherently take place within a truth-oriented process of deliberation. One cannot enter into truth-oriented deliberation with the attitude that says "Whatever this process of fair debate and majority decision yields will likely be what we ought to do, so I will wait and see what that is."[14] A participant in a process of truth-oriented deliberation must be able to enter into sifting reasons and arguments rather than detachedly regarding the process as a black box.

Drawing on the account of truth-orientation earlier in the chapter, I can now point out that for political deliberation to be truth-oriented, it is crucial that there be sufficient initial presuppositions to license its question "What should we do?" and sufficient acknowledgment of our fallibility. As I have just argued, a commitment to democracy, as I have specified it, is sufficient to mark out a truth-susceptible practical question. What about acknowledging our fallibility?

To recognize our fallibility, it is not enough to deliberate flexibly and remain open to revising or reformulating the democratic ideals that initially orient us; it is also important to recognize that even the best-constituted democratic process might settle on a false view about what we ought to do. This implies, in turn, that there are truth-conditions pertaining to what we ought (through our democratic institutions) to do that are logically independent of the democratic process. These are the process-independent standards of justice, charity, environmental and economic stewardship, and so on.

So now the puzzle takes a more focused form: How can truth-oriented democratic deliberation be subject to process-independent standards yet capable of constitutively affecting what we ought to do? To show how it can, I need to explain how Rawls's influential dichotomy between "pure" and "perfect or imperfect" procedures fails to exhaust the possibilities.

Rawls's important distinctions among ways in which procedures can be related to right answers—whether just, true, or correct answers—are as follows. "Pure" procedures are ones for which, as Rawls says, "there is no independent criterion for the right result: instead there is a correct or fair procedure such that the outcome is likewise correct or fair, whatever it is, provided that the procedure has been properly followed."[15] Impure procedures, on the other hand, are ones with respect to which the right answers are fully given in advance. Among the impure, there are in turn two types: "perfect" procedures are guaranteed to reach those independently given answers and "imperfect" procedures carry no such guarantee.[16]

It would be impossible to reconcile truth-orientation with individualized popular sovereignty if Rawls's dichotomy between pure and impure procedures exhausted the conceptual possibilities. As I have just shown, pure procedures do not allow their participants to orient themselves toward truth, while impure procedures cannot have any affect on which answers are correct. Fortunately, however, logical space remains for a third possibility. In between a situation in which all practical truths in a given domain are fixed independently of a procedure and a situation in which none of them are—leaving truth to be wholly determined by how the procedure comes out—lies a vast range in which, while some aspects of the truth are fixed independently of the procedure, the procedure nonetheless has some truth-determining effect. I call procedures that thus fall in between impure ones and pure ones "normatively fruitful procedures."[17] This middle, mixed case is particularly important with regard to practical questions, to which many considerations are typically relevant yet for which we generally seek an all-things-considered answer that takes those considerations appropriately into account.

Outside of the democratic context, an intuitively compelling case of normatively fruitful practical deliberation is that of a couple deciding whether to get married. On the one hand, there are many factors fixed independently of their deliberations that bear on their decision. Do they love one another? Will their careers allow them to live in the same city? Is either of them currently married to someone else? And so on. For some couples, such independent considerations might be dispositive. For many couples, however, the whole set of such considerations, listed independently of their deliberations, might leave matters up in the air, some pointing in one direction, some pointing in the other, with none of them ruling out a "yes" or a "no" answer to their practical question. For these couples, it may well be that whether or not they should get married (hence the truth-value of the claim that they should) depends on what they decide after discussing the matter and deliberating together.[18] In the case of marriage, this dependence may be asymmetrical: Perhaps their deciding, after due discussion, that they ought to get married is a *necessary* condition for it being appropriate for them to marry but not a *sufficient* one. To be sure, part of our deference to the participants in such a decision may simply result from applying an epistemic rule of thumb to the effect that those close to a matter are likely to know more about it. Such a rule of thumb is liable to being rebutted by what the *actual* facts are. Part of the reason for the deference, though, is intrinsic. Marriage, it might just turn out (in the culture or cultures relevant to interpreting the couple's intentions), is the kind of status that should not be entered into unless the parties have *actually* arrived, through joint deliberation, at a state of mutual consent and affirmation.[19]

The questions of policy faced by democratic states often fall into this normatively fruitful middle range, in which what ought to be done depends both on factors fixed independently of democratic deliberation and on the outcome of democratic deliberation itself. This can be because of the importance of respecting individuals as self-originating sources of claims. A less individualistic explanation that we might well also accept from within our commitment to democracy is simply that whether a government ought to enforce a given policy may depend in some contexts on whether a duly constituted majority of the appropriate kind has actually spoken in favor of so doing.

Importantly for the truth-orientation of democratic deliberation, there does not seem to be any general way to separate out which aspects of which questions are settled by the legislature and which are independently settled. To be sure, we can imagine extreme cases at either pole. A legislature that approves of slavery has simply done something wrong. By contrast, a legislature that is deciding whether to fund an award for prominent national philosophers may obviously face a question to which no right answer is given independently of democratic debate. In most legislative debates, however, matters of both types will intermingle, making the boundaries between them indiscernible. For instance, suppose the Congress, rather than the DOT, had debated whether to include antidiscrimination language in the Biaggi Amendment. Arguably, not discriminating against the disabled is a moral requirement that stands independently of whatever the legislature might have decided; but arguably, how to phrase or specify the requirement of "special efforts" is a question that depends at least in part on what the legislators and the public conclude after due reflection. With the truth of what we ought to do depending *both* on external standards *and* on how actual democratic deliberation turns out, democratic processes are normatively fruitful ones.[20]

## Agency Continuation of Public Reasoning

It is now apparent how agencies can reasonably take up the conclusions of democratic procedures as provisional premises of truth-oriented noninstrumental reasoning about what we ought to do. This is a reasonable attitude because a legitimate legislative decision can affect what we ought to do. If the legislature says that we ought to make special efforts to make transportation accessible to the disabled, then perhaps we should. This kind of inference is of course not always secure. If one knows that the legislation resulted from back-room trading or from a secret exchange of blackmail threats, then it will stand rebutted.† When it seems acceptable, however, agency officials will be reasonable if they revise their views so as to take on this new assumption and proceed to reason from that revised starting-point about what we ought to do. This assumption will be like the substantive presuppositions needed to get any truth-oriented deliberation about what we ought to do off the ground: helping to shape the question but subject to revision on reflection.

By handing off to the agencies premises with which their reasoning can work, the legislature can enlist them as cooperative partners in our efforts to decide, together, what we ought to do. In thus extending the strands of populism and rationalism to the level of agency policy-making, I have not

---

† Specifying informative conditions for when to take the legislature's decision to be a reliable indicator of what we ought to do would be a difficult task. As the following chapter will argue, we must not exclude the results of bargaining or compromise, as such, from playing a role in affecting what we ought to do.

forgotten about the importance of republican checks. These will still be necessary to prevent the agencies from dominating us. What I have been about, though, is trying to find an appropriate way of formulating the norms of reasoning that ought also to constrain agency decision-making. I rejected the narrowly instrumental constraint of agency instrumentalism, and in rejecting the ersatz populism of cost-benefit analysis highlighted the need to invite the agencies to engage in intelligent deliberation about ends. That need, however, seemed to stand in conflict with the agencies' subordinate status vis-à-vis legislatures. Now, with the aid of the idea of normatively fruitful procedures, one can see that this conflict is only apparent. Agencies are subordinate to the legislature, as far as reasoning goes, mainly in the sense that the agencies' work comes as a second step after the legislature has taken a first one. This is not to say that the legislature's enactment is not to be taken as authoritative by the agencies, excluding certain types of reconsideration.[21] Nor is it to deny that this authority will need legal enforcement. Still, how we think about agency reasoning hinges on the difference between excluding certain matters from reconsideration because one provisionally takes a practical premise to be true and doing so just because one has been told to do so.

So far, my theory of democratic deliberation has taken account of the multiplicity of individuals only in an abstract and indirect way by considering the division of democratic deliberation into stages. Now it is time to face up to our multiplicity more squarely and to begin to recognize the concrete differences among us and among our political views that make politics both necessary and difficult. A first step in examining joint deliberation among multiple people with differing views will be to see how the process of compromise can contribute to democratic deliberation.

# CHAPTER 11

# Deep Compromise

The last few chapters' emphasis on how to conceive of the rational constraints that should apply to agency policy-making, while moving us toward a broader understanding of democratic reasoning, may have given the impression that democracy as democratic autonomy would be as civil as a proverbial gentleman's club, as free of intractable internal conflict as a herd of sheep, and as disinterestedly rational as an academic seminar.[1] It is time to correct this impression. Citizens in any democracy will have deeply conflicting interests that unavoidably lead them to argue in self-interested ways. The depth of their conflicts and the depth of existing injustices may rightly call for angry protests, unrestrained verbal attacks on opponents, and ways of trying to combat the entrenched powers that exercise domination. The conception of democracy that I am pursuing has not forgotten these facts. The republican insistence on dispersing power among a number of different institutions so as to reduce the possibility that the government itself dominates or is captured by one dominant social force is what motivated my looking into the structure of agency decision-making in the first place. Accepting the need for the republican device of dispersing powers, I turned away from a unitary conception of democracy and from an idealized, monistic conception of popular sovereignty. The need to rely on majority rule to bring closure to political debates has not been forgotten, either: I will discuss its place in due course. We will not understand its place aright, however, unless we recognize how democratic deliberation can begin to *cope* with the many kinds of disagreement that divide us.

Democracy has a dual role with respect to disagreement; one is to lessen it so that we can come to decisions that are workable, the other is to accommodate us to disagreement so that we can recognize as legitimate even decisions we disagree with. While different theorists of deliberative democracy have laid the emphasis more on one of these roles than the other, I am not aware of any who have wholly neglected either.[2] Who seriously thinks that democratic deliberation can remove all disagreement, and what theorist of democratic institutions thinks that discussion therein does or ought to leave all initial disagreement unmitigated?

We disagree, of course, about the ends of policy and not just about the means. Hence, in illustrating the kind of process-independent standards that apply to democratic decisions—justice, charity, environmental and economic stewardship—I have tried to indicate a sufficient range so that each of my readers will recognize at least some one of them as naming a standard that should apply. For there are individuals who would deny that there ought to be any collective stewardship of the environment or that the government ought to concern itself with distributive justice, let alone with charity. Disagreement about ends also shows up at more specific levels. Different people would specify differently the goal of maintaining clean air or the goal of ensuring workplace safety. And even now, decades after the Biaggi Amendment, people differ about the appropriate way to characterize the goal of making transportation and other services accessible to the disabled (who are the disabled, anyway?).[3] When we disagree about ends, does that mean that collective deliberation about ends is not possible?

I have argued for the general possibility of rational deliberation about ends. Further, I have argued that our populist task is to settle on collective ends, to decide on the ends of policy as well as on means. If disagreement among individuals about ends stymies collective reasoning about ends, then recognizing the depth of disagreement prevalent in society should lead us to conclude that the ideal of a rationalist populism is impossible of attainment.

Having taken you this far with democracy as democratic autonomy, with its aspect of rationalist populism, I obviously do not think that initial disagreements about ends blocks joint deliberation about them. The task of this chapter is to explain why not. I will set out a general conception of deep compromise—compromise that extends to ends—that shows how interpersonal deliberation about ends can be more like its intrapersonal counterpart than one might have suspected.[4] I will first set out the notion of deep compromise and then examine in a general way the motivational assumptions that must hold for such compromise to be possible. At the close of the chapter, I will explain how deep compromise remains a possibility under conditions of pluralism.

## Compromise and Deep Compromise

Compromise has a bad reputation. In large part, it deserves it; venal politicians all too often compromise their principles for the sake of personal gain or glory. Neither true principles nor fundamental human rights ought to be compromised even for the sake of social welfare; yet examples of when they have been, such as the U.S. slavery compromises of 1789 and 1830, are the ones that have shaped our thinking about compromise in general. Nonetheless, there remains an important middle range of politics in which our deciding what to do depends on a mutual willingness to forge compromises for the right sorts of reasons. My purpose here is not to praise compromise as such—for many compromises are venal or unfair or immoral—but rather to clarify the possibilities for joint political deliberation that compromise affords. In particular, I will develop the notion of deep compromise, which is central to democratic deliberation and helps it constitute joint deliberation of ends. In order to highlight the distinctive characteristics of deep compromise, I will distinguish it from the kind of compromise involved in framing a *modus vivendi*.[5]

It is a great mistake, and a common one, to contrast deliberation with bargaining in the political context. One political theorist describes democratic deliberation by noting that "deliberative 'conversations' fall somewhere between two extremes: *bargaining*, which involves exchanging threats and promises, and *arguing*, which concerns either matters of principle or matters of fact and causality."[6] Political deliberation should be viewed as bargaining facilitated by argument and hence as lying between argument and bargaining in the way that cappuccino lies between coffee and milk. We should not suppose that political deliberation represents some wholly distinct, third alternative that does not partake of bargaining and arguing. Thus, it is within the sometimes raucous blend of bargaining and argument that constitutes democratic deliberation that deep compromise arises.

One reason that the nature of political compromise has not been well understood is that instrumentalist understandings of practical rationality have flattened out our ways of describing compromises. As I have argued, an intelligent approach to public reasoning about policy requires being open to revising our collective aims through a process of collective reasoning. Accordingly, the sort of compromise important in democratic deliberation cannot be modeled in a way that holds ends fixed. It follows that we must think our way clear of instrumentalist assumptions about defining compromise and demonstrating its benefits. In addition, we need to remember the importance of shifting to the categories of end and means, leaving that of preference rankings behind. Since we aim to look inside the process of democratic deliberation, we are interested in more than just how individuals would rank alternative outcomes. We also want to know what they seek for the sake of what and whether it is possible for them to compromise rationally about final ends, which they seek for their own sakes.

Accordingly, I am not here interested in "bargaining theory," which, like game theory, considers the situation we would be in, collectively, absent the possibility of collective reasoning. Typically taking individuals' preference rankings as fixed and abstracting from how any particular bargain might be reached or imposed, bargaining theory abstractly studies such properties as the stability or fairness of a given allocation of goods to individuals. By contrast, what I am interested in here is actual processes of compromise among flesh-and-blood individuals who arrive at compromises by changing their minds.

So understood, compromise of any kind involves a kind of responsiveness to the other. What kind? Not a merely opportunistic one. If two people, each on their way to dinner, run into each other, come to realize this, and spontaneously resolve to go and eat together, that joint resolution does involve a kind of responsiveness to one another but does not intuitively strike us as a compromise. A spiteful response to another is not productive of compromise, either. If, in pursuit of a place to eat together, one of the parties insists on going to a Thai restaurant precisely because he knows his partner for the evening gets indigestion from spicy food (whereas he much likes it himself), he is not compromising with his companion but slyly trying to stick it to him. Intuitively, then, compromise in general seems to be a modification in one's practical commitments that one would not have made but for one's concern or respect for the other or for the joint entity or enterprise one shares with him or her.[7] Some degree of mutual goodwill and mutual respect is needed for the parties to negotiation to consider compromising their position in any way. A valued, shared identity beyond what is implied by mutual goodwill and respect is not needed but can certainly help.

Note two points about this general conception of compromise. First, compromise, thus understood, is different from simply coming to appreciate the other's arguments and modifying one's view accordingly, for the latter is a way of coming to agreement rather than a way of mitigating disagreement. Since a reasoner's general concern to believe the truth can suffice to explain being led by arguments one takes to be sound, such changes in view can occur even absent any respect or goodwill directed toward or shared with the other. The notion of compromise, again, seems to involve the idea of changes that one would not have accepted *but for* this kind of concern and respect. Second, notice that I have been describing the attitudes involved as unilateral. That is as it should be, as far as the definition goes. If the two men end up going to the Thai restaurant, the spiteful one will not have compromised but the other one presumably will. Although fair compromises are almost always mutual, not all compromises are fair. This one surely is not.

Within this general category of compromise, I can now distinguish two types. *Bare compromise*, which is characteristic of a *modus vivendi* and of which logrolling is a common example, is a change of the relevant kind in one's support of policies or implementing means without a corresponding change in one's ends. A simple domestic example will illustrate. Suppose that the children need to be picked up at school at six o'clock but the mother is a member of a basketball league that practices and plays only at that time and the father is taking art classes that meet only at that time. A bare compromise, in this case, might involve each spouse taking turns missing the after-work activity. Bare compromise thus does not involve any reconsideration of what is worth seeking for its own sake, only a willingness to accept less satisfactory means to the ends one started with.

*Deep compromise*, by contrast, is a change in one's support of policies or implementing means that is accompanied and explained or supported by a change in one's ends that itself counts as a compromise.[8] That is, a deep compromise builds a new policy position on an underlying compromise at the level of ends. As a result, a participant in a deep compromise can regard the compromise policy as intrinsically supported, at least to some degree, by an end that he or she has actually adopted out of concern or respect for the other either as an individual or as a fellow member of some valued identity or enterprise.[9] To vary the domestic example just given, suppose that the wife had been pursuing competitive, league basketball for its own sake. It was a commitment she took seriously. She would take care to show up for the extra practices before tournaments and to get enough sleep before big games. Further, it was a commitment she considered on its own terms, without regard to other goods that this league play might be serving, such as working out aggressions or providing vigorous exercise. Given the conflict about picking up the children at school, this commitment is one that she might compromise, especially if the husband compromises too or if the husband cannot realistically do so. She might, for instance, decide that it was acceptable to play pickup basketball during the day and give up on competitive league play. Because this would still be a way of playing basketball, this compromise does not go *very* deep, but it goes deep enough to affect her ends, for she had been committed to the league competition for its own sake. If we assume that she would not have accepted this compromise except out of her love for her husband or out of loyalty to the whole family, then this serves to illustrate deep compromise, as I have defined the notion. Patently, as I said it would be, it is one question whether a deep compromise has occurred and another whether it should have.

Deep compromises are common at various levels in democratic politics. A course of argument that has been repeated in several jurisdictions around the world lately concerning state sanctioning of relationships between same-sex partners provides a more serious, political illustration of deep compromise—though one of doubtful mutuality. Reasonable compromise has been at least one-sidedly involved in most of these debates. In giving a schematic version of these arguments, I mean neither to endorse the sort of compromise that has resulted nor to criticize it from either of the two opposing sides but just to illustrate how political compromise can extend to ends.

Here is roughly what seems typically to have happened. Initially, advocates of homosexual rights pushed for recognition of the unions of gays as being marriages just like those of more traditional couples, with all the pertaining legal rights and privileges. In addition to wanting this possibility for the sake of the legal advantages it offers to gay couples, they sought it for its own sake, as an element in the recognition they believe that society owes them as equals. Initially, their most virulent opponents opposed any such recognition, opposing, for its own sake, the granting of any such recognition to couples they deem united around sinful behavior. In several jurisdictions, however, a compromise has been reached that affords some legal recognition of and protection for the unions of homosexual couples who seek state sanctioning of their relationships but refrains from calling these unions "marriages." While proponents of gay rights may complain that no such compromise should have been accepted, as it fails to obtain full recognition of gays as equals, it is clear that, given the political situation even in the jurisdictions that have taken this step, this move did represent a serious compromise of the other side's position as well. In this case, the aspect of deep compromise is asymmetrical. The record shows that some of the legislators initially wholly opposed to gay marriages changed their minds on the basis of hearing from gay people about their plight. Some, at least, reacted in an empathetic way to the hate mail they received on account of even being openly undecided on this issue: "If I am faced with such hate merely for being willing to entertain sanctioning gay marriages, just imagine what it must feel like to be gay!" The legislators so persuaded described themselves as voting their consciences even though it would imperil their seats. In short, it seems that some of the legislators initially opposed to gay rights ended up voting for the compromise because their concern or respect for members of the other side led them to take more seriously their opponents' arguments about the importance of their obtaining equal respect. Instead of still regarding even state recognition of any kind as a position to be opposed for its own sake (as wrong), these swing legislators came to see it as an acceptable means to expressing and promoting respect for homosexuals. Further, the nature of the qualification here responds to the practical exigencies of mitigating disagreement between the parties. The opposition to gay marriage (under that label) is not wholly withdrawn but is simply qualified so as to allow for the kind of second-best recognition afforded by the idea of state-sanctioned "unions." Such is a true move of deep compromise: Opponents of gay marriage who reason in this way have qualified their initial end so as to mitigate disagreement with the proponents.[10]

Deep compromise represents a possibility for reasonably revising ends that, by definition, exists only for groups of people in which mutual respect, concern, or shared identity is strong enough for them to try to work together. Further, it is a possibility that can be realized only if people deliberate together in a strong sense: they must not only mutually offer reasons to one another but also must respond to those reasons in a way that indicates that they have taken them seriously. Only where deep compromise is significantly possible, let us say, does "joint deliberation about ends" exist. (Note that this is not yet deliberation about joint or shared ends.)

## The Benefits and Justification of Deep Compromise

You will remember that I have already argued that democratic deliberation ought to extend to ends. For this to be possible, it seems that deep compromise must be possible. In now turning to examine the potential benefits of deep compromise, then, my point is not to raise the question of whether or not we should accept it as part of the repertoire of democratic deliberation. Rather, the point is to link this discussion of deep compromise to my earlier discussions of practical intelligence, rationality, and justification. To be sure, if one were in doubt about the usefulness of deep compromise, these considerations might count as offering commonsensical arguments in its favor. A serious weighing of whether to allow deep compromise would have to take account of all the ways that power imbalances, entrenched ideologies, and venal vices lead people to compromise their ends or commitments when they should not. As I see it, however, deep compromise is possible, and, given its possibility, its existence in democratic societies is almost inevitable. Hence, while we should of course try to right power imbalances, unsettle false ideas, and combat venality, we should also look to see how deep compromise can contribute to democratic deliberation and how its results may sometimes be justified.

The possibility of deep compromise allows for a flexibly intelligent approach to practical reasoning by a group of people. Instead of a collection of individuals each responding intelligently in an uncoordinated way to the practical challenges of a situation, deep compromise provides a way for them to do so in a coordinated and cooperative fashion. In the deliberations that led to the second set of rules under the Biaggi Amendment, this sort of flexibility showed itself in a willingness not to define the goal of nondiscrimination against the disabled, once articulated, in an absolute or literally unbending way. The disabled were not to be put in the position of having the same choice of seats in every bus, or the same means of getting down to train platforms, that the nondisabled enjoy. Although such extremes were indeed suggested by the ideal of nondiscrimination, those advocating that idea were willing, as I have noted, to accept a compromise specification of this end: not that each and every component and part of all ordinary transportation modes be made accessible to the disabled but that each mode, "taken in its entirety," be made accessible. This willingness to compromise a principle showed what looks to be a sensible flexibility in response to the other side's concerns about cost.

Neither the benefits nor the fairness of deep compromise can be made out by reference to a fixed set of individual preferences or ends, the typical approach of formalized bargaining theory and of cooperation in the context of repeated prisoner's dilemma games. Academics working in these areas tend to assume that the benefits of cooperation are to be measured by reference to individual "objective functions" that are taken as fixed. An essential aspect of deep compromise, however, is that it allows bargaining parties to revise their ends or "objective functions" in light of considerations brought forward by others. This means that there is no adequate way to measure the benefits of such cooperation without going outside the idea of satisfying individuals' actual preferences: Doing so by reference to the antecedent conceptions of the good will underestimate the value of the compromising, while doing so by reference to the resultant conceptions will exaggerate it. What one needs is some independently established conception of the good, whether that is thought of in terms of true human needs, the preferences people would have if fully informed and fully rational, or the fundamental values of liberalism.

In a way guided by such a substantive conception of the good, the rationality of deep compromise can be tested in the same general way as can other forms of reasoning about ends, namely by reference to the resulting coherence, or lack thereof, with what people remain committed to on reflection. In order to avoid biasing this test in favor of any compromise, once it is adopted, we should insist that the reflection take account of the process of compromise itself: Does one accept that set of considerations, on reflection, as an appropriate basis on which to have changed one's mind? This proviso is needed to help filter out the sort of self-deceptive adaptation known as a "sour grapes" reaction.[11] With that second-order supplement, the main case for the rationality of a change in view can be made out (or denied) on the same kind of basis as an individual's change in ends. Can the change be supported but its mutual fit with the commitments retained on reflection? Note that my argument does not depend on finding a criterion to sort rational compromises from irrational ones, or good ones from bad ones, but depends simply on the significant possibility of rational, deep compromise.

To see how this might work out in democratic politics, suppose that most citizens are at least implicitly committed to the following core idea of liberal democracy: that each person's political views ought to count for something in a democracy. In a democracy sufficiently well ordered for citizens to have this commitment, certain cases of deep compromise can be justified because they allow each party to get something close to what its political views call for. That is, a successful deep compromise can often serve as a way of treating all citizens as self-originating sources of claims. An example currently under contention in the United States concerns government funding for stem-cell research. Since these cells are derived from human embryos, abortion foes oppose all such research. Since the cells have the potential to differentiate into any kind of human tissue, they offer tremendous promise of better treatment of diseases. The Congress is now considering whether to accept a compromise that would allow the research but only using lines of stem cells already being cultivated in labs. Neither harvesting further cells from aborted embryos nor fertilizing eggs in order to create new blastocysts would be allowed in federally funded research programs. It is currently being debated, on both sides, whether this compromise actually does provide each side with substantially what it cares about. If the compromise is accepted, in the end, that may well be for arbitrary reasons; but it could be because the prolife side recognizes the importance of the medical research involved, deciding that this compromise adequately removes incentives for destroying human life, while the proresearch side decides that, considering the serious worries and doubts about the permissibility of abortion, they can do enough with the existing stem-cell lines. If that were what happened, then each side could decide, on reflection, that their aims were substantially well served by the compromise, and each side could accept, on reflection, that important considerations raised by the other had reasonably led them to accept this compromise. To be sure, if this intermediate proposal is accepted as a deep compromise by both sides, it will not be known to history as a compromise but as a resolution of the problem.

To clarify my purpose in speaking of the rationality of deep compromises, let me refer for a moment to a broader moral backdrop. It has sometimes been argued that politics is a "tragic" enterprise and that politicians need to be willing to get their hands dirty—that is, to sacrifice their principles in order to prevent disasters and to keep the political machine moving.[12] In discussing the incommensurability of values in chapter 7, I affirmed that tragic choices do exist. Yet it vastly oversimplifies our situation to suggest either (with Max Weber) that an "ethic of ultimate ends" or principle stands over and against a politician's ethic of responsibility or (with Isaiah Berlin) that our principles or ultimate commitments clash with one another like armored Titans. Contrary to the first suggestion, each of us, whether participating actively in politics or not, tends to have a wide variety of principled commitments or ends, and these multiply conflict with one another in more and less serious ways all of the time. The idea that there is a simple idea of "welfare" or "good consequences" that abstracts from all of these multiple conflicts has been foisted on us by utilitarian philosophers and must be resisted. Contrary to the second suggestion, since these principles and commitments do constantly conflict, sometimes in contingent little ways and sometimes in less avoidable and tractable ways, we do learn rationally to cope with these conflicts; and when we do, we do not treat generally our ideals and commitments as idols carved in stone; rather, we are often willing to reshape them. This being so, compromises, as such, should not be regarded as morally suspect; and political compromises should not be viewed as being any more tainted than those that can arise in individual deliberation.

Accordingly, we must judge each proposed compromise on its merits. Sometimes, as I have repeatedly said, the content of the compromise will be unacceptable—on account of its injustice, meanness, or rashness, say. And sometimes a compromise will be criticizable on account of the process that produced it having been duplicitous, arm-twisting, or irrational. Sometimes, however, deep compromises can be freely and rationally accepted as the result of a process of joint deliberation that is open and public. My aim has simply been to make a start at articulating the conditions of rationality that apply to deep compromise.

When deep compromises meet this test of reflective rationality and are recognized by the participants as doing so, they offer a better chance of generating results that each party considers justified or fully legitimate than do bare compromises. Where compromises are reached without benefit of mutually responsive deliberation about ends, one is stuck with what, at the collective level, is just a contest of wants. Some people want gay couples' unions sanctioned by the states, others do not; some will favor stem-cell research, some not; and it is just a question of who can muster the most votes. Bare compromises made just in order to carry a majority will not be regarded by the parties as being supported by reasons. They will be seen, instead, as having been exacted by the power—the threat-advantage—of the other side. Accordingly, openness to deep compromise both helps to engage thinking about what is justified and makes it at least somewhat more likely that people will arrive at conclusions that they each consider justified. In this way, judicious use of our capacity for deep compromise can facilitate political justification.

So far, my assertion that we have this capacity has rested on a briefly stated assumption about respect or caring for others or for shared identities or projects. It is time to examine this assumption more deeply.

## Motivations for Deep Compromise

Since deep compromise allows for a flexibly intelligent approach that can yield rationally defensible changes in ends and to conclusions that are mutually considered justified, I must next ask to what extent we can reasonably hope for deep compromise to work. Is it realistic to hope that deep compromise will play an important role in democratic politics? I will argue that it is. While the core of my argument will deploy some simple psychological assumptions, I want before presenting them to clear away some competing general views about human psychology, some more-or-less ideological views about human nature that get in the way of a reasonable appraisal of the chances of deep compromise.

In bringing out this possibility for joint political action, I aim to describe "the possibility that when politics goes well, we can know a good in common that we cannot know alone" but to do so without either romanticizing the possibilities of individual convergence or excessively idealizing the nature of the political collective.[13] Indeed, there are four overly simple sets of assumptions about human nature to be avoided here: pessimistic and optimistic versions of individualism and collectivism. The pessimistic individualist regards individuals as confronting each other in politics from behind the fixed barricades of interest. From this perspective, deliberation can make headway only if it somehow informs individuals about hitherto unrecognized ways of pursuing their strategic interests.[14] The optimistic, romantic individualist, by contrast, has faith that individuals' interests do not really clash at any deep level. That being so, what is needed is for individuals just to have the chance freely to express themselves in an uninhibited way. If they have a chance to do that in a noncoercive setting, then they can merge their views in civic friendship. The optimistic collectivist thinks in terms of the body politic as a unit that can act coherently and effectively, without worrying overly much about individuals' differing views.[15] The pessimistic collectivist, by contrast, worries that the powers of conformist and mass culture will iron out all interesting individuality.[16]

As I say, I resist each of these four overly simple assumptions about human nature. Against both sides, I insist on the primacy and possibility of forging a collective, democratic will in a way that takes individual rights, views, and claims seriously. My position opposes the collectivists, for it insists that the collective will be built up from an individual basis. (In the following chapter I will examine the mechanics of this.) My position opposes the individualists, for it insists on the importance of forging a collective will via a process of democratic deliberation. Pessimistic individualists wrongly regard this work as impossible, because they view individuals' interests as fixed independently of deliberation. Romantic individualists, for their part, fail to recognize just how much work collective deliberation can be. Since my view thus depends on the possibility of deep compromise, it will be well now to confront the pessimistic individualists' contrary assumptions.

As I mentioned when discussing the cost-benefit analyst's conception of preferences in chapter 9, the sort of aggregative theorist likely to invoke a pessimistic individualism is also likely to equivocate on the notion of an individual's interests. The equivocation is that between preference satisfaction, as such, and welfare or well-being. Preferences, as I noted, can range over any subject matter. One may have so-called existence preferences about whether spotted newts or unreconstructed racists continue to exist. One may prefer that one's loved ones, or one's nephew's school district, or one's favorite team's stadium receive some sort of benefit. Preferences, so construed, bear no relation to one's self-interest if the latter is conceived as something that, in its nature, is likely to clash with the self-interests of others. The preferences of all individuals might all converge on an identical ranking of alternative social futures. Further, preferences so construed have *no* intrinsic conceptual connection to individual welfare or well-being. Out of love, out of self-hatred, or out of any of a number of other motives, one may prefer to sacrifice one's own well-being to benefit others. Finally, preferences of this sort are just the kind of thing we expect to change all the time. Interests, by contrast, are thought of by the pessimistic individualist as being more fixed than this. They are fixed, presumably, by relatively permanent features of human nature and of the individual's situation, combining to determine what contributes to his or her well-being. Now, the trouble with this notion of interests is that although we can, indeed, develop a rough sketch of human well-being that seems to hold relatively fixed,[17] this idea of well-being is so sketchy that it is constantly in need of, and subject to, deliberative specification and revision. Hence there is no basis for the pessimistic individualist's view of individuals as hunkering down in the trenches to defend their fixed interests.

My own assumptions about individual motivation are two: first, that individual motivation is relatively malleable and relatively prone to being reshaped and redirected in deliberation; and second, that individual citizens in a reasonably just democracy are generally disposed to cooperate with one another. Let me take the more general point about malleability first.

Our motivations shift with our decisions and choices, and these decisions and choices are often the result of reasoning; hence there is room for practical reasoning to shape our motivations. To say this is just to spell out an implication of my account in chapter 7 of deliberation about ends, for the notion of an end was defined there partly in terms of what the individual would pursue under certain circumstances. This counterfactual presents one version of the idea of motivation. Accordingly, my account there of how deliberation can shape and shift ends was, at the same time, an account of how deliberation can shift and shape motivation. The idea of specification, of which that account made much use, also comes in to help explain, to those who have doubts about this, how reasoning can have such efficacy. Even Humean instrumentalists allow that motivation to achieve some end converts readily into motivation to pursue a *way* of achieving that end. When an end is specified, the resulting, more specific end represents a way of achieving the initial one. Hence the Humean instrumentalist should allow that motivation transfers via specification. The fact that some specifications can, as I showed, generate new final ends by promoting mere means to that status does not disturb this general point about motivational transfer.[18]

My more specific assumption about individuals' motivations is that citizens in a reasonably well-ordered society (which, by the arguments of part I, must be a democracy) are generally disposed to cooperate with one another. By this I mean not that all citizens are always, in all circumstances, disposed to some degree to cooperate with one another but that in many circumstances to a significant degree the great majority of citizens are so disposed. I believe that this assumption holds for most of the well-functioning democracies today, to a sufficient degree that we may realistically invoke it in explaining how political will is democratically formed in those places. One is disposed to cooperate with another if, by virtue of one's concern and respect for the other, or by virtue of one's attachment to an identity or project one shares with the other, one is disposed to modify one's plans and intentions in ways that accommodate the other's aims. Well-ordered democracies underwrite this kind of mutual concern and respect by embodying it in their institutions. Citizens of a reasonably well-functioning democracy accordingly have some good reason to feel some degree of solidarity with each other, and they normally do. This does not mean that they are never mean, spiteful, uncooperative, or simply obstinate. This background of institutionally supported, mutual concern and respect, however, makes it explicable that citizens of well-functioning democracies are generally disposed to cooperate with each other. At some level, they identify themselves as sharing in the cooperative project of collective self-governance.

The role in my argument of this assumption of a cooperative disposition is quite a modest one. It would be fatuous to proceed otherwise, as examples of recalcitrant conflict surround us. In my argument, the function of a cooperative disposition is just to get the parties to the bargaining table, so to speak. Our general willingness to consider modifying our plans to accommodate the needs and concerns of others gives us a significant reason, in many contexts, to deliberate with them about how we should proceed. This general disposition, shared by most citizens of well-functioning democracies, brings them to the threshold of joint deliberation. While many kinds of concern can override or cancel our willingness to cooperate with others in this way, the point, again, is that this sort of willingness to cooperate helps get the bargaining going in many contexts.

Once joint deliberation has begun, then, given the further assumption of the malleability of our aims, this cooperative deliberation may well lead to a mutually responsive modification of the participants' ends and motivations. Our ends are malleable to an important extent, and we—if we are citizens of a reasonably well-ordered democracy—tend to be at least somewhat disposed to cooperate with our fellow citizens. This being so, there is a decent prospect that our joint deliberation will yield pragmatically useful and rationally well-supported deep compromises.

Putting the point in metaphysically rather portentous language, it is central to this process of principled compromise that it enables the individuals involved to construct their (sense of their) selves—or their conception of the good—in dialogue as they go along. This fact is what essentially distinguishes this approach from the pessimistic and optimistic forms of individualism and collectivism set out earlier. I have already spelled out how it departs from a pessimistic individualism; assuming individual citizens have enough good will toward one another to enter into discussions or negotiations, it supposes that they can get around initial conflicts. In supposing this, however, my account hardly shifts over into an optimistic individualism by expecting a result in which each individual is seen to be able fully to express uncompromisingly his or her total individuality. Rather, each individual must typically give up something, in the time-honored fashion, to arrive at a resolution each finds acceptable. In this way, one sees the result is truly built up from the views of individuals, rather than via their acting as a single body. This picture of deep compromise partakes neither of a brute, optimistic confidence in the collective body's united wisdom nor of a pessimistic fear of collectively imposed conformism that irons out all dissent. While the resulting picture of reasonable compromise, in which individuals are open to reformulating their practical identities in ways that respond to the considerations the others raise, is at one level completely familiar, it is novel both in relation to the going theories of policy reasoning and in relation to the going ways of talking, in the loosely metaphysical way I have been indulging in about political identities.

In fact, most recent discussion of individuals' political identities has emphasized their multiplicity and incommensurable difference. Can a proposal about democratic deliberation that depends on the possibility of deep compromise survive in contemporary conditions of pluralism?

## Pluralism and Compromise

A serious skeptical challenge to the possibility of forging compromises at the level of ends in democratic deliberation arises from the existence of fundamental differences among the conceptions of value and of the universe that orient citizens in a diverse country. Lobbyists for the disabled and for transportation providers may be able to reach deep compromises, but what

about our prospects for reaching deep compromises with the fundamentalists in Hawkins County who objected to textbooks touting the dignity and
worth of human beings?

Some care is needed to pinpoint exactly what sort of trouble this pluralism might cause. (Here I follow recent convention and speak of "pluralism" as a fact rather than a doctrine.) After all, intractable conflict can easily arise among those who share exactly the same conceptions of the good,
as is familiar from cases of brothers wanting the same woman, neighboring
farmers wanting exclusive access to the same spring, and members of the
same political party each wanting to control a key committee.[19] As these
cases should also remind us, no set of realistic conditions will guarantee
that a reasonable resolution of conflict is reached; all that we can expect are
conditions that make it reasonable to deliberate together in search of a reasonable compromise. In the preceding sections, I have sketched a general
argument about the possibility and value of forging agreements through
deep compromise. Conditions of pluralism might interfere with the process
that my argument envisions in one of two ways. First, pluralism might undercut the mutual solidarity or goodwill that is important to motivate people to deliberate together. Since those with different worldviews will tend
to have less in common than those who share worldviews, the former will
be less apt to feel solidarity with one another. Second, pluralism might
make it more difficult to construe our democratic deliberation as being oriented toward generating true conclusions about what we ought to do.
"True from whose perspective?" will be the question. For both these reasons, the conditions of pluralism might be thought to undercut the possibility of forging deep compromise in a process of joint reasoning. Although these two reasons for doubt are quite distinct, I will address them
together.

My first line of response rests on the commonsensical point that it must
be possible to reach deep compromises despite pluralism, because we do it
all the time in pluralist societies. In the United States, we did so in working
out disability policy and could well do so again—despite a more obvious
involvement of pluralist battle lines—in the case of stem-cell research. Another example of deep compromise that succeeded in the face of dimensions
of ideological and ethnic difference is the early civil rights legislation shep-
herded to passage by the then senate majority leader Lyndon Johnson.[20]
Most of the southern senators were firmly opposed to any civil rights legislation, while civil rights advocates pressed for measures that would have
strongly empowered the federal government to punish civil rights abuses.
Johnson helped forge a compromise that cut deeply: A number of key
southern legislators had to be persuaded to accept the principle that the
federal government ought to oversee the enforcement of civil rights laws,

while the liberal supporters of strong enforcement powers had to be persuaded to give those up and accept a more symbolic provision.*

What accounts for this possibility of deep compromise? One way to answer this question would be to take the pluralist bull by the horns. In our postmodernist era, many are in the grip of metaphysical doubts that appear to be raised about objectivity, reason, and truth by the conditions of pluralism; and these doubts cling to the cognitivist claims of a conception of deliberative democracy such as the one I have been elaborating. One valuable way to address these doubts is to attack them head on, whether by undercutting the inference to relativist conclusions from the facts of pluralism[21] or by defending an objective, comprehensive conception of the basis of political decision.[22] These are both valuable enterprises. For my purposes, here, however, I do not need to establish or presuppose such universalist bases for combating pluralism—beyond, that is, what is involved in the commitment to the ideals of democracy.

Instead, I recur to and build on the argument of the previous chapter, which defended a more modest conception of practical truth. In so defending the possibility of deep compromise, however, I will simultaneously take on an objection that the postmodernists' concern raises but that may also have arisen independently: How can deliberation involving deep compromise be truth-oriented.[23]

In the last chapter, I argued that the fundamental liberal values underlying democracy provide sufficient structure to the question "What should we do?" that answers to it may be regarded as candidates for truth.[24] Hence those who believe in democracy because they believe in the importance of respecting persons as free, equal, and autonomous can deliberate together in a truth-oriented way. The principles of freedom, equality, and mutual respect for autonomy that—as I have argued—underlie our commitment to democracy as the only legitimate form of government also suffice to limn a conception of the public good, general adherence to which, in turn, suffices to ground cooperative, truth-oriented deliberation. These democratic ideals define a vague conception of the public good that is widely shared in well-ordered democracies, even pluralist ones.

Now my claim is this: In reasonably well-ordered democracies, even pluralist ones, citizens will sufficiently share the vague conception of the public good that underlies democracy to make deep compromise possible. Further, citizens in a reasonably well-ordered democracy will recognize that they share this basic commitment to democracy. This mutual recognition of a

---

* I adduce the example to help prove the possibility of deep compromise, not its rightness. With hindsight, Johnson's compromise can be viewed as a key step toward the ultimate success of the civil rights movement. It can also be viewed as a case of selling out to powerful racists.

shared, albeit schematic conception of the public good is sufficient to make deep compromise possible, even across the deep fault lines of pluralism. Publicly shared belief in such a conception of democracy also helps explain the actual success of deep compromises in the United States and elsewhere. We can see in the three ways how this shared basis helps enable deep compromises within truth-oriented deliberation.

First, since the ideal of mutual respect lies at the core of the liberal-democratic commitment, a mutual recognition of commitment to it can be expected to promote effective attitudes of mutual respect.[25] Mutual condescension is probably eroded by this mutual recognition; but mutual respect should be strengthened by it. The helpfulness in moral development of the mutually respectful aspects of etiquette bear out this claim.[26]

Second, mutual recognition as fellow citizens in a democratic jurisdiction provides at least a decent basis for forming a valued conception of shared identity. Whether this conception of shared democratic identity is a strong force shaping motivations will presumably depend on other factors. It will depend on whether the jurisdiction is too poor for fair cooperation among its citizens to be possible; and it will depend on whether its democratic institutions are reasonably just.[27] When conditions are favorable in these ways, however, we may hope that shared identity as a democratic citizen will itself be a possible basis for willingness to engage in deep compromise.

Finally, if this shared democratic project has gone at all well, then we may hope that citizens of the jurisdiction develop a modicum of concern for one another *as* fellow citizens. They may be troubled if a fellow citizen is kidnapped or suffers deprivation in a way over and above how they worry about non–fellow citizens. This mutual caring can reinforce mutual respect and a shared sense of valued identity in motivating a willingness to engage in deep compromise.†

To suppose that there is a core of shared values that suffices for joint deliberation to be truth-oriented is not to deny that values, including the relevant ones, are incommensurable.‡ Even the values involved in the democratic ideal, such as freedom, equality, and autonomy, are indeed distinct and are mutually incommensurable. There are different ways they might be specified, suggesting different priority relations among them in different circumstances.[28] In my own development of the ideal of democracy, I have

---

† Mutual caring is of course of distinctive importance for the substance of policy. As Musgrave points out, policy oriented by mutual caring as well as mutual respect will often be more interventionistic than policy oriented by mutual respect alone. See his contribution to James M. Buchanan and Richard A. Musgrave, *Public Finance and Public Choice: Two Contrasting Visions of the State* (Cambridge: MIT Press, 1999).

‡ I discuss the distinct issue of incommensurable worldviews note 29 to this chapter.

specified them in a connected fashion that, I hope, is relatively persuasive; but I do not assume that all citizens accept democracy as democratic autonomy. Even so, they share enough substantial commitment that they can deliberate about how these elements of the democratic ideal ought to be specified; and when they address more concrete policy problems, a vague conception of this ideal can serve to orient their question about what we ought to do. In that respect, the point is to be able to ask a truth-susceptible question, not to answer it. As I have argued, generating rational answers to practical questions does not depend on commensurating the values involved. Proposed answers can be defended, instead, on the basis of their mutual fit with the web of other commitments that, on reflection, appear to matter. Deep compromises can be justified on the same footing. Without a commensurating standard, there will be no easy formula for determining whether a compromise is fair; but no easy formula should have been expected.

So what about those fundamentalists in Hawkins County and the liberals who oppose them? As I have previously suggested, the prospect of finding a resolution to the textbook controversy that they can deem acceptable, given their views as they are, seem quite dim. The only hope for a deliberative resolution of the dispute between these opponents is for some change of view to be rationally induced. Since my hypothesis about the basis for deep compromise in democratic societies hangs on the core importance of the liberal ideal, I will examine how the change might come on the fundamentalists' side. It seems to me that there are two main possibilities. Either the fundamentalists have a basic belief in democracy or they do not. Suppose that they do, at least as far as governing their county is concerned, but that they have deep suspicion about federal power. Then, it seems to me, it should be possible to deploy arguments along the basic lines of the initial chapters of this book to try to convince them that they implicitly, in fact, already do believe in the equal dignity and worth of human beings.§ And if, in fact, they do implicitly believe in this, they may have been willing to listen to such an argument. Since belief in human dignity is not, in fact, incompatible with piety, it should further be possible to convince them that they are not being inconsistent to believe in both Christianity and democracy. Accordingly, it might be possible to convince them on this basis that they should not regard the idea of the equal dignity and worth of human beings as anathema. If we instead suppose that the fundamentalists have no allegiance to democracy at all, then I am not commit-

§ I am assuming that their problems with these notions stemmed from the Christian ideal of humility. If they are simply racists, then debate with them would need to proceed along different lines.

ted to showing that it is possible for liberal democrats to reach a deep compromise with them. It *might* be though, in this particular case, for the liberal democrats might be able to find support for the ideal of equal human dignity in the Gospels. In that case, it would be their willingness to take up the fundamentalists' conception with respect and tact that would be crucial to bringing them around.[29]

I suggest, in short, that the democratic conception of the public good is sufficiently shared by the citizens of well-ordered democratic societies that it provides a strong motivational basis for deep compromise as well as a sufficient conceptual basis (as argued in the previous chapter) for truth-oriented democratic deliberation. Although this stipulation of a basic commitment to democracy does constrain pluralism, it by no means rules it out. It is thick enough to get truth-oriented deliberation going but vague enough to leave room for all sorts of incommensurable conceptions of the good.[30] Accordingly, appeal to this democratic conception of the public good explains how, for my purposes, democratic deliberation can deliberatively forge deep compromises under pluralist conditions.

# CHAPTER 12

# Forging Joint Intentions
# and Shared Ends

The possibility of deep compromise is crucial to our ability to reach political agreement through deliberation, especially under conditions of pluralism, which mean that we often start out quite far apart. Yet the notion of deep compromise cannot serve to model our agreements. As I defined it in the last chapter, it is not even necessarily mutual: One party to a bargain can engage in deep compromise, shifting his or her ends out of concern or respect for the other, while the other does not. Hence, while deep compromise can facilitate agreement, it cannot represent its structure.

I turn now to a pair of notions that can serve as ways of representing political agreements: joint intentions and shared ends. My principal purpose in doing so is to articulate the conceptual tools needed by an account of democratic reasoning that avoids both of the poles I have already rejected: the view that "the state" or "the people" may simply be viewed as a reasoner just like any human individual and the diametrically opposed view that wholly rejects such talk of collective reasoning and looks instead only to the aggregation of individual decisions (as in social choice theory) or to their strategic interdependence (as in game theory). We must, instead, find a way to model collective, political deliberation by individual reasoners with potentially distinct views. In doing so, we need to understand the structure of the intentions that issue from such deliberation, which cannot simply be the intentions of the state or simply the set of individuals' intentions. Perhaps, in the end, we will be talking about the government's intentions: but the liberal and populist aspects of democracy as democratic autonomy demand that we try to understand the government's intentions as growing out of what each of us, as distinct individuals, think ought to be done.

This chapter aims only to articulate the conceptual middle ground between blithely collectivist and narrowly individualist conceptions of intention. It does not yet try to solve the problem of whether even legislative decisions can count as expressing the will of the people. To approach that question, I will first have to face up to the indirectness of representative government (in chapter 14) and the necessity of relying on majority rule (in chapter 15). The latter, especially, will cast a shadow on the rosy picture of consensus that may seem to emerge—despite my caveats—from this chapter, for it reminds us that democratic governments rarely, if ever, generate intentions that all citizens endorse. All I mean to describe, here, is the right way to think about such jointness as does emerge.

In addition to laying out these conceptual structures, this chapter will also undertake two small substantive tasks. In the course of explaining how joint intentions can be reached, I will argue that features of the process can help us understand how democratic deliberation can be normatively fruitful; and in addition to setting out the idea of shared ends, I will argue that some are needed if democratic government is to function well.

## The Structure of Joint Intentions

Whether or not practical reasoning issues directly in action—a matter disputed among philosophers—it at least issues in intentions. Individual practical reasoning issues in individual intentions, which govern individual action.[1] Accordingly, we need to understand how individual citizens can come together in democratic institutions in such a way as to forge joint intentions about governmental action.

If democracy as democratic autonomy is to be feasible, it will have to be plausible to understand the actions of democratic governments as joint actions of at least some of the citizens in something like the same sense that dancing the tango and building a house typically are joint actions. Although such examples of joint action are highly familiar from everyday life, they have oddly been neglected by philosophers until quite recently—perhaps on account of Western philosophy's individualistic bias.[2] Because of the relative newness of the problem of joint action within the philosophy of action and philosophy of mind, there is little consensus on what it is that needs explaining. Indeed, the field of joint action offers a wide variety of forms for study. There are joint actions of different types or levels. I am not attempting a comprehensive look at this nascent field. Instead, I will pick out two notions of joint intention crucial to understanding different stages of democratic deliberation, a cooperative-agreement form and a tacitly informal form.

In adapting some recent work on the concept of joint intentions to help model what goes on in democratic decision, I will be abstracting for the moment from the question, otherwise crucial, of how to conceptualize the position of the minority voters, those who lose out when the votes are counted. In developing the relevant notion of joint intentions, I will, for now, just speak of agreement among some subset of citizens—a subset that surely will turn out to be less than the whole. Only once we have in our hands the conceptual tools needed to grasp the abstract structure of joint intentions, as this notion applies to deliberative decision in populist democracy, may we sensibly step back to ask about those citizens who do not, in fact, join in the resulting joint intentions. The point of the first step is not to provide anything even parallel to a principle of social choice. Rather, what we first need is a psychological category that may begin to suggest an appropriate alternative to, say, the idea of a "social ranking" or a "social preference."

The category of intention provides a way of representing decisions that is more in keeping with our focus on intelligent deliberation than is either that of a social ranking or a social preference. It does not multiply terms needlessly to add "intention" alongside "end" and "means." Rather, an intention is naturally thought of as the result of deliberation that considers end and means and hence as a form of decision that incorporates at least an implicit reference to pursued end and selected means within it. Thus, an intention paradigmatically takes the form *to do action A for the sake of end E*.[3] I argued in the previous chapter that collective deliberation will do well to involve the kind of joint deliberation about ends produced by a process of deep compromise. Now I shall examine the sort of joint intentions such deliberation can yield.

In modeling democratic decision-making, there is no need to push for an understanding of the resulting joint intention that reduces it entirely to individualistic terms, and there is considerable reason for doubting that this reduction would be possible. Having a democracy up and running at all requires the prior existence of broad and deep joint agreements about how to proceed. This set of background agreements informs the process of reaching deep compromises and forming joint intentions about how to direct the use of the powers that have been constitutionally created.

If all goes well, the process of democratic deliberation results in an agreement about what to do, the content of which might be spelled out in a piece of legislation or in a party platform. (This agreement is seldom unanimous; but, again, I am temporarily abstracting from that.) A distinctive feature of deliberative democracy is that the participants are to some degree responsive to reasons offered by other people, whether in reaching deep compromises or more shallowly. When deliberation thus yields agreement, those party to it will think that it names what we ought to do. Having played a part in forming it, they will naturally come to have an intention each to do his or her individual part, as determined by the agreement, for they take it seriously as a commitment about what we shall do. What it means to "play one's part" will vary with the context and with the content of the agreement. For example, if the agreement is to push for a patients' bill of rights, then the parties agree to favor some appropriate version of such a proposal, once one is drafted. If the agreement is to ban discrimination of certain kinds against the disabled, then those party to it indicate that they at least undertake not to engage in the relevant kinds of discrimination themselves. And if the agreement is to delegate standard-setting on carcinogens in the workplace to an administrative agency, subject to regular legislative oversight, then legislators joining in this agreement intend to follow up in this way, at least if they are on the relevant committee. Further, if this agreement is the result of deliberation, then we may presume that the parties to it believe that fulfilling the intention embodied in the agreement is possible, so long as enough of them do their parts. Finally, if this deliberation has been democratic, it should meet certain publicity constraints.[4] In the case of the democratic decision, the publicity ought to be actual, not merely potential. That is, the individual intentions and beliefs that support the public agreement should be common knowledge among the participants.

This constellation of facts—an agreement that we do something with regard to which (1) each of the parties intends to do his or her part as required by the joint plan; (2) each of the parties believes that the joint action can be carried out if enough do their parts; and (3) these intentions and beliefs are common knowledge—exemplifies the kind of joint intention that is important in democratic politics.[5] Call this the "cooperative agreement" account of joint intention, as it explicitly rests on a nonanalyzed notion of our agreeing to do something. Successful democratic deliberation will issue in joint intentions of this kind. Joint intentions of this sort are built up from individual intentions but are not reducible to them. The primitive element of agreement—as on constitutional essentials—and the layer of mutual awareness takes this notion of joint intention out of the purely individualist camp; but the dependence on individual intentions and the forward-looking focus on individuals doing their parts denies it membership in the collectivist camp as well. The populist aspect of democracy is picked up in the thought that, if enough people play their parts, *we* will succeed in doing something together.

To explain how democratic deliberation can forge joint intentions, I will describe four stages of the democratic process: formulating proposals; discussing their merits; coming to an informal agreement; and converting informal agreement into official decision. I will show how joint intentions can emerge from this process. An important task for this account is to elucidate the interplay of rational and populist elements. It is not enough just to insist that both discussion of a proposal's merits and free decision have their places. There needs also to be some explanation of how the overall process can be normatively fruitful, in the sense explained in chapter 10: some account of how it is that the process of forging joint intentions can affect what it is that ought to be done. One of the virtues of the cooperative agreement account of joint intention is that it facilitates this explanatory task.

Where will it begin? A narrowly instrumental, aggregative view of democracy might start with desires or preferences of citizens; a purely cognitive view might start with their opinions and views; and a noncognitive view focused mainly on the value of fair procedures might start with their attempts to exert their influence. By contrast, a view that sees deliberative democracy in terms of practical reasoning will naturally start with *proposals* that individuals, or their representatives, make about what we ought to do. Typically, but not necessarily, these proposals will arise out of the desires, preferences, or ends of the people who make them. These proposals, whether they take the form of nominating candidates for election or introducing bills for legislative consideration, are public actions in a dual sense. First, they are obviously actions essentially open to public inspection and awareness, in a way that desires or opinions may not be. Second, I am assuming that the relevant proposals are restricted as to their content: They are proposals *about* what we are to do, together.

The notion of a proposal has some simple implications that are helpful to understand in relation to the forging of joint intentions. A proposal is a public act, whereby, among other things, one implies that one is willing to accept that some steps necessary to achieving the proposal be taken. If I propose that John be the one to carry our petition to the authorities, then I openly imply that I am willing to hand John my copies of the petition. If what I am proposing is a joint action, then I imply that I am willing to do my part, as necessary, to carry out the proposal—subject, of course, to various escape clauses, necessary largely because I cannot foresee all the difficulties that may arise in bringing the proposal to fruition. If I propose that we marry, I imply that I will get myself to the altar on time—unless I discover that you are still married to someone else. A proposal may indeed be put forward insincerely, as the study of strategic voting shows; but an insincere proposal insincerely implies that one would undertake the necessary steps. The disappointed bride will not only feel generally jilted but will also have special cause to complain about being stood up at the altar.

This "willingness" involved in a proposal is not yet an intention to do my part. When I propose marriage to you, it would be unusually presumptuous of me already to intend to arrive at the church on time. More normally, this willingness will still have a conditional character: I intend to do my part, as required, *if* the proposal is accepted.[6] In politics, if I propose that we raise the tax rate, I imply my willingness to pay additional taxes— but to do so only if my proposal is accepted by the political process!

The second stage of deliberative democracy is for the proposals to be discussed on the merits. Since, as I have shown, political rationality ought not to be understood as merely instrumental, it is important to recognize that the ends in terms of which the public good gets interpreted are themselves up for discussion. Indeed, many of the most significant political proposals will imply or suggest ways in which the public good ought to be reconceived. Thus, evaluating proposals in terms of how they serve the public good is not simply a matter of comparing them on the basis of an independent standard. In this case, too, as Rawls puts it, "there is no way to get beyond deliberative rationality."[7] Nonetheless, it remains possible to consider whether the proposal well serves the public ends that, people think, ought to be pursued.

The third stage is to arrive at some informal agreement about what we ought to do. This informal agreement might be incomplete in substance and reflect the participation only of some of the participants. What matters, on the conception I am putting forward, is that there be some movement toward consensus, at least among subgroups, before a formal decision is attempted. This often occurs by way of refining and weeding out options. In some contexts, informal agreement is all that is needed to form joint intentions. Examining how this is possible will prove crucial to understanding how it is that democratic deliberation can affect what ought to be done. Before I look at this, it is important to note that in democratic policymaking, things do not stop there.

Thus, the fourth stage in the democratic formation of policy is one that converts informal mutual agreement into an explicit and effective decision that is shared by those party to it. In the process, such informal and perhaps fragmentary informal agreements as exist are acknowledged and folded into the decision. In a democratic body, this occurs by the use of majority rule. Consonantly with the account I have given of the first stage, that of putting forward proposals, I would describe each individual's vote as an acceptance of the proposal for which he or she votes.[8] This acceptance has two sides to it, corresponding to the two sides of citizenship that Rousseau identified: One accepts it as a member of the sovereign body, so that if enough of one's peers do likewise, the measure will prevail; and one also accepts it as a subject, indicating one's willingness to do one's part, as defined by the measure, should it prevail.[9]

This characterization of the democratic process as forging intentions that are joint as among the victorious majority at least gives us an appropriate conceptualization of the kind of mark we ought to aim at. Under realistic conditions, unfortunately, there are various reasons why individuals' votes may fail to indicate real acceptance of the candidate or option they voted for. Least interesting is the fact that they may not have been paying sufficient attention to what they were voting for. In that case, they at least have had an opportunity to accept something and have indicated, misleadingly, that they do accept it. The case of the notorious butterfly ballot in certain

Florida counties in the 2000 presidential election—which required close attention indeed—shows that this problem is not trivial; but it is not foolish to insist that voters ought to pay attention to what they are voting on.

Even more serious worries arise from agenda-shaping and strategic voting. In setting out these four stages of democratic deliberation, I have been speaking as if democratic decision occurred in one unified forum. In fact, however, large-scale governments tend to involve multiple fora in which majority rule is invoked: elections, legislative committees, the entire legislature, executive commissions, and so forth. I will show in chapter 16 that this stepwise division of deliberative labor can make important positive contributions to democratic reasoning. It also threatens the claim that a vote indicates acceptance, however, for it entails that those voting in one forum may be limited to options or candidates that are chosen by those in another forum. For this reason, voters are not infrequently faced with what they consider to be a choice among unacceptable evils. Part of what is needed to minimize this problem and to regain democratic control over complex government is to reassert popular influence over agenda formation and candidate selection. A second reason that an attentive vote may not indicate acceptance is that it may be cast strategically. Now, the vote for Gore by a Nader supporter is strategic in a sense; but the fact that one would rank Nader higher than Gore does not indicate that one finds Gore unacceptable. That remains an open question; however, to vote for an extravagant version of a proposed tax cut over a more reasonable one with the hope that, in a second round of voting, the extravagant one, and thus tax cuts in general, will be defeated, is hardly to accept the idea of a tax cut. Accordingly, while a vote may count as an acceptance of the proposal for which it is cast, this need not be the case.

These problems of agenda-shaping and strategic voting remind us of the importance of the distributed conception of popular sovereignty. One reason that no one institutional stage of the democratic process can be regarded as the privileged mouthpiece of the people is that no one institution can control the agenda it faces. To address these problems, we should see to it that democratic deliberation extends broadly to the public sphere, where discussion generates alternatives. The egalitarian commitment of democracy entails that we should strive to ensure that imbalances of power do not give certain groups undue influence over the public agenda. In short, while there is no way to get rid of strategic voting and agenda manipulation within a legislative assembly or elsewhere, the deleterious aspects of these phenomena can be mitigated by promoting democracy—by which I do not just mean majority rule—more broadly.

Accordingly, while individuals participating in democratic deliberation and majority decision will not always indicate by their votes which proposals they accept, they will tend to do so under idealized conditions, namely when voters are attentive and people have a fair chance to influence the agenda via open discussions in the public sphere.

This process of explicit, joint acknowledgement and endorsement of an agreement via the procedure of majority rule provides all that is needed to yield a proper, partially joint intention as the outcome of the democratic process. The application of majority rule formalizes an agreement that has been forged by deliberation. It is an agreement with regard to which all those in the majority are committed to each doing their parts, as defined by that agreement. Although these individual intentions were initially conditioned upon enough other people coming to agree, the application of majority rule will satisfy the antecedent in these conditional intentions. Finally, properly applying majority rule depends on a normative background that places it within something like a constitution and explains how it operates as part of the rule of law. As such, the operation of majority rule implies a public awareness of the commitments of each, as expressed in the vote. For this reason, then, the justified operation of majority rule will also satisfy the mutual knowledge condition of a genuine partially joint intention—an intention jointly held, at least, by the members of the successful majority.

This way of modeling democratic deliberation as directed toward the formation of partially joint intentions appropriately combines a respect for the distinctness of individual citizens with an acknowledgment of the fact that their participation in a democracy involves them in a common project. This model provides a relatively precise way of thinking about what is going on in joint deliberation—and one that neither imposes a reductive individualism nor facilely assumes a natural collectivity. Rather, it describes how joint intentions may be forged via individual participation in democratic deliberation. A further advantage of this way of thinking about democratic deliberation, as I have said, is that it helps explain how deliberation affects what ought to be done. Let me explain how.

## The Normative Fruitfulness of Joint Deliberation

Crucial to any potential normative shift is the third stage in the process I have just described, namely that of forming informal agreements. Recall that the cooperative agreement account of joint intentions takes the idea of our agreeing on a plan of joint action to be a primitive and adds conditions about commitment, mutual belief in possibility, and mutual awareness to assure that such an agreement really amounts to a joint intention. Joint intentions, so understood, thus stand apart from the kind of tacit, informal agreement that can arise, say, when two people wordlessly agree to play "horse" on a basketball court.[10] In looking at the third stage of democratic deliberation set out earlier, however, it is necessary to look at just this sort of informal agreement, to consider what is involved in this more basic form of shared intention.

A mere coincidence in plans is totally different from an agreement of the relevant kind. A group of waiting passengers might become mutually aware that each intended to fly to Chicago. Their mutually acknowledged awareness of this would by no means constitute an agreement to do so together. Intuitively, a central requisite or implication of agreeing to do something together is being mutually obligated in some sense and to some degree. As Margaret Gilbert writes, "genuine travelling together involves rights and duties that are something other than moral rights and duties." The rights and duties involved are not "moral," at least in the sense that they are not part of the general rights and duties of all moral agents. Rather, they result in some way from the interaction of the people who agree, tacitly or explicitly, to do something together. The idea of two people agreeing to do something together involves more than just the facts that each intends that they do it together (e.g., attend the conference) and that they each know this. Minimally, it also involves the notion that their so intending is "in accordance with and because of" their each so intending to do so.[11] Deep compromise involves such responsiveness, as its participants shift their objectives in accordance with and because of what the others intend. Even when such opposed views are not initially involved, however, the process of agreeing what to do together always involves a responsiveness to the intentions of the other or others. It is from this kind of mutual responsiveness that something like obligations arise.

Adapting some principles from the law of contracts, we can distinguish two ways that responding to others can give rise to the kind of obligation that converts mutual awareness of intentions into something normatively significant enough to count as an agreement: assurance and reliance.[12] If the first party desired assurance that the other would do his part, and the second deliberately took steps to reassure the other that he would, and both know this, then this may give rise to an agreement in which the second is obligated to do her part. If the assurance was thus provided on both sides, then it can be a symmetrically binding mutual agreement. On this possibility, then, explicitly reassuring a party who desires that reassurance is what gives rise to obligation. A second route to an obligation-involving agreement, instead of arising from a preexisting worry or desire for reassurance, looks to the results of an initial declaration of intention. Roughly speaking, if the first party's declaration of intention leads the second reasonably to make commitments that relied on the first party's following through, such that the second would suffer some loss if the first party did not, then that may give rise to an agreement in which the first is obligated to do his or her part. If the reliance is mutual, then so also may be the obligations arising out of the agreement. Both routes toward obligation involve an important kind of responsiveness between the two people involved, based on their mutual awareness of what each other intends, or says he or she intends. One response is to a need for reassurance; another response is a result of having felt assured.

In a deliberative ideal of democracy, it is above all responsiveness to the arguments and proposals of others that will be crucial in creating informal agreements. Let me briefly give another example to sketch how I see assurance and reliance phenomena arising in political debate. Some of it is pragmatic and some more cognitive. First comes the formation of shared intentions within the various competing political factions. Consider the issue of health-care reform. Various groups in the legislature would like to put forward a more free-market-oriented and less costly, albeit less comprehensive, reform package than the one proposed by the president. After much discussion of the merits of alternative proposals and much strategic jockeying back and forth, different coalitions of legislators will coalesce around different proposals for different reform bills. In the course of debate over the merits and tactics of these alternatives, they will publicly declare themselves for one or another of these alternatives, arguing that their favorite is the one that we, as a nation, should enact. Some legislators will want to be assured that enough protection for their elderly constituents will be built into the legislation and will be so assured. At this agreement-forging stage, deliberative democracy depends on a considerable degree of trust in the knowledge and the normative judgment of others. Now, once some proposals come to be favored, other legislators will withdraw particular proposals of their own, reasonably relying on their faction's leaders to provide a bill sufficiently friendly to free-marketers. In these ways, the legislators, sometimes via open pledges but sometimes more tacitly, will build shared intentions (of the more basic kind) to pursue their faction's proposal as what ought to be done. Each of them will put forward their faction's bill as what they propose we should do because, as he or she believes, it is in the public interest. (Whether this implied or explicit declaration is likely to be either cogent or sincere in actual legislatures is not now my concern.) Some of this assurance and reliance is backward-looking, focused on the process of judgment that leads one person or group to favor one alternative over another: "I have looked into it." Some of it is prospective, focused on the question of whether the relevant people or groups will do their parts as required for the plan to work. Both of these types of assurance and reliance, however, are focused on the collective action to be taken—the proposal to be enacted—and not just on the enacting of it. The shifts made in reliance on others or in response to others' assurances are shifts in what it is that

individuals think we ought to do. In this way, therefore, the types of assurance and reliance that arise in political discussion can give rise to informal
but normatively significant agreements about what we ought to do.

The situation is this: The nature of the road down which we have traveled
in our deliberations affects how we ought to continue. If individuals were
conceived as having fixed preferences or ends, shifting only in their view
about how to satisfy these, this situation would be difficult to understand.
It would be rational, instead, to insist on ignoring the "sunk costs" of past
discussion and to focus only on future effects. If your reliance on another
has led you to risk an asset on the other's word, then the risk of default
could be factored into an analysis of the consequences of the various options. All this talk of assurance and reliance and the obligations to which
they give rise would, on this picture, seem a needless duplication. Once we
acknowledge, however, that a mutual, cooperative shift of aims and ends is
occurring in democratic deliberation, the picture changes radically. Once
someone has shifted their ends in order to accommodate you, you owe them
something; and what you owe them is not appropriately measured by reference to their resultant set of ends. Suppose your spouse decides to give
up his or her career plans in order to stay home with the children and to
allow you to pursue your ambitions. In this case, you directly owe him or
her a debt of gratitude that should affect your future action. If, later, he or
she becomes reconciled to this life, no longer wishing for a career, still, that
would not cancel this debt. Similarly, where advocates of gay marriage have
given up pushing for the full marriage label and instead joined a coalition
in favor of civil union for gay couples, the opponents of gay marriage are
under some obligation to them to work out a version of civil union that
genuinely addresses their underlying concerns. Each side having modified
its intentions "in accordance with and because of" the position of the other,
each thereby comes under some obligation to follow through on the joint
intention that results. In this way, then, the formation of informal agreements can affect what it is that democratic bodies ought to do. This is not
to pull a normative rabbit out of a positive hat. Rather, this explanation of
how assurance and reliance modifies what ought to be done depends on
invoking well-established, highly general norms to the effect that such implicit promises ought to be kept and that such favors ought to be met with
gratitude.

If we start to think about democratic deliberation in terms of the forging
of joint intentions, we will see that this notion aptly applies at many different levels besides that of the legislature as a whole. Political parties, factions, committees, departments, agencies, and even the public at large engage
in efforts to formulate joint intentions. The personnel participating in any
given process of agreement is sometimes as fluid and shifting as a group of

teenagers planning a party. In modern governments, in which decisions are typically made in successive tiers, the structure of related joint intentions will be highly complex. This is a fertile field for potential exploration; all I hope to have done is to have described an appropriate way to think about democratic decision as a movement toward collectivity by individual citizens deliberating with one another.

Understanding democratic deliberation as a process of forging partially joint intentions, in short, satisfies two crucial theoretical needs. First, it models the product of democratic deliberation in a metaphysically appropriate way, without falling either into reductive individualism or obscurantist collectivism. Second, it helps explain the normative fruitfulness of democratic deliberation. What room does it make for joint deliberation about the ends of policy?

## Shared Ends

A process that yields shared intentions need not generate shared ends, but it easily could. Although an intention in the paradigmatic individual case takes the form *to do action A for the sake of end E*, what is shared in a joint intention may bear only on the action to be taken and not on the end. We may all agree on what ought to be done but each have quite different reasons for coming to this conclusion. Indeed, this possibility is crucial to democratic deliberation and to public justification under conditions of pluralism.[13] In particular, there is no need for us all to agree on an ultimate end that should regulate political activity.

Nevertheless, as I shall argue, it is often useful, and indeed practically necessary, for us to try to agree on some intermediate ends—ends that are final but not ultimate—in order effectively to carry out our collective projects. Legislators try to do so (within a projected majority group) when they build statements of purpose into complex pieces of legislation. These articulate some of the principal ends to be kept in view when the legislation is implemented. "In order to promote the economic health of the inner cities, the Small Business Administration is hereby empowered to give grants . . ." That such purposes are to be treated as final ends is clear, in such cases, because of two facts: first, that the more detailed and directly action-guided aspects of the bill are explicitly put forward as being chosen for their sakes; and second, that these purposes, collectively, are taken to articulate sufficient grounds for undertaking the described actions.

The shared ends that are most important in politics, it seems, are ones that are tied in this way to articulating reasons for a range of actions. It is much rarer for political institutions to articulate a set of final ends just as such. Political candidates and political parties sometimes do, to be sure. I will focus, however, on what I take to be the more common case, in which shared ends arise as part of shared intentions.

In such cases, I do not need any new conceptual apparatus to analyze the idea of shared ends. Rather, I may simply build on the idea of a joint intention developed in the previous section. Thus, ends are shared when the content of the agreement, regarding which people intend to do their parts and which they mutually believe will succeed if enough of them do, extends beyond actions to state the end or ends for the sake of which the actions are to be undertaken.

In a system of government in which power is dispersed and important decisions are delegated, effective implementation of government programs depends on the existence of some level of agreement about intermediate final ends guiding policy. Sometimes this agreement will have been forged in the legislature, and sometimes it needs to come later. In the case of the rulemaking needed to give force to the Biaggi Amendment, for instance, it was necessary to resolve what the purposes were for making transportation available to the disabled: simply to provide point-to-point convenience or also combat discrimination against the disabled? Without such a rough agreement at the level of ends, it would have been very difficult to find a reasonable basis on which to proceed.

The point, here, is a quite general one pertaining to the coordination of multiple agents. Mere statement of an action to be done often provides insufficient basis to prevent those attempting to collaborate from frustrating one another. Enriching the initial resolution by spelling out shared ends can help a lot. Arriving at a plan that decently coordinates the joint action of several people requires spelling things out at more than one level. It is not enough just to say, for instance, that we will paint the house together. We need to arrive at "meshing subplans" for doing so, indicating who will buy the paint, whether we need to scrape before putting on the new paint, and what color to use.[14] It will be no good if I scrape the north side just after you have put new paint over the old paint there and similarly frustrating if I keep trying to paint the house yellow while you go on reapplying the old green color. These examples have to do with the subplans, or the means—including the constitutive means—to the end of painting the house. Yet the participants' choice of causal means or specification of constitutive means will of course depend on what they they take the purposes of the whole project to be. Suppose we have the following "convergent" or "overlapping" or "incompletely theorized" agreement. You think that we should repaint the house because the green on it now is insufficiently weatherproof, and I think we should repaint the house because the current green needs some retouching to look nice. If that is where we leave things, then there will be no surprise if each of us goes out and buys different types and colors of paint. In addition, your weatherproofing goal may lead you to be glad of every additional layer of paint you can get on the house, whereas my aesthetic concern may lead me to scrape off old paint so as to get a nice-looking uniform surface. In short, if our more final ends diverge, it is highly likely that areas of the subplans that we have not explicitly worked out together will simply provide us room for getting in each other's way. In painting a house, we can probably work these matters out, especially if we have enough experience with house-painting to ask the right questions of each other. In running a government, things are otherwise. There are so many questions to ask, and so many unforeseeable contingencies, that there is always ample ground for jointly frustrating action. Accordingly, government action often depends on some layer of agreed ends if it is to be effective at all.

As in my more general discussion in chapter 10 of delegated decision-making, there is no pretense, here, that agreement at the level of intermediate ends will somehow solve the problem of statutory interpretation. A statute that contains a statement of purposes as well as prescriptive clauses poses a more complex interpretive problem than one that does not. Without a more general shared orientation (as might be provided by the general commitment to democracy), adding a statement of purposes would be like adding a rule to interpret a rule; we would land in a vain regress in search of a touchstone of interpretation. But the points of the preceding paragraph must be understood more pragmatically and as taking for granted a common language. The lesson was simply this: that if we mean to succeed in a joint project with others, we will often need to put some effort into articulating our aims.[15] The articulation of shared ends by, say, the legislature, is of course only a first step. That the legislature has articulated some purposes by no means guarantees that the agencies will take them seriously in exercising the discretion delegated to them. They are subject to incentives and pressures of their own, which may pull in other directions. What I have shown, though, is that agreeing on intermediate ends is, in many contexts, a necessary condition of democratic control of policy-making.

That completes my survey of the rational tools most important in democratic decision-making. I have explained how practical reasoning can extend to ends and how such noninstrumental reasoning is essential, for various reasons and in various respects, within democratic deliberation. Arguments acknowledging the burden of legitimacy carried by lawmaking show that, because controversial issues pertaining to setting public ends will inevitably seep over to the agencies, the agencies ought to be constrained by norms of noninstrumental, rather than instrumental, reasoning. A more general consideration of the nature of practical reasoning shows that a flexible openness to refashioning ends is a crucial prerequisite of practical intelligence. A shared orientation at least to the vague ideals underlying democracy underwrites the truth-orientedness of democratic deliberation, together with the mutual respect and concern that—we may hope—stems from sharing in the democratic project of collective self-governance, can lead individuals reasonably to enter into deep compromises, in which they revise their ends in order to come to agreement with others. The sorts of agreements they forge are joint intentions within coalitions. In order for these agreements successfully to constrain subsequent policy-making, they will often need to include agreement on intermediate ends. With these general ideas about noninstrumental reasoning, truth-oriented deliberation, deep compromise, joint intentions, and shared ends in hand, I can now turn to a more concrete look at the institutions in which democratic decision-making is embodied.

# PART III

# INSTITUTING PUBLIC REASONING

# CHAPTER 13

# The Public

In chapter 4, I argued for a qualified populism. Democracy ought to be organized so that decisions result from a fair process in which citizens participate sufficiently so that it is true to say that they together decide what ought to be done. Only a democracy so organized adequately respects persons' autonomy. The relevant process of decision cannot be concentrated in a single institutional body, such as the legislature. Rather, the process of formulating the people's will, or of jointly deciding what should be done, must be regarded as being distributed across a wide range of political institutions. Institutions that make laws that put citizens under new duties must be regarded as part of this distributed process of political will-formation: It is not enough that they be subject to the contestatory checks that republicans would recommend.

There are many ways that distributed popular sovereignty might be institutionalized.[1] While it would be a pretty piece of work to generate conditions to indicate which of the possible modes of political organization are acceptable and which not, such generality is beyond my grasp. I will be content to start with arrangements familiar in existing democracies and to ask whether a suitably reformed version of such institutions could satisfy the ideals of democracy as democratic autonomy.

I will argue for an affirmative answer. This answer will depend on each of the relevant parts fitting together appropriately. Here is a brief preview: Reasons, arguments, views, and proposals need to be developed in the informal public sphere. In public political discussion, citizens form associations, factions, and coalitions that built initial, internally joint resolutions about what we should do. Each aspect of the formal, institutionalized process of political decision is and ought to be subject to fair influence by the views of the public and ought, in addition, to have its own particular mode of responding to public input. Elected legislatures are most directly subject to influence by the public. For that reason, they have a natural primacy. The rule of law must constrain the administrative agencies to stick to working out ways of specifying the provisions of legislation (in the rulemaking context) or to specifying ways of accomplishing the tasks that the legislature has delegated to them (in contexts such as central banking and foreign policy, where rulemaking is less used). Administrative agencies must also themselves be guided by public input. In addition to soliciting comments on proposed rules, they must invite representatives of the interested public to help draft them, at least in a range of important cases. The fully specified rules, in turn, should be the subject of open, public reflection.

In this view, the rationalist aspect of democracy as democratic autonomy strongly shapes the way in which populism is worked out. Thus, it is central to this picture of democratic will-formation that it depends on dividing our deliberative labor into stages. Proposals, views, and concerns that arise in vague form in public discussion are to be put in the form of proposed laws by legislators, who then vote them up or down. Deploying their substantive expertise, the agencies are then to help specify these provisions further. And while this reasoning is divided into stages, it is also an ongoing and dynamic process. Modes of feedback and reflective oversight, in which the public and the legislature remain aware of and involved to a degree in more detailed policy-making, are essential to the whole process counting as one of popular will-formation.

What we need to do, then, is to examine each aspect of this process as a potential contributor to public reasoning in which citizens adequately participate—in different ways in different stages—as free and equal citizens. I will take up each stage of the process in turn.

I begin with the public. Especially in light of the essentially reflective nature of noninstrumental deliberation, the public is the institution, or institutionally supported entity, most important to the entire process of democratic deliberation. Before considering how public reflection can frame the process of democratic deliberation, I need first to describe the general idea of a public that emerges from the role that the notion is called on to play in the theory of deliberative democracy and then to examine more concretely the institutional conditions of one's existence. Finally, I will turn to a corollary of the public's human embodiment, its openness to the rhetorical appeal to public emotions.

## The General Nature of a Public

Because our primary concern should be with whether or not a public capable of reflection exists, we should start with the substantive, rather than with the adjective "public."[2] Only if a public does exist can one set about drawing the lines between what properly concerns it (and hence is "public" in one sense) and what does not (and hence is by contrast "private") or between what is addressed to it (and hence is "public" in another sense) and what is not. My interest is in the structural conditions for the existence of a public; laying these out will tell a lot about what public reflection must look like. While focusing on the noun will bring these out, this procedure does risk reification. Having in chapter 3 drawn from the social choice theory the lesson that the people's will has no coherent definition apart from a set of deliberative institutions that help construct it, I hope to be safe against anyone thinking that I think of the people or the public as a self-sufficient and univocal entity standing over against the organs of government. As Dewey wrote, "the wrong place to look [for the public] is in the realm of alleged causal agency, of authorship, of forces which are supposed to produce a state by an intrinsic *vis genetrix* [originative power]."[3] Having otherwise characterized the democratic state, I now turn back, as Dewey did, to look for the public. As I say, looking for the public will help us focus on the relevant conditions of existence.

I must reject two understandings of "the public" as unsuited to my purposes: the overly organic ancient *res publica* understanding that did not draw a distinction between state and society and the overly atomistic modern understanding that reduces the public to a set of individuals. Importantly, my purpose in defining "the public" is neither to develop a criterion of justification nor simply to engage in sociology but rather to think in a realistic way about how to institute democratic reasoning. Other conceptions of the public may be better suited for other purposes.

Ancient Greek and Roman conceptions of the public developed without having to face the kind of division of deliberative labor required in the complex modern state. In the Athenian democracy, since citizens were chosen for public office by lot and all citizens could, if necessary, meet together in assembly, there was little need for the distinction between state and society. Although the Roman Empire contrasted both in scale and in its mode of selecting legislators, Roman jurists employing the idea of the public retained the Athenian identification of the public interests with the interests of the state. Contrary to this ancient line, a premise of this essay has been that assuring the proper alignment of the decisions of the state with the will of the people is a primary topic of democratic theory and the primary challenge of democratic constitutional design. The ideal of treating individuals as self-originating sources of claims implies that each individual's views and interests matter as such in a proper construction of the public good. This constraint on the public good helps differentiate it from the good of the state, which might not take such account of individuals. In thinking about the public good in the modern world, for the purposes of articulating a theory of democracy for modern nations, we must acknowledge this distinction, in part by focusing on the freedoms that shield individuals against an overly powerful state apparatus. Accordingly, we must reject this ancient identification: The public, in the sense that matters here, stands in an uneasy relationship to the state.[4]

It would overcorrect for this ancient organicism to define "the public" simply as the set of all citizens. Such is the tendency of much recent writing in liberal political theory, when it takes up the topic of "public reasoning."[5] On this view, "public reasoning" simply is reasoning addressed to each citizen. This liberal ideal of justification is too sociologically thin to convey anything useful about what it takes for a public to exist, except for there being a jurisdiction of which they are citizens. That presupposition it problematizes by its abstract understanding of a "set" of citizens, in relation to which any geographic boundary seems arbitrary. While that problematizing is productive for pursuing issues of globalization and secession, it is premature; we need a better understanding, first, of the simple case of a single democratic jurisdiction. A more crucial failing of this thin liberal gloss of public reasoning is that it fails to imply that the individuals in question mutually recognize the adequacy or acceptability of the reasons they address to each other.[6] Without any mutual recognition, there is no public in the sense that matters here, for there is no moment of collective reflection. This atomistic definition of public reasoning therefore fails to carry with it an understanding of the public that is adequate to my purposes.

The kind of publicity I am seeking to explicate is also stronger than the hypothetical publicity that is central in the tradition of Kantian liberalism. Kant influentially held that unless a policy *could* be defended publicly, it is unjust.[7] This is an important theme but one that is largely superseded by the populist demand that policy *actually* be defended publicly, except in certain special cases.* What I seek to clarify is how the public actually reflectively endorses—or spurns—the decisions arrived at by democratic governments.

Actual, mutually aware public endorsement is needed in order to follow through on the populist theme that democratic government should articulate the will of the people. In a more restricted setting, the requirement of mutual awareness is built into the idea of a joint intention, which I used in the preceding chapter to characterize the product of democratic deliberation. While that analysis indicated how we might view legislative enactments as expressing the joint intentions of coalitions of legislators, the normative push of our basic ideals of democracy is toward understanding democratic enactments as reflecting the will of the people as a whole. In addition, the need for a reflective level of endorsement arises from the nature of nonin-

---

* The reason for the hedge is that some status quo policies are never discussed at all in a given generation's lifetime. Consider how certain aspects of the institution of marriage remained unquestioned for centuries until debates about gay unions began to unsettle the notion.

strumental practical reasoning (as set out in chapter 7). For various reasons—not least because of the necessity of employing majority rule—we cannot expect that the entire public self-consciously join in joint policy intentions. We can, however, expect that public reflection involve a layer of mutual awareness.

The public on which democratic reasoning depends, therefore, must be self-aware. Dewey wrote that "the primary problem of the public [is] to achieve such recognition of itself as will give it weight."[8] There is no need to wax metaphysical about the public's self-recognition. Consonantly with the way in which joint intentions are being built up out of mutually recognized individual intentions, the public's self-recognition can be built up out of a certain mutual awareness among its members.[9]

In order for the public to be a potential arena for practical reasoning, the content of this mutual awareness must include some shared normative commitments, however schematic. If all that unites us is a mutual awareness that we hate each other, then we cannot count as constituting a public. In Northern Ireland and in Rwanda, public reasoning has largely broken down at the national level. If some vestige remains, it is because some thin layer of shared commitment remains. Certainly since the eighteenth century, the public has always been conceived as a forum for the mutual assessment of reasons.[10] Public reasoning hence requires a basis in *some* substantive agreement, such that those involved may reason with one another.[11] This condition coincides with what is required, as I showed in chapter 10, for democratic deliberation to be oriented toward the truth. For democracy to be truly deliberative, I argued, there must be some basis of substantive agreement that allows those addressing one another in debate to pursue a question about what they *ought* to do, as opposed to merely arriving, through strategic maneuver, at a decision about what they *will* do. A public that is to complete the process of democratic reasoning by reflectively endorsing—or rejecting—governmental decisions must similarly be oriented by *some* substantive agreement. What defines a public, then, is a mutual awareness of what it is that others accept or endorse: not just that a commitment be endorsed by each but that each is aware of the fact that each is committed to it.[12]

Rather than thinking about this mutual awareness on a literally individualistic basis, as is encouraged by thinking of the public as a set of individuals, we should think of it more holistically or approximately. Even where a thriving public exists, it is always the case that some of the individual citizens dissent from any commitment one might pick as a core or defining one for that public. Further, there is the set of questions surrounding who counts as a citizen. Certainly, the concept of a public does not demand that those in a coma be addressed, or young children. Understanding the public in an initial way, then, as the body of citizenry united in their mutually aware, nearly universal acceptance of some practical commitments, I may begin to examine the structural conditions that are practically necessary for the public's existence.

## The Concrete Existence of a Public

While a mutually acknowledged layer of substantive agreement—however thin—is the condition for the existence of a public that ties in most directly with my theory of deliberative democracy, there are other, more concrete aspects of the idea that are also important to understanding it: the conditions of inclusive political equality, constitutionally protected freedom and openness, and civic virtue.[13] I do not try to lay down where the concept of "the public" ends and the conditions necessary for an effective democratic public to exist begin. What matters is that each of these aspects must be provided for in order for a democratic public to be able to reflect on policy matters. They are also aspects of the public that both require and admit of institutional support.

A public is an inclusively egalitarian entity. Members of a public stand on an equal footing and do not regard themselves as a privileged few. In addressing each other, members of a public address each other as equals, with no claim of intrinsic authority. This ideal again reflects the idea's Enlightenment origins. Especially since it is compatible with admitting the existence of other modes of addressing people, it is an ideal we should retain. In its eighteenth-century guise, this aspect of the idea of the public was realized in a highly narrow way. The public was conceived as an inclusive domain of white male property-holders and intellectuals. We should want to be more inclusive today.

This aspect of the idea of a public obviously needs and can benefit from institutional support. The law can and should build in the presumption that all are equal before it and that no one stands above it. The task of putting people under new duties, in particular, needs to be removed from the hands of aristocrats and landowners and placed under the control of democratic government. Principles of nondiscrimination need to be promulgated and enforced so as to reinforce the idea that people are to be treated equally. New fora, such as coffeehouse gatherings, newspapers, and radio call-in shows, need to be developed in which people can actually carry out the idea of addressing one another as equals. Since I am concerned specifically with a democratic public, I should add that everyone's voting rights need to be protected and the principle of "one person, one vote" respected, in order that people may address one another as equals in the political process. Many of these aspects of the fundamental equality of a public deserve constitutional protection.

A public is also an entity in which its members can address one another openly and freely. Constitutional protections are even more central to establishing and protecting the openness and freedom on which a public's existence depends. There are four kinds of constitutional guarantee to consider under this heading: those protecting (1) the publicity of decisions; (2) the openness of the political process; (3) the freedom of the press; and (4) the freedoms of speech and of association.[14]

To begin with, the public must have a shared matter to reflect about. Specifically, unless people become aware of the decisions their government has reached or is reaching, they will be in no position either to accept or reject them, whether mutually or simply as individuals. Hence the first requisite of public reflection in a democracy is publicity in the mundane sense. Proposed items of legislation and administrative rules must generally be effectively promulgated so that they become available to all interested citizens. The same of course holds of ratified legislation and administrative rules that go into force. Of course, there are exceptions. There are government actions, including ones with the general form of law, with respect to which secrecy is justified.[15] Many of these cases involve actions, such as foreign-policy maneuvers, that do not impinge very directly on citizens. In such cases, the considerations of due notice that underlie the ideal of the rule of law are somewhat attenuated. In any case, the general point is unassailable, that the public cannot react to a policy unless it is made known to them.

Openness of the policy-making process is a separate concern, which raises the distinct issue of motivation. People may not feel it worth their while to think about a given policy unless they think that their reaction will be attended to. Unless the policy-making process is appropriately open to public input, then, efforts at public reflection will be undercut. In a large society, effective openness requires not only that deliberations be open to the public, as opposed to occurring behind closed doors, but also that freedom of the press be sufficiently well enforced that the media can feel free both to make public what is going on and to comment critically on it. It does not suffice literally just to open the doors of the committee room and the staff office. It takes a more complex, interactive process for the process of policy-making to be laid open to the public. Given that we all have competing claims on our time, a democratic public will atrophy unless the political process is open to its input.

Freedom of the press deserves attention in its own right as a condition crucially supporting the existence of a public. A free press is an indispensable aid to promulgating policies and publicizing the policy-making process as it is underway. It is also an important vehicle wherein public opinion gets articulated and communicated to government officials. In the last role, the news media are just that—media that facilitate the expression of public opinion—as opposed to being its authoritative or privileged mouthpiece. Looking to the past, we can see that freedom of the press entails other conditions that do not universally obtain, such as a relatively educated, literate citizenry who feel free to develop their political views without fear of oppression.[16] Looking toward the future, it may be that given the rise of internet chat groups that need the sponsorship of no media organization, the traditional media are less indispensable in giving voice to public opinion than they once were; still, it is difficult to imagine these chat groups having reliable public policy information to discuss were it not for the more traditional news media.

Equal in importance to freedom for the press is firm protection of individuals' rights to express their policy views without fear of governmental reprisal and to associate with one another to discuss, develop, and pursue their political agendas. The importance of protecting individual freedom of speech is simply obvious in this context. Freedom of association should be regarded as an equally necessary support for the existence of a public, once one remembers the vast complexity of policy problems and the need we each have to rely on the judgment of others in developing our own political views.

These conditions I have mentioned—publicity, openness, freedom of the press, and freedom of speech and association—match the historical conditions that, toward the end of the eighteenth century, accompanied the birth of the modern public as the addressee and, ideally, as the formulator of political opinion in a democratic republic. These conditions include the initial broadening of political enfranchisement sufficiently to give a foothold to the Enlightenment egalitarianism that would eventually argue for universal suffrage, the decline of absolutist privilege sufficiently to give individuals confidence that their rights and freedoms would receive proper protection in independent courts of law, and the rise of a popular press to help express and disseminate public opinion. The form of equality essential to the existence of a democratic public is that which entails the equal protection of the constitutional rights just enumerated.

The conditions laid out so far support the possibility that the body of citizens sufficiently agree that they can reason with one another, that they do so on a footing of equality rather than legally recognized privilege, and that they may do so via protected means of freely sharing relevant information. The remaining conditions for the effective existence of a democratic public are attitudinal: that a group *can* reason freely with one another in an inclusive way does not yet indicate that they *will*; yet a public will not form unless people are motivated to take advantage of this possibility. At this general level, the necessary motivational conditions are captured by two aspects of civic virtue that have been well described by Gutmann and Thompson: the virtues of civic integrity and civic magnanimity.[17]

The virtues of civic integrity crucially support the effort to reason with others in public by helping ensure that people taking positions in political debate actually believe the reasons that they profess. Hence one requirement of civic integrity is to argue sincerely, as opposed to cynically tailoring what one says to what one's audience wants to hear or mouthing opinions that one is not prepared to act on. One cannot move toward joint intention in any way grounded by shared normative standards if one does not even believe that the position one espouses is supported by the normative standards one recognizes, standards to which one is sufficiently committed that one would indeed intend to do one's part in the joint action if the view were collectively adopted. A second requirement of civic integrity is that one recognize the implicit generality of the reasons to which one appeals in political argument. The footing of equality on which members of a public address one another is inimical to the idea of someone making a particular exception for himself or herself. Each participant's openness to tracing these general implications, which may lead to specifying or otherwise revising the ends or principles appealed to, is necessary if the public argument is to have any chance of moving toward reasonable agreement.

The virtues of civic magnanimity support public deliberation in a more other-directed way. The first virtue of civic magnanimity is the willingness to acknowledge the sincerity of one's opponents in political debate. For there to be successful joint deliberation about what we should do, it is important that each party recognize that the others are also concerned to promote a view about what we ought to do, as opposed to simply trying to grab for private advantage. Democracy as a whole depends on this virtue being sufficiently widespread that participants in democratic deliberation can regard one another as putting forward opposed views about what we should do. A further aspect of civic magnanimity characterized by Gutmann and Thompson is open-mindedness. Given that we often disagree about what we ought to do, public reasoning about politics would be futile without a considerable degree of open-mindedness on the part of the participants.[18] Willingness to search for deep compromise is a particularly important form of open-mindedness.

In sum, the effective existence of a public depends, first, on the existence of a modicum of background agreement that makes it possible for citizens to discuss political questions in a way that allows each to regard himself or herself and each of the others as reasoning about what we ought to do. Second, it depends on a political process in which citizens face one another on a footing of equality—each addressing all. Third, the open promulgation of policies and their being openly arrived at is also crucial to there being a common subject matter for discussion, a *res publica* to stand as the focus of citizen attention. Freedom of the press and of expression and of association is necessary for people to be free to discuss this matter in a way that responds to the reasons they recognize and not simply to the perceived preferences of the powerful. Finally, civic integrity and civic magnanimity are virtues that are practically necessary for this discussion to progress toward a mutual acceptance of conclusions about what we ought to do and hence are necessary to motivate involvement in public discussion.

The dependence of the existence of a public on constitutional structures and protections has important implications regarding which groupings of people may appropriately be regarded as "publics." In the sense developed here, there is not currently a global public—which is not to say that there should not be. That is not because there is no level of universal moral agreement. Rather, it is because there is no international constitutional regime that effectively (1) requires that all the policies fundamentally shaping the international order be openly made; (2) protects the freedom of everyone around the world to address one another on policy questions; or (3) places them on a footing of equality in so doing. There are both Canadian and Quebecois publics, but there are not either Basque or Kurdish publics. To note these facts is, again, not to make a normative judgment about the significance of national or provincial boundaries. As I noted in the introduction, I do not suppose that this study has much useful to say about which people ought to control which pieces of territory. Whether all the people of the globe ought, democratically, to control the globe is a difficult question perhaps better approached piecemeal via concrete legal innovations (such as the Law of the Sea Treaty or the controversial International Criminal Court) rather than at one theoretical swoop. The account developed here does imply that legitimate global democracy would ultimately depend on developing, at a global level, the sorts of constitutional guarantees of equality, freedom, and openness just canvassed.

## Public Reflection

If all that were required for democratic reflection were a way of feeding back information about costs and obstacles to other centers of decision, that is easily enough arranged. Legislative oversight of agency functions is a traditional task, and agencies may also be required to generate "impact statements" of various kinds that detail the costs of certain classes of regulation. Similarly, citizens' groups play a vital role in getting information about the actions of elected representatives back to the voters. These groups can keep track of representatives' votes, rating them on the issues of concern to their membership.

Although such simple and tested institutional and informal mechanisms do help supplement the top-down picture that proceeds from elections to legislation to administrative rulemaking, they do not speak to the core question of democratic reflection. They do not explain how it is that we, as a democracy, can reflect on our policy choices and decide whether our collective aims, once specified in implementable form, are still worth pursuing. Feedback mechanisms and devices that promote citizen participation, as important as they are, do not suffice to underwrite the claim that we have reflectively endorsed any given policy decision. In general, practical reasoning does not proceed unidirectionally from first settling ends to finally selecting means; rather, practical reasoning essentially involves a reflective rethinking of ends in light of available means, acknowledged obstacles, and unintended effects.[19] Without an account of public reflection, our picture of democratic deliberation would be missing the central feature that justifies its claim to count as a mode of truth-oriented reasoning. Without rational public reflection, however, democratic reasoning about the ends of policy would fail, and democratic autonomy would be impossible.[20]

Intuitively, we do speak of a public's acceptance or rejection of political decisions. It appears that the U.S. public has accepted the legitimacy of George W. Bush's accession to the presidency, despite the serious grounds for doubt. (Again, this talk is approximative or holistic in a hard-to-pin-down way; it does not imply that every U.S. citizen accepts this.) A quarter-century ago, it became plain that the U.S. public rejected the legitimacy of Richard Nixon's stonewalling response to the Watergate investigations. Publics in western Europe have accepted the membership of their nations in the European Union but are somewhat more divided on extending its membership eastward. While these sorts of judgment are commonsensical enough, there is no readily specifiable basis for them.

A sharply specified basis would be essential if I were looking to public acceptance to determine the legitimacy of the law. Although, in the long run, public acceptance of the law is important to its legitimacy, that is not my theoretical tack. Rather, public deliberation, not public consent, is my normative focus; I need to ascertain whether it makes sense to claim that public deliberation in a democracy can contain a reflective moment, in which people step back to consider whether they accept or reject the way that public ends have been revised. It is not a question of a criterion but a question of capacity: Do the people have a capacity for reflection of the kind that, in individuals, allows for the revision of ends? Can the people, having started down a path of pursuing a given policy and enacting it into law, retain the capacity to revise the ends that the policy embodies?

The answer is yes, if the people exists as a public. That is a primary function of a public, to reflect on policies proposed, policies undertaken, and the purposes for which they are proposed and undertaken. In the case of providing transportation to the disabled, one would say that the American public has accepted the idea of mainstreaming the disabled into ordinary modes of transportation. Ramps, elevators, and reserved parking spaces, far from being the focus of political protests, are accepted and indeed taken for granted as aspects of the ways we move about. In accepting these means of access, we also understand what they are for, and we accept the idea that the disabled should have access to the same modes of transportation as the rest of society. While in this case, it might have been possible for people to infer the ends from the means and then come to accept the ends as well, in other cases it is important that the government has publicly articulated the ends of policy. If the deep compromises that are being worked out and tried with regard to gay unions or stem-cell research are ever to gain public acceptance, for instance, this will crucially depend on some level of public understanding of the reasons behind the compromise. Thus, a people's ability to reflect on policy crucially depends on the conditions of openness and publicity that frame a public.†

## The Role of Emotion in Public Reflection

I argued in chapter 6 that deliberative democracy depends on mutual persuasion and can live with its artful deployment. Apart from the unequal distribution of persuasive abilities, however, there is a further feature of political rhetoric that disturbs many, namely its appeal to the emotions of the audience. Yet they should not be disturbed, nor would they be if they thought the matter over in a cool hour. I will argue that, far from being inimical to democratic reasoning, the appeal to emotion is indispensable to it.

At the outset, one must concede that the appeal to emotion offers a broad avenue for deceptive manipulation. This concession does not undercut the importance of emotional appeals to democratic reasoning in any way, however, for nonemotional appeals are equally susceptible to deceitful use. As we are forced all too often to recognize, "damn lies" and cynical deceptions are forwarded just as often by cooked statistics and manipulated experimental results as by emotional demagoguery.

There are three reasons that an appeal to emotions is necessary in democratic reasoning: first, emotions are necessarily involved in the process of reaching deep compromise; second, emotions carry important political perceptions not otherwise accessible to us; and, third, emotion is equally an aspect of the collective embodiment of reflection as it is of the individual.

---

† Whether nondemocratic publics, or peoples that enjoy some but not all of the conditions I have identified for the existence of a public, can also reflect is a question I leave aside. My claim is that at least a democratic public can reflect on the ends of policy.

Taking these points in turn, the first is obvious enough once we recall that deep compromise entails that the participants alter their ends on the basis of considerations adduced by others. Because of the nature of our practical commitment to our ends, our emotions are implicated in them. To give up an end will generally generate a layer of disappointment. To revise one is to become excited by a newly conceived prospect, to set one's hopes in a different direction than one had before—it is, in other words, to experience an emotional shift. To adduce considerations in favor of revising ends in a certain way is to make this prospect seem promising and attractive or to make failure to attain it seem awful, unfortunate, or fearful.[21] Reasoning toward deep compromise, then, will necessarily involve an appeal to the emotions of the participants, intended or not. Intending to make an appeal to the emotions of the participants, as does one who deploys the art of rhetoric, need not in any way disturb the persuader's concentration on giving reasons. To make a prospect seem promising or awful *is* to give reasons for or against it. As I argued in chapter 6, mutuality in the giving of reasons should constrain persuasive political rhetoric in general and its appeal to emotions in particular; but participants in political discussion should expect that appeals will be made to their emotions.

Concrete and particular considerations are especially effective in generating emotional response. Again, like general rhetorical appeals or dispassionate displays of statistics, particular stories and exemplars can be used deceptively or unfairly, as in the elder Bush's use of Willy Horton, a convict who committed rape after being released from prison by the Massachusetts government of Bush's opponent in the presidential race, Michael Dukakis. Particular cases are sometimes pregnant with spurious generalizations. Still, there are many kinds of input essential to the political process that can come only in the form of emotionally laden particular observations. Responsible collective deliberation demands that we see the horrors of Auschwitz, or My Lai, or the World Trade Center for what they are and take guidance from the feelings of outrage and horror that arise from responding to the particularities of these places and bodies and stories. In the writing of environmental or safety regulations, sound scientific and economic data need to be coupled with a sensitive listening to the stories of emphysema sufferers and those paralyzed from vehicle rollovers caused by defective tires. It is only via our emotional reactions that we fully arrive at a judgment of the significance of such cases; and what we learn from our emotions about such cases can often be conveyed in no other way.[22] We need to reason in an emotionally informed way, seeking perspective without assuming that "the cool hour" is authoritative or privileged.[23]

More generally, the emotions play a necessary role in rational reflection. This is as true of individual reflection as of collective reflections.[24] The reflective moment in reasoning is the point at which one stops to consider whether one can accept the revised view to which the considerations one has reviewed have led one. At this reflective moment, the deliberative emotions play an indispensable holistic role. Suppose that the arguments adduced support a certain deep compromise. The question for reflection is whether one can live with that compromise, after duly thinking about it. In answering such a question, a reasonable deliberator does well to listen to his or her emotions. If the thought of accepting the compromise is accompanied by a feeling of disgust, outrage, or even of vague dread, that is an indication that the individual deliberator had perhaps best not accept it. Such emotions are not groundless but help each of us to arrive at a holistic assessment of a welter of complex and incommensurable considerations. The same is true of the public's motley collective reflection. Public outrage bespeaks public rejection; public joy accompanies a strong form of public acceptance. Individual reflection is essentially embodied in flesh-and-blood deliberators.[25] Democratic reason's embodiment is more multifarious, embracing many individuals but also the hearing rooms that collect them and the information media that connect them; still, there is an important sense in which, as Iris Marion Young observes, "rhetoric constitutes the flesh and blood of any political communication."[26] Rhetoric forges the emotional connections between speakers and listeners that enables the public to experience collective emotions.

The political use of rhetoric thus is no enemy to democratic reasoning but rather completes it. It is essential both to its generation of deep compromise and, more deeply, to the collectively reflective aspect wherein democratic decisions are accepted or rejected by the public. Without rhetoric, there would be no public reflection.

In this chapter, I have concentrated on the possibility that the public can reflect on governmental policies because the moment of reflection is a distinctive component of the theory of noninstrumental reasoning on which I am building. This focus should not obscure the important function of the public in initiating proposals and political ideas. These are chewed over in "the informal political sphere" long before surfacing as concrete legislative initiatives. In the following chapters, I will often describe places in which public input importantly affects and enters institutionalized processes of democratic deliberation. It enters most boisterously and effectively during political elections. Given the populist strand of my conception of democracy, however, I must ask why we must have elections. Is the institution of indirect, representative democracy really compatible with democracy as democratic autonomy?

# CHAPTER 14

## Representative Government

Explicit lawmaking begins in democratically elected legislatures. What requirements on representative government flow from the ideal of democracy as democratic autonomy? And is this ideal even compatible with indirect, representative government? The qualified populism that I have accepted rejects monism but still affirms that voting is a method for citizens to participate directly in making law, which is then the will of the people. How can this ideal be realized at all in a system of representative government? In answering this question, it is necessary to consider how elections ought to be structured, in what respect must legislators be representative of the public, and whether legislative decisions can fairly be viewed as articulating the will of the people.

## Indirect Liberal Democracy

In his thorough study of the idea of representative government, Bernard Manin concludes that "representative democracy is not a system in which the community governs itself, but a system in which public policies and decisions are made subject to the verdict of the people."[1] I think that Manin is wrong about this. Part of my task, then, will be to explore both the reasons that support his conclusion and the reasons it understates the contribution of elected legislatures to popular rule. Regarding the institution of representative government as contributory to rule by the people will turn out to have implications for how we ought to understand the nature of representation, how we ought to structure elections, and what sort of role should be assigned to the legislature.

What Manin's thorough historical work demonstrates beyond question is that government by elected representatives is not a necessary or inherent part of the idea of democracy. To the contrary, in past centuries, including those in which many of what we now call "the Western democracies" were founded, democracy was still associated with the ancient Greek custom of selecting legislators by lot, whereas the election of representative assemblies was associated with aristocracy. The common practice of imposing property-holding and age qualifications on candidates for office reinforced a general assumption that those elected would be in some degree wiser, on average, than the populace at large. While this specific claim of distinction may no longer be credible, its residue is our general lack of any assumption that legislatures should look, in all respects, like microcosms of their nation or constituency. Still, I shall argue, there is an important respect in which legislatures ought to be representative of their constituency.

A feature that further differentiates representative government from direct democracy is that the former guarantees a significant degree of independence for the judgment of the legislators. Generally speaking, this independence is assured by refraining from using either of two sorts of device that would seriously limit it; imperative mandates and recalls.[2] Although the possibility has been discussed, off and on, of binding representatives by imperative mandates or instructions generated by the electorate, the leading systems of representative government omit or forbid this sort of practice. The case is similar with the tenure of representatives, which runs typically for a fixed term without being subject to being cut short on the initiative on the electorate. Accordingly, elected representatives approach their legislative work without being specifically bound to the will of the people either by advance instructions or by the thought that they are subject to recall at any moment if they displease the electorate. In this way, some independence on the part of the representatives is assured. Compensatingly, all thriving democracies set the tenure of representatives at a period of a number of years—a period well short of life tenure—and help make the legislators somewhat beholden to the electorate by firmly protecting the freedom of individuals and associations to criticize their representatives publicly.[3] The influence that matters is influence over the decisions made by legislators, not just influence over the composition of the legislature.[4] Hence the representatives, while somewhat independent, are not wholly beyond being influenced by the public at large. We should encourage political entrepreneurship such as that exercised by Mario Biaggi in framing his amendment while keeping it on a long public leash.

In discussing how representative government contributes to rule by the people, I will assume that it does not assure that the legislators are in all ways a microcosm of the electorate and that, in the qualified way just described, it protects the independence of the legislators' judgment. Distinctive dedication to public service and to political debate is to be hoped for in legislators; and independence of judgment is necessary in order for them to carry democratic deliberation to the next stage. In these respects, certainly, representative government is like neither town-meeting democracies nor like ancient democracies in which the magistrates were selected by lot.

There are good reasons why we no longer select our legislators by lot. Contemporary legislators occupy a position intermediate between that of ancient magistrates and the ancient lawgivers. The latter effectively established ancient constitutions but also laid down the general lines of law. The magistrates selected by lot were in a position closer to that of contemporary administrators. To be sure, they needed to address questions of foreign and economic policy; but they were not charged with creating complex regulatory and benefits programs that had the general force of law. On account of this difference, it would overly tax citizens of contemporary democracies to choose our legislatures by lot, the way we select our juries. Further, elected legislators have time during political campaigns to build alliances with citizen's groups. While this opens opportunities for corruption and undue influence, it also gives the legislators the ability to work effectively on building coalitions. To thrust ordinary citizens into the position of making laws, today, would be to subject them to a maelstrom of pressures with which they would not be able adequately to cope. In addition, elected legislators also are in a position to develop some substantive expertise over time in their committee work and otherwise. Randomly selected legislators would not be. Crucially, this absence of legislative expertise would show itself in a marked handing-over to the executive branch—even more so than is now common—of the task of drafting proposed legislation. The randomly selected legislators could vote among alternatives; but the alternatives would be largely crafted by others.

So, under modern conditions, what does it mean to say either that the community governs itself, or that it does not? Perhaps one was thinking of plebiscitary democracy: but again, on that model, who sets the agenda of questions being put to the people, and by what process?[5] Self-rule—certainly in politics and perhaps in general—always needs to rely on a constitutional structure that gives some shape to the relevant "self." In chapter 4, I argued that democracy must be conceived of as a form of government in which each of us plays an active role in deciding what we ought to do. To ensure this possibility, it must operate via fair processes that treat citizens as free and equal and that respect their autonomy by inviting them to rule by reasoning with one another within those processes. The principal reason to think of democracy as a form of government in which we govern ourselves is that we need to remember that it is up to each of us to influence policy by reasoning with one another. A community governs itself democratically, then, when it affords adequate opportunity for citizens to engage and deliberate with each other, via fair procedures, in the process of making laws.

What the liberal demand for fair procedures means is probably most obvious in the case of legislative elections. Let me begin with the noncontroversial ramifications of this demand. Treating citizens as free, therein, demands that they be able to speak their minds in favor of one candidate or another, or one platform or another, without fear of reprisal or sanction. The government has an active duty to see to it that this freedom is secured to each. Citizens must also be free to associate in political gatherings. For the process to treat individuals as equal, what matters above all is that the process be governed by the principle of "one person, one vote." In addition, as I argued in chapter 6, background justice must be established so as to prevent rich individuals and powerful corporations from having a grossly disproportionate influence on electoral outcomes.

Supposing, then, that we stick with legislators subject to a periodic necessity of going up for election but free of constraint by mandates and recalls. Such legislators are subject to public influence in two principal ways: via the electoral process and via public suasion. Taking the latter first, an elementary point is that all, or almost all, legislative proceedings ought to be open to the public and a matter of public record.[6] Only if they are can citizens and citizens' associations enter their comments on proposed legislation or protest about steps taken. In addition to being open to the public, the legislature ought also to hold hearings at which interested members of the public are invited to comment on draft legislation—hardly a revolutionary idea, I know, but nonetheless an important aspect of public influence on legislation. When such hearings are held, we might add, legislators ought to listen.

How the electoral process ought to be structured so as fairly to allow public influence on legislatures is a more difficult and complex subject. To address it, I will first need to settle the respect in which legislatures ought to be fairly representative of the people.

## Citizens' Views as the Object of Representation

In order effectively to play their role in a system of reasoned popular rule, legislatures must be fairly representative of the range of citizens' political views. That is because it crucially lies to the legislature to forge the deep compromises that will orient subsequent policy-making. Such compromises can and should be made on a fair basis, such as only a system of fair election can begin to approximate.

It would simplify matters greatly if political differences could, without too much distortion, be arrayed on a single dimension, whether left to right or backward to forward. If that were what the problem of political decision looked like, then we would not have to worry ourselves much about the respect in which the legislators ought to be representative of the people. Instead, we could rest content with a two-party system and count on the inherent pressures of vote-getting to cause the parties to try to move toward the middle, or median, voter.[7] For many reasons, however, such simplification of political disagreement is excessive. One of the reasons is that a complicated ethnic and gender-based politics has been overlaid on whatever vestiges remain of the economic, class-based divisions on which the traditional ideas of "right" and "left" were based.[8] Another is that new issues are constantly arising—about providing transportation to the disabled, protecting Arctic wildlife, or whether to fund stem-cell research—that raise questions askew to any antecedently salient dimension of difference.[9]

Equally clearly, we ought not to abandon the complacent hope of letting the election process automatically bring majorities toward the median position only to fall into the anxious extreme of demanding that the legislatures be like the people they represent in every salient respect. In her marvelous study of the idea of political representation, Hanna Fenichel Pitkin noted the great historical influence of the idea that the legislative assembly should "mirror" the populace, quoting John Adams's famous statement that the representative body "should be an exact portrait, in miniature, of the people at large, as it should think, feel, reason, and act like them." As Pitkin argued, this ideal, so unqualifiedly put, "may well be chimerical, and therefore dangerous."[10] At the very least, it can encourage hypocrisy, as when Huey Long removed his silk pajamas in order to pose in faded cotton for the photographers.[11] As I noted at the beginning of this section, the institutions of representative government arose independently of democracy. It has always been part of their baggage of assumptions that the legislators would not, in fact, be entirely average men and women but would be people of some distinction—if not the finest political minds—who were interested in governing. If average people were wanted, they could be selected by lot, as in ancient Greece. It is, in effect, because we recognize the importance of the governing done by legislatures that we seek and accept above-average political excellences in our legislators. Since likeness in all respects to the populace is to be rejected as a spurious and chimerical goal for legislatures, representativeness with respect to what, then, should matter most?

As I have already indicated, the general answer flows from the overall account I have been developing of the nature of democracy: What needs fairly to be represented are the citizens' political positions—not the ones they might have in idealized isolation from any political system but the ones they actually do have.[12] These are the rough proposals that citizens would make about what we ought to do. Like acts of voting, as analyzed in chapter 12, these positions have the structure of conditional intentions: that we do thus-and-so, an endeavor in which I will do my part. Like intentions in general, these positions have full practical intentionality, picking out both a joint action to be done and an end for the sake of which it is to be done. Democratic deliberation at all levels must refine such intentions. For representative government to be a vehicle of rule by the people, it must work from the intentions of individuals toward an initial formulation of a joint intention.

To represent, instead, only the preferences or interests of people would indeed be to count them, but not as participants in the process of forging joint decisions. As I showed in chapter 9, preference-based accounts tend to presume, falsely, that preferences rest on "complete thinking," which in turn implies that the individual whose preferences are being polled has already completed his or her deliberation, taking into account all that needs to be taken into account. Such an idealized agent is not a collaborator in a collective process of deliberation that recognizes the need for ongoing principled compromise. Interest-based conceptions of representation similarly presuppose an independent fixity of individual's positions that clashes with the sort of mutual accommodation that is required. While constitutional design must take account of the challenges posed by the existence of multiple factions with relatively fixed interests—and prominently did so in the case of the United States—the aim of a constitutional framer should be to tame the potential excesses of factionalism rather than to represent interest-based factions as such.

The general account of representation I offer here dovetails with the expressive theory of voting endorsed in the introduction. Because so many people vote, one individual's vote has little or no influence on whether his or her preferences are satisfied by political outcomes or whether or nor his or her interests are served thereby. To understand voting behavior, then, we need to see its expressive aspect. People vote to express their attachment to certain political views. Now, this fact, coupled with the secret ballot, can be a license to irresponsible voting. Here, again, we must hope that citizens are, in general, sufficiently attached to the democratic project, and have sufficient concern and respect for one another, that the expression of simply malicious, bigoted, or spiteful views will be somewhat curbed and that people will orient themselves toward the rough idea of the public good that the democratic ideals mark out. However weak or strong this civilizing effect of a shared commitment to democracy may be, though, it will be appropriate to understand citizens' votes as expressing their political views, their views about what we ought to do and ought not to do via the political process.

In an argument due to Brennan and Hamlin, this expressive function of voting serves as the basis for showing that representative government is the best form of government, not merely second-best to direct democracy.[13] As I have mentioned, we reasonably depend on legislators to inform themselves about the detailed issues they face. Voters are rationally ignorant about many of these details, as it makes sense to leave them to specialists one can trust. Direct voting on political alternatives would let this ignorance be dispositive and would leave the result hostage to all sorts of quirky prejudice that voters might feel free to express in their votes. Since expressive votes are not linked to individuals' interests, there is no telling what they might express. "In the limit," Brennan and Hamlin remark, "direct expressive voting on policies yields normatively arbitrary outcomes."[14] By meeting voters halfway, a system of representative government can do considerably better. In such a system, politicians not only develop some issue expertise; they also take the initiative in framing proposals that they think people will approve. They provide alternative conceptions or interpretations of the public good around which the citizens' expression of their views, in voting, can coalesce.

In short, it is not citizens' intellectual qualities, preferences, or interests that ought fairly to be represented in legislative assemblies, it is their political views. In other words, that is the respect in which these assemblies ought to be representative. Once elected the legislators will, we suppose, use their own judgment. They can thus only represent citizens' views to the extent they share them or at least take them seriously. This consideration provides one part of the answer to the question of why it is that legislative assemblies ought to contain more than one or ten representatives but less than ten thousand.[15] They need to be small enough to engage effectively together in deliberative processes of compromise but large enough that the many dimensions of citizens' political views can be fairly represented.

## How Can Citizens' Views Be Fairly Represented?

To see more concretely what is involved in the idea of fairly representing citizens' views, it will help to consider how this conception of the point of representativeness sheds a new light on the old debate about proportional representation versus single-member districts.

Our ideal of political equality, it seems, is too highly contested to settle this question. The principal equality-based objection to single-member districts is that a salient minority, one that is in all districts a minority, might end up being entirely closed out of government, its voice not being present in the legislative assembly.[16] If we think in terms of fixed individual preferences and the influence individuals have over political outcomes, however, it will turn out that systems of proportional representation also leave some with a potential complaint of inequality.

One influential position is that it does not much matter which of these two systems we adopt, because the full range of citizen opinion will have a chance to express itself one way or another. In systems of proportional representation, a fuller range of opinion is represented in legislative assemblies; but in systems with single-member districts, that full range can find expression at party conventions where platforms are crafted and candidates endorsed.[17]

This argument fails adequately to account for the importance of seeing to it that the most important compromises take place within fair procedures that treat persons as equals. In jurisdictions where open political primaries have replaced party nominating caucuses, the selection of party candidates can benefit from the fairness of a one-person-one-vote system widely open to the citizenry. Party conventions and platform committees do not tend to work that way, however. If the platform committee members are elected at all, they are elected by the faithful at party congresses, rather than more broadly by the electorate.* Thus, while it is indeed true that the broader range of public opinion that systems of single-member districts tend to keep out of the legislature can be taken account of in party meetings, that is precisely not where it should be taken account of. If politics were simply a matter of individuals with fixed preferences interacting so as to attempt to influence outcomes, it would not matter so much where their influence is felt; but since, to the contrary, politics is crucially a matter of deliberatively forging deep compromises, we need to try to ensure that the range of citizens' views is fairly represented in this process, and most especially at the point where the compromises that are most basic and that will guide subsequent lawmaking are made. That point is in the legislature. Hence, a system of proportional representation will tend to better serve to fairly represent citizens' views than will a system of single-member districts.

That being said, I hasten to note that this is but one consideration among many. Against proportional representation, it will be objected that systems of proportional representation bring instability and indecision. Postwar Italy comes to mind as a country in which shifting coalitions in parliament bring about constant changes of regime, arguably leading to a debilitating indecisiveness and ineffectiveness of government. Further, systems of proportional representation raise all sorts of possibilities for irrationalities and perverse results that can arise within the legislature, as when, for example, a small swing party throws its coalition-building weight around.[18] Finally, going more to the heart of my concern with deep compromise, it may be that systems of proportional representation encourage a tight form of party

---

* A two-tier system of electoral representation is conceivable, in which mass ballots among party members are held to select representatives to a platform committee, as well as nominees who, then bound by their platforms, offer themselves in a general election for an assembly. That would be a third possibility besides the two I am discussing.

discipline that is itself inimical to the spirit of compromise within legislatures. These are all complex and difficult empirical questions that would have to be taken seriously before picking one system of representation over another. My purpose is not to design anyone's constitution but just to begin to illustrate what is involved in the idea of fairly representing citizens' political views.

I have been emphasizing that individuals' political views are not held fixed but rather shift during democratic deliberation. Unwillingness to change our minds, including our conceptions of what ends are worth seeking for their own sakes, would be a sign of a lack of practical intelligence. That being so, fairly representing citizens' political views is a more complex and difficult matter than I have so far acknowledged. Prior to 1970, it seems likely that few U.S. citizens had any firm view, one way or another, as to whether special efforts ought to be made to make transportation systems accessible to the disabled, let alone views about what sort of efforts would be appropriate and what ends should guide the effort. We will not have determinate views on problems we have not encountered.

When speaking about the need fairly to represent individuals' political views, then, I have been supposing that these views typically involve some relatively general commitments that are potentially relevant to a wide range of issues that might arise, and that these will tend to organize a person's more particular views. To these relatively general commitments—to a safe environment, a thriving business economy, or bettering the lot of the little guy—candidates and political parties can appeal. Views of this broad kind do seem both normatively and empirically significant in politics. We must not assume, however, that the views individuals either have or would have on more particular issues follow from their more general commitments in any discernible fashion. Someone's views on an issue such as oil drilling in the Arctic National Wildlife Refuge, or funding research on stem cells, or reforming disability benefits for children might end up depending more crucially on particular aspects of his or her life experience and quite concrete ranges of his or her normative commitments.

Taking account of these facts requires us to broaden somewhat our account of what it is that needs to be represented in democratic assemblies. To adapt Iris Young's term, we can say that someone's entire perspective shapes the way in which their political views will adapt to new problems and evolve over time.[19] Because democracy, conceived as democratic autonomy, aims to enlist citizens in a dynamic and intelligent process of reformulating public ends over time, it would be very important to see to it that their experiential perspectives, as well as their overt and explicit political views, are fairly represented in legislatures, as well.

The fact that individuals' perspectives orient the ways their political views would be articulated and adapted in the face of new challenges suggests that this dimension of representation deserves independent attention. At one extreme, if the proposal of representing perspectives were pushed without qualification, it would lead us back to the mirror imagery that we have rejected. Different people have different perspectives that arise from their differential wealth, curiosity, social privilege, intelligence, gender, town of birth, and exposure to late-night television. At the opposite extreme, if the proposal of representing views as enriched by perspectives is to be qualified, one way to do so would be to hope that a wide enough range of perspectives is represented in the candidates for office. These candidates, after all, put themselves forward as flesh-and-blood people who evince their perspectives and persona even while they are stating, or claiming to state, their political views. To this extent, representation of various perspectives is already taken care of.[20] In between these extremes, however, lies a more contextual and specific position. In some historical contexts, including that of the present-day United States, a powerful case can be made that certain perspectives—those of women, minorities, and other marginalized groups—have been systematically underrepresented in, not to say suppressed by, the political process. When that has been the case, fair representation of their views and perspectives will require some targeted measures, including some that are aimed at nominating members of the relevant groups for office and getting them elected.[21]

In sum, fair legislative representation of citizens' views and perspectives through a fair system of election is essential to the legislature being able to play its part in a system whereby we rule ourselves via fair procedures that treat individuals as free and equal autonomous beings. Further, the process of legislation must be public and open to more immediate channels whereby people's arguments can be heard. This is another way in which the process must account for the fact that people's political views are not antecedently fully fixed or determinate. Having, with luck, elected legislators who fairly represent the range of the public's views and perspectives, and keeping open this possibility for direct communication, legislators should then be allowed to frame deep compromises and to vote on the basis of their best judgment about what it is that we ought to do. Within such a context, they thereby can help frame the will of the people.

# CHAPTER 15

## Majority Rule as a Closure Device

For all the importance of legislators being willing to forge deep compromises through a process of collective reasoning, there is no doubt but that they will have to resort to voting, at the end of the day, to determine which proposals will have the force of law. Some form of majority rule is the obviously favored candidate for a closure device. Does reliance on majority rule seriously impede, or render impossible, achieving the ideal of a rationalist populism? Is legislative use of majority rule compatible with democracy as democratic autonomy? There are two distinct aspects of this question. First, is legislative use of majority rule compatible with the populist demand for rule by the people? Second, is it compatible with the rationalist demand for truth-oriented democratic deliberation?

### Majority Rule in Populist Government

The question about the compatibility between majority rule and populism might seem a strange one, as many have simply equated populism with unfettered majority rule. My interpretation of populism, however, has been different. Instead, it has demanded that democratic government be such that each individual is treated as a free and equal autonomous participant in a fair process of lawmaking. Together with the rationalist strand, this generates a hope for unanimity or consensus. Hence the question about the compatibility between majority rule and populism is a question about why consensus among the legislators is not what would be required to achieve the ideals of democracy as democratic autonomy. How can majority rule play a role in forging the will of the entire people?

At an abstract level, the answer to this question is the same as the answer to the parallel question about representative government: because majority rule is an eminently fair and sensible procedure by which to make collective decisions. I have disavowed any search for an antecedently existent will of the people and resisted the relevance of unanimity as a standard. The qualified populism that is built into democracy as democratic autonomy centers on the importance of enlisting the participation of each citizen in a fair process of decision. Majority rule can be part of such a process so long as it is, itself, fair.[1]

Whether legislative use of majority rule is a fair procedure depends on the fairness of the electoral and deliberative processes that lead up to the use of majority rule. In arguing, in this chapter, for the potential fairness of majority rule, I will be supposing that the last chapter's requirement of fair representation of the citizens views is met by the electoral process. I will also be supposing that a suitable analogue of the requirements of deliberative equality set out in chapter 6 is met within the legislature, so that individual legislators have a fair chance to make their views heard.[2]

Accordingly, the question I am now raising about majority rule stands at some considerable remove from the social theorist's question about whether majority rule is a uniquely supportable social choice function.[3] In his influential attack on populism, Riker argued that it is not.[4] Majority rule can be shown to have considerable virtues of decisiveness and fairness when only two alternatives are involved; but when (as in all realistic cases) more than two are involved, he argued, it is subject to strategic manipulations that deprive it of fairness and meaning.

What this shows is that majority rule cannot begin to do all the heavy lifting needed for democratic decision. Much of this work must go on, instead, in the deliberative processes in which legislators generate proposed legislation and craft deep compromises. This work is necessary in order to generate one relatively definite option to consider out of the millions of possible ways any given bill could be drafted. (Should it say "special efforts to make transportation accessible" or "extraordinary measures to provide transportation"?) Again, I am here looking at majority rule as a closure device, not as a decision procedure to sort among options. Making this point vivid, and reflecting some traditional wisdom on the subject, is the fact that existing legislatures generally contrive to see to it that votes are held on binary, yes-or-no propositions: Should this bill be passed? Should it be amended as proposed? Should it be reported from committee to the body as a whole?[5] This is as it should be—or, at least, this is a satisfactory way of dividing the deliberative labor so that majority rule can play a conditionally justified role. The bargaining process that accompanies the framing of proposals and the setting of the agenda will presumably involve all sorts of opportunity for strategic manipulation. Such fairness as applies to that process must be a matter, first, of the representativeness of the views being forwarded and, second, of the roughly equal deliberative resources (such as time at the microphone) accorded to the participants.

Having thus cleared away worries about manipulation and hence arbitrariness by locating them elsewhere, I can return to the basic argument for the fairness of majority rule. Thus, compare majority rule to alternative closure rules that differ from it only in the percentage of affirmative votes they require for one alternative to be selected over the other. Compared to such alternatives, majority rule maximizes the chance that each individual has of being decisive, for if less than a majority can either select or block one of the alternatives, a smaller group in that instance is being decisive.[6] In a legislative context, requiring more than a straight majority in order to pass a measure ends up unduly privileging the status quo. As Robert Dahl remarks, "the status quo always has so many built-in advantages that surely it doesn't need the additional advantage of a biased decision rule!"[7]

Employing a consensus standard in lieu of a unanimity one would carry a subtler form of pro-status-quo bias. Consensus represents a looser constraint than unanimity, more open to conventions about developing "a sense of the meeting" and allowing more room to weight differentially contributions to debate that differ in quality.[8] Absent pluralism, or in small bodies of defined purpose such as certain regulatory commissions, use of consensus may be an appropriate way to build on ends that are shared but tacit. Under conditions of pluralism, however, and in application to legislative assemblies, the attractive features of consensus are overwhelmed by the danger that this appeal to tacit norms will simply provide yet another way for hegemonic influences to control the result. And in any case, pluralist conditions will disturb the appeals to background norms that are needed to facilitate the development of a "sense of the meeting" and to arrive at a common sense of which arguments were weightier. Thus, under modern conditions, consensus is likely to be either biased in favor of the factions that control the chair or else equally paralyzing as a demand for unanimity and hence for that reason biased in favor of the status quo.

The use of majority rule as a closure device cannot ensure that the process of drafting, compromise, and debate that led up to it was a fair one. Supposing that it was fair, however, the use of majority rule to answer binary questions such as whether to pass a given bill is fair. If the process of debate was fair, and if the legislature is fairly representative of the people, then the fairness of employing majority rule as a closure device can be shown by reference to the argument from maximal self-determination. Having limited the use of majority rule to settle binary questions, the possibility of strategic voting is removed. While, as I have admitted, possibilities for strategic manipulation abound elsewhere in the process, they will not be introduced into the process by employing majority rule as a closure device to produce decisions on binary questions.

What else might one sensibly mean by "rule by the people?"[9] Remember, one cannot sensibly have in mind the thought that "the People" is some special sort of entity—whether comprising all citizens or only a majority of them—with a will of its own that is conceptually independent of and genetically antecedent to political institutions.[10] Hence one will want to have in mind that the will of the people is definable and expressible only via a set of constitutional procedures, which ought to be fair and to answer to the fundamental ideals that underlie democracy. Majority rule seems an eminently fair closure rule to rely on in such procedures in the context of a fairly representative legislature, and defensible on the same sort of normative, individualistic basis on which our basic commitment to democracy rests. Therefore, majority rule is better regarded as a feature that helps constitute (within this context) our idea of "the will of the people" than as a feature potentially at odds with popular rule.

Recall that, in democracy as democratic autonomy, the importance of thinking about the will of the people has nothing to do with discovering a latent will, constituting an infallible one, or solving the problem of authority by equating obedience to the popular will with liberty. Rather, in the conception of democracy that I have been pursuing, the idea of the will of the people has a twofold function. It reminds us that government decisions are to be made via a process allowing the active participation of citizens, who are treated as free, equal, and autonomous; and it orients our task within democratic deliberation: We are aiming to decide what we ought to do. The latter way of conceiving of our task casts it as one of collective will-formation but also as a truth-oriented task. Is majority rule compatible with truth-orientation?

## Majority Rule and Truth-Orientation

The question about the compatibility between the use of majority rule and democratic deliberation's orientation to truth factors into three. From the point of view of the participants in the process of debate and decision, there are two questions to ask. First, is it a coherent possibility to orient one's deliberations to truth when one knows that majority rule will bring closure? Second, if it is, under what conditions may we hope that participants do orient themselves to truth? A third question arises from the contrasting perspective of constitutional design. If one were designing a governmental process to be oriented toward figuring out the truth about what we should do, what would justify including majority rule as the closure device to generate legislative decisions?

The general concern about incompatibility is a serious one. As I write these words, I see the problem in the public reactions to the proposed U.S. compromise on stem-cell research. The commentators' general take on the issue seems to be that the compromise—limiting federally funded research to that on existing stem-cell lines—will satisfy neither side. Representatives of one side or the other, anticipating legislative debate on the matter, have been voicing their dissatisfaction. Researchers emphasize how much the compromise hems them in and how much research will simply shift to the private (nonfederally subsidized) sector and to other countries. Prolifers complain that the acceptance of any research on cells derived from embryos violates the sanctity of human life. Surprisingly little of the discussion in the popular press has addressed the merits of the compromise. If one grants that there are important goods and ills at stake on either side, some compromise may be called for. Is this a good one or not? The intellectual process of sorting out the answer to that question seems to have been short-circuited by the attempt to sway enough legislators' votes in order to win what will assuredly be a rather narrow majority for or against this compromise. Here one can see how, by a logic of backward induction, knowing that an issue will be settled by majority rule can stunt the truth-orientation of debate. Instead of attempting to figure out how their pet causes and concerns ought to be balanced with those of other groups, factions often simply push for what they can get, subject only to the need of building a winning coalition.

Although this is a serious problem, it does not indicate any incoherence on the part of participants who orient themselves to truth. For one thing, it may be that the members of a factions are such true believers in their cause—such ideologues—that they sincerely believe that whatever result best serves it is the one that ought to be done. These ideologues will not enter in to the spirit of compromise; but neither do they think of themselves as simply trying to maximize the interests of the members of their group. Rather, they believe that they are pushing for what, in fact, ought to be done. If these ideologues are forced to accept compromises rather than having to accept an even worse outcome from majority rule, these will be bare compromises, not deep ones. Hence such ideologues can maintain a general orientation to truth within the process of democratic deliberation leading up to the use of majority rule but are limited in their participation in mutual, truth-oriented deliberation. They are oriented by what they take to be facts about what we ought to do rather than simply by what they want; but their truth-orientation is crimped by their insufficient sense of their own fallibility.

Legislators who are not ideologues in this sense may be more thoroughly truth-oriented in their approach to democratic deliberation. As I have argued, any truth-orientation in democratic deliberation ultimately depends on a layer of shared values or ends, the liberal democratic values of freedom, equality, and respect for individual autonomy. Without this thin layer of shared values, we would not be able to pursue the question "What should we do?" When that layer of shared commitment to the democratic project is present, however, it will also serve to provide a basis for mutual respect. Legislators who share this commitment to democracy will have reason to treat their colleagues' positions respectfully, as those of individuals whose claims and arguments deserve to be taken seriously (and as representatives of individuals whose views deserve to be taken seriously). When this democratic commitment is not superseded or overridden by some pocket of ideology, then it will generate the kind of mutual concern and respect that can in turn generate deep compromise. And when legislators are willing to consider deep compromises, they can engage in a more thoroughly truth-oriented way with their opponents' arguments. The stem-cell debate can illustrate the kinds of attitudes I have in mind. Prolifers in favor of banning the research entirely could move out from the assumption that their opponents have an important concern in mind, namely the promotion of possible cures for Parkinson's, Alzheimer's, and other terrible diseases. If this is indeed an important concern, then that implies that the policy we ought to accept is not necessarily the one that enforces the prolife line most strongly. Out of concern and respect for their opponents' position on this matter, prolife-leaning legislators could reexamine their own principles to see if some acceptable accommodation could be reached. In particular, they could examine the moral argument suggested by the compromise, which is that while it is wrong to kill embryos for the sake of harvesting stem cells and wrong to spur creating embryos for the purpose of harvesting them, it is morally permissible to conduct research on cells derived from embryos that are already dead. In the other direction, legislators in favor of fewer restrictions on research could start out from the supposition that the prolife concerns are worth taking seriously. Since we are all fallible, perhaps they are correct in thinking that a human life begins at conception. If this is a serious possibility, then what we ought to do is not to pursue stem-cell research unrestricted by reference to concerns about the embryos from which the cells are harvested. Perhaps we should find a position that curtails the moral risk involved in such research. Does the proposed compromise serve well at locating such a position?

Opponents thus willing to engage in a process of deep compromise with one another can take up one another's arguments in a truth-oriented way. For such legislators, the process of building coalitions will dictate when they stop trying to compromise, but it will not infect their orientation to truth in the process of deliberation.

So much for the first question, about the conceptual coherence of truth-orientation within a process of deliberation closed by majority rule. In answering it, I have already been drawn onto the territory of the second, motivational question; for I have shown that a robust truth-orientation within the legislative process depends on an effective degree of mutual concern and respect. This is needed in order to prevent those who anticipate being in the majority from simply exploiting the power that this position affords.

Whether these motivational conditions will actually be met will depend on a host of sociological and political conditions. Liberal democracy here depends on the civic virtue of citizens and legislators, on the accumulated social capital of mutual trust, and on political arrangements and a political history that combine to prevent any one group from becoming a "permanent" or ossified minority, whom the majority can effectively ignore since they are so predictably on the losing side.[11] These are three large topics—civic virtue, social trust, and the nonentrenchment of power—that I have neither the expertise nor the space to go into. I will content myself with explaining why the form of liberal democracy defended here—democracy as democratic autonomy—is less inimical to the fulfillment of these concerns than are some other forms of liberal individualism, real or imagined.

Civic virtue, as is often pointed out, is a notion that cannot be developed—and therefore, a set of traits that cannot be promoted—without taking on board some substantive value commitments. A neutralist liberalism, it is said, would undercut these traits, which are necessary to the ongoing thriving of democratic institutions.[12] The liberal democracy that I have defended is avowedly nonneutralist and hence does accept the need to set out from substantive value commitments. Furthermore, it is a cognitivist, truth-oriented liberalism, not a liberalism based on subjective wants or preferences. For this reason, it is also open to building further on its initial value commitments. On account of its frank nonneutrality and its rationalism, then, the version of liberal democracy defended here is far less corrosive of the values of civic virtue than is a neutralist, subjectivist liberalism.

Social trust is eroded not so much by neutrality as by self-interested defection. Much recent work in political theory on the basis of trust has framed the question from within Hobbesian or standardly economic premises about self-interested individuals: Under what conditions is it self-interestedly rational to be trustworthy?[13] Social institutions and devices see to it that the answer is not "never." Still, those suspicious of this kind of self-interested individualism have argued that trust is neither well modeled nor well secured on such a basis. Rather, they suggest, mutual trust is an attitude more akin to an emotion than a rationally calculated response to strategic interaction.[14] However this may be, I simply point out that the theory of liberal democracy I have been developing has already committed itself to not viewing individuals as maximizers of self-interest. Instead they are moved both by views about what we ought to do and by mutual concern and respect.[15]

Liberalism is sometimes said to promote the entrenchment of economic power by arguing for unfettered freedom for the capitalist. Again, while the charge is true with respect to some forms of liberalism, it does not hit home against democracy as democratic autonomy. In my initial glosses of freedom in chapter 2, I firmly rejected the idea that freedom consisted in individuals doing whatever they like. Rather, democracy as democratic autonomy has taken on board the republican distinction between liberty and license, which makes it possible to see nonarbitrary democratic rule as enhancing freedom, on balance, rather than undermining it. Regulations that favor the economically oppressed, therefore, cannot be ruled out on the basis of the kind of ideal of freedom that democracy as democratic autonomy presupposes. I have also rejected the idea that there is a natural way in which economic arrangements, including property and contract law, would sort themselves out in the absence of government. Furthermore, the liberalism incorporated into democracy as democratic autonomy builds on equality as well as freedom. A key part of government's task, therefore, must be to evolve and enforce fair and just laws constituting economic rights; and basic economic institutions that are fair from the perspective of free and equal citizens may well need to regulate the capitalist and the corporation in various ways.[16] Finally, nothing in my account so far has implied that business corporations ought to be regarded as having any political rights of their own.*

In short, while nothing in my account of democracy as democratic autonomy will ensure that favorable motivational conditions of virtue, trust, and nonentrenchment exist to encourage legislators to take up one another's arguments in a mutually respectful and caring way, nothing in this ideal mitigates strongly against the possibility, either.

These conclusions about motivation bear upon the issue of designing democratic institutions so as to include the use of majority rule as a closure device but do not settle it. From that perspective, it is necessary again to ask whether reliance on majority rule is compatible with an orientation to truth.

Estlund has argued that the use of majority rule is legitimate precisely because it is a way of generating reliable answers about what we ought to do—at least where important questions of justice are at stake.[17] Although constrained by basic considerations of fairness and by a liberal recognition of the facts of pluralism, which undercut anyone's claim to privileged insight, majority procedures are sufficiently reliable that we ought to accept their conclusions as legitimate. The essential basis for taking majoritarian procedures to be reliable is provided by the Condorcet jury theorem, which I considered in chapter 5 in connection with a radical majoritarianism that would leave out mutual deliberation.[18] The jury theorem is a powerful theoretical result that shows that, under favorable conditions, majority rule multiplies citizens' individual reliability by virtue of the law of large numbers. In its original form, the theorem assumed that voters's views are sta-

---

* This is a difficult question, in part because of practical difficulties in distinguishing business corporations from citizens' associations, which are often also incorporated. Multinational business corporations also often have nonprofit affiliates. I am indebted to Nicholas Crosson for discussion of these issues.

tistically independent of one another—an assumption that will patently be violated if citizens form their views via a process of joint deliberation. Yet Estlund is fully aware of the ways that deliberation can epistemically improve our views—as well as having a nuanced grasp of when it might not.[19] He has shown that the theorem's basic result can survive mutual influence so long as voters are discriminating about whom they defer to.[20]

Confining myself to the same restricted confined context in which I made the case for majority rule's fairness, I may rest some confidence in the jury theorem in arguing for its reliability. This restricted context has two features that are important to the validity of this appeal. First, majority rule is invoked only on binary questions, such as when legislation is voted up or down. Although the jury theorem has been recently extended to cases in which there are more than two options,[21] this extension seems not fully to have confronted the issue of strategic or manipulative voting, which arises where there are more than two options. As in the case of my argument in the previous section for majority rule's fairness, however, we may shove the burden of providing for nonmanipulativeness onto the deliberative side of the process—which must bear it in any case—and confine our attention to binary votes, which are not subject to strategic manipulation. In addition, this restricted context for majority rule—namely as a rule of closure for legislative debates—helps secure one of the jury theorem's other needed assumptions, namely that the voters are reasonably competent, as opposed to being infected by false views.[22] This restriction helps in two ways. The first picks up my assumption that the legislators sufficiently share the fundamental democratic commitments to be able to share a truth-oriented attitude toward deliberation. If that is so, then they escape the whole domain of error that would consist in not believing in the democratic ideals. Second, we may hope that elections serve to select legislators who are at least somewhat more reliable in discerning what we ought to do than are average members of the public.[23]

This appeal to the jury theorem to defend the epistemic reliability of majority rule can be supplemented by reference to the idea, defended in chapter 10, that democratic procedures are normatively fruitful. That is, rather than being either pure procedures with respect to what ought to be done, constituting what ought to be done with no conceptual possibility of error, or imperfect procedures with respect to what ought to be done, aiming at, but in no way influencing, what ought to be done, they are both fallible and partly constitutive of what ought to be done. As I further argued, there is no reliable way for us to separate out the issues with respect to which fair democratic procedures are dispositive about what ought to be done and those with respect to which they are fallible. If this is the situation, then I can continue to appeal to the jury theorem, for it merely supposes that there are truth-conditions that apply to political questions, whether wholly independent of how the political process goes or not; but I can simultaneously appeal to a much simpler argument that speaks to the point of view of the constitutional designer. If the truth about what we ought to do depends on how a fair democratic process of deliberation actually comes out, then, given my conclusion in the previous section that majority rule ought to be regarded as part of a fair democratic process, a constitutional designer ought to build in a place for majority rule as a device for bringing legislative debate to closure. There is no more reliable way to find out what the majoritarian process will approve than to let it run.

Because there is no way of telling for which issues a fair majoritarian process decides the truth about what we ought to do, accepting its normative fruitfulness does not disturb our regarding it as fallible. Neither— given all the ways the assumptions need to be hedged—does the appeal to the jury theorem.[24] Since we will rightly regard the result as fallible—and in fact have no trouble in doing so—we will rightly conclude that the search for political truth continues after the votes are taken. The political process allows for this by allowing for laws to be revoked or amended, as happens when legislators fail to be reelected or become aware of their constituents' disapproval of existing laws. Yet the use of majority rule to close legislative debates is not just a "pause" in the search for truth; it is an important part of that deliberative search.[25]

## The Minority Voter

Even though majority rule, in this confined context, is a reasonably reliable procedure and may be publicly recognized as such, the strength of its reliability is not so great as to make it reasonable for those on the losing side generally to conclude—as Rousseau would have had them do—that they must have been mistaken about what we ought to do. If the losers have been sincerely engaged in a process of joint deliberation about what we ought to do, then they will most likely continue sincerely to believe that we ought to do something other than what the majority has decided on.[26] Does the plight of the minority, or losing, voter indicate that the populist aim of articulating the will of the people has failed?[27]

The answer is no. Again, the qualified populist is looking neither to discover the antecedent popular will nor to construct a unanimous basis for political rule. Rather, what matters is that our collective decisions fairly enlist us as free and equal, active participants. If that has been done, that is all that is required.

From the point of view of the losing voters, the fairness of the process ought to stand as a powerful argument for the legitimacy of the decision. One can regard a decision as legitimate without agreeing that it represents what ought to be done.[28] If the ideals of freedom, equality, and autonomy that shape the constitution are also ones that these voters do, in fact, accept, then this reason to regard the results as legitimate will move these losing voters. In a well-ordered democracy, people will generally subscribe to these ideals. It will greatly enhance the legitimacy of applications of majority rule from the point of view of the losers if (1) the process of debate allows for a fair hearing of all; (2) the process is contrived in such a way that majorities in formation need to take account of the views of the others; and (3) the formulation of alternatives and the process of debate is conducted in a way that encourages reasonable compromise among all participants, who may thus view themselves as cooperatively engaged in a process of determining "what we should do."[29] In addition, the constitutional system should be arranged so as to avoid the formation of permanent or ossified minorities, whether as a result of historically entrenched discrimination or excessive dominance of the political system by a single political party. In this last respect, proportional representation (argued for in the previous chapter) is again helpful.[30] Under these favorable conditions, losers under majority rule will generally have strong reason to regard the result as legitimate. To be sure, this reason may be overridden, in their minds, by other reasons they take to be stronger, as when the majority decision, in their view, sanctions genocide. Deliberative democracy depends on the fact that democratic deliberation is oriented in part to standards external to the political process and hence on the possibility that these dissenters might be right in such a case. A theory of democracy does not require a proof that the majority decision is always going to be regarded as legitimate by all, however, but does require a sufficient explanation of why the losers would generally have sufficiently strong reason to regard majority decisions as legitimate so that the democratic process can function smoothly. The strong argument for the legitimacy of the result, which appeals despite their disapproval of that result, is an indication that it is not wrong so to regard majority decisions.

From the point of view of this challenge by minority voters, the ways I have restricted the role of majority rule are again crucial: Majority rule comes in not as a self-sufficient method of decision but as a device for bringing closure to a fair process of democratic deliberation that occurs within a deliberative body, one whose makeup and procedures are fairly delineated by a constitution that appropriately protects the freedom, equality, and autonomy of citizens. If these conditions are met by the background institutions, then majority rule within legislative assemblies can indeed be a vehicle for rule by the people.

# CHAPTER 16

# Democratic Rulemaking

In the introduction, I sketched the magnitude of the problem posed by administrative discretion. At this point in the argument, the stage has been set for a solution. It is time to assemble the players so as to describe the conditions necessary to avoiding bureaucratic domination. There are four main elements of my story that need now to be combined. First, I have shown in an abstract way how the normative fruitfulness of democratic deliberation allows the legislature's conclusions to be handed off to the agencies as premises to guide further truth-oriented deliberation about what we ought to do.[1] For instance, once the legislature had spoken, it was reasonable for officials in the Department of Transportation to presume that transportation ought to be made available to the disabled and to go on from there to figure out how best to do this. Second, in characterizing types of practical reasoning, I distinguished different patterns of constraint. A narrowly instrumental constraint that attempted to keep controversial decisions about public ends out of the agencies is, I argued, naive; but the broadly instrumental constraint that builds on the idea of specifying ends will prove useful. Third, I have shown how flexible agency deliberation can and often does extend beyond specifying legislatively set ends to establishing new ends in a rationally defensible way. In the second round of rulemaking under the Biaggi Amendment, this involved articulating a new, superordinate (or more final) end, that of avoiding discrimination against the disabled, to help guide the specification of the legislatively mandated end, that of making special efforts to make transportation accessible to the disabled. Yet this move came about largely because of the bureaucratic entrepreneurship of the DOT's acting assistant secretary for environment, safety, and consumer affairs, Martin Convisser, and the creative agenda management of the DOT's general counsel, Linda Kamm. Hence, while they were indeed engaged in a flexible remaking of aims, such processes should be more closely guided by public input than was this one. Finally, I have followed the process of formulating the public will through the electoral process to the passage of legislation.

This, too, can involve flexible practical intelligence that refashions aims—most particularly so in the fashioning of deep compromises, such as those involved in policies pertaining to gay unions and stem-cell research.

These four themes need now to come together to generate complementary constraints on agency policy-making. I will begin by explaining how the formal constraints of the rule of law can combine with the rational constraint of specification to assure that the handoff is successful and that the agencies faithfully work within the parameters set by the legislature. Next I will turn to the kinds of reform needed in order to make it plausible to view the agencies as helping articulate the popular will. Finally, I will take a further look at the division of deliberative labor involved in delegating decision-making authority to the agencies and the kind of justified reliance on expertise that it involves.[2]

In discussing the constraints on delegation to agencies that are needed in order for agency decision to be democratic, I am presuming that some level of delegation to agencies is appropriate. A more substantive discussion of policy would compare situations in which delegation is relatively useful to those in which it is relatively inappropriate.[3] In addition, a more complete account of democratic policy-making would have to cover other means that administrative agencies have of exercising and delegating discretionary authority, such as the executive order, the informal directive, and the privatization of government functions.[4] Administrative rulemaking represents a more central problem, however, as it is necessary to achieving the rule of law. My aim in this section, then, is to see how the ideal of the rule of law can work together with the appropriate rationality constraint to provide a way in which administrative discretion may be realistically constrained so as to conform to and express the ideal of rule by the people.

## Democratic Rulemaking

If administrative decisions were not significantly constrained to remain faithful to the legislative decisions empowering them and to encourage continuing democratic participation, then the achievement of democracy at the legislative level would be a hollow victory. This possibility is not merely hypothetical; in too many countries, such as Peru at least some time back, only a thin veneer of democracy exists. A legislature and maybe a president are elected, but the all-important task of giving definite shape to the laws is left to the control of entrenched elites that control the administrative bureaucracies. A crucial part of the needed constraint on the agencies comes under the heading of the rule of law.

By itself, the ideal of fidelity to the law would gain little handle on the practical issues of administrative discretion. Most (although not all) uses of administrative discretion are not illegal (*ultra vires*).[5] Yet the ideal of the rule of law sets the stage for a fuller conception of administrative policy-making in which the requirement of fidelity to the law is supplemented by an appropriate rationality constraint that would govern the ways agencies carry out their discretionary work. In this section, I will develop the alternative rationality constraint that, together with the ideal of the rule of law, will help reconcile administrative discretion to rule by the people. In brief: I will argue that while the agencies should be encouraged to engage in open-ended deliberation about ends that may extend to establishing new, super-ordinate ones to guide policy-making, they ought to do so only in service of a process of deliberation that is limited to specifying the directives contained in the statutes they are purporting to implement. This understanding of democratic rationality in administrative decision is comparatively realistic. In addition, as I will show, it affords a natural place for continuing citizen participation in an ongoing process of deep compromise.

I should emphasize that I see the constraints that I will be describing in this chapter as supplementing an important range of opportunities to contest, appeal, and change agency policy. The constraints I will be emphasizing are not meant to displace opportunities for protest, judicial challenge, or legislative oversight but rather to supplement them.[6] In establishing the need for republicanism to be liberal and populist, we do not leave behind the core features of republicanism, including the dispersal and checking of power.[7]

On certain conceptions of legality, the rule of law and democracy are inherently connected, perhaps because legality is thought of as intimately tied to legitimacy, and legitimacy, in turn, depends on democracy.[8] As I will be using the term "rule of law," however, the question of the relation between the rule of law and democracy is more open than this. While the legitimacy of laws does depend on democracy, there is a thinner understanding of the rule of law that does not carry with it all of the commitments of legitimate legality. This narrower, traditional interpretation of the rule of law may be summed up under three headings: generality, predictability, and regular process.[9] As I noted in chapter 3, laws must be general, so as not to single out any individual person or firm for special punishment or favors. General law must be uniform across persons, treating like cases alike. While generality will help with predictability, it is not sufficient for it. Predictability is required in order that citizens be able reasonably to rely on the law in planning their conduct. To this end, law must be promulgated in a public way by regular procedures. In order that laws be accessible to citizens' planning, they must be promulgated in advance of their sanctions coming into effect; there may be no ex post facto laws, at least not ones imposing punishments.[10] It is unfair to impose punishments on people who, when they acted, had no basis for understanding their behavior as criminal. Imposing punishments in the absence of any law declaring behavior illegal is similarly unfair. A final prerequisite of predictability and fairness is that laws must not be unduly vague.* Generality must not become meaningless abstraction. Finally, the requirements of regular process must ensure, at the second order, that existing laws are applied fairly and with at least a minimum of consistency. Ways of institutionalizing regular process differ. In general, they support open procedures bound by rules of evidence that allow for affected parties to present their arguments and challenge their opponents. While satisfying the requirement of regular process seems not to require democracy, it does require a somewhat independent judiciary. It depends on judicial officials who are subject to rules helping ensure their impartiality and shielding them from bribery and other undue attempts at influence. These three requirements, then, of generality, predictability, and regular process make up the narrow, traditional notion of the rule of law that I will use here. Although the precise institutional details of their interpretation will of course vary, these three requirements hang together. All are directed toward regularity in the content and application of the law.

The ideal of the rule of law bears an obvious connection with the ideal of freedom and the way it puts all lawmaking under a burden of legitimation.[11] Governments purport to put citizens under new duties. A basic respect for their freedom demands that citizens be able to discern these new duties, that they be able to take them into account in planning their activities, and that they not be imposed arbitrarily.

For democracy to be possible, and for bureaucratic domination to be avoided, three requirements relevant to the administrative agencies must be met. First, the agencies must themselves make rules in a way that accords with the threefold requirements of the rule of law. The rules must be general, they must provide a predictable basis for citizen action, and they must be generated via a regular and fair process. Second, the rules that agencies make must be appropriately constrained and guided by statutes passed by democratically elected legislatures. Third, we cannot rely solely on abstract ideals of democratic rationality; we must also be able to put into place workable processes that stand a good chance of seeing to it that these ideals are realized in a way that reflects the will of the people. Only if these three conditions—the effective rule of law, fidelity to statutes, and apposite procedures—are met will the combined result of legislative and agency action remain even rudimentarily subject to democratic control.

---

* As will emerge hereafter, the rationality constraint that I will invoke, which requires that the agencies specify the aims of the statutes, imposes some "backward-looking" constraint on acceptable levels of vagueness.

Ideals of rationality enter in, here, as an unavoidable way of spelling out what the second of these three conditions requires. Narrowly instrumental rationality does not provide a workable interpretation of the way that legislation might appropriately constrain agency discretion; but broadly instrumental rationality, and in particular the idea of specification, provides a realistic and sufficiently flexible limit on what agency deliberation is about. Requiring that the agencies specify the directives contained in the statute avoids naiveté, as it makes room for determining public ends in needed ways while at the same time preserving fidelity to the legislatively enacted law. Although, as I have argued, ends can be revised via specification, it remains the case that a specification of an intention represents a *way* of carrying out that intention. By definition, an action that satisfies a specification of some aim will satisfy that aim.[12] This, then, is what we must require or expect of administrative rulemaking: that it limit itself to specifying legislation; and this is the ideal of rationality that we must hold agencies up to: that they find defensible and appropriate ways of specifying the directives embodied in the legislation they are charged with implementing.

Nothing in this rational requirement precludes the agencies from engaging in the kind of reasoning pursued by Martin Convisser at the DOT. Agencies will remain free to engage in open-ended deliberation about ends relevant to the policy issues at hand, sometimes articulating and establishing (for purposes of making policy) new superordinate ends—ones that are put forward as ones to which the policies in question ought to be directed. The point is simply that their doing so must be in service of specifying a way to implement or elaborate the directives of the governing statute.[13]

This trio of conditions of the rule of law, fidelity to statute, and apposite procedures, interpreted via the rational relation of specification, has backward-looking implications for legislation, which must be respected if the handoff of decision from the legislature to the agencies is to be successful. These implications emerge especially clearly from the German constitutional law on the subject, where they are actually spelled out, although with a somewhat more instrumentalist conception of rationality in mind.[14] According to the German constitution of 1948, the authorizing legislation under which the administrative rule is written must state clear goals, apply to a clearly defined subject matter, and set definite limits on the range of possible implementations.[15] These conditions are crucial for any democracy. Unless the statutes state clear goals, apply to a defined subject matter, and set definite limits to the range of possible interpretations, the decision-making in the democratically elected legislature will have come to naught. Unless the statutes that the legislature passes give the agencies some definite guidance, any claim that the rule of law is also rule by the people will be ridiculous.† Laws that are too vague cannot even be reasonably specified.[16] The practical question, here, is not whether any legal texts whatsoever can constrain action but whether the statutes passed by legislators are definite enough to provide a positive basis from which agency deliberation can proceed. Such definiteness is required if the democratic rule of law is to exist at the agency level.

Bringing agency decision-making under the rule of law with the help of the rational constraint of specification is only the first step. It assures that the legislature's decision is, indeed, effectively handed off to the agencies. What then? In answering this question, I will address the sorts of reform needed for procedures to be apposite.

## Incorporating a Popular Voice

The requirement that the agencies develop specifications of the laws they implement helps maintain their fidelity to legislative decisions while taking account of their unavoidable role in determining collective ends. It is plain, however, that the specification constraint does not suffice to reconcile agency policy-making to rule by the people, for there are always too many possible and plausible ways in which a given piece of legislation might be specified. The specification constraint just sets some limits to the task faced by agencies. It remains to ask if that task can be carried out democratically. It is necessary to examine whether and how democratic input can be brought to bear on administrative rulemaking in such a way as simultaneously to take further account of citizens' voices and to keep agency decision within bounds set by the legislature, thereby fulfilling the demanding ideal of nondomination that arises from interpreting the concept of nonarbitrary power in a liberal-populist way.

We may assume that something like the process established in the United States by the Administrative Procedures Act (APA) of 1946 must be in place to ensure that administrative rulemaking is regular, fair, and at least minimally democratic. An all-important presupposition of this Act is that the statutes that the agencies are to implement have themselves been publicly promulgated. Without publicity, its procedures would afford no avenue for influence by the people. Against this presumed background of legislative

---

† I will not pause, here, to battle those postmodernists who hold that no text, legal or otherwise, binds any interpreter—that statutes do not even succeed in stating vague ends. Such views overreact to the failure of narrow conceptions of rationality that stemmed from the logical positivists.

publicity, the APA requires agencies that set about implementing statutes of a regulatory and programmatic kind first to publish draft rules in order to garner comments from the public. Although there are important national variations, I will assume that democracy requires such a process of inviting public comment regarding proposed rules to be published in furtherance of statutes that have themselves been made public.[17] The assumption of such a process helps fix ideas as I proceed to ask how administrative rulemaking should be constrained in order for it to be truly democratic.

Notice-and-comment rulemaking as under the APA does not provide sufficiently for public participation. The interested members of the public can certainly make their voices heard through this process. What is less clear is how their voices will then influence the revision of proposed rules. Even if agencies are required to respond to all comments, we may suspect that in many cases the responses are merely *pro forma*. Sometimes, in fact, agencies go to tremendous effort to catalogue and take account of all of the arguments and objections raised in the public comments. From what point of view? There seem to be two likely possibilities: the point of view of the general sort of consequentialism built into tools such as cost-benefit analysis or the point of view of the "mission" of the agency or of the program whose legislation is to be interpreted via the proposed rules. Although these sorts of normative perspective can provide a somewhat helpful way of assessing the force of public comments on proposed rules, they fail to invite the public in as full participants in the process of rulemaking.

In order to participate more seriously in a process of continued deep compromise at the rulemaking stage, representatives of the public would need to be able to engage with one another and with agency representatives in a face-to-face process of debate and negotiation. In the United States, this kind of thing has been tried, using a procedure created by the Negotiated Rulemaking Act of 1990.[18] Although this process has its defects, and has not been in use long enough for a clear verdict on its usefulness to have emerged, it does illustrate how democratic deliberation might be extended to agency policy-making. The Act provides that in cases in which the issue is clear and there is a relatively small group of identifiable interested parties, agencies may involve these so-called stakeholders in the *drafting* of administrative rules. The drafting committee is not limited to previously identified stakeholders; anyone who can make out a significant interest in the matter at issue may ask to participate. The drafting committee is provided with a "facilitator." Stakeholders who are at a serious financial or technical disadvantage may, in certain circumstances, apply for aid. The drafters are meant to come to a consensus, though they are given some leeway in defining what they will take consensus to be. This process of negotiation supplements, rather than supplanting, the stage of notice and comment, for rules that are so drafted still go through the ordinary process before becoming law. To date, negotiated rulemaking has been most common in environmental regulation.

Negotiated rulemaking certainly answers to the abstract requirements of citizen participation in an ongoing process of deep compromise in which our collective ends are refined beyond the level of specificity attained in statutes. The requirement of consensus introduces a strong pressure in favor of cooperative compromise. Whereas consensus is too demanding and too potentially discriminating a standard to employ in legislative assemblies, which are writing on a comparatively blank slate, it is a more reachable and safe goal in the contexts in which negotiated rulemaking is employed. Consensus is more easily reachable there because the statute under which the rules are to be written already provides a basic framework or outline that constrains debate. The push for consensus here seems to involve less danger of implicit discrimination than it would at the legislative level, for two reasons. First, this context is one step removed from the competitive world of electoral politics, hence from the raw exercise of power and influence that can come from threats to influence elections. Second, although a consensus standard depends on tacitly shared norms that allow the potentially invidious appeal to such notions as "the sense of the meeting," this danger of discrimination is here mitigated by the fact that there is in this context a perfectly innocent and democratically unimpugnable source from which to draw shared norms to serve this limited purpose, to wit, the statute being interpreted. The common mission of working out rules that interpret the statute, rather than the general norms of a hegemonic broader culture, can here get the practice of consensus-seeking off the ground.

A crucial question pertaining to such a process of negotiated rulemaking is whether it marks out a workable and acceptable way of representing the voices of the citizens. Making the process in principle open to anyone who asserts an interest may not suffice if there is insufficient publicity about the process or if people lack the knowledge they need to participate meaningfully in the process or the focused incentive to do so. Organized citizens' groups such as labor unions and environmentalists' organizations can considerably alleviate both of these problems.[19] A more difficult question is whether such a process can adequately represent the point of view of the diffuse public—the vast majority of people who may not have a specific "stake" in the controversy surrounding the interpretation of a given piece of legislation.[20] One line of response to this problem is to appoint members to the negotiation panels who are chosen in order to represent the diffuse public. Another is to rely on the media to publicize the workings of such panels, so that at least there may be some long-term reaction from the broader public.

The other side of the coin is the empowerment of interest groups in the process of negotiated rulemaking. The conception of democratic representation developed in chapter 14 implies that we should not be too worried about this. It would empower these negotiation committees excessively if agencies were bound to accept their product.[21] That would heighten the danger that agencies would become "captured" by the interests they are meant to regulate. To avert this danger, we should think about negotiated rulemaking as a *supplement* to the ordinary notice-and-comment process, one that leaves the ultimate authority over the final issuance of administrative rules with the administrative agency. We must distinguish, further, between *representing* the voices of the various affected interests, which is an important democratic desideratum at this level, and allowing those voices to *dictate* the results. As the concept of deep compromise implies, we do not face a forced choice between collaboration guided by a shared sense of the common good and interest-group representation characterized by self-interested bargaining. Democratic deliberation will combine both of those aspects in a process of mutual accommodation. Negotiated rulemaking provides a way of continuing this process at the agency level, illustrating how this process can be open, in a populist way, to active participation by citizens.

Apposite rulemaking procedures must find some such way of inviting interested members of the public to participate in the process of specifying statutory directives. One may object, however, that this analysis does not account for the power that bureaucracies have by virtue of their accumulated expertise. Is this not inimical to populist rule? Is it not a source of bureaucratic domination? Not necessarily, as I will now explain.

## The Diverse Delegation of Political Judgment

By accepting that we must live with administrative agencies, I have implicitly rejected that version of the liberal ideal that defines itself by "its commitment to a form of power which is 'horizontal' and reciprocal rather than 'vertical' and managerial."[22] It is debilitatingly naive to suppose that modern governments can accomplish the kinds of tasks we want them to fulfill without relying on a vertical division of labor between legislatures making laws and administrative agencies implementing them and in so doing exercising fundamentally important discretionary authority in further settling social ends. A liberal democrat's aim should not be to spurn "vertical" and managerial authority but instead to constrain it so as to make it compatible with the "horizontal" egalitarian and participative demands of the democratic ideal. Further, as a republican might add, vertically dividing power is one way of dispersing it and thereby preventing too much power from being concentrated in one set of hands—say that of the legislative majority.

This idea of a vertical division of labor, however, only begins to capture the kind of deliberative work that modern democracies must rely on administrative agencies to accomplish. While the metaphor of a vertical dimension reflects the fact that legislatures must rely on agencies to work out the (often controversial) details, it omits the equally important fact that we rely on a multitude of different agencies, each enjoying a different substantive jurisdiction and expertise. Without such a substantive division of deliberative labor among agencies, our problems of collective policy deliberation would be intractable. Hence, in examining how the role of administrative agencies complicates and challenges the ideal of rule by the people, we must attend not only to the vertical delegation of authority involved but also to the broader pattern of substantively divided deliberative labor and to the question of when democratic deference to substantive agency expertise and to specialized agency concern is appropriate.

Any attempt to set out the conditions under which it is appropriate to defer to agency expertise in the controversial process of specifying public ends would be misbegotten if we ought never to defer to expertise on evaluative matters.[23] Of course, since we are reserving room for public contestation, judicial review, and legislative oversight, we are not talking about final or unconditional deference. But the substantive division of deliberative labor among the agencies does depend on some level of deference to their end-setting expertise.

Deference—whether to the legislature's judgment or to the agencies'— obviously ought not to extend to thinking of either set of institutions as constituting pure procedures, infallible in their judgments about what we ought to do. In his doctoral dissertation, in the course of discussing ideal-observer procedures, Rawls put the point this way: "The main objection in each case is always the following: how do we know that the entity in question will always behave in accordance with what is right[?] This is a question ... which we always can ask, and which we always do ask, and it shows that we do not, in actual practice, hand over the determination of right and wrong to any other agency whatsoever."[24] Now, the openness of the question of whether the authority has acted rightly does argue against analyzing the notion of rightness or wrongness in terms of what the authority would approve or judge. I, too, have insisted that there are standards external to any actual democratic process that partially determine what we ought to do.

Neither severally nor together, however, do these points imply that there is no significant sense in which we may hand over the determination of right and wrong to some agency—even to an administrative one! No one would suggest that we think about agency deliberation as a pure procedure, wholly constitutive or self-sufficiently determinative of what we ought to do; and the conceptual analysis of (political) rightness and wrongness is not

what is here at issue. Yet, as the possibility of normatively fruitful procedures shows, the fact that there are standards external to a procedure does
not show that the relevant truth conditions are wholly independent of how
that procedure actually works out. Thus, just as we rely on elected legislatures to determine some aspects of what we ought to do, so too might we
do so with the administrative agencies—especially if they meet the rationalist and populist constraints I developed in the previous two sections.

Because we cannot disentangle the matters on which fair democratic procedure is dispositive and those on which it is merely fallible, such faith as
we place in our democratic institutions' ability to make correct determinations about what we ought to do must always be highly fallible. And that
is even supposing that they meet all the conditions of fairness, openness,
and rationality that I have been developing. Nonetheless, there remains an
important sense in which we appropriately hand matters over to them for
determination. It derives from one of the reasons for turning political matters over to an institutionally divided process in the first place: Political
matters are far too complex to reflect upon all at once. Some matters—the
constitutional essentials—we need to have relatively fixed views about even
in order to constitute the relevant "we." Within that framework, we have
to work things out in a generally stepwise and incremental fashion in order
to take adequate account of all the conflicting considerations that impinge
and in order to learn adequately from unfolding experience.[25]

Still, perhaps the reader will object to the idea that agency experts could
play a determinative role. Since the notion of determination is perhaps vi-
ciously vague, I do not insist on it. What matters, for my purposes, is that
there are good reasons for us to hope that agencies develop substantive
evaluative expertise in the course of pursuing projects that we, through our
legislature, have decided that they ought to pursue. Expertise in empirical
matters is obviously important as well—just less controversial.‡

For it to be appropriate and legitimate for us to rely on agency evaluative
expertise, two main kinds of condition must be fulfilled: the condition of
mandate and the condition of reasonable trust.

The first fundamental institutional condition for the legitimacy of deference to agency evaluative expertise is that the existence of the agency and
the general delineation of its mission have the mandate of the democratic
legislature. The very existence of officials whose job it is to monitor the
plight of refugees internationally or to control levels of air pollution should
reflect the collective, democratic will as expressed by the legislature. (Note

---

‡ What is less controversial about the idea of empirical expertise is the idea of relying on
it. As Matthew Adler has pointed out to me, however, it is often controversial which side in
a policy debate possesses superior empirical expertise; witness the debates over global warming.

that I am using the term "agency" generically, without trying to be precise in distinguishing agencies from departments, bureaus, commissions, or offices.) In most democratic states—though not elsewhere—it can generally be taken for granted that this condition is met. Administrative agencies are, in these states, creatures of statutory law, hence reflect at least a one-time democratic decision that there ought to be an organization devoted to the specific set of concerns with which the agency is charged.

The sort of evaluative expertise I am talking about, here, is the kind that develops in the course of specifying the ends that the agency is charged with pursuing. This kind of expertise is less easy to codify than empirical expertise. What is involved is the kind of deeper understanding of a range of goods that comes from experience in seeking to promote or respect them in a range of concrete contexts. Civil servants come to know the goods they are charged with promoting and the ills they are charged with avoiding. Officials working on policy pertaining to refugees are in a position to understand all of the ambiguous ills and dangers faced by those in refugee camps in a more nuanced and exact way than those of us whose knowledge of their situation comes only from the mass media. Officials in charge of air pollution abatement are better positioned than are most members of the public to discriminate different ways one might understand what "air pollution" is. In all of these cases, those with responsibility for promoting a range of goods or with avoiding a range of ills have acquired not just information about how to do so or about the collateral effects of achieving or failing to achieve their goal but also an understanding of the detailed contours of the goods and ills in question. Each expert of this kind develops an expertise in distinguishing and classifying versions of the good or ill in which he or she specializes: the refugee worker in forms of displacement and despair (removal for safety, temporary exile, being exiled and unwanted by the host country, etc.) and the pollution control worker in forms of air pollution (view-decreasing, health-threatening, climate-affecting, etc.). Through experience, each will also develop a sense for which aspects of good and ill are particularly relevant in which sorts of situation. In short, through their responsibility and specialization, one skill these workers develop is a ready ability to pick out different ways that the general goals with which they are charged might be specified and a sense of when one specification or another is apt in given circumstances.

Since citizens' political views change over time, however, a one-time democratic endorsement does not suffice to assure an adequate mandate for deference to agency evaluative expertise. Some way must be found of ensuring that the existence of the agency and the general definition of its mission be subject to recurrent legislative review, revision, and rejection or endorsement. Such devices commonly include oversight hearings, "sunset" statutes that require that programs expire after a term of years unless renewed, and, most important, legislative supervision of annual agency budgets. Where such devices of legislative control are effectively in place, agency officials are generally positioned to develop expertise in those goods and ills with which we, acting through our legislature, have decided that we are concerned.

When this condition of legislative mandate is met, we may say—presuming the correctness of my conclusion in the previous chapters about democratic legislatures—that we have in effect given these officials the responsibility to look out for a range of goods and ills. Accordingly, our democratic deliberation of deliberative responsibility implies that an official should be especially concerned with the goods and ills under his or her agency's purview. Although this duty seems obvious, it is not well understood. Not long ago, the U.S. Congress called for "an ethics investigation" of an official in the Small Business Administration (SBA) who pushed for weakening environmental standards regulating petroleum storage facilities— on the grounds that his actions that were intended to favor chemical wholesalers and gasoline distributors. While that might indeed be a substantively appropriate objection to his position on this matter, which was subject to interagency negotiation, it hardly reflects a lapse in his professional role. As his supervisor declared, with strong surface plausibility, "he has done what his job description says he should do, which is to represent the interests of small business."[26] Part of what we do when we set up administrative agencies with differing missions and jurisdictions is to assign to each of them a different substantive set of concerns to promote and to specify. We should not expect officials charged with responsibility over one set of problems to approach policy analysis in the same way as those charged with any other set of problems.§

The special concern and responsibility that each agency has neither frees it from a generalized responsibility to the public good in general nor precludes it from keeping the general public good in mind. What I have been endorsing, here, is the development of special evaluative expertise, not monomania. Some particularly contested matters, such as the SBA regulation just mentioned, will be the subject of interagency negotiation before administrative rules are finally settled, thus helping ensure that different sides of the question are heard. In all cases, officials are charged with pursuing their special mission in a way consistent with the public good, generally—if vaguely—conceived. Legislative oversight and methods of promoting direct

---

§ That cost-benefit analysis is insensitive to prior legislative decision in this way is an additional reason to reject its ability to serve as a fundamental standard for policy-making. Correspondingly, however, it makes it a powerful tool for checking up on agencies and making comparisons among them.

participation can help ensure that the point of view of the broader public is not forgotten.

This picture of our division of the responsibility of refining our democratic intentions implies that our working conception of the public good—which, idealizing, may be said to have a unified moment in legislative decision—begins within the administrative agencies to ramify. Different agencies will arrive at differing specifications of goods and ills with which they both deal. In general, this difference will reflect a fruitful result of deliberative specification rather than any kind of inconsistency. Thus, if the environmental protection agency defines or interprets traffic congestion in a way that centers on its tendency to produce unhealthy concentrations of pollutants and transportation department officials define or interpret it instead in a way focused on the time lost by commuters, this is just what we would expect from the division of responsibility between these two agencies. Rather than trying to insist that there be some uniform definition or interpretation of what "traffic congestion" really is, we should welcome this fact that it can be differently specified for different purposes. (I will return to this issue of consistency across agencies and programs in the next chapter, with reference to risk assessments.)

While this first condition for the legitimate exercise of agency expertise in specifying public ends is quite obvious and is relatively easily fulfilled, the second is more elusive and less easy to assess. It has to do with trust.

Division of responsibility, as opposed to a mere division of labor, requires trust because it means ceding space for discretion to the other agents. This concession creates the kind of vulnerability to the actions of the entrusted that characterizes trust. We must trust that they will do a good job in exercising the discretion they have been allowed. There are two levels in trust we are asked to place in agency officials. First-order trust of these officials demands that we entrust to them policy-making with regard to the environmental ends, or the small-business ends, or whatever ends define the agency's mission. Trust at this level must rest, in large part, on the professionalism and integrity of the officials. More interesting and problematic is second-order trust. As I have argued, we must also entrust officials with well specifying the ends they have been (at the first order) entrusted with pursuing.[27] It is at this second-order level that the sensitive aspect of "handing over our moral judgment to others" comes more obviously into play. The crucial question is: How should we understand the situation in which the role or responsibility of the entrusted officials is to specify those very goods or ills that they have been entrusted with pursuing?

The conception of deliberative democracy that I have been developing implies that what we are trusting officials with is a role in a truth-oriented process of determining the public good. Although they are to be authorized to determine the public good, still their efforts to specify it for their range of concerns should attempt to get things right. Hence, at some level, what we are being asked to trust is their epistemic authority. The necessary role the agencies play in our democratic division of deliberative labor, however, implies that this cannot be the whole story.

The reason that the needed trust in officials cannot be fully cashed out as trust in their reliability is that, by the very nature of the task they are undertaking, we lack sufficient independent standards of reliability. If we were antecedently fully settled on our interpretation of our ends, we could fairly judge the "reliability" of agency judgments by how faithfully and effectively they serve those ends. The conundrum we face in interpreting trust in agency decision, however, arises precisely from the fact that we need them to continue specifying and interpreting our collective ends. This is a process the reliability or effectiveness of which is not reasonably judged on the basis of the vague conception of collective ends embodied in legislation. The purported bottom-line question, whether it is "rational" to trust officials to help us specify our political ends, then, has no unqualified answer.[28] Even if, at some metaphysical level, a process-independent right answer existed as to which judgments the agency officials should make, our trust in their judgment cannot be adequately understood, psychologically, as our trusting that they will arrive at the right answers. Rather, we must trust the *way* they arrive at their judgments.[29]

The epistemic trust that is required, then, is neither a simple trust in the reliability of agency decision-making nor a bare trust that agencies will keep in mind the goods they have been entrusted with, such that any decision that they made on that basis would be acceptable. Rather, to repeat, we need to trust that agency officials will work in an appropriate and sound *way* with the values and goals that have been entrusted to them.

Given all the dangers—of corruption, self-aggrandizement, and routinization, to name just a few—to which administrative bureaucracies are susceptible, what could possibly make it reasonable to trust them in this way? And who needs to trust them? Each of us? I think it would be a futile and thankless task to elaborate some more precise criterion pertaining to what threshold percentage or proportion of citizens had to trust a given agency to what extent. What we are left with is the question of when it would be generally reasonable for people to trust the agencies to specify appropriately the goods they have been entrusted with. The answer, at one level, is obviously "it depends." An agency charged with attempting to better the lot of an oppressed group is probably not reasonably trustworthy in that task unless among its officials are some who share that group's concrete perspective. The case of children offers a special challenge in this respect.

At a general level, however, we can institute some procedural measures that can help ensure that the agencies are trustworthy in their noninstrumental elaboration of those aspects of the public good that fall under their purview. There are two main types. First, I have shown have that trusting officials to specify and interpret the ends they are directed to pursue requires trusting the people involved to have the kinds of substantive ethical and political commitments that help give us confidence that they will carry out this task in an appropriate way. One important way that these substantive commitments are lined up with those of a majority of the electorate is by giving the majority party or coalition the power to appoint some of the key figures at the top of government agencies. The second general set of measures we can take to bolster the relevant form of agency trustworthiness, balancing the first, is to enhance agency professionalism. If most agency personnel were subject to political appointment, as in systems overly prone to patronage, that would substantially cancel the benefits of substantive area expertise, which takes time to develop, and whose legitimacy in influencing democratic will-formation I am now examining. Important in complementing this kind of control by appointment, then, is a second set of legal mechanisms that protect the long-term integrity of the civil service. These will include measures to protect the tenure of civil servants, to regulate their conflicts of interest, and to provide that their meetings be open.[30]

The effective establishment of mechanisms to promote political control of key appointments and enhance the integrity of agency officials and openness of agency process will surely not guarantee widespread trust in government officials. The agencies still might not be worthy of the trust; and even if they were, general cynicism about government tends to undercut even reasonably based trust. Existing cynicism, however, seems to have been nourished partly by the kind of instrumentalist approach I have criticized, according to which agency officials are meant to be engaged in a quasi-scientific, value-neutral enterprise.[31] We may hope that a more forthright acknowledgement of the kinds of deliberation about collective ends that need to go on in agencies, together with a more vigorous effort than now common to involve the public in this process, would do much to invalidate such cynicism.

In the previous sections, I have explained how public reasoning can be handed off from the legislature to the agencies and how the people can more effectively than at present make their voices heard in agency lawmaking. When the appropriate conditions are met, these constraints and reforms would allow us to say that agency policy-making is not incompatible with rule by the people and is subject to serious democratic constraint. In my view, however, these conditions do not go far enough to ensure that the agencies are not exercising bureaucratic domination. Even in combination, the constraints of the rule of law and of rationally specifying of statutes and the institutional innovation of a widespread use of negotiated rulemaking would leave considerable room for agency discretion.

Only if the further conditions of mandate and trust are met can we be reasonably confident that the agencies are not exercising arbitrary power. Under these conditions, their crucial evaluative judgments would be internally guided by goods and values that we, the people, have asked them to look after. In these circumstances, agency deliberation about ends would count as a continuation of fair processes of democratic deliberation. If all these conditions held, then it would be possible to escape bureaucratic domination.

Under these favorable conditions, as I have suggested, we would be trusting the agencies to engage in a ramifying process of specifying our collective ends. Ends that are broadly agreed upon in the legislature will get variously interpreted and specified in different agencies with different substantive concerns and different contexts of operation. To bring out the distinctive patterns of reasoning involved in this kind of ramifying specification, it will help to contrast it with a standard approach to decision-making involving risk.

# CHAPTER 17

## The Democratic Treatment of Risk

To illustrate the power of democratic reasoning that specifies our public ends in a ramifying way, drawing on agency evaluative expertise as it goes, I sketch in this chapter how it would apply to the regulation of risk. To take on this topic is to push the idea of specifying public ends about as far as it can go. Whereas quantitative approaches easily allow multiplying the value of outcomes by the probability of their occurrence, a qualitative, noninstrumental approach to public reasoning such as the one I have been developing does not. Hence it might appear that the kind of approach I have been developing here is inept at dealing with risk regulation. Not so, I shall argue. My aim is not to achieve total hegemony for noninstrumental reasoning. As I have indicated all along, empirical research and narrowly instrumental reasoning are essential contributors to intelligent practical reasoning and important tools of public accounting. Rather, my aim is to show that the qualitative approach developed here does not fall down when it comes to choices involving risk and uncertainty; to the contrary, it offers an attractive alternative to consider alongside the standard decision-theoretic approaches, an alternative that would allow us to frame these issues in a more democratic fashion.

### Risk Rationalism

Standard rational-choice approaches are on their strongest ground in accounting for decision-making involving risk. Indeed, both Frank P. Ramsey's pathbreaking work on probability in the 1930s and standard methods for generating cardinal utility functions to represent preferences take it that a person's choices reveal his or her preferences *simultaneously with* his or her attitudes toward risk.[1] Preference-based rational choice theory thus fundamentally treats of individuals' approaches to situations involving risk.

Preference-based theories in general, as I noted in chapter 9, can be developed in either of two ways. Insofar as such a theory aspires to be a normative foundation for decision-making, it is pushed in the direction of supposing that all preferences are completely thought through, having taken account of all organic relationships among values. In the context of policy-making, however, such an idealization renders the theory useless, for no one's completely thought-through preferences are known. Accordingly, the version of preference-based theory that is relevant in risk regulation, as in other areas of direct policy-making, is that which accepts the less than completely thought-through preferences.[2] These may be revealed by our actual willingness to pay for listable harms and benefits, such as the loss of life or of a limb or the saving of time spent commuting, or by our survey responses in which we say what we would be willing to pay. This preference information can then be coupled with empirical information about the likelihood of harm and benefit of various magnitudes resulting from a project.

With decision-making involving risk and uncertainty, the tremendous usefulness of this approach lies in its ability to multiply the numbers assigned to a project's harms and benefits by the probability of their occurrence and then add up the products.* The result is the expected value of the project. This approach affords a systematic basis for handling trade-offs involving risk that otherwise seem difficult to make, such as those involved in a bridge project that would save each of half a million commuters fifteen minutes of daily driving but would cost a billion dollars to build and pose a significant risk of bridge-workers dying. More generally, this approach affords a way to rationalize regulatory policy involving risks of various kinds, most notably fatal ones. The dual challenges this risk-rationalist approach poses to my alternative account of democratic deliberation are the following. First, can my qualitative account provide an adequate alternative basis for achieving consistency among government programs that regulate risk? Second, can my qualitative account of the progressive specification of public ends cope in a rational way with isolated choices involving risk?[3]

The first challenge is powerful, for the kind of consistency among projects that is promoted by risk rationalists is demanding and simple. Using money as an indexing device (or *numéraire*), they insist that, generally speaking, society should be willing to incur the same dollar cost per marginal life saved, marginal limb loss averted, or marginal amount of time saved for commuters. Comparing different government programs for their degree of

---

* The case of uncertainty, that is, risks of unknown magnitude, can be assimilated to this framework by employing subjective probabilities. See, for example, R. Duncan Luce and Howard Raiffa, *Games and Decisions: Introduction and Critical Survey* (New York: Wiley, 1957).

consistency in this respect provides a powerful way of raising questions about the rationality of the pattern of our collective decisions.

In general terms, the second challenge asks whether an adequate alternative means of regularizing and rationalizing agency decision can possibly be found. Here the concern is not rational consistency, as such, but rational perspicuity in service of public and hence democratic control. Crucial to how we respond to the second challenge is how we understand the sort of rational systematization that it is appropriate to seek in public policy. Justice Breyer, in a book arguing powerfully for the consistency that risk rationalism can bring, articulately develops this second, institutional argument. Rationalizing agency decisions along risk-rationalist lines, he argues, can make agency decisions more transparent and more easily subject to democratic influence. He proposes that a centralized interagency body be formed, drawing on a cadre of technically well-trained civil servants who cycle in and out of the various agencies that regulate risk, to review proposed regulations with the goal of promoting uniformity in the marginal amounts spent to save lives in different programs.[4] He intends this approach not to constrain or limit democracy in the name of impartial reason but rather to put in place a rationalizing mechanism that will ultimately serve democracy better than does the current, relatively decentralized and apparently haphazard system of risk regulation. He suggests that "the existence of a single, rationalizing group of administrators can thus facilitate democratic control, for it would reduce a mass of individual decisions to a smaller number of policy choices, publicize the criteria used to make those choices, and thereby make it easier for Congress, or the public, to understand what the Executive Branch is doing and why. . . . To systematize . . . is to empower the public."[5]

## Consistency and Context

Justice Breyer's vision of how democratic control may be extended to administrative decision is diametrically opposed to that defended here. I have developed the idea of an institutionally distributed rule by the people that accommodates the fact that the agencies play an essential role in interpreting and specifying our collective ends. Breyer, in contrast, seems to hope that the important democratic control may be exercised adequately at a single stage—presumably the legislative—which will have the job of setting broad goals and program priorities. Should we build bridges? Should we regulate carcinogens in the workplace? The detailed pursuit of these programs that undertake or regulate risky activities can then be rationally and consistently carried out by reference to the trade-off rates indicated in individuals' preferences. Breyer's institutionally situated version of risk rationalism, in other words, represents a special case (focused on risk regulation) of the kind of instrumentalist view I criticized in chapter 9.

The risk rationalist's hope seems to be that the issues of concern to the demos (or its legislative representatives) can be reduced to simple enough choices that the significant decision-making can be completed at the legislative stage, leaving to the executive branch only the technical task of allocating the money to the marginally most effective programs. Against this kind of position, my argument all along has been that the issues cannot be reduced to such simple terms. Instead, we have no choice but to rely on the agencies to engage in a continuing process of interpretation and specification. To do otherwise is, as I have argued, to fall into stupidity by supposing that the preferences available independently of the process of collective deliberation are sufficiently thought through so as to need no revision when brought into contact with the kinds of issues and obstacles that arise in pursuing detailed collective resolutions. If Justice Breyer's position were just that it is useful to have a central body that is charged with comparing the marginal costs of reducing various specifiable risks across the range of government programs, it would be unobjectionable. That degree of systematization ought to be accepted and encouraged. Breyer's proposal is not so modest, however, for it reflects the risk rationalist's global ambition to "systematize" policy-making.

Consistency of the kind that risk rationalists favor is a virtue, but it is not the cardinal virtue they make it out to be. As I have conceded all along, quantitative analysis of costs and benefits that unearths information of this kind can be useful in at least raising an important question about government programs. If, on one context, we are willing to incur $100,000 in costs for each additional life saved by a government program, while in another context we incur ten or a hundred times that amount for each additional life saved, there had better be a good reason for the disparity. Otherwise, we should shift our resources into the program that offers us more life-saving "bang" per buck. Rational choice theorists and risk-benefit analysts do us a real service by raising this kind of question. We should of course utilize our resources in the ways that are most effective in producing desired change, provided that we do not have strong reason not to do so.

Where I differ with the risk rationalists in assessing this proviso's importance is that unlike them, I believe that we often do have strong reason not to equalize cost-benefit ratios along the suggested lines. My difference with the risk rationalists is not an empirical one. The issue hangs, instead, on how we conceive of the other reasons that might arise under the proviso, blocking the straightforward application of rational choice theory. The risk rationalists seem to suppose that these reasons will be rare and peripheral. To the contrary, I want to stress two central and common kinds of contextual reason for accepting some cross-program disparity in the marginal cost of reducing certain harms or achieving certain benefits, neither of which is readily cognizable by my risk-rationalist opponents: (1) a disparity can result from a legitimate and useful process of democratic ramification of policy-making authority and (2) a disparity can result from contextual discriminations—brought to light by this same process—within the (typically broad) categories of harm and benefit involved, discriminations that undercut the claim that all harms or benefits within the initially characterized category ought to be treated equally. Let me briefly explain each of these possibilities in turn.

The first of these points pertains to the political context in which risk-regulation decisions are being made. What I argued in the previous chapter was that under favorable conditions we may regard the administrative agencies as vehicles through which we collaborate in an institutionally divided process of specifying the ends of policy. If we cannot so regard them, then it is likely that we are subject to some degree of bureaucratic domination, in which case risk analysis would provide us with a powerful critical weapon. I do not counsel laying down our weapons of contestation and criticism; but I want us to see that more collaborative, democratic means of collective decision are also available. So suppose that the conditions are favorable and that we can regard the agencies as working with us to specify the ends of policy. If so, then we have entrusted agencies with specific mandates, around which substantive evaluative expertise will grow.

If that is a fair description of the situation of the administrative agencies in a well-justified democratic setting, then there is every reason to expect that different agencies will specify values differently. The Department of Transportation will work out one working understanding of what it means to improve the situation of the disabled, and the Department of Health and Human Services (now administering the SSI program) will work out another. Not only will the relevant statutory definitions of "disability" differ in these different contexts but the specification of what it means to discriminate against the disabled, or effectively to help them, will also reasonably differ in the different contexts. It is an intrinsic feature of institutionally dividing the complex collective process of democratic reasoning that some branches of the process will work out different results on some general topic than do others. There being no monistic place at which the popular will is articulated once and for all, this kind of diversity in evaluative judgment just comes with the territory of a modern, democratic government.

Furthermore—and here I come to the second point about contexts—there are good reasons, wholly apart from this institutional division of labor, why our evaluative judgments are not readily amenable to the kind of consistency that the risk rationalist would impose on them. In order to attain the simple systematization to which they aspire, the risk rationalists hope to contain the ways that preferences interact with context. They can easily cope with all sorts of trade-off, which can be sorted out with sufficiently fine-grained willingness-to-pay information. What poses more of a problem, however, is the ways that context can interfere with the additive separability of different evaluative dimensions.[6] Starting with risk to life, for instance, we would notice quickly enough that people's willingness to pay varies systematically with whether the risk flows in a predictable way from voluntarily undertaken activity, such as driving a car. When we start caring about a good more in one context than we do in another, holding fixed all other goods and ills, however, then the model of risk rationality is in trouble. Idealized, completely thought-through preferences would not have this problem, for when one faces a failure of additive separability, one can simply chop the relevant outcomes, or goods and bads, more finely.[7] One can differentiate between the bad of unpredictable loss of life involuntarily incurred from the bad of predictable loss of life incurred in voluntarily undertaken activity. And indeed, when prompted by findings of empirical psychology, risk analysts do sometimes recognize a few other dimensions that seem generally to matter to people when they assess a risk: whether its objective probability is knowable, whether it arises from a dreaded source, and whether it was voluntarily incurred.[8] But these are just the baby steps in attempting to take account of the ways our evaluative judgments take context into account: Completely thought-through preferences would have to be very fine-grained, indeed. Realistically available preference information, by contrast, will reveal its crudity in the many ways in which the factors it distinguishes fail to be additively separable in the many contexts in which they organically interact.

The standard trope of the risk rationalist is to ignore the other goods and ills that might organically affect, in a given context, how much we are willing to pay for reducing the risk to life (or any other kind of risk). Risk rationalists fortify their presentations with long tables listing the disparate amounts of money spent per life saved in different government programs.[9] Often the disparities revealed are indeed quite shocking and probably do point out the need for some reallocation of government resources. But the charge of inconsistency fails to individuate the relevant goods and ills finely enough. We might rightly care about who is responsible for imposing the risk. In particular, it could reasonably matter to us whether a risk is one that we impose via our government. For instance, one category that consistently generates high dollar amounts per life saved is that of drinking-water safety standards. More is spent per life saved in that context than in reducing comparable dangers in the workplace. While part of this disparity may result from tunnel vision and arbitrariness in government agendas,[10] part of it may be a justifiable reflection of the public's judgment that we should pay more to prevent ourselves from being responsible for deaths than we should to prevent others from being responsible for deaths. Or again, we might reasonably care about the difference between achieving a risk reduction by requiring air bags to be installed in automobiles and achieving the same level of risk reduction by requiring drivers to wear helmets. The latter, we would rightly feel, impinges more drastically on more people's freedom in a way that we cannot explain except contextually. In short, other things are seldom equal, as other values, evaluatively significant features of responsibility, and significant distinctions among the means to be employed in reducing the risk are frequently significant. For these reasons, while comparing the dollars spent for reducing a given risk across different programs is a useful way of pointing up potential misallocations of public resources, it does not represent a reasonable general basis for making policy, even in the risk-reduction field.

What the risk rationalist does is to combine the relatively crude informational base offered by revealed preferences with a rhetoric that suggests that certain very abstractly described values, such as risk to life or limb, ought to be uniformly treated across different contexts. The consistency standard that they wield, however, would rightly apply only once we had arrived at completely thought-through preferences, which would fully take organic, contextual effects into account. Completely thought-through preferences are not available in advance or in abstraction from collective deliberation, however; instead, we need to work out our views in a flexibly intelligent way as we go. Only once we actually start to face such questions as how to make transportation accessible to the disabled, how to maintain clean air, or how to instruct our peace-keeping infantry will we be in a position to deal with these contextual issues. At that point, as I have argued, we must rely on a combination of fresh, open-ended citizen input, substantive agency evaluative expertise, and reinforced procedural means of contestation.

## Noninstrumental Risk Rationality

These reasons for resisting risk rationality's consistency demand do not yet amount to a positive case for the rationality of dealing with risk regulation by means of a qualitative, ramifying specification of the ends of policy. In the course of making the standard economists' sort of point that we do, in fact, seem to feel comfortable making trade-offs involving deadly risks, Breyer notes that "we believe it worth installing guard rails on bridges, but not worth coating the Grand Canyon in soft plastic to catch those who might fall over the edge."[11] I want to run with the Grand Canyon example, and I will use it to illustrate the advantages of the qualitative approach that pursues a ramifying specification of the goods and ills involved in policy decisions.

The values relevant to deciding on safety measures at the canyon rim are ones that it would be fully appropriate for the National Park Service to try to specify in light of concerns special to the context. There are many reasons why we might refrain from coating the Grand Canyon with soft plastic, starting with its prohibitive cost. Less drastically, however, we might install cyclone fencing along visited parts of the canyon rim and along the burro trails leading down to the Colorado River. That we do not do so may say something about our estimate of the risks to life that the fencing would avert and the monetary costs of installing the fence, but it more importantly reflects the nonmonetary values there at stake, especially the relatively un-spoiled natural majesty of the canyon. Installing cyclone fences along its rim would spoil the experience of majesty and beauty that attracts people to visit the canyon in the first place. Some of these aesthetic considerations could be captured as monetizable costs of building such fences. Some of what is going on, however, is attributable to the two kinds of contextual effect I have mentioned.

Thus, in furtherance of a democratic decision to create a national park to protect the canyon's beauty and to enable visitors to experience it, the U.S. Congress has delegated to the National Park Service the promotion of these aims. It is in line with the priorities that we should expect the Park Service to pursue that trade-offs involving risk to life be approached as part of a process of coming to a reasonable working understanding of how to pro-mote these goals. It will require the Park Service, working in consultation with the public and with relevant associations, to think through more com-pletely the trade-offs that are involved. We must expect, however, that this more complete thinking will be both contextually bound and will be ap-propriately framed by the Park Service's special mission. We should not expect, in other words, that the marginal dollar cost incurred per life saved by precautions taken in Grand Canyon National Park to be equal to the marginal amount elsewhere incurred, for other things are not evaluatively equal and the relatively more complete thinking arrived at is, in each case, contextually limited.

About the direct contextual interaction of the values that matter, here, I can only speculate. Intuitively, it seems to me, we are attracted to the Canyon in part because of its awesomeness. It is not a tamed tract of nature like Central Park. It is part of the appeal of awesome natural features, such as the Grand Canyon or Mount Rainier, that they dwarf human beings and, as a consequence, threaten our lives when we visit them. For this kind of reason, I might intelligibly judge that a life lost to a fall into the Canyon or to an avalanche on Mount Rainier is a somewhat less terrible thing than a life lost to heat prostration in the middle of Central Park. (I say this as someone who owes a deep debt of gratitude to a mountain rescue team.) What might reasonably account for this differential evaluation would not be some further good or ill produced. It is not that the fall would enhance the awesomeness of the Canyon or that the collapse would detract from the landscaped peacefulness of Central Park. Rather, it could well be the context that mattered: A death in the Grand Canyon or on Mount Rainier is perhaps less awful, from some suitably objective point of view, than a death in Central Park.

By no means should we invite bureaucrats to indulge in such speculations about values. What we can reasonably do, however, is to hope that such contextually specific features of people's evaluative judgments will find their way into agency decision-making indirectly, through public hearings and processes of negotiated rulemaking. These kinds of contextually specific judgment, then, can reinforce specific legislative mandates as a basis for proceeding on a qualitative basis that does not strive above all for inter-agency consistency with regard to some abstractly characterized values.

Ramifying specification of our public ends is perfectly suited to take account of this kind of contextually variable set of evaluative considerations. Our concern with preventing accidents can reasonably be given one interpretation in the context of protecting people who voluntarily visit national parks in the hopes of enjoying natural beauty unhemmed by artificial contrivances and another interpretation in the context of preventing meltdowns of nuclear reactors. Our concern to promote public health can reasonably be interpreted one way in setting safety standards for public supplies of drinking water and another way in establishing guidelines for children's toys. These variations no more add up to a contradiction than does wearing one kind of clothing to the office and another to a picnic.

Positively, what underwrites the potential rationality of this kind of ramifying specification is the same sort of basis to which my account of non-instrumental reasoning has appealed all along, namely mutual fit with the considerations we take, on reflection, to be important. In this respect, there is no difference between articulating the aims of transportation policy regarding the disabled and those of drinking-water regulation. Intelligent deliberation pertaining to risk regulation requires all the same predictive or risk information that risk rationalism does: This indicates where the opportunities and obstacles lie. Further, as I have been indicating, we may intrinsically care, in differential ways, about the existence of various kinds of risk. Duly informed by this information about risk, the regulator can proceed intelligently to specify the relevant public ends.

In this process, contextually specific solutions will be arrived at. If the issue is what to do about people falling into the Grand Canyon, the concern with safety is framed within the Park Service's mission to make it possible for visitors to appreciate the Canyon's unique beauties. Accordingly, rather than surveying all available safety measures with a neutral eye to the degree of accident reduction generated per dollar cost, the Park Service's deliberations will naturally and appropriately favor those means that prevent accidents without seriously interfering with this mission. Warning signs, of the relatively restrained kind we find in keeping with the park's natural beauty will, I assume, represent one kind of possibility.

In some public policy contexts, quantitative study will be a more central part of the process. When an agency must set the number of parts per billion of a given chemical that may be accepted in the workplace or to establish flammability standards for airline seat cushions, the nature of the task calls for the careful collection of data that bears on the probability of relevant risks under alternative standards. Here as well, however, the distinct missions with which the respective agencies have been charged will rightly color the way they make use of this data. If the clean air statute has handed the environmental protection agency the vague directive to see to it that air quality "does not degrade," this gives special significance to some *status quo ante* as both a mandatory target and a level beyond which cleanliness need not go. In the case of airline regulation, by contrast, the public's expectation—as expressed through the way that the safety agency is meant, for instance, to investigate every crash—may be that no airline fatality is to be regarded as acceptable. This does not, of course, mean that the public would mandate measures that would force all airlines into bankruptcy; but it does mean that when the safety rules are negotiated in consultation with the airlines and representatives of passenger groups, no expected fatality level is to be found acceptable in itself.

This kind of case, pitting a public goal against the cost to private industry of achieving it through mandatory means, may seem to be where push comes to shove and ultimate, normative recourse to quantitative risk analysis is needed, after all. It is not so. To be sure, legislatures of modern democracies are all too often inarticulate about what they are entrusting agencies to do. Yet the situation of an agency like the Federal Aviation Administration (FAA) is not all that different from the one facing the National Park Service in promoting safety to the visitors of the Grand Canyon. In neither case does the mission of the agency boil down to the promotion of one simple value, whether it is the safety of the public, the preservation of natural beauty, or the maintenance of a thriving airline industry. Although the Park Service must preserve the natural beauty of the parks, maximizing that goal would mean keeping people out of them; whereas presumably an important reason that it is to protect this beauty is so that people can appreciate it. How many people has recently become a salient, problematic question. Hence the Park Service is charged with finding a reasonable way to accommodate the competing goals of preservation and enjoyment. It is the same with the FAA, which is charged with the task (not easy at the moment) of finding a reasonable way to accommodate the goals of passenger safety and airline economic health.

I have denied that finding a way of commensurating values is necessary to making rational choices involving such value conflicts or trade-offs. Rationally specifying ends offers another route. Further, since there is no objective basis on which to commensurate values, and since subjective preferences that might serve instead are always incompletely thought through, it is more intelligent to try to work these matters out via a process of collective, democratic deliberation than to trust to the spurious systematization of risk rationality. It is true that, in contrast to the risk rationalists, I have no all-purpose "method" to offer that will allow generally trained policy analysts to churn out answers. Instead, I assert our need to depend on the substantive expertise that agency officials gain from experience in coping with a given range of problems, as well as on the context set by legislative definitions of agency and program missions and on continuing public involvement in the drafting of regulations. From this it should not be concluded, however, that the risk rationalists' approach enjoys a kind of overall rationality that mine lacks. They, too, depend on making a place for the kind of substantive trading-off that I put front and center; it is just that in their case the process of reaching a reasonable accommodation of conflicting ends is supposed to take place privately, in the hearts and minds of individuals, who then reveal their judgments in market behavior or in surveys, whereas on my proposal it occurs in contextualized public fora, open to public input and contestation. Relying on a fair process of democratic deliberation to work out our views on such matters is indispensable to our doing so intelligently and responsibly.

# CHAPTER 18

# Conclusion

Democracy is a demanding ideal. If all of its demands are met in some jurisdiction, then its citizens will rule themselves by reasoning together about what to do. Then, too, bureaucracies will not dominate the citizens but rather will play an indispensable part in their figuring out what they ought to do.

I have woven together the four strands of the democratic ideal—liberalism, republicanism, rationalism, and populism—into a conception of democracy as democratic autonomy. I have elaborated a conception of democratic reasoning both for its own sake, to help us understand what it is to reason together democratically, and also for the sake of addressing the problem of bureaucratic domination. In the end, the two problems converge. Only if all four of the component ideals of democracy are adequately and harmoniously realized can we decide what to do by reasoning together democratically; and only if all four ideals are adequately and harmoniously realized can bureaucratic domination be prevented.

Whether these four aspects of democracy are anywhere adequately and harmoniously realized is an open question. I know of no jurisdiction that could serve as an obvious paradigm. Thus it is that although the ideal of democracy has triumphed in the world, the reality lags behind. Yet the four-part ideal of democracy as democratic autonomy is eminently realizable.

To remind you of the reasons why all four aspects are necessary to democratic reasoning and to preventing bureaucratic domination, and to assess the distance that most existing regimes have yet to travel, I will briefly review each strand in turn.

## The Four Component Ideals

*Liberalism.* I start with the liberal strand, as the liberal's twin ideals of freedom and equality together make the most basic case for democracy. I have developed the idea of freedom in three layers, each important and none deductively derivable from the others. The basic idea of freedom places a burden of legitimation on governments and on all institutions that purport to put people under new duties. The more specific, republican interpretation of freedom as nondomination constrains governments—not to leave things in a privileged "natural" state but to exercise their power nonarbitrarily. More specifically still, the liberal insists on a range of fundamental freedoms. Freedoms of conscience and of expression are essential to individuals even in developing and discussing political views. Freedoms of association and movement are essential to the formation of a public that can reflect on political matters. The freedoms to vote and to stand for elective office must also not be taken for granted.

In many jurisdictions that today count themselves as democratic, these fundamental freedoms are only imperfectly realized. Voting rights violations are still found in the United States and elsewhere. In the United States, however, these fundamental freedoms are at least all on the books. As to freedom from domination, I will be able to assess it only once I put all four strands together to ask about bureaucratic domination.

The equality that matters in a democracy is formal as well as informal and qualitative as well as quantitative. Informally, a spirit of equality must shape the public sphere. Citizens must be willing to address one another as equals in democratic debate. While important legal buttresses of this attitude, formally enforcing the ideal of equality before the law, can help, the attitude counts more, in the end. More formally, quantitative equality must be enforced in the constitution of elections and of votes within legislatures. In both of these contexts, some version of "one person, one vote," must prevail. In the context of electing legislators, specifically, the procedures that institute this rule must serve political equality by seeing to it that legislatures represent the views of citizens fairly. This concern, I have argued, speaks in favor of systems of proportional representation. In contexts tainted by historical or ongoing injustices against the poor, weak, or marginalized, it will also call for special, remedial measures to see to it that hitherto silenced perspectives are adequately represented. And throughout, qualitative equality in the process of democratic deliberation must be assured by conditions of background justice.

On the matter of equality, almost every nation has far to go. Whether citizens are willing to address one another as equals is a matter highly dependent on the accidents of history. How to foster such an attitude in a nation riven by ethnic conflict, by the legacy of *latifundia*, or by persisting aristocratic privilege is no easy question. In nations more favorably circumstanced in these respects, electoral reforms may well be needed to assure fair representation of citizen views and perspectives. And even where the history is favorable and the electoral system is fair, grossly unequal concentrations of wealth and economic power that make their weight felt, unchecked, in the political arena often destroy the qualitative equality of democratic deliberation.

In the case of these ideals of freedom and equality, as well as that of the other component ideals of democracy, my aim has not been to generate a precise scorecard by which to rate a government's progress toward full democracy so much as to articulate a set of aims toward which we, as democrats, should aim. Although these aims have many elements and fit together in complex ways, they remain too vague to give rise to precise comparative measures. In the spirit of the overall account of democratic reasoning I have developed here, they are put forward, rather, to help guide the processes in which we specify our ongoing democratic projects. As we do so, our specifications would naturally ramify in another way besides that produced by agency specialization: They will ramify internationally, as different jurisdictions work out different ways of realizing the complex ideal of democracy as democratic autonomy.[1]

*Republicanism.* The republican interpretation of freedom as nondomination gives rise to at least four themes that have been important to this discussion. At a basic level, it argues for the separation and dispersal of power. Hence, even if complexity did not force a division of democratic deliberation on us, the republican strand of democracy would advise it. While governmental power ought to be divided and dispersed, this is not because only governments threaten to dominate us. Economic and corporate forms of domination are among those that this republican ideal—in concert with that of background distributive justice—condemns. Avoidance of domination, by Pettit's definition, requires that power be exercised nonarbitrarily. In the governmental context, this requires that lawmaking decisions emerge from a fair process of deliberation in which people have been able to participate as free, equal, and autonomous citizens. In this way, republicanism builds in liberalism. A fair process of this kind does not demand consensus or unanimity. In fact, those criteria for decision are inherently biased in favor of the status quo. Rather, majority rule is a more fair device to use—at least in bringing closure to legislative debates. In addition, there need to be ample opportunities for citizens to contest governmental decisions. Legislative elections must be periodic. Legislative and administrative decisions must be open and public, so that citizens can assess them. Opportunities for administrative and judicial appeal should be available. Program-authorizing legislation and administrative rules should be subject to periodic review and renewal.

My impression is that, in the wake of the American republic's founding, most of these republican devices have become quite widespread. The crucial issue is that of bureaucratic domination. Given how abstruse and specialized many agency decisions are—whether in setting antipollution regulations for wood stoves, overseeing airline deregulation, or guiding soldiers' treatment of noncombatants—what is most doubtful is whether the citizenry is sufficiently informed or aware of these decisions to be able effectively to contest them. Here we must rely on citizens' associations that specialize in one issue or another; but we must also rely, as I have argued, on enabling a more proactive public role in influencing these agency decisions to begin with.

*Rationalism.* The ideal of respect for autonomy, placed in a democratic setting, begets the further ideal of making democratic decisions by reasoning with one another. We owe it to one another to offer reasons in favor of our views about what we ought to do and to listen respectfully to the views of others. Like all reasoning, this ought to be truth-oriented; and that is not possible without some at least schematic layer of substantive agreement. Since this book has been discussing what an adequate realization of the ideal of democracy requires, much of the discussion has supposed that this agreement centers around that ideal. Such thin agreement is compatible with a broad plurality of incommensurable worldviews that unite only on this point; it is not compatible, however, with antidemocratic views, past, present, or future. Given such a thin, shared basis, public discussion can really count as a case of our reasoning together: It can count as oriented to the truth about what we ought to do.

Crucially, as I have argued, our democratic deliberations do not hold fixed or take for granted a set of political ends. Rather, these deliberations are devoted to establishing and revising our ends, both severally and jointly. Noninstrumental reasoning—reasoning that extends both to specifying final ends and establishing new ones—is possible, and is needed in democratic politics alongside more commonly accepted, instrumental modes of reasoning. On account of the many ways in which we disagree with one another, both pedestrianly due to conflicting interests and more loftily over matters of principle, it is often necessary, if we are to settle certain policy questions reasonably, that we do so by reasoning toward a deep compromise, in which the participants shift their ends out of concern or respect for the others or for their shared democratic project. Fully achieving the practical promise of noninstrumental democratic deliberation thus requires not only that citizens believe in democratic ideals but also that they come—on the basis of this shared belief or on some other basis—to be moved by feelings of solidarity, mutual concern, or mutual respect. On account of its noninstrumental nature, the rationality of the whole process of democratic deliberation importantly depends on the public reflecting on the ends that have been adopted and the decisions that have been reached. This dependence reinforces the importance of the liberal strand, for the existence of a public capable of reflection importantly depends on a range of supports familiar from liberal constitutionalism.

The rationalist theme converges with the republican one to require that our democratic deliberation be dispersed over a range of institutions and that the divisions of deliberative responsibility involved be clear ones. Administrative agencies must be constrained not only to act under statutory authorization (as opposed to acting *ultra vires*) but also to pursue rational ways of specifying the statutory directives under whose authorization they make law. This in turn implies that legislatures must provide them with sufficiently definite guidelines that they have something to work with. That the decision-making is thus vertically divided does not interfere with the truth-orientation of the whole process, for, under favorable conditions, the agencies can take the legislature's work as providing premises for their further noninstrumental reasoning about what we ought to do. Our truth-oriented deliberation about what to do also tolerates a horizontal specialization among agencies, which may be expected to specify values and principles differently. The nonuniformity that results is a natural concomitant of the impossibility of carrying on our democratic deliberations monistically. Both with respect to vertical delegation and with respect to horizontal division of concern, the legislative mandates need to be clear, not only for the sake of further agency deliberation but also for the sake of possible citizen contestation. Citizens cannot meaningfully contest agency decisions unless they know what parameters the agency was legislatively told to work within and what concerns it was justifiably giving precedence.

It is with respect to this ideal of democratic reasoning that existing democracies fall farthest short. To begin with, there are many reasons to worry about individuals' capacity to enter into democratic deliberation. Does everyone have a view about what we ought to do, or are people more likely to harbor a mishmash of conflicting, half-baked political thoughts? Since, as I have argued, values are multiple and incommensurable, we have no reason to expect anyone to hold a neatly ordered or complete political view; yet many are simply apathetic and ignorant. If so, that reinforces the case for representative, as opposed to direct, democracy, in at least a second-best way. A further concern is that even if people do have views about what we ought to do, it is their narrow self-interest, and not those views, that will control their political action. While this is indeed a worry, and will remain one with regard to institutions of contestation and of direct participation (such as negotiated rulemaking), at the electoral level it is largely canceled by the causal insignificance of each person's vote, which frees people to vote along expressive lines.

When we turn our attention to the official aspects of government, we have reason to doubt the prevalence of the rational spirit there, as well. Do legislators sufficiently respect or care for one another, or for their joint democratic project, to enter reasonably into the spirit of deep compromise? Whether or not they do will vary by issue and will remain hostage to particular facts about political parties and their influence. As to whether rational deliberation about ends, more generally, can go on, we can be more confident, as it does seem to go on all the time in government. The question is usually whether the reasoning is fairly representative of the views of the people rather than whether it has been reasoning at all. In the case of administrative agencies, as well, I am convinced that rational establishment and specification of public ends is quite common. This process has remained too free from public influence and control, however—and hence too prone to yielding bureaucratic domination—because we have lacked a sufficiently open, public recognition that this is the kind of reasoning that the agencies rightly must undertake. It is largely in the hopes of furthering this recognition that I have written this book.

*Populism.* If the other three strands of the democratic ideal—its liberalism, republicanism, and rationalism—are each fully realized, then it becomes much easier to conceive how rule by the people can exist. I have argued that democracy ought to be a form of rule by the people, in which citizens participate in making the laws, which thus comes to represent the will of the people. I have explained how the process of democratic will-formation is distributed across the whole range of democratic institutions. These include the institutions allowing for contestation and appeal, for the reflective moment is crucial to our joint deliberation about ends. Because only a public can reflect in the relevant way, this means that rule by the people must be rule by a public. Our democratic will-formation is also distributed along the more explicit vertical and horizontal lines mentioned earlier. Forging a democratic will requires an openness to forming joint intentions with others, but it also requires the use of majority rule, which limits the set of others with whom explicitly joint intentions are ever formed. The reason that this openness matters, then, is not that the will of the people must literally be the will of each and every one of us. As I have argued, the criterion of unanimity is to be rejected. Rather, the openness matters because we must be willing to engage in a fair, deliberative process of deciding, together, what we ought to do. What counts as a fair procedure will naturally vary, depending on what part of the governmental process we are talking about.

The populist ideal applies to all lawmaking that purports to put citizens under new duties. Accordingly, it applies, in general, to the rulemaking undertaken by the administrative agencies. This means that citizen participation in agency rulemaking via fair procedures (and in other agency decision-making having the force of law) is not merely needed to supplement reactive modes of contestation; it is also definitionally required for bureaucratic power to be nonarbitrary.

Having taken up populism last, many of its points of vulnerability have already come up where it intersects with the three other strands of democracy as democratic autonomy. It depends on fair procedures, a modicum of shared assumptions, shared mutual respect or goodwill, and a willingness and capacity to reason with one another. Better achieving the populist aspect of the democratic ideal will require institutional reforms in many jurisdictions. In particular, it may require electoral reform to ensure that legislatures more fairly represent citizens' views and reform of administrative law so as to allow and promote the more widespread use of participative mechanisms such as negotiated rulemaking.

While it seems fairly obvious that no nation currently lives up to this four-part ideal of democracy as democratic autonomy, it also seems that with the cooperation of historical and cultural circumstance, and with a due eye to sociological and educational prerequisites of reform, this ideal could be achieved. Far from being beyond human reach, it should regulate the ways we pursue our democratic projects, here and now.

## Pulling the Strands Together

Having reviewed each of these strands of democracy as democratic autonomy, I can now offer a complete perspective on the resulting account of democratic reasoning and the concomitant picture of how we might avoid bureaucratic domination.

*Democratic reasoning.* The conception of democratic reasoning that I have defended here contrasts with going understandings of public reason and public reasoning. It is a conception of noninstrumental reasoning in which ends are newly established, revised, and specified in a flexible consideration of the obstacles that arise in settling on acceptable means to our ends. It is a conception of reasoning that is essentially democratic, as it describes how our collective reasoning is distributed through democratic procedures of electing representatives, voting on legislation, and delegating the power to elaborate and implement it. And it is a conception of reflective reasoning that is essentially embodied in these institutions and in a public capable of reflection and of emotional discernment.

In being focused on the interaction of end-setting and means-selection, this conception of practical reasoning departs from those technical conceptions, dominant in economics and decision theory, that employ preference rankings as their primitive. As I have argued, views employing the preference primitive to model the whole of public reasoning either idealistically assume that people have thought through all the important issues already or else fail to invite individuals to join in a flexible, truth-oriented process of joint deliberation. If truth-oriented deliberation about public ends were in principle impossible, these views might count as offering a decent fall-back; but since it is possible, they should be relegated to the secondary status of useful accounting tools.

As a noninstrumentalist account of public reasoning, the conception developed here also contrasts with those that would model democratic reasoning in a simple, top-down fashion in which the people, via the legislature, set the ends and the agencies confine themselves to selecting means to those ends. Not only is this view naively unrealistic, as I initially claimed, but one can now also see that it fails adequately to carry the people's deliberative control to the level of agency decision-making. That control depends on the public's continuing involvement in a truth-oriented and hence open-ended process of deliberation about ends.

As a distributed account of public reasoning, my account contrasts with organicist conceptions that would treat the state like a large person, monistic conceptions that conceive of the people as reasoning together in some unitary forum, and narrowly individualist conceptions that reconstruct the idea of public reason solely in terms of the idea of reasons or reasoning acceptable to each individual. The organicist conception is simply dangerous, while the monistic conception is an unrealistic oversimplification. The narrowly individualist idea of reasons or reasoning acceptable to all, by contrast, has its important places within our complex democratic ideal. It can play a useful role in foundational, social-contract reconstructions of the fundamental principles of democracy and social justice—an enterprise I have not attempted here. It also is important to articulating what is involved in the virtues of civic integrity and civic magnanimity that, I argued, are constitutive supports for the existence of a public. What this abstract, narrowly individualistic idea about public reason cannot do, however, is give us a useful working criterion of political truth. We cannot start out looking, as such, for what can be supported by reasons acceptable to all. To the contrary, we must be willing to enter into democratic deliberation in a spirit of openness to working out reasonable deep compromises, in the course of which what reasons people find acceptable change as their ends change. We have to engage in this work of joint political reasoning in order to arrive at results that are acceptable to the public; but the importance of referring to the public, here, is not to reimport the rejected criterion of unanimity but instead to insist on the moment of reflection.

As a reflective conception of democratic reasoning, in this sense, my view contrasts with conceptions of reasoning that make it out simply in terms of logical and inferential relations among beliefs or commitments.[2] Decision theory, and the other preference-based views it has spawned, tends in that direction: Its favorite trope is axiomatization. In stark contrast, I view non-instrumental reasoning as essentially embodied in an entity that can reflect and as not being subject to axiomatizable principles that might be abstracted from that embodiment. The embodiment of political deliberation, as I have insisted, is spread out across a wide variety of institutions staffed by many two-eared persons. The public is the institution that is most importantly reflective. Because the public is an embodied entity that reflects, its emotions play an essential role in democratic deliberation. It is for this reason that persuasive rhetoric, which is designed to elicit these emotions, is to be welcomed and regulated rather than regretted or banned.

*Avoiding bureaucratic domination.* We are dominated to the extent that we are subject to the arbitrary power of others, most egregiously so when that power purports to impose duties on us. Power is arbitrary when it is not adequately controlled by a fair process of decision in which those subject to it are treated as free and equal and their fundamental rights and liberties are protected. The only adequate way to control agency decisions along these lines, I have argued, is to carry democratic deliberation through to the agency level.

I am now in a better position to locate the worry about bureaucratic domination than I was at the outset. The worry is not that the agencies are not capable of reasoning, including reasoning of the relevant, noninstrumental kind. When, with encouragement from HEW, Martin Convisser helped articulate the goal of nondiscriminatory access to transportation for the disabled, he did establish a new end, and he did so on a rationally defensible basis. What was missing from the process, rather, was public participation and control. Since, as I have suggested, the public seems to have accepted the innovation that Convisser helped write into the regulations under the Biaggi Amendment, this particular exercise of discretion will appear to us benign. There are countless other cases, however, where we will instead have good grounds to complain of the abuse of administrative power. These are the sorts of cases that are dramatized, in the United States, whenever presidential administrations change and the new administration undoes many of the administrative rules that were pushed through at the close of the old. To prevent bureaucratic domination, we cannot simply hope that such rules as are adopted find overall public acceptance. Indeed, it is fundamental to the concept of domination that it does not entail that power is abused but only that it is not subject to controls that would prevent its being arbitrarily abused.

To prevent bureaucratic domination, then, we must do three things. Most fundamentally, we must conceive of agency deliberation as an integral part of our distributed democratic reasoning about what we ought to do. Conceiving it as such, we ought to arrange it so that it can fulfill this role. This means, first of all, that legislatures must take care to pass statutes sufficiently definite that agencies can coherently take them up in the next stage of democratic deliberation. This does not demand much by way of the avoidance of vagueness only—no more than what is demanded, for instance, by the

German constitution. Second, this means that we need to reconceive the rational constraint within which agencies should work. Instead of being constrained to a narrow standard of instrumental rationality—a demand that turns out to be futile and to frustrate populism—they should be constrained to specifying statutory directives within a broader process of non-instrumental reasoning. Third, we must arrange for vehicles of fair citizen participation that are appropriate to this mode of reasoning. This is a mode of reasoning that calls for the continuing crafting of deep compromises, but within a special evaluative framework established by the relevant statute. In particular, interested citizens, or the groups and associations that informally represent them, need to be invited to participate in a process of negotiated rulemaking so that this mutual adjustment of final ends can occur within a process in which the people are afforded, indirectly, a fair opportunity to participate.

Only if agency reasoning is thus incorporated, in theory and in practice, as a stage within the people's democratic reasoning will the problem of bureaucratic domination be adequately addressed. Only if administrative decision-making is thus brought within the ambit of democratic reasoning can we truly say that we live in a democracy, which implies rule by the people. Thus, only if democratic deliberation extends from the coffeehouse to the conference room, from campaign rallies to departmental hallways, will it be the case that we rule ourselves. Only then could we truly say that we enjoy a democratic autonomy.

# NOTES

## CHAPTER 1

1. See, for example, William H. Riker, *Liberalism against Populism: A Confrontation between the Theory of Democracy and the Theory of Social Choice* (Prospect Heights, Ill.: Waveland Press, 1988 [reprint]), 9.
2. I follow the definition of "domination" offered in Philip Pettit, *Republicanism: A Theory of Freedom and Government* (Oxford: Oxford University Press, 1997). That "protection from the arbitrary use of political authority and coercive power" is a central aim of democracy is also a theme in David Held, *Models of Democracy*, 2d ed. (Stanford: Stanford University Press, 1996): see especially p. 300.
3. Pettit, *Republicanism*, 56. The nature of this "appropriate connection" is considered chapter 3.
4. Hernando de Soto, "Some Lessons in Democracy—For the U.S.," *New York Times*, April 1, 1990, sec. 4, p. 2.
5. For additional cases, see David Schoenbrod, *Power without Responsibility: How Congress Abuses the People through Delegation* (New Haven: Yale University Press, 1993).
6. Account and quotations drawn from Bob Woodward and Benjamin Weiser, "Costs Soar for Children's Disability Program," *Washington Post*, February 4, 1994, p. A1.
7. In *Sullivan v. Zebley*, 493 U.S. 521 (1990), the U.S. Supreme Court also stepped in and declared that, for the purposes of the act, development that was not "age appropriate" could count as disability, prompting an upsurge in the number of children applying for coverage.
8. Robert Pear, "After a Review, 95,000 Children Will Lose Cash Disability Benefits," *New York Times*, August 15, 1997, p. A1.
9. With regard to the U.S. federal government, see the ongoing debate between Schoenbrod, *Power without Responsibility*, and Jerry L. Mashaw, *Greed, Chaos, and Governance: Using Public Choice to Improve Public Law* (New Haven: Yale University Press, 1997). Somewhat more abstract discussions of when and to what extent delegating power is appropriate may be found in David Epstein and Sharyn O'Halloran, *Delegating Powers: A Transaction Cost Politics Ap-*

*proach to Policy Making under Separate Powers* (Cambridge, England: Cambridge University Press, 1999), and Cass R. Sunstein and Edna Ullmann-Margalit, "Second-Order Decisions," *Ethics*, 110 (1999); 5–31.

10. Dramatic cases of economic interests overriding democratic wishes occurred under the aegis of the "Competitiveness Council" chaired by Vice President Dan Quayle in the 1980s. The Council was known to reinstate provisions in regulations that had been specifically considered and rejected by the Congress.

11. A classic statement of the issue of bureaucratic domination is that in Theodore J. Lowi, *The End of Liberalism: Ideology, Policy, and the Crisis of Public Authority* (New York: Norton, 1979). Richard B. Stewart, "The Reformation of American Administrative Law," *Harvard Law Review* 88 (1975): 1669–813, gives a particularly powerful articulation of the problem in its modern guise. In somewhat more general terms, Max Weber noted that "democracy inevitably comes into conflict with the bureaucratic tendencies which, by its fight against notable rule, democracy has produced." *From Max Weber*, edited by H. H. Gerth and C. Wright Mills (New York: Oxford University Press, 1974), 226.

12. Robert A. Dahl, *Democracy and Its Critics* (New Haven: Yale University Press, 1989), 187–91, argues that the Netherlands, New Zealand, and Switzerland, which lack judicial review of national legislation, are not obviously defective democracies.

13. Ibid., 189–90; Jeremy Waldron, *The Dignity of Legislation* (Cambridge, England: Cambridge University Press, 1999), 63.

14. *John Locke, Two Treatises of Government*, edited by Peter Laslett (1698, reprint, New York: Mentor, 1965), book 2, sec. 137.

15. See Pettit, *Republicanism*, 180–83.

16. Weber, *From Max Weber*, 212–3.

17. A theme of Richard Neustradt, *Presidential Power: The Politics of Leadership* (New York: Wiley Press, 1960), is that the power of the president is typically exaggerated because people fail to note just how much the president depends on not only cooperation with the Congress but also cooperation with those in the executive agencies to get anything done.

18. On the general theme of law being democratically made, see Waldron, *The Dignity of Legislation*.

19. Weber, *From Max Weber*, 224.

20. Alexander Hamilton, James Madison, and John Jay, *The Federalist Papers*, edited by Clinton Rossiter (New York: New American Library, 1961), 77.

21. Madison's reversal of traditional views about the appropriate size for democratic republics is well set out in Samuel Beer, *To Make a Nation: The Rediscovery of American Federalism* (Cambridge: Harvard University Press, 1993), 255–61.

22. Jean-Jacques Rousseau, *The Social Contract and Discourses*, translated by G. D. H. Cole (New York: Dutton, 1973), III.iv, p. 217.

23. Hamilton, Madison, and Jay, *The Federalist Papers*, no. 51, p. 324.

24. James M. Buchanan and Gordon Tullock, *The Calculus of Consent: Logical Foundations of Constitutional Democracy* (1962; reprint, Ann Arbor: University of Michigan Press, 1965), 12, 14.

25. This description is Buchanan's in James M. Buchanan and Richard A. Musgrave,

*Public Finance and Public Choice: Two Contrasting Visions of the State* (Cambridge: MIT Press, 1999), 21.

26. Buchanan and Musgrave, *Public Finance and Public Choice*, 113–7.
27. James M. Buchanan and Roger D. Congleton, *Politics by Principle, Not Interest* (Cambridge, England: Cambridge University Press, 1998), ix.
28. Geoffrey Brennan and Loren Lomasky, *Democracy and Decision* (Cambridge, England: Cambridge University Press, 1993).
29. Geoffrey Brennan and Alan Hamlin, *Democratic Devices and Desires* (Cambridge, England: Cambridge University Press, 2000), 115–6.
30. John Rawls, *The Law of Peoples* (Cambridge: Harvard University Press, 1999), 4.
31. Such is the tendency of Mashaw, *Greed, Chaos, and Governance*, especially pp. 138–140.
32. I am hardly the first to employ the label "democratic autonomy." My version of "democratic autonomy" differs from the view offered under that label in Held, *Models of Democracy*, chap. 9, in two ways. First, I limit my use of the term "autonomy" more closely to what is contained in the concept of reasoned, or reason-responsive, self-rule. Second, as the many parts of the value-based aspect of argument in Part I for my interpretation of democracy as democratic autonomy indicates, I do not agree with Held's apparent view (p. 298) that democracy can be defended as transcending value disagreements. I do not deceive myself into thinking that everyone subscribes to the values of freedom, equality, and autonomy that support democracy as democratic autonomy; but my argument is that those who believe in democracy implicitly seem to do so and in any case ought to do so. Those who do not will not be impressed by the problem of bureaucratic domination as I pose it, hence will be uninterested in its solution. They may stop reading now. Peter Breiner, "Democratic Autonomy, Political Ethics, and Moral Luck," *Political Theory* 17 (1989): 550–74, uses the term "democratic autonomy," as I do, to apply to collective, democratic self-rule. I dissent from his claim (at 571) that the notion of democratic autonomy rests on Rousseau's idea of the general will.
33. Henry S. Richardson, "Autonomy's Many Normative Presuppositions," *American Philosophical Quarterly* 38 (2001): 287–303.
34. Henry S. Richardson, *Practical Reasoning about Final Ends* (Cambridge, England: Cambridge University Press, 1994).
35. Buchanan and Tullock, *The Calculus of Consent*, 31–32.
36. Ibid., *The Calculus of Consent*, 32.
37. Sometimes, as in Gerald F. Gaus, *Justificatory Liberalism: An Essay on Epistemology and Political Theory* (New York: Oxford University Press, 1996), attention has focused on the modes of reasoning involved in justifying fundamental political principles. At other times, the attention rests instead on whether deep disagreements among citizens disrupts possibilities for reasoning and on what principles and virtues may guide us when they do: see, e.g., Amy Gutmann and Dennis Thompson, *Democracy and Disagreement* (Cambridge: Harvard University Press, 1996). Yet another strand of the deliberative democracy movement emphasizes the epistemic benefits of democratic procedures. See, e.g., David

Estlund, "Beyond Fairness and Deliberation: The Epistemic Dimension of Democratic Authority," in *Deliberative Democracy: Essays on Reason and Politics*, edited by James F. Bohman and William Rehg (Cambridge: MIT Press, 1997), 173–204. Yet while there is criticism all round of narrow, instrumental models of democratic reasoning, there has yet to be an adequate development of the noninstrumental alternative mode(s) of reasoning open to us in a democracy. That is the insufficiency to which I refer in the text.

## CHAPTER 2

1. Thomas Aquinas, *Summa Theologica*, translated by Fathers of the English Dominican Province, 5 vols. (Westminister, Md.: Christian Classics, 1981), 2: 1014. Aquinas thus makes room for what Nussbaum calls "local specification": see Martha C. Nussbaum, "Aristotelian Social Democracy," in *Liberalism and the Good*, edited by R. Bruce Douglass, Gerald M. Mara, and Henry S. Richardson (New York: Routledge, 1990), 203–52, 236. On the same theme in Locke, see Jeremy Waldron, *The Dignity of Legislation* (Cambridge, England: Cambridge University Press, 1999), 66.
2. This way of framing the normative problem of political authority I owe to Joseph Raz, *The Morality of Freedom* (Oxford: Oxford University Press, 1986), chaps. 2–3.
3. For the distinction between "equal concern and respect" and "treating people equally" and the suggestion that the former is a more basic and less controversial normative requirement, see Ronald Dworkin, *Taking Rights Seriously* (Cambridge: Harvard University Press, 1978), 370.
4. This is the "egalitarian plateau" referred to by Will Kymlicka, *Contemporary Political Philosophy* (New York: Oxford University Press, 1990), 5.
5. Philip Pettit, *Republicanism: A Theory of Freedom and Government* (Oxford: Oxford University Press, 1997).
6. Isaiah Berlin, *Four Essays on Liberty* (Oxford: Oxford University Press, 1979).
7. It does not seem promising to think of freedom in terms of the presence of self-interference. Whether nondomination is rightly counted as a distinct form of liberty, as opposed to counting as a constitutive support of positive liberty, is questioned by Gopal Sreenivasan, "A Proliferation of Liberties," *Philosophy and Phenomenological Research* 63 (2001): 229–37. For my purposes, it is not necessary to settle the question; what matters is that domination is to be avoided. I am attempting to build my case for democratic autonomy on a basis that is less question-begging than a robust assertion of the importance of positive liberty would be. In the end, however, I make a case for a kind of collective self-mastery.
8. Pettit, *Republicanism*, 22.
9. Ibid., 22–23. It will be objected that domination always interferes in a background way, if not actively. Even if that is so, Pettit does real service by highlighting the evils of the dominator's *capacity* to interfere.
10. Herbert Spencer, *Political Writings*, edited by J. Offer (Cambridge, England: Cambridge University Press, 1994), 6–7.

11. Pettit, *Republicanism*, 53–4.
12. This kind of case in which morality requires not minding one's own business is discussed in Sarah Buss, "Appearing Respectful: The Moral Significance of Manners," *Ethics* 109 (1999): 795–826.
13. On these compromises in American history, see Morton Horwitz, *The Transformation of American Law* (Cambridge: Harvard University Press, 1977). On the fact that property law has no single, natural interpretation, see the set of puzzles about the Lockean theory of property laid out with disarming frankness in Robert Nozick, *Anarchy, State, and Utopia* (New York: Basic Books, 1974), 174–5.
14. John Rawls, *A Theory of Justice*, rev. ed. (Cambridge: Harvard University Press, 1999), 7.
15. Less crude than many defenders of negative liberty, James Buchanan recognizes that the government needs to support the legal infrastructure of the market: see James M. Buchanan and Richard A. Musgrave, *Public Finance and Public Choice: Two Contrasting Visions of the State* (Cambridge: MIT Press, 1999), 83–4. Buchanan tends more to one-sidedness.
16. Pettit, *Republicanism*, 43.
17. Richard Price, *Political Writings*, edited by D. O. Thomas (Cambridge, England: Cambridge University Press, 1991), quoted in Pettit, *Republicanism*, 34.
18. Ibid., 35.
19. On the idea of a normative power, see Wesley N. Hohfeld, "Some Fundamental Legal Conceptions as Applied in Judicial Reasoning," *Yale Law Journal* 23 (1913): 16–59.
20. Pettit, *Republicanism*, 52, 79.
21. Ibid., 59.
22. Ibid., 49.
23. Ibid., 41.

CHAPTER 3

1. Philip Pettit, *Republicanism: A Theory of Freedom and Government* (Oxford: Oxford University Press, 1997), 56.
2. Ibid., 56.
3. See, e.g., R. Bruce Douglass, Gerald M. Mara, and Henry S. Richardson, eds., *Liberalism and the Good* (New York: Routledge, 1990).
4. I articulated some of my reasons in Henry S. Richardson, "The Problem of Liberalism and the Good," introduction to *Liberalism and the Good*, edited by R. Bruce Douglass, Gerald M. Mara, and Henry S. Richardson (New York: Routledge, 1990), 1–28. Rawls, whose earlier work had led some to think of liberalism as neutral about the good, clarifies his own willingness to argue from a political conception of the good in *Political Liberalism* (New York: Columbia University Press, 1996). There he instead draws a line, which does not concern me here, between political and comprehensive conceptions of the good.
5. Rawls, *Political Liberalism*, 139, describes fair cooperation among free and equal citizens as "very great values."

6. Pettit, *Republicanism*, 88. I take up Pettit's own interpretation of nonarbitrariness in the final section of this chapter.
7. See, e.g., R. M. Hare, *Moral Thinking: Its Levels, Method, and Point* (Oxford: Oxford University Press, 1981).
8. See the discussion of Buchanan's public choice theory in the introduction.
9. Knut Wicksell, *Finanztheoretische Untersuchungen* (Jena: Fischer, 1896). Wicksell is credited in James M. Buchanan and Gordon Tullock, *The Calculus of Consent: Logical Foundations of Constitutional Democracy* (1962; reprint, Ann Arbor: University of Michigan Press, 1965), 8. Intriguingly, Wicksell is described as "the last common ancestor" of Buchanan and Richard Musgrave, a public sector economist far more sympathetic to social democracy and the welfare state, in James M. Buchanan and Richard A. Musgrave, *Public Finance and Public Choice: Two Contrasting Visions of the State* (Cambridge: MIT Press, 1999), 7.
10. John Rawls, *A Theory of Justice*, rev. ed. (Cambridge: Harvard University Press, 1999), 249–50.
11. Wicksell's unanimity criterion is related to the hypothetical Pareto-improvement standard employed by cost-benefit analysis. I discuss the latter in chapter 9.
12. Rawls, *A Theory of Justice*, p. 3.
13. On the place of compromise within democratic deliberation, see chapter 11. In stressing the importance of redressing injustice, environmental devastation, war, and dangerous economic imprudence through legislation, I am disagreeing with the remarkable claim in James M. Buchanan and Roger D. Congleton, *Politics by Principle, Not Interest* (Cambridge, England: Cambridge University Press, 1998), 9, that "there is no social purpose to the law." "But," they there suggest, "if social values do exist separately, there is little basis for democracy itself to have independent normative significance." Not so, I am in the course of arguing; and in chapter 10 I argue that democracy *depends* for its normative significance on values that exist separately from individual views or preferences.
14. See Jürgen Habermas, *Between Facts and Norms: Contributions to a Discourse Theory of Law and Democracy*, translated by William Rehg (Cambridge: MIT Press, 1996), 161, 496. It is doubtful that Habermas means this idea to serve as a guide for concrete procedures of political deliberation. It is more sensibly taken as playing a role in a philosophical conception of political justification, the kind of role also played by Rawls's idea of "overlapping consensus" (see Rawls, *Political Liberalism*, chap. 4). Mistaking these ideas for conceptions of concrete political processes, Chantal Mouffe, *The Democratic Paradox* (London: Verso, 2000), chides both Habermas and Rawls for neglecting the inherently adversarial and conflictual aspect of politics. They do not. Rather, their notions of ideal consensus help describe what it would be to justify a political *theory*. Actual politics they do understand to be highly conflictual. Habermas makes that clearer in "Three Normative Models of Democracy," in *The Inclusion of the Other: Studies in Political Theory* (Cambridge: M.I.T. Press, 1998), 239–52.
15. See Jean-Jacques Rousseau, *The Social Contract and Discourses*, translated by G. D. H. Cole (New York: Dutton, 1973), IV.ii, p. 250.
16. See ibid., 2.3, p. 185.

17. Pettit, *Republicanism*, 56, flirts with the notion that "an interest or idea" being "factional or sectional" is at least an "operational test" of its being arbitrary.
18. For a fuller account of the ideal of the rule of law, see chapter 16.
19. Friedrich A. Hayek, *The Constitution of Liberty* (1960; reprint, Chicago: University of Chicago Press, 1971), 149–53. I criticize Hayek's treatment of generality in Henry S. Richardson, "Administrative Policy-Making: Rule of Law or Bureaucracy?" in *Recrafting the Rule of Law: The Limits of Legal Order*, edited by David Dyzenhaus (Oxford: Hart Press, 1999), 309–30.
20. Buchanan and Congleton, *Politics by Principle*, 44. As to legislation that imposes duties rather than distributing benefits, Buchanan and Congleton tie themselves in knots. With respect to a program of military conscription, they write that "clearly, the generality norm here requires that all persons, in a well-defined age bracket, be accorded like treatment" (45). They do not explain, however, how it is that their generality requirement allows exempting those outside this age bracket from conscription. In effect, they are here sweeping under the rug the main problems that face any theory that takes as its central requirement the principle that governments ought to treat people equally.
21. Richard Musgrave raises similar doubts about Buchanan and Congleton's "generality principle" in Buchanan and Musgrave, *Public Finance and Public Choice*, 137, 232.
22. As I have noted earlier, my stance conflicts with some remarks of Pettit's that seem to cast liberal democratic institutions in a merely heuristic role: Pettit, *Republicanism*, 56–7.
23. See, e.g., Michael J. Sandel, *Democracy's Discontent: America in Search of a Public Philosophy* (Cambridge: Harvard University Press, 1996), part 1.
24. Kenneth J. Arrow, *Social Choice and Individual Values*, 2d ed. (New Haven: Yale University Press, 1963). For a lucid restatement of Arrow's theorem and its proof, see Amartya K. Sen, *Collective Choice and Social Welfare* (reprint, Amsterdam: North-Holland, 1984), chap. 3. My exposition will follow Sen's.
25. Sen, *Collective Choice and Social Welfare*, 38. The discussion of the voting paradoxes goes back at least to Condorcet.
26. For a presentation of the logical problems that focuses on agenda-setting, see R. McKelvey, "General Conditions for Global Instransitivities in Formal Voting Models," *Econometrica* 47 (1979): 1085–110.
27. A classic work is Duncan Black, *The Theory of Committees and Elections* (Cambridge, England: Cambridge University Press, 1958).
28. William H. Riker, *Liberalism against Populism: A Confrontation between the Theory of Democracy and the Theory of Social Choice* (Prospect Heights, Ill.: Waveland Press, 1988 [reprint]), 137.
29. Grounds for resisting this move to skepticism from Arrow's impossibility theorem are offered by Jules Coleman and John Ferejohn, "Democracy and Social Choice," *Ethics* 97 (October 1986): 6–25; S. L. Hurley, *Natural Reasons: Personality and Polity* (New York: Oxford University Press, 1989), 333–42; and Mathias Risse, "Arrow's Theorem, Indeterminacy, and Multiplicity Reconsidered," *Ethics* 111 (2001): 706–34. These authors point out, in various ways, that a cognitivist or truth-oriented conception of democratic deliberation (such as that developed in chapters 5 and 10) disturbs the inference to skepticism.

30. I will pursue this defense of the idea of the public good against Riker further in the next chapter. While I am agreeing with him in stressing the importance of liberalism, I will be arguing, against his title theme, that there is an important sense of populism that remains consistent with liberalism.

31. In addition, the consideration of fallibility mentioned in the preceding paragraph implies that condition (P) is not rightly taken as a restriction on what we ought to do. See Hurley, *Natural Reasons*, 338.

32. For the thought that principles of liberal constitutionalism generate "gag rules" of this kind, see Stephen Holmes, "Gag Rules and the Politics of Omission," in *Constitutionalism and Democracy*, edited by Jon Elster and Rune Slagstad (Cambridge, England: Cambridge University Press, 1988), 19–58.

33. For example, Jon Riley, *Liberal Utilitarianism: Social Choice Theory and J. S. Mill's Philosophy* (Cambridge, England: Cambridge University Press, 1988) gives an argument from within Mill's utilitarian liberalism for rejecting (U). Geoffrey Brennan and Alan Hamlin, *Democratic Devices and Desires* (Cambridge, England: Cambridge University Press, 2000), 106–7, argue on a more general basis that surely some configurations of preference are socially and ethically unacceptable.

34. Cass R. Sunstein, *The Partial Constitution* (Cambridge: Harvard University Press, 1993), Frank Michelman, "The Supreme Court 1985 Term," *Harvard Law Review* 100 (1986): 4–77.

35. See, e.g., Amy Gutmann and Dennis Thompson, *Democracy and Disagreement* (Cambridge Harvard University Press, 1996), 52–63.

36. Philip Pettit, "Democracy, Electoral and Contestatory," in *Designing Democratic Institutions*, edited by Ian Shapiro and Stephen Macedo (New York: New York University Press, 2000), 107.

37. Ibid., 108.

38. Pettit does not say whether the standard is rejectability as irrelevant by any, by all, or by whom.

39. Gutmann and Thompson, in *Democracy and Disagreement*, overestimate the amount of theoretical work that can be done by the idea of reasons that all can accept.

40. Pettit, *Republicanism*, 56–7, seems to reject the liberal interpretation's insistence on building democratic mechanisms into the interpretation of nonarbitrariness, for he there writes that "politics is the only heuristic available for determining whether the interference of the state is arbitrary or not": the only heuristic, perhaps, but merely a heuristic nonetheless.

## CHAPTER 4

1. I generally follow Christopher Morris's advice and avoid the term "popular sovereignty," which connotes a unitary source of normative authority that would clash with the liberal and republican aspects of democracy as democratic autonomy. See Christopher W. Morris, "The Very Idea of Popular Sovereignty," in *Democracy*, edited by Ellen Frankel Paul, Fred D. Miller, and Jeffrey Paul (Cambridge, England: Cambridge University Press, 2000), 1–26.

2. Not all contemporary republicans wholly resist populist ideas. See Cass R. Sunstein, *The Partial Constitution* (Cambridge: Harvard University Press, 1993), and Frank I. Michelman, "How Can the People Ever Make the Laws? A Critique of Deliberative Democracy," in *Deliberative Democracy: Essays on Reason and Politics*, edited by James Bohman and William Rehg (Cambridge: MIT Press, 1997), 145–71. In the latter work, as I will show, Michelman argues that an unqualified or total populism is incoherent; still, he seems sympathetic to the sort of qualified populism I will argue for here.

3. Philip Pettit, *Republicanism: A Theory of Freedom and Government* (Oxford: Oxford University Press, 1997), 81.

4. William H. Riker, *Liberalism against Populism: A Confrontation between the Theory of Democracy and the Theory of Social Choice* (Prospect Heights, Ill.: Waveland Press, 1988 [reprint]), xi.

5. I do, however, sympathize with the views ascribed to Rousseau in Jürgen Habermas, *Between Facts and Norms: Contributions to a Discourse Theory of Law and Democracy*, translated by William Rehg (Cambridge: MIT Press, 1996) concerning democratic populism in general (32) and mutual transformation through democratic participation (102).

6. Jean-Jacques Rousseau, *The Social Contract and Discourses*, translated by G. D. H. Cole (New York: Dutton, 1973), I.viii, p. 178; I.vii, p. 177.

7. See, e.g., Rousseau, *The Social Contract and Discourses*, II.iii, p. 184: "The general will is always upright [*droite*] and always tends to the public advantage; but it does not follow that the deliberations of the people always have the same rectitude."

8. Ibid., IV.ii, p. 250.

9. See, e.g., Gopal Sreenivasan, "What Is the General Will?" *Philosophical Review* 109 (2000): 545–81.

10. Riker, *Liberalism against Populism*, 14, argues that one must add the dangerous Rousseauvian claims to distinguish populism from a simply liberal-republican embrace of majoritarian procedures. The use I will make of the populist ideal of the will of the people will show that this is not the case.

11. Hobbes makes a parallel point about the freedom attributed to the ancient Romans in *Leviathan*, edited by Edwin Curley (Indianapolis: Hackett, 1994), II.xxi, p. 140.

12. E.g., by Jules Coleman and John Ferejohn, "Democracy and Social Choice," *Ethics* 97 (October 1986): 6–25; Joshua Cohen, "An Epistemic Conception of Democracy," *Ethics* 97 (October 1986): 26–38; and Geoffrey Brennan and Alan Hamlin, *Democratic Devices and Desires* (Cambridge, England: Cambridge University Press, 2000), 142–45, 239–41. The first two articles defend populism against Riker by giving an epistemic interpretation of democratic procedures, taking them to be reliable indicators of the common good. Although chapter 15 will give a hedged reliability argument for the use of majority rule, I do not believe that democratic procedures, as such, can soundly be defended on the basis of their reliability. As I explain in chapter 10, I am committed to seeing them neither as pure procedures nor as imperfect ones but as what I call "normatively fruitful" ones.

13. Aristotle, *De Anima* III.10. Aristotle's claim that the apparent good is always

the object of choice has been interestingly disputed in recent years: see, e.g., Michael Stocker, "Desiring the Bad: An Essay in Moral Psychology," *Journal of Philosophy* 76 (1979): 738–53, and J. David Velleman, "The Guise of the Good," *Nous* 26, no. 1 (1992): 3–26. The point of doubt, however, concerns whether we always act for the sake of some good or apparent good and not whether it is useful to differentiate between the will and that at which it aims, which is often or typically a good or apparent good.

14. Immanuel Kant, "An Answer to the Question: What Is Enlightenment?" in *Practical Philosophy*, translated and edited by Mary J. Gregor (Cambridge, England: Cambridge University Press, 1996), 17.

15. John Rawls, "Kantian Constructivism in Moral Theory: The Dewey Lectures 1980," *Journal of Philosophy* 77, no. 9 (1980): 543.

16. This same consideration in favor of political participation makes it unacceptable to delegate all political decisions to rulers selected by lot, another neutral procedural device.

17. This is a variant of the idea of a Queen for a Day discussed in David Estlund, "Beyond Fairness and Deliberation: The Epistemic Dimension of Democratic Authority," in *Deliberative Democracy: Essays on Reason and Politics*, edited by James F. Bohman and William Rehg (Cambridge: MIT Press, 1997), 191–4. On 193, Estlund writes, "I know of no strong moral argument against [Queen for a Day] as compared with ordinary voting." See also David Estlund, "Jeremy Waldron on Law and Disagreement," *Philosophical Studies* 99 (2000): 111–28. In the text I construct part of an implicit argument against it; the remainder comes in my discussion in chapter 14 of the importance of representing a variety of citizens' views within the legislature. The random selection of a Dictator for a day should be contrasted with the use of lot to select magistrates, common in ancient democracies and discussed by Bernard Manin, *The Principles of Representative Government* (Cambridge, England: Cambridge University Press, 1997), chaps. 1–2. On more limited, contemporary uses of random decisional devices, see Lyn Carson and Brian Martin, *Random Selection in Politics* (Westport, Conn.: Praeger, 1999).

18. See, e.g., Margaret Gilbert, *On Social Facts* (Princeton: Princeton University Press, 1989); Michael E. Bratman, "Shared Cooperative Activity," *Philosophical Review* 101 (April 1992): 327–41; and Raimo Tuomela, *Cooperation: A Philosophical Study* (Dordrecht: Kluwer, 2000). I will put this recent work to use in chapter 12.

19. D'Agostino writes that "majoritarian techniques cannot reliably give a transitive social ordering of regimes and therefore cannot provide an adequate basis for constitutional decision-making"; *Free Public Reason: Making It Up as We Go* (New York: Oxford University Press, 1996), 96. I concur. Majority rule has its place within a constitution, not as the basis of one.

20. As pointed out in Mathias Risse, "Arrow's Theorem, Indeterminacy, and Multiplicity Reconsidered," *Ethics* 111 (2001): 733, while Arrovian considerations do disturb a populism that would define the will of the people in terms of some privileged, abstract procedure, the liberal procedures I have invoked are actual and concrete rather than abstract and depend on a background of settled individual rights.

21. In suggesting that the idea of the will of the people be interpreted via the notion

of procedures that treat citizens as free and equal, I follow Joshua Cohen, "Democracy and Liberty," in *Deliberative Democracy*, edited by Jon Elster (Cambridge, England: Cambridge University Press, 1998), 185–6, who defines democracy as holding that legitimate decisions must be "collective" in the sense that they are "authorized by *citizens as a body*" and defends a "*deliberative* conception" of democracy, defined as one in which "a decision is collective just in case it emerges from arrangements of binding collective choice that establish conditions of *free public reasoning among equals who are governed by the decisions.*"

22. See also Habermas, *Between Facts and Norms*, 455.

23. Michelman, "How Can the People Ever Make the Laws?" 174. Of course, contrary to Michelman's title, I take his insight to be a critique not of deliberative democracy in general but only of an implausibly radical form thereof.

24. See Henry S. Richardson, "Autonomy's Many Normative Presuppositions," *American Philosophical Quarterly* 38 (2001): 287–303.

25. Here, we work our way back to Kant, though without his idea of hypothetical generalization; see Immanuel Kant, *Practical Philosophy*, 387, Ak. 6:230.

26. Bruce Ackerman, *We the People*, vol. 1, *Foundations* (Cambridge: Harvard University Press, 1991), Vol. 2, *Transformations* (Cambridge: Harvard University Press, 1998).

27. Ibid., 1:181.

28. Ackerman's dualism is endorsed in John Rawls, *Political Liberalism* (New York: Columbia University Press, 1996), 231.

29. Ackerman, *We the People*, 1:182.

30. Ibid., 1:6.

31. Ibid., 2:39–40.

32. Ibid., 1:242. See Frank I. Michelman, "Constitutional Fidelity/Democratic Agency," *Fordham Law Review* 55 (1997): 1541–2.

33. A philosophical metaphor for this situation is that of Neurath's boat at sea: Any plank can be replaced, but attempting to replace all at once will sink the ship. Putting some few fundamental planks beyond amendment does not interfere with rule by the people, especially if those planks are derived from the same fundamental liberalism that generates the demand for populism.

34. Pettit, *Republicanism*, 186.

35. For reasons to doubt that the possibility of reflective revision is sufficient for individual autonomy, see, e.g., John Christman, "Autonomy and Personal History," *Canadian Journal of Philosophy* 21 (1991): 1–24, and Paul Benson, "Autonomy and Oppressive Socialization," *Social Theory and Practice* 17 (1991): 385–408.

36. On the individual case, see Richardson, "Autonomy's Many Normative Presuppositions."

## CHAPTER 5

1. In focusing on "reasoning" rather than "deliberation," I follow Joshua Cohen, "Democracy and Liberty," in *Deliberative Democracy*, edited by Jon Elster (Cambridge, England: Cambridge University Press, 1998), 193.

2. See, e.g., Jon Elster, "The Market and the Forum: Three Varieties of Political Theory," in *Foundations of Social Choice Theory*, edited by Jon Elster and Aanand Hyllund (Cambridge, England: Cambridge University Press), 103–32; Cass R. Sunstein, "Preferences and Politics," *Philosophy and Public Affairs* 20, no. 1 (winter 1991): 3–34; and Bernard Manin, "On Legitimacy and Political Deliberation," translated by Elly Stein and Jane Mansbridge, *Political Theory* 15, no. 3 (August 1987): 338–68.

3. I am grateful to Benjamin Challinor Richardson for this example.

4. See, e.g., John Dryzek, *Discursive Democracy: Politics, Policy, and Political Science* (Cambridge, England: Cambridge University Press, 1990) and Jürgen Habermas, *Between Facts and Norms: Contributions to a Discourse Theory of Law and Democracy*, translated by William Rehg (Cambridge: MIT Press, 1996).

5. The development of the idea of "communicative rationality" in Jürgen Habermas, *The Theory of Communicative Action*, vol. 1, *Reason and the Rationalization of Society* (Boston: Beacon Press, 1984), does manage to cast it as a form of reasoning. It succeeds in doing so at the cost of quite an extreme idealization (referring to an "ideal speech situation" in which claims are subject only to "the forceless force of the better argument"). Habermas skips over the quite ordinary ways in which even individuals can reason noninstrumentally (see chapter 7 herein). Only from such a realistically accessible basis can we arrive at a realistic account of collective noninstrumental reasoning.

6. Someone who is clear about strengthening the conception of fair procedures is Joshua Cohen. See, e.g., Cohen, "Democracy and Liberty."

7. Liberal proceduralist themes come to the fore in Thomas Christiano, *The Rule of the Many: Fundamental Issues in Democratic Theory* (Boulder, Colo.: Westview Press, 1996). Like the liberal proceduralist in the text, Christiano is not hostile to the deliberative theme but simply regards democratic deliberation as an obvious aspect of the operation of fair, liberal procedures.

8. The Asarco case is discussed in Robert B. Reich, "Policy Making in a Democracy," in *The Power of Public Ideas*, edited by Robert B. Reich (Cambridge: Ballinger, 1988), 123–56, and in Army Gutmann and Dennis Thompson, *Democracy and Disagreement* (Cambridge: Harvard University Press, 1996), 167–98.

9. The question about what follows listening is asked with reference to Habermas's conception of ideal discourse by John Patrick Diggins, *The Promise of Pragmatism: Modernism and the Crisis of Knowledge and Authority* (Chicago: University of Chicago Press, 1994), 445.

10. As I mentioned in the introduction, I take this point about the link between reasoning and truth-orientation from David M. Estlund, "Who's Afraid of Deliberative Democracy? On the Strategic/deliberative Dichotomy in Recent Constitutional Jurisprudence," *Texas Law Review* 71 (June 1993): 1437–77.

11. See Henry S. Richardson, *Practical Reasoning about Final Ends* (Cambridge, England: Cambridge University Press, 1994), 31.

12. Of course, as Popper's philosophy of science emphasized, a reasoner will also want to determine which propositions are false: see Karl R. Popper, *The Logic of Scientific Discovery*, rev. ed. New York: Harper and Row, 1968), chapter 4. My point is that the idea of reasoning must be understood by reference to the concept of truth.

13. For a defense and explication of the general practical "ought," see Richardson, *Practical Reasoning about Final Ends*, sec. 6.

14. I am here considering epistemic arguments for individuals to reason with one another, as opposed to epistemic arguments for other aspects of democratic procedures, such as majority rule. I discuss such arguments in chapter 15.

15. Aristotle, *Politics* 1281b1–23.

16. See, e.g., Karl Marx, *The German Ideology*, edited by C. J. Arthur (New York: International, 1970), 65–66.

17. James Bohman, *Public Deliberation: Pluralism, Complexity, and Democracy* (Cambridge: MIT Press, 1996), 27.

18. On the dangers of rhetorical bullying, see Diego Gambetta, " 'Claro': An Essay on Discursive Machismo," in *Deliberative Democracy*, edited by Jon Elster (Cambridge, England: Cambridge University Press, 1998), 19–43.

19. See Martha C. Nussbaum, *Love's Knowledge: Essays on Philosophy and Literature* (New York: Oxford University Press, 1990).

20. See, e.g., Iris Marion Young, "Communication and the Other: Beyond Deliberative Democracy," in *Democracy and Difference: Contesting the Boundaries of the Political*, edited by Seyla Benhabib (Princeton: Princeton University Press, 1996), 120–35; and John Dryzek, *Deliberative Democracy and Beyond: Liberals, Critics, Contestations* (Oxford: Oxford University Press, 2000), chap. 3. I discuss techniques for responding to difference in chapter 11.

21. John Broome, "Normative Requirements," in *Normativity*, edited by Jonathan Dancy (Oxford: Blackwell, 2000), has convinced me that not all the considerations that bear on what ought to be done are useful classified as reasons.

22. Marie Jean Antoine Nicolas de Caritat Condorcet, "A Survey of the Principles Underlying the Draft Constitution," translated and excerpted in *Condorcet: Foundations of Social Choice and Political Theory*, edited by Iain McLean and Fiona Hewitt (Aldershot, England: Elgar, 1994), 190–227. Lucid presentations of the theorem are given in David Estlund, "Opinion Leaders, Independence and Condorcet's Jury Theorem," *Theory and Decision* 36 (1994): 131–62; and in Christian List and Robert E. Goodin, "Epistemic Democracy: Generalizing the Condorcet Jury Theorem," *Journal of Political Philosophy* 9 (2001): 276–306.

23. List and Goodin, in "Epistemic Democracy," claim to have extended the Condorcet jury theorem to the multioption case.

24. Estlund, "Opinion Leaders," shows how the jury theorem can be extended to cases in which statistical independence fails. In brief, his suggestion is that majority rule can still be reliable so long as people are discriminating about whom they defer to.

25. It should be clear, here, that the ideal of treating citizens as self-originating sources of claims is an ideal commitment of democracy and not a thesis about the genesis of individuals' commitments or practical identity. In particular, contrary to the suggestion of Iris Marion Young, "Review of Nussbaum, *Sex and Social Justice*," *Ethics* 111 (2001): 821, it does not stand opposed to, say, feminist views that emphasize that individuals' practical identities cannot be understood apart from social context.

26. See, e.g., John Rawls, *Political Liberalism* (New York: Columbia University Press, 1996), and "The Idea of Public Reason Revisited," in *The Law of Peoples*

(Cambridge: Harvard University Press, 1999), 129–80; Bohman, *Public Deliberation*, chap. 2; Robert Audi and Nicholas Wolterstorff, *Religion in the Public Sphere: The Place of Religious Convictions in Political Debate* (Lanham, Md.: Rowman and Littlefield, 1997).

27. Gutmann and Thompson, *Democracy and Disagreement*, 64.
28. This is the direction in which Rawls moves in "The Idea of Public Reason Revisited," in *The Law of Peoples*, 129–80.
29. Gutmann and Thompson, *Democracy and Disagreement*, 79–80.

## CHAPTER 6

1. Thomas Christiano, *The Rule of the Many: Fundamental Issues in Democratic Theory* (Boulder, Colo.: Westview Press, 1996), 91.
2. In addition to the sources cited there, see the discussion of the principle of anonymity in William H. Riker, *Liberalism against Populism: A Confrontation between the Theory of Democracy and the Theory of Social Choice* (Prospect Heights, Ill.: Waveland Press, 1988 [reprint]), 51–56.
3. An exception, in this respect, is Jürgen Habermas, "Three Normative Models of Democracy," in *Inclusion of the Other: Studies in Political Theory* (Cambridge: MIT Press, 1998), 239–52.
4. Jürgen Habermas, *Moral Consciousness and Communicative Action*, translated by Christian Lenhardt and Shierry Weber Nicholsen, with an introduction by Thomas McCarthy (Cambridge: MIT Press, 1990), 88–89.
5. Joshua Cohen, "The Economic Basis of Deliberative Democracy," *Social Philosophy and Policy* 6, no. 2 (1989): 33.
6. James Bohman, *Public Deliberation: Pluralism, Complexity, and Democracy* (Cambridge: MIT Press, 1996), 120–21.
7. Ibid., 121–32.
8. Christiano, *The Rule of the Many*, 92, 93.
9. See John Rawls, *A Theory of Justice*, rev. ed. (Cambridge: Harvard University Press, 1999), 313; Cohen, "The Economic Basis of Deliberative Democracy." Bohman, too, turns to the background conditions in speaking about how to prevent political poverty: see Bohman, *Public Deliberation*, 131, 133.
10. Rawls, *A Theory of Justice*, 313.
11. Rawls has recently stressed the difference between a "welfare state" that aims simply to provide a minimum standard of living and a "property-owning democracy," the aim of which is to promote the steady dispersal of the ownership of capital and resources over time so as "to carry out the idea of society as a fair system of cooperation over time among citizens as free and equal persons." Rawls, *A Theory of Justice*, xv.
12. Here I draw on Bohman's adaptation of Sen's idea of capabilities in developing an account of political poverty: see Bohman, *Public Deliberation*, 123–132.
13. Rawls, *A Theory of Justice*, 197–200, 245–7, 313; John Rawls, *Political Liberalism* (New York: Columbia University Press, 1996), 318, 326–8.
14. Here I broach Plato's "ancient quarrel" with the rhetoricians: see his dialogues, the *Gorgias*, and *The Republic*. For direct rebuttal of Plato, see Martha C. Nuss-

baum, *Love's Knowledge: Essays on Philosophy and Literature* (New York: Oxford University Press, 1990), esp. 14–18. Habermas's opposition to rhetoric seems to rest on a number of mistaken conceptions. In part, it rests on an overly rigid use of the distinction between "illocutionary acts," the aim of which one accomplishes simply by saying what one says, and "perlocutionary acts" that have ulterior purposes such as persuasion or manipulation. As noted in Joseph Heath, *Communicative Action and Rational Choice* (Cambridge: MIT Press, 2000), 50, "in many cases it is very difficult to say where one component of the act stops and the other starts, making it hard to believe that these could constitute the goal states of two mutually exclusive action orientations."

15. Iris Marion Young, *Inclusion and Democracy* (Oxford: Oxford University Press, 2000), 67–69, mentions the ability of the art of rhetoric to tailor a message to a particular audience as one reason to regard it as having an important role in deliberative democracy. Making inconsistent promises, of course, is another matter altogether.

16. On Hitler's abuse of rhetoric, see Thomas Spragens, *Reason and Democracy* (Durham, N.C.: Duke University Press, 1990), cited by Young, *Inclusion and Democracy*, 63.

17. David Estlund, "Political Quality," *Social Philosophy and Policy* 17 (2000): 127–60.

18. See Young, *Inclusion and Democracy*, 70–7. The relatively novel idea would be for officials to organize fora to elicit life stories: television is full of unofficial fora that do that, albeit in a way that focuses on the lurid.

19. Here, I adapt Robert Nozick's famous argument that "liberty upsets patterns" to support a quite un-Nozickean conclusion about the importance of focusing on the basic political structure, which establishes background justice. See Robert Nozick, *Anarchy, State, and Utopia* (New York: Basic Books, 1974), 160–4.

## CHAPTER 7

1. Peter Oelbaum, "Munich's Electronic Timetable Information System," in *Transport for People with Mobility Handicaps: Information and Communication* (Strasbourg: European Conference of Ministers of Transport, 1991), 83–90.

2. Anne Crichton and Lyn Jongbloed, *Disability and Social Policy in Canada* (North York, Ontario: Captus Press, 1998).

3. Agneta Stahl and Per Gunnar Andersson, "Solutions in Sweden," in *Transport for People with Mobility Handicaps*, 91–9.

4. *Improving Transport for People with Mobility Handicaps* (Strasbourg: European Conference of Ministers of Transport, 1999).

5. Robert A. Katzmann, *Institutional Disability: The Saga of Transportation Policy for the Disabled* (Washington, D.C.: Brookings, 1986). As Katzmann makes clear at the opening of this book, he is concerned with the issue of bureaucratic domination from the perspective of populist democracy.

6. Ibid., 29.

7. An obligingly uncompromising version of this kind of argument against mandatory disability regulations is provided by Richard A. Epstein, *Forbidden*

*Grounds: The Case against Employment Discrimination Laws* (Cambridge: Harvard University Press, 1992). In the context of employment discrimination law, Epstein suggests that it would be more efficient to write checks to disabled persons than to require employers to make special accommodations for them.

8. Henry S. Richardson, *Practical Reasoning about Final Ends* (Cambridge, England: Cambridge University Press, 1994).

9. John Dewey, "Theory of Valuation," 1939; reprinted in *The Later Works, 1925–1953*, vol. 13, edited by Jo Ann Boydston (Carbondale: Southern Illinois University Press, 1988), 189–251.

10. See Martha C. Nussbaum, *Women and Human Development: The Capabilities Approach* (Cambridge, England: Cambridge University Press, 2000), 119–22.

11. One economist who has pled for a richer set of psychological categories is Amartya Sen: see, e.g., Amartya Sen, "Rational Fools," in *Choice, Welfare, and Measurement* (Cambridge: MIT Press, 1982), 84–106.

12. I will here be summarizing some aspects of my account in Richardson, *Practical Reasoning about Final Ends*, secs. 7, 13, 26.

13. There are complications. Mark Murphy has pointed out to me that there are some projects that we would undertake only because they realize two distinct goods. In such cases, I think it is open to us to frame an end that conjoins the two goods in question. Ends are psychological creatures, and are subject to being individuated the way we think about them.

14. Sen helpfully defines "antisymmetry" in Amartya K. Sen, *Collective Choice and Social Welfare*, (reprint, Amsterdam: North-Holland, 1984), 8. Thanks to Gopal Sreenivasan and our seminar for correction, here.

15. See Thomas E. Hill, Jr., *Respect, Pluralism, and Justice* (Oxford: Oxford University Press, 2000), 77–80. I am grateful to J. David Velleman for having raised the criticism to which I am here attempting to respond.

16. For a development of the contrast between teleological reasoning and reasoning that respects ideals, see, e.g., Elizabeth Anderson, *Value in Ethics and Economics* (Cambridge: Harvard University Press, 1993). I by no means deny that this contrast is important in many contexts, including sorting out the issues of objectification that preoccupy Anderson; I am simply pointing out that I have defined "final ends" broadly enough to encompass both sides of the contrast.

17. Martha Nussbaum has attempted to work out a conception of human flourishing of this sort that lists but also unifies the basic sorts of functioning that are essential to living a good human life. See, most recently, *Women and Human Development*, chap. 1. In her view, the responsibility of governments centers on assuring that each citizen has a threshold capability for functioning in each of the component ways. Against this focus on capabilities, I argue, in Henry S. Richardson, "Some Limitations of Nussbaum's Capabilities," *Quinnipiac Law Review* 19 (2000): 309–32, that governments ought sometimes to concern themselves directly with citizens' functioning. In the body of this book, however, I take no position on this question.

18. This much I concede to those, such as Sarah W. Broadie, *Ethics with Aristotle* (New York: Oxford University Press, 1991), who argue that our conception of an ultimate end does not play a useful role. In Richardson, *Practical Reasoning*

*about Final Ends*, chap. 10, I argue that we can and do deliberate about and from ultimate ends.

19. See, e.g., Anthony Kenny, *Will, Freedom and Power* (Oxford: Blackwell, 1975).

20. See Broadie, *Ethics with Aristotle*, 226.

21. Aristotle, *Nicomachean Ethics*, 1112b17.

22. In so reflecting, we are employing what Dewey, as in "The Need for Recovery in Philosophy," in *The Middle Works, 1899–1929*, edited by Jo Ann Boydston (1917; reprint, Carbondale: Southern Illinois University Press, 1980), 3–48, would call "practical intelligence" and Rawls would call "deliberative rationality," as in *A Theory of Justice* (Cambridge: Harvard University Press, 1971), 560.

23. See David Wiggins, "Deliberation and Practical Reason," in *Essays on Aristotle's Ethics*, edited by Amélie Oksenberg Rorty (1975–76; reprint, Berkeley: University of California Press, 1980), 241–66.

24. Aristotle and Aquinas both emphasize the importance of specifying norms. In modern times, see Aurel Kolnai, "Deliberation Is of Ends," in *Ethics, Value, and Reality: Selected Papers of Aurel Kolnai* (Indianapolis: Hackett, 1978), 44–62; and Wiggins, "Deliberation and Practical Reason." I define specification more precisely in "Specifying Norms as a Way to Resolve Concrete Ethical Problems," *Philosophy and Public Affairs* 19 (fall 1990): 279–310, and I clarify the relation between specification and other modes of interpreting norms in "Specifying, Balancing, and Interpreting Bioethical Principles," *Journal of Medicine and Philosophy* 25 (2000): 285–307.

25. I quote the relevant passage in Richardson, *Practical Reasoning about Final Ends*, 7.

26. For some elaboration of this point, see Henry S. Richardson, "Commensurability," in *Encyclopedia of Ethics*, edited by Lawrence Becker (New York: Routledge, 2001), 258–62.

27. Plato seems to take this position in the *Protagoras* and Aristotle in *De Anima*. Mill and Sidgwick are more definite. On their argument that commensurability is a prerequisite of rational choice, see Richardson, *Practical Reasoning about Final Ends*, sec. 18.

28. See Martha C. Nussbaum, *The Fragility of Goodness: Luck and Ethics in Greek Tragedy and Philosophy* (Cambridge, England: Cambridge University Press, 1986). I develop this argument for incommensurability in Richardson, *Practical Reasoning about Final Ends*, sec. 17.

29. For a rigorous and economical argument against thinking of all relevant practical considerations as reasons that might be weighed against one another, see John Broome, "Normative Requirements," in *Normativity*, edited by Jonathan Dancy (Oxford: Blackwell, 2000), 78–99.

30. Katzmann, *Institutional Disability*, 94.

31. Ibid., 113–4.

32. Ibid., 109.

33. Ibid., 115.

34. I here recast the politician example in Richardson, *Practical Reasoning about Final Ends*, 84.

35. Richardson, *Practical Reasoning about Final Ends*, sec. 26.
36. I argue this point in ibid., 180–2.
37. Thus I refrain from postulating that coherence provides a standard or index on the basis of which alternative revisions can be ranked. Elijah Millgram has recently complained that "without such an [index or standard], telling you to choose the most coherent [practical or theoretical] theory of the batch is telling you almost nothing" Elijah Millgram, "Coherence: The Price of the Ticket," *Journal of Philosophy* 97 (2000): 82. Because I think that is true I refrain from giving such advice. My reason for pointing to a basis of reasoning in coherence stems not from the clear guidance thereby to be obtained but from the fact, explained in the text, that coherence reasons (reasons of mutual fit) can be distinguished from the reasons embodied in an ordering of finality.

CHAPTER 8

1. Jürgen Habermas, *Between Facts and Norms: Contributions to a Discourse Theory of Law and Democracy*, translated by William Rehg (Cambridge: MIT Press, 1996), 298–99.
2. Herbert A. Simon, *Administrative Behavior: A Study of Decision-Making Processes in Administrative Organizations* (New York: Free Press, 1997), 65. Simon, however, is not a clear proponent of agency instrumentalism, for he recognizes that one cannot just say "Let the legislature make the value judgments and the administrative agencies make the factual ones."
3. For Weber's distinction between an instrumentally sensible "ethic of responsibility" and an "ethic of ultimate ends," see Max Weber, *From Max Weber*, edited by H. H. Gerth and C. Wright Mills (New York: Oxford University Press, 1974), 121.
4. Max Weber, *Economy and Society: An Outline of Interpretive Sociology*, translated by G. Roth and C. Wittich (Berkeley: University of California Press, 1968). In characterizing Weber as not allowing for rational deliberation about ends, I follow what I take to be the main thrust of his account of *Zweckrationalität*. As noted in *Stefan Gosepath, Aufgeklärtes Eigeninteresse* (Frankfurt: Suhrkamp, 1992), 36n., however, Weber's initial definition of *Zweckrationalität* in section 2 of *Economy and Society* purports also to embrace at least the weighing of ends against each other. In the account of bureaucracy into which this notion is incorporated, however, this further possibility for reason recedes from view.
5. Thomas Christiano, *The Rule of the Many: Fundamental Issues in Democratic Theory* (Boulder, Colo.: Westview Press, 1996), 216.
6. Thus, while I agree with David Schoenbrod, *Power without Responsibility: How Congress Abuses the People through Delegation* (New Haven: Yale University Press, 1993), that there is much that might be done to lessen the vagueness of statutes passed by the U.S. Congress, I believe he rests too much hope in the possibility of putting a stop to the delegation of lawmaking power.
7. See chapter 16 for a more exact statement of this requirement for limiting vagueness.

8. Aristotle, *Nicomachean Ethics*, translated by Terence Irwin (Indianapolis: Hackett, 1985), 1112b17.

## CHAPTER 9

1. Value incommensurability, combined with the cultural pluralism endemic to modern democracies, makes it essential to the approach I am now considering that it takes individuals' preferences as the inputs and constructs its index on that basis, rather than assessing costs and benefits on the basis of a candidate objective conception of welfare, as proposed, for instance, by Matthew D. Adler and Eric A. Posner, "Implementing Cost-Benefit Analysis When Preferences Are Distorted," in *Cost-Benefit Analysis: Legal, Economic, and Philosophical Perspectives*, edited by Matthew D. Adler and Eric A. Posner (Chicago: University of Chicago Press, 2001), 269–311.

2. The remainder of this chapter draws freely on Henry S. Richardson, "The Stupidity of the Cost-Benefit Standard," *Journal of Legal Studies* 29 (2000): 971–1003.

3. See Richard A. Epstein, *Forbidden Grounds: The Case against Employment Discrimination Laws* (Cambridge: Harvard University Press, 1992), 493–4.

4. Is there anyone who accords CBA this kind of importance as an underlying standard for policy-making? Judge Posner did at one point; see Richard A. Posner, *The Economics of Justice* (Cambridge: Harvard University Press, 1981). In his reply to an earlier version of this chapter, however, Posner retreats from defending CBA as a decision-making standard and instead insists on the point that I explicitly concede, that CBA is a useful tool of evaluation: Richard A. Posner, "Cost-Benefit Analysis: Definition, Justification, and Comment on Conference Papers," in Adler and Posner, *Cost-Benefit Analysis*, 338–40.

5. *See John Dewey, "The Need for Recovery in Philosophy," in The Middle Works, 1899–1929*, edited by Jo Ann Boydston (1917; reprint, Carbondale: Southern Illinois University Press, 1980), 3–48.

6. As will become apparent, it will not matter, for the purposes of my argument, whether the normative standard underlying CBA is put in terms of the sum of compensating variations or the sum of equivalent variations or, for that matter, simply in terms of the Marshallian demand curve. On these variations, see, e.g., Yew-Kwang Ng, *Welfare Economics: Introduction and Development of Basic Concepts* (London: MacMillan, 1983), 87–90. This mode of aggregation is similar in spirit to the Wicksell unanimity criterion I examined in chapter 3. In both cases, since all that needs to be shown is the *possibility* of compensating individuals so as to get everyone on board, distributive issues arise where the compensation is not actually carried out—especially when a project differentially impacts the rich and the poor: see, e.g., Cass R. Sunstein, "Cognition and Cost-Benefit Analysis," in Adler and Posner, *Cost-Benefit Analysis*, 250–1, 254.

7. Dewey describes "the continuum of end-means" in "Theory of Valuation," 1939; reprinted in *The Later Works, 1925–1953*, vol. 13, edited by Jo Ann Boydston (Carbondale: Southern Illinois University Press, 1988), sec. 6.

8. Amartya Sen, *Choice, Welfare, and Measurement* (Cambridge: MIT Press, 1982), 60–61.
9. See Elijah Millgram, *Practical Induction* (Cambridge: Harvard University Press, 1997).
10. Kenneth J. Arrow, "Utilities, Attitudes, Choices: A Review Note," in *Individual Choice under Certainty and Uncertainty*, in *Collected Papers of Kenneth J. Arrow* (Cambridge: Harvard University Press, 1984), 57.
11. See G. H. von Wright, *The Logic of Preference* (Edinburgh: Edinburgh University Press, 1963), 23.
12. My thanks to David Estlund for pointing out this possibility.
13. See, e.g., Elizabeth Anderson, *Value in Ethics and Economics* (Cambridge: Harvard University Press, 1993).
14. Since the focus of my attack is this fixity of CBA's informational base, the reader may feel that I have proved too much; for the *actual* Pareto improvement standard has the same informational base. And surely I am not against actual Pareto efficiency? My answer hinges on the distinction between preferences that are completely thought through and those that are not. I might concede that actual Pareto efficiency relative to completely-thought-through preferences would be an unassailable basis for approving of a proposal. What my discussion of the need for practical intelligence has highlighted, however, is that we always stand at some considerable distance from having completely-thought-through preferences. If we switch to a more realistic informational basis, then, and take preferences more-or-less as they are, then we should not accept that actual Pareto efficiency offers a sufficient or unassailable standard for policy decision.

CHAPTER 10

1. This tension between truth and deference is a version of the more general tension between agency and authority that is well articulated in Carol C. Gould, *Rethinking Democracy: Freedom and Social Cooperation in Politics, Economy, and Society* (Cambridge, England: Cambridge University Press, 1988), chap. 8.
2. In this paragraph, I explain the relatively narrow grounds on which I depart from the view defended in David Estlund, "Beyond Fairness and Deliberation: The Epistemic Dimension of Democratic Authority," in *Deliberative Democracy: Essays on Reason and Politics*, edited by James F. Bohman and William Rehg (Cambridge: MIT Press, 1997), 173–204, to which I am otherwise much indebted. According to Estlund, the procedure of a fair, democratic legislature is a reliable but imperfect way of getting at what justice (as the overriding political virtue?) requires but is a perfect procedure for producing legitimate results. For the reasons explained in the text, instead of making this cut between justice and legitimacy, I argue later in this chapter that, with respect to what we ought to do, democratic legislatures are neither pure procedures (for they are subject to check by independent standards) nor imperfect procedures (for their actions play a role in constituting what it is that we ought to do). Estlund's claim that a fair democratic legislature's judgment is quite reliable in discerning what we ought to do (or what is required by justice?) would provide an alter-

native basis to the one I offer for agencies putting tentative faith in their conclusions. I discuss his reliability argument in chapter 15.

3. See Richard Rorty, "Pragmatism, Davidson, and Truth," in *Objectivity, Relativism, and Truth* (Cambridge, England: Cambridge University Press, 1991), 128.

4. See, e.g., Hilary Putnam, *Reason, Truth and History* (Cambridge, England:
Cambridge University Press, 1981).

5. In Gilbert Harman and Judith Jarvis Thompson, *Moral Relativism and Moral
Objectivity* (Cambridge, Mass.: Blackwell, 1996), 41, Harman protests that such
disquotational truth-conditions are not "objective"; but he there has to admit
that he cannot pinpoint the significant difference between "objective" and "non-
objective" truth-conditions.

6. See C. J. Misak, *Truth and the End of Inquiry: A Peircean Account of Truth*
(Oxford: Oxford University Press, 1991), which, though defending an
"account" of truth along these Peircean lines, refrains for just this reason from
claiming that this is a "definition" of truth.

7. See, e.g., Donald Davidson, *Inquiries into Truth and Interpretation:* corrected
ed. (reprint, 1984, Oxford: Oxford University Press, 1986).

8. Here I build on Henry S. Richardson, "Truth and Ends in Dewey's Pragmatism," in *Pragmatism*, edited by Cheryl Misak (Calgary, Alberta: University of
Calgary Press, 2000), 109–47.

9. John McDowell has compellingly described one way to unite these three aspects
of truth in a single account. He claims that the idea of disquotation already
carries with it normativity: "What makes it correct among speakers of English
to make a claim with the words 'Snow is white' . . . is that snow is (indeed)
white"; "Toward Rehabilitating Objectivity," in *Rorty and His Critics*, edited
by Robert Brandom (Oxford: Blackwell, 2000), 116. Further, he points out (at
117), the cautionary "use" of "true" may be expressed by combining disquotation with negation and possibility operators: "Rorty's cautionary use is exemplified in a form of words such as ' "All life forms are carbon-based" may
not (after all) be true'; but one could achieve exactly the same effect by saying
'There may be (after all) some life forms that are not carbon based.' " While
McDowell's argument insightfully provides one way to knit the three aspects
together, it leans more heavily than he admits on our already understanding the
point of making correct assertions and avoiding false ones, the aim around which
our practices of inquiry are built. Accordingly, a complete account of truth
cannot actually rest on the disquotational aspect—the deflationary correspondence aspect—alone but must embed that aspect within a border understanding
of our practices of inquiry, and understanding that helps account for the normativity involved. While this disquotational aspect captures the aim of these
practices (to see things as they are), and the cautionary aspect reflects the ever-
present possibility of failure, the correspondence aspect is necessary to getting
going the idea of a practice having such a point.

10. Edna Ullmann-Margalit and Sidney Morgenbesser, "Picking and Choosing," *Social Research* 44 (1977): 757–85.

11. Immanuel Kant, *Groundwork of the Metaphysics of Morals*, translated by H. J.
Paton (New York: Harper and Row, 1964).

12. This point is, of course, debated: see the classic discussion in Philippa Foot,

"Morality as a System of Hypothetical Imperatives," in *Virtues and Vices and Other Essays in Moral Philosophy* (Berkeley: University of California Press, 1978), 157–73, and John McDowell, "Are Moral Requirements Hypothetical Imperatives?" in *Mind, Value, and Reality* (Cambridge: Harvard University Press, 1998), 77–94.

13. Compare Christine M. Korsgaard, "Self-Constitution in the Ethics of Plato and Kant," *Journal of Ethics* 3 (1999): 1–29. Compare, also, the way in which even a strategic conception of rationality depends on shared substantive beliefs—as is explained in Joseph Heath, "The Structure of Normative Control," *Law and Philosophy* 17 (1998): 419–42.

14. David M. Estlund, "Who's Afraid of Deliberative Democracy? On the Strategic/deliberative Dichotomy in Recent Constitutional Jurisprudence," *Texas Law Review* 71 (June 1993): 1449, makes this point effectively.

15. John Rawls, *A Theory of Justice* (Cambridge: Harvard University Press, 1971), 85–6.

16. A system of democratic republican government is described as an imperfect procedure, in just the sense employed in the text, in Philip Pettit, "Democracy, Electoral and Contestatory," in *Designing Democratic Institutions*, edited by Ian Shapiro and Stephen Macedo (New York: New York University Press, 2000), 137–8. I have criticized the independent criterion of correct political action on which Pettit bases this suggestion in chapter 3.

17. See Henry S. Richardson, "Democratic Intentions," in *Deliberative Democracy: Essays on Reason and Politics*, edited by James Bohman and William Rehg (Cambridge: MIT Press, 1997), 349–82. In the terms of Raz's discussion of authority in Joseph Raz, *The Morality of Freedom* (Oxford: Oxford University Press, 1986), chap. 2: I am not denying that "all authoritative directives should be based on reasons which already independently apply to the subjects of the directives and are relevant to their action in the circumstances governed by the directive" (47); I am asserting that democratic decisions, once taken, can generate new reasons.

18. What the couple *would* decide upon due deliberation is yet another factor that is independent of their actual deliberations, and we can easily imagine that the appeal to hypothetical deliberation, even idealized hypothetical deliberation, leaves matters indeterminate. Once serious deliberation about ends is allowed, there will be little temptation to suppose that the reasoning of an ideal deliberator can be axiomatized or otherwise captured in terms of criteria that would guarantee a determinate answer to every practical question, given full information.

19. Compare also the implications of an individual's conscientious beliefs about what her obligations are. I am greatly indebted, here, to my colleague Mark Murphy's work on that topic; see "The Conscience Principle," *Journal of Philosophical Research* 22 (1997): 387–407.

20. If I am right that the democratic processes are rightly regarded as normatively fruitful with respect to what we ought to do, this raises a further difficulty with attempts to defend the processes on the basis of their reliability concerning what we ought to do.

21. On authority as excluding a range of considerations, see Raz, *The Morality of Freedom*, 46.

## CHAPTER 11

1. Recent theories of deliberative democracy, in general, have come in for these sorts of criticism. On the tendency to suppose civility, see John Dryzek, *Deliberative Democracy and Beyond: Liberals, Critics, Contestations* (Oxford: Oxford University Press, 2000), chap. 3; but see David M. Estlund, "Deliberation Down and Dirty: Must Political Expression Be Civil?" in *The Boundaries of Freedom of Expression and Order in American Democracy*, edited by Thomas R. Hensley (Kent, Ohio: Kent State University Press, 2001), 49–67, for a deliberative theorist who accepts the importance of uncivil inputs. On the supposed tendency to minimize conflict, see Chantal Mouffe, *The Democratic Paradox* (London: Verso, 2000). And on the tendency to think that disinterested rationality can displace the exercise of power, see Jane Mansbridge, "Using Power/Fighting Power: The Polity," in *Democracy and Difference: Contesting the Boundaries of the Political*, edited by Seyla Benhabib (Princeton: Princeton University Press, 1996), 46–66.
2. Accommodation to disagreement is emphasized by Amy Gutmann and Dennis Thompson, *Democracy and Disagreement* (Cambridge: Harvard University Press, 1996), and by Thomas Christiano, "Justice and Disagreement at the Foundations of Political Authority," *Ethics* 110 (1999): 165–87. Lessening of disagreement is emphasized by Joshua Cohen, "Democracy and Liberty," in *Deliberative Democracy*, edited by Jon Elster (Cambridge, England: Cambridge University Press, 1998), 185–231, and Jürgen Habermas, *Between Facts and Norms: Contributions to a Discourse Theory of Law and Democracy*, translated by William Rehg (Cambridge: MIT Press, 1996).
3. For a philosophical discussion of the nature of disability, see Anita Silvers, "(In)Equality, (Ab)Normality, and the Americans with Disabilities Act," *Journal of Medicine and Philosophy* 21 (1996): 209–24.
4. In Henry S. Richardson, "The Stupidity of the Cost-Benefit Standard," *Journal of Legal Studies* 29 (2000): 971–1003, and in earlier versions of this chapter, I used the label "principled compromise." That phrase, however, misleadingly suggests that the compromise is honorable or morally sound. Rather, I have in mind compromise that goes to the level of ends; whether it is honorable or sound is a separate question. I am grateful to Scott J. Shapiro for discussion of the terminology and of the concepts involved.
5. I am grateful to Susan Wolf for pressing me to make these distinctions.
6. Diego Gambetta, " 'Claro': An Essay on Discursive Machismo," in Elster, *Deliberative Democracy* (Cambridge, England: Cambridge University Press, 1998), 19.
7. This and the following two definitions are based on those in Richardson, "The Stupidity of the Cost-Benefit Standard."
8. J. Patrick Dobel, *Compromise and Political Action: Political Morality in Liberal and Democratic Life* (Savage, Md.: Rowman and Littlefield, 1990), chap. 4, ar-

gues for the political virtues of compromise that extends to the level of ends and moral commitments. Dobel does not define this sort of compromise in the two-level way that I do, but the spirit of his discussion is much the same.

9. Arthur Kuflik, "Morality and Compromise," in *Compromise in Ethics, Law, and Politics,* edited by J. Roland Pennock and John W. Chapman (New York: New York University Press, 1979), 38–65, suggests that while compromise typically involves both a process of give-and-take and a result characterizable as involving mutual concession, the notion of a compromise is sufficiently flexible that one or the other of these features may be sufficient. Martin Benjamin, *Splitting the Difference: Compromise and Integrity in Ethics and Politics* (Lawrence: University Press of Kansas, 1990) is more restrictive. Benjamin argues that a result found mutually satisfactory, because a "synthesis" of the initial positions, should not be counted as a compromise (7). I suggest, however, that it is a mistake to lump all results found mutually satisfactory under this one heading, for this ignores types of give-and-take and mutual concession that can have preceded despite the mutual satisfactoriness of the result. Renouncing some of one's ends in response to the arguments and needs of the other can also be a kind of concession. Thus, what I'm calling "deep compromise" would count as compromise on Kuflik's permissive analysis and should also count as a compromise on a more sensitive version of the stricter test, in which both mutual give-and-take and a result involving "concession" are taken to be necessary features.

10. On the other side of the debate about gay marriage, it is not so clear that deep compromise either has occurred or is called for. Probably the acceptance of the compromise by most advocates of gay marriage was simply strategic, representing a realistic acceptance of what is now politically feasible. Further, many of these advocates are unwilling to frame their goal around the traditional institution of marriage, and would prefer to pressure legislators to reform the whole institution.

11. The classic discussion is Jon Elster, *Sour Grapes: Studies in the Subversion of Rationality* (Cambridge, England: Cambridge University Press, 1983), chap. 3. It is no easy matter to devise a filter that will rule out all cases of sour grapes yet allow for adequate opportunity for learning from experience. Indeed, it is not fully clear where the conceptual difference between the two is supposed to lie. The test of reflective acceptance of the process of adaptation or change will at least rule out the most egregious cases of self-deception. While there are, indeed, worries about individual autonomy that attend any case of potential sour grapes adaptation, these attend any adaptation of preferences and commitments to circumstance and not just ones that flow from one's respect or concern for others. So any account of practical reasoning, and not just a democratic one, will need to develop a distinction between self-deceptive and pathological cases of sour grapes and beneficial and open-eyed learning from experience. I do not try to develop such an account here; but I would assert that the line cannot be drawn without drawing on substantive assumptions about the good.

12. This theme is importantly discussed in Isaiah Berlin, "On the Pursuit of the Ideal," *New York Review of Books,* March 17, 1988, 11–18, and Michael Walzer,

"Political Action: The Problem of Dirty Hands," *Philosophy and Public Affairs* 2 (1973): 160–80.

13. Michael J. Sandel, *Liberalism and the Limits of Justice* (Cambridge, England: Cambridge University Press, 1982), 183.

14. Pessimistic individualism seems endemic to contemporary political science, in which game theory is all the rage.

15. Rousseau, of course, pursued the metaphor of the body politic; and think of the way "realists" in foreign policy deploy the idea of "national interest."

16. Benjamin Constant and Alexis de Tocqueville famously worried about conformism as a deleterious effect in politics, while John Stuart Mill and Karl Popper worried about the repression of individuality by the coercive power of the state.

17. See, e.g., Martha C. Nussbaum, "Aristotelian Social Democracy," in *Liberalism and the Good*, edited by R. Bruce Douglass, Gerald M. Mara, and Henry S. Richardson (New York: Routledge, 1990), 203–52.

18. For a fuller defense of the claim that motivation readily transfers via specification, see Henry S. Richardson, *Practical Reasoning about Final Ends* (Cambridge, England: Cambridge University Press, 1994), sec. 11.

19. Thus, Bohman is wrong to claim that the " 'fact of pluralism' is what makes majority rule necessary to conclude real deliberation"; *Public Deliberation: Pluralism, Complexity, and Democracy* (Cambridge: MIT Press, 1996), 180.

20. I take the example from Dobel, *Compromise and Political Action*, 184.

21. See, e.g., Martha C. Nussbaum, "Skepticism about Practical Reason in Literature and the Law," *Harvard Law Review* 107, no. 3 (January 1994): 714–44.

22. See, e.g., the perfectionist liberalism of Joseph Raz, *The Morality of Freedom* (Oxford: Oxford University Press, 1986).

23. Gerald F. Gaus, "Reason, Justification, and Consensus: Why Democracy Can't Have It All," in *Deliberative Democracy: Essays on Reason and Politics*, edited by James Bohman and William Rehg (Cambridge: MIT Press, 1997), 231, seems to imply that a process of negotiation, such as might be aimed at compromise, cannot be truth-oriented. That he excludes this possibility may be a result of his not recognizing the possibility of deep compromise: see Gerald F. Gaus, *Justificatory Liberalism: An Essay on Epistemology and Political Theory* (New York: Oxford University Press, 1996), 272.

24. Compare John Rawls, *Political Liberalism* (New York: Columbia University Press, 1996), 139, which refers to "the very great values" of the political, around which he builds a conception of objectivity. Whereas Rawls aims to build on precepts that, he hopes, "we do, in fact, accept," my hope is more conditional. I aim to build on precepts that we must accept if we are taking seriously this whole question about how best to conceive of democratic deliberation and rule by the people. I accept these precepts, have argued for them briefly, and hope that my readers accept them, too; but I do not assume that all my readers do.

25. For elaborate psychological arguments that serve to back up this commonsensical claim (while also trying to do much more), see John Rawls, *A Theory of Justice*, rev. ed. (Cambridge: Harvard University Press, 1999), part 3.

26. See Sarah Buss, "Appearing Respectful: The Moral Significance of Manners," *Ethics* 109 (1999): 795–826.

27. As Rawls suggests, under these conditions, a shared acceptance of fundamental terms of fair political cooperation may suffice to ground the existence of "a people" that is ethnically and doxastically diverse; *The Law of Peoples* (Cambridge: Harvard University Press, 1999), 25.

28. The great example of work specifying the ideals of freedom, equality, and autonomy in a coherent and powerful fashion without presupposing or generating any commensurating value is, of course, Rawls, *A Theory of Justice*. For a description of that work that makes this apparent, see Henry S. Richardson, "Beyond Good and Right: Toward a Constructive Ethical Pragmatism," *Philosophy and Public Affairs* 24 (1995): 108–41.

29. In Richardson, *Practical Reasoning about Final Ends*, chaps. 6–13, addressing the question of whether deep disagreement blocks rational deliberation about ends, I argued that general considerations of holism in understanding guarantee that there will always be such an opening for rational deliberation to get a foothold, granting sufficient mutual concern or goodwill. In the case I was discussing there, which involved a dispute over the treatment of female rape complaints between a Western liberal and a traditionally minded Pakistani Muslim, this condition of mutual concern and respect was trivially satisfied, or perhaps, rather, substituted for by the fact that the discussion was limited to the case of a single person who had internalized both sets of values. For some reason to doubt the general considerations about interpreting others that I was there deploying, see Gopal Sreenivasan, "Understanding Alien Morals," *Philosophy and Phenomenological Research* 62 (2001): 1–32. In the text, I do not claim that such an opening is *always* available, just that deep disagreement does not preclude mutual deliberation leading to deep compromise.

30. I borrow the idea of basic commitments that are "thick, but vague" from Nussbaum, "Aristotelian Social Democracy," 217.

CHAPTER 12

1. That is, practical reasoning that fails to issue in an intention is defective. This section is adapted from the latter part of Henry S. Richardson, "Democratic Intentions," in *Deliberative Democracy: Essays on Reason and Politics*, edited by James Bohman and William Rehg (Cambridge: MIT Press, 1997), 349–82.

2. Annette Baier, *The Commons of the Mind: The Paul Carus Lecture, Series 19* (Chicago: Open Court 1997), decries the tendency toward individualism in the philosophy of mind.

3. See Sarah W. Broadie, *Ethics with Aristotle* (New York: Oxford University Press, 1991), 226.

4. James Bohman, *Public Deliberation: Pluralism, Complexity, and Democracy* (Cambridge: MIT Press, 1996) develops the importance of publicity constraints in a deliberative context.

5. I owe this way of thinking of a joint intention to Raimo Tuomela, who has studied it extensively. See, e.g., Raimo Tuomela, "We Will Do It: An Analysis of Group-Intentions," *Philosophy and Phenomenological Research* 51 (1991): 249–77, and Raimo Tuomela, *Cooperation: A Philosophical Study* (Dordrecht:

Kluwer, 2000). Building in a layer of common knowledge is appropriate in a democratic setting, which aims at publicity. For a sparer analysis of joint action that centers solely on the idea of individuals intending to do their parts, see Christopher Kutz, "Acting Together," *Philosophy and Phenomenological Research* 61 (2000): 1–31.

6. On the centrality of such conditional commitment to shared action, see Margaret Gilbert, *On Social Facts* (Princeton: Princeton University Press, 1989), 199.

7. John Rawls, *A Theory of Justice* (Cambridge: Harvard University Press, 1971), 560.

8. Or, to be pedantic, each vote is what would be an acceptance if enough other people vote the same way. The vote is a performative act of communication, as noted in Thomas Christiano, "Voting and Democracy," *Canadian Journal of Philosophy* 25, no. 3 (September 1995): 395–414; but what is accomplished by it obviously depends on what other people do.

9. See Jean-Jacques Rousseau, *The Social Contract and Discourses*, translated by G. D. H. Cole (New York: Dutton, 1973), III.xiii, p. 237.

10. See Michael E. Bratman, "Shared Cooperative Activity," *Philosophical Review* 101 (1992): 327–41.

11. Michael Bratman, "Shared Intention and Mutual Obligation," in *Faces of Intention: Selected Essays of Intention and Agency* (Cambridge, England: Cambridge University Press, 1999), 130–41. I postpone until the following section discussion of Bratman's further, important proviso that each must have "meshing subplans"—compatible ideas about how they will do their parts in carrying out the overall plan—that are part of the basis of their agreement.

12. The assurance possibility is discussed in Bratman, "Shared Intention and Mutual Obligation," with reference to T. M. Scanlon, "Promises and Practices," *Philosophy and Public Affairs* 19 (1990): 199–226. The possibility of supplementing assurance with reliance as an additional element of agreement I draw from contract law. I gloss over some of the interesting complexity of Scanlon's "principle of fidelity," which Bratman discusses more fully. I am not aiming at a descriptively reductive analysis of the origins of a normative claim; rather, I am attempting to describe enough about the normatively relevant features of joint deliberation to allow us to recognize in a rough way—given some general views we share about our obligations—how obligations enter in. If we do so, I shall suggest, we shall see how a mutual responsiveness is essential to the process. I am indebted to Matthias Kettner for discussion of this question.

13. Somewhat different versions of the possibility of agreement on what is to be done but not on the grounds for doing it have been put forward by John Rawls, *Political Liberalism* (New York: Columbia University Press, 1996), chap. 4 ("overlapping consensus"); Cass R. Sunstein, *Legal Reasoning and Political Conflict* (New York: Oxford University Press, 1996), chap. 2; and Fred D'Agostino, *Free Public Reason: Making It Up as We Go* (New York: Oxford University Press, 1996), 30 ("convergent justification").

14. See Bratman, "Shared Cooperative Activity."

15. Put side-by-side with the point made at the beginning of this section about the importance, given pluralism, of reaching agreements on actions without always pushing for agreement on ends or rationale, what I am saying is that some

agreement on final ends is needed but that pushing for full agreement on final ends will be vain and probably counterproductive.

## CHAPTER 13

1. For an indication of some dimensions of the variety of democratic regimes, see Arend Lijphart, *Patterns of Democracy: Government Forms and Performance in Thirty-Six Countries* (New Haven: Yale University Press, 1999). Because democracy as democratic autonomy embraces a republican insistence on dispersing and checking power and because I defend (in the following chapter) proportional representation, the view defended here more closely resembles the "consensus democracy" Lijphart prefers than the "Westminster democracy" to which he opposes it.

2. Since my interest is ultimately in the nature of holistic reflection by the entire body of citizens, I steer clear of talk of "the many particular and diverse publics appearing in modern mass democracies"; Iris Marion Young, *Inclusion and Democracy* (Oxford: Oxford University Press, 2000), 69. The point Young is there making could be made using the term "audience."

3. John Dewey, *The Public and Its Problems* (Athens, Ohio: Ohio University Press, 1991), 37.

4. On the distinction between the ancient doctrine of the *res publica* and the modern conception of the public good, see Stephen Holmes, *Benjamin Constant and the Making of Modern Liberalism* (New Haven: Yale University Press, 1984).

5. See, e.g., Gerald F. Gaus, *Justificatory Liberalism: An Essay on Epistemology and Political Theory* (New York: Oxford University Press, 1996), 121 (public reasoning as generating beliefs "justified from the standpoint of everyone"), and Fred D'Agostino, *Free Public Reason: Making It Up as We Go* (New York: Oxford University Press, 1996), 6–7. Interestingly, Rawls puts forward a less individualistic and more structural notion of public reasoning when he writes that the "reason" of a political society is its "way of formulating its plans, of putting its ends in an order of priority and of making its decisions accordingly"; *Political Liberalism* (New York: Columbia University Press, 1996), 212. That gloss of a society's reason is oddly permissive; some ways of collectively formulating plans and setting priorities would not count as exercizes in reason. Collective priorities might be set by lottery, for instance.

6. I do not mean to imply that those cited in note 5 fail to account for such mutual addressing of reasons in their views; it is just that their working definitions of a public fail to carry this implication.

7. In Immanuel Kant, *Perpetual Peace and Other Essays*, translated by Ted Humphrey (Indianapolis: Hackett, 1983), 135 (Ak. 381), Kant puts forward as "the transcendental formula of public right" the proposition that "all actions that affect the rights of other men are wrong if their maxim is not consistent with publicity." This is to put forward a hypothetical publicity standard, as we must ask, regarding any given policy, whether it *would* be consistent with publicity. This is not to say, of course, that one cannot build a moral case for actual

publicity in the conduct of policy-making on a Kantian basis. For a full exploration of the requirements of publicity in this sense of making deliberations public, see Amy Gutmann and Dennis Thompson, *Democracy and Disagreement* (Cambridge: Harvard University Press, 1996), chap. 3.

8. Dewey, *The Public and Its Problems*, 77. I differ somewhat with Dewey's description of the reason the public needs "weight." He there writes that the weight is needed with regard to the selection of representatives. To the contrary, in my so-far unidirectional and in this respect uncontroversial story, I take it that individuals as such have weight—equal weight—in the selection of representatives and that it is they, and not "the public," who need to be represented. Where "the public" does need to be represented, in my view, is in the more diffuse channels of political reflection to be described in this chapter.

9. Compare the sort of awareness described by Rawls's first-level characterization of the idea of publicity: "This level is achieved when society is effectively regulated by public principles of justice: citizens accept and know that others likewise accept those principles, and this knowledge in turn is publicly recognized." *Political Liberalism* (New York: Columbia University Press, 1993), 66.

10. The idea that the public is a forum for the assessment of reasons has been powerfully developed by Habermas, according to whom a public space opens up whenever individuals encounter each other not merely strategically but in the mode of seeking an agreement on the basis of reasons that they mutually recognize as valid and acceptable reasons. Jürgen Habermas, *Between Facts and Norms: Contributions to a Discourse Theory of Law and Democracy*, translated by William Rehg (Cambridge): MIT Press, 1996), 361, 119.

11. See Joseph Heath, *Communicative Action and Rational Choice* (Cambridge: MIT Press, 2000), who reconstructs Habermas's distinction between the strategic and the communicative in an illuminating fashion, reinforcing the need for an initial agreement in norms even while defending Habermas's style of transcendental argument.

12. Compare the characterization of the "epistemic populist's" conditions for the existence of a popular will in Joshua Cohen, "An Epistemic Conception of Democracy," *Ethics* 97 (October 1986): 26–38.

13. The account of the public I give in the text is a brief sketch. For a detailed account of the historical evolution of the institution of a public—albeit one more oriented by the aim of distinguishing "public" from "private" than the one here—see Jürgen Habermas, *The Structural Transformation of the Public Sphere: An Inquiry into a Category of Bourgeois Society* (Cambridge: MIT Press, 1989).

14. On the links between fundamental liberties and a deliberative conception of democracy, see Joshua Cohen, "Democracy and Liberty," in *Deliberative Democracy*, edited by Jon Elster (Cambridge, England: Cambridge University Press, 1998), 185–231.

15. For a nuanced and persuasive discussion of these exceptions to publicity requirements, see Gutmann and Thompson, *Democracy and Disagreement*, chap. 3.

16. See Holmes, *Benjamin Constant*, 243.

17. Gutmann and Thompson, *Democracy and Disagreement*, 79–85. In what fol-

lows, I simply recast Gutmann and Thompson's characterizations of these civic virtues in my own terms so as to link them with my account of deliberative democracy.

18. If we confine ourselves just to the virtues that seem necessary supports of democratic deliberation, it seems possible that this open-mindedness could be quite unevenly distributed among the citizenry. Democratic deliberation can exist without it satisfying all of the requirements of fairness and reasonableness.

19. On the theme of unintended effects, see Peter Breiner, "Democratic Autonomy, Political Ethics, and Moral Luck," *Political Theory* 17 (1989): 550–74.

20. In emphasizing that an account of democratic deliberation depends on the interaction of the formal institutions of representative government with the informal public sphere, I follow the otherwise rather different account in Habermas, *Between Facts and Norms*, especially chaps. 7–8.

21. The connections between emotions and practical judgment that I assume in the text, while not universally accepted by philosophers, are nonetheless not particularly controversial. The connection between emotions and ends, for instance, is accepted both by Aristotle, who believes in cognitive practical judgment, and Hume, who does not. That practical judgments involve emotions is well argued, e.g., by Michael Stocker, "Emotional Thoughts," *American Philosophical Quarterly* 24 (1987): 59–69. This conclusion can hold true independently of whether one also accepts the stronger Stoic thesis, revived by Martha Nussbaum, that certain emotions are identical with certain practical judgments. See Martha C. Nussbaum, *Upheavals of Thought: The Intelligence of Emotions* (Cambridge, England: Cambridge University Press, 2001).

22. It is because emotions can be essential to what is said that I have avoided describing or defining rhetoric as concerned with *how* something is said as opposed to *what* is said—as it is, for instance, by Young, *Inclusion and Democracy*, 64–5. Of course rhetoric is concerned with how things are said; but it concedes too much to noncognitivist views of the emotions (see note 21) to suppose that how something is said can be separated from what is said.

23. For criticism of the ideal of the "cool hour," see Martha C. Nussbaum, *Love's Knowledge: Essays on Philosophy and Literature* (New York: Oxford University Press, 1990), especially 335–64.

24. See Richardson, *Practical Reasoning about Final Ends* (Cambridge, England: Cambridge University Press, 1994), sec. 27.

25. For the moment, at least; I do not mean to take a stand, here, against the possibility of reflective deliberators made of silicon and steel.

26. Young, *Inclusion and Democracy*, 65.

CHAPTER 14

1. Bernard Manin, *The Principles of Representative Government* (Cambridge, England: Cambridge University Press, 1997), 192.

2. See ibid., 163.

3. Ibid., 169, 175.

4. See Thomas Christiano, *The Rule of the Many: Fundamental Issues in Democratic Theory* (Boulder, Colo.: Westview Press, 1996), 233.

5. For additional objections to reliance on referenda, see Philip Pettit, "Democracy, Electoral and Contestatory," in *Designing Democratic Institutions*, edited by Ian Shapiro and Stephen Macedo (New York: New York University Press, 2000), 134.

6. The importance of such publicity, and the kinds of secrecy exceptions to which it is subject, is well discussed in Amy Gutmann and Dennis Thompson, *Democracy and Disagreement* (Cambridge: Harvard University Press, 1996), chap. 3.

7. I refer to the median voter theorem, which is discussed with considerable nuance in Geoffrey Brennan and Alan Hamlin, *Democratic Devices and Desires* (Cambridge, England: Cambridge University Press, 2000).

8. See Anne Phillips, *The Politics of Presence* (Oxford: Oxford University Press, 1995), 41–42.

9. Hence even if the pull toward the median survives multiple dimensions of difference, it will be sharply attenuated by the constant arising of new dimensions. For references to some of the relevant theoretical findings, see William H. Riker, *Liberalism against Populism: A Confrontation between the Theory of Democracy and the Theory of Social Choice* (Prospect Heights, Ill.: Waveland Press, 1988 [reprint]), 62.

10. Hanna Fenichel Pitkin, *The Concept of Representation* (Berkeley: University of California Press, 1971), 86.

11. Ibid., 79.

12. Compare Christiano, who speaks of the "equal" representation of citizens' "views": *The Rule of the Many*, 91. Since which views people actually have will depend on the system of representation in force, we here see again the incoherence of the radical democratic hope that democracy might go "all the way down." This influence on views of the process of course does not imply, however, that any system of representation fairly represents the views of the people it represents.

13. Brennan and Hamlin, *Democratic Devices and Desires*, chap. 9. I adapt the argument somewhat to fit my own framework. Brennan, it will be recalled, was one of the main proponents of the theory of expressive voting.

14. Ibid., 180.

15. This question of the appropriate size for a representative assembly is raised by Jeremy Waldron, *The Dignity of Legislation* (Cambridge, England: Cambridge University Press, 1999), 80.

16. See Lani Guinier, *The Tyranny of the Majority* (New York: Free Press, 1994).

17. See Charles R. Beitz, *Political Equality: An Essay in Democratic Theory* (Princeton: Princeton University Press, 1989) and the discussion of this argument in Phillips, *The Politics of Presence*, 50–1.

18. The relevant "voting power" literature is summarized in Brennan and Hamlin, *Democratic Devices and Desires*, 197.

19. Iris Marion Young, *Inclusion and Democracy* (Oxford: Oxford University Press, 2000), 133–41.

20. For acceptance, from a totally different perspective, of this idea that voters respond to candidates as concrete persons, see Brennan and Hamlin, *Democratic Devices and Desires*, 178.
21. This argument for special measures to compensate for oppression is developed by Will Kymlicka, *Multicultural Citizenship* (Oxford: Oxford University Press, 1995), chap. 7, and by Young, *Inclusion and Democracy*, 141–8.

CHAPTER 15

1. For a lucid discussion of classic views on the naturalness and fairness, or artificiality and arbitrariness, of majority rule, see Jeremy Waldron, *The Dignity of Legislation* (Cambridge, England: Cambridge University Press, 1999).
2. Whether the requirement of giving legislators equal political resources is compatible, say, with a seniority system in the awarding of key committee posts is not a straightforward question. The matter of seniority bears on how a party's political position evolves, with some continuity, over time. It is important for democratic deliberation that parties articulate political positions; and some employment of seniority preferment may help with this process.
3. In understanding majority rule as an element in a concretely institutionalized process, rather than as a social choice function, I follow Elaine Mates Spitz, "Majority Rule: The Virtue of Numbers," *Ethics* 89 (1978): 113.
4. William H. Riker, *Liberalism against Populism: A Confrontation between the Theory of Democracy and the Theory of Social Choice* (Prospect Heights, Ill.: Waveland Press, 1988 [reprint]). See my discussion of Riker in chapter 4.
5. For discussion of the ways existing legislatures channel the use of majority rule see Joseph M. Bessette, *The Mild Voice of Reason: Deliberative Democracy and American National Government* (Chicago: University of Chicago Press, 1994). On my desk, I have a plaque awarded to my father in December 1994 for his leadership "in the fight to restore majority rule to the U.S. Senate." This highlights the degree to which other devices besides majority rule are at work in most actual legislative bodies.
6. Douglas W. Rae, "Decision-Rules and Individual Values in Constitutional Choice," *American Political Science Review* 63 (1969): 40–56, cited in Robert A. Dahl, *Democracy and Its Critics* (New Haven: Yale University Press, 1989), 138. See also Carol C. Gould, *Rethinking Democracy: Freedom and Social Cooperation in Politics, Economy, and Society* (Cambridge, England: Cambridge University Press, 1988), 236, and David Estlund, "Jeremy Waldron on Law and Disagreement," *Philosophical Studies* 99 (2000): 120–1.
7. Dahl, *Democracy and Its Critics*, 140.
8. Michael J. Sheeran, *Beyond Majority Rule: Voteless Decisions in the Religious Society of Friends*, 2d ed. (Philadelphia: Philadelphia Yearly Meeting of the Religious Society of Friends, 1996).
9. See Richard Wollheim, "A Paradox in the Theory of Democracy," in *Philosophy, Politics, and Society, Second Series*, edited by Peter Laslett and W. G. Runciman. (Oxford: Blackwell, 1969), 73, who presents this interpretation of "rule by the people" as rather commonsensical.

10. See Frank I. Michelman, "How Can the People Ever Make the Laws? A Critique of Deliberative Democracy," in *Deliberative Democracy: Essays on Reason and Politics*, edited by James Bohman and William Rehg (Cambridge: MIT Press, 1997), n. 9. Although Michelman purports to find a version of this thought in Richard Parker, his quotation from Parker actually reveals him to be asserting that "there is no such entity as 'the majority.' "

11. The problem of such a minority is a concern of Arend Lijphart, *Patterns of Democracy: Government Forms and Performance in Thirty-Six Countries* (New Haven: Yale University Press, 1999), especially 31–2. On the importance of civic virtue, see William A. Galston, *Liberal Purposes: Goods, Virtues, and Diversity in the Liberal State* (Cambridge, England: Cambridge University Press, 1991), and Amy Gutmann and Dennis Thompson, *Democracy and Disagreement* (Cambridge: Harvard University Press, 1996), especially 81–85. The idea of social capital, in the sense referred to here, was influentially set out in Robert Putnam, "Bowling Alone: America's Declining Social Capital," *Journal of Democracy* 6 (1995): 65–78. See also Mark E. Warren, ed., *Democracy and Trust* (Cambridge, England: Cambridge University Press, 1999).

12. See, e.g., Michael J. Sandel, *Democracy's Discontent: America in Search of a Public Philosophy* (Cambridge: Harvard University Press, 1996).

13. Russell Hardin, "Trustworthiness," *Ethics* 107 (1996): 26–42.

14. See, e.g., Lawrence C. Becker, "Trust as Noncognitive Security about Motives," *Ethics* 107 (1996): 43–61.

15. Hence my liberalism is more Rawlsian than Hobbesian in its assumptions about human motivation.

16. I allude, of course, to Rawls's magisterial account of such matters in *A Theory of Justice*, rev. ed. (Cambridge: Harvard University Press, 1999).

17. David Estlund, "Beyond Fairness and Deliberation: The Epistemic Dimension of Democratic Authority," in *Deliberative Democracy: Essays on Reason and Politics*, edited by James F. Bohman and William Rehg (Cambridge: MIT Press, 1997), 173–204. While Estlund emphasizes that the reliability of majority procedures goes to matters of justice and hence helps build a case for taking those procedures to be dispositive of legitimacy, it is not clear to me why justice should be singled out among other virtues of political institutions or how Estlund's appeal to Condorcet's jury theorem limits reliability to considerations of justice. The argument depends on citizens being minimally reliable when they vote. When they do, justice will presumably be but one consideration among many bearing upon what they think we ought to do.

18. There is a long tradition of debate about the democratic appeal to the jury theorem. John Stuart Mill was critical of the theorem's relevance to democracy. Others more optimistic include Brian Barry, "The Public Interest," *Proceedings of the Aristotelian Society* suppl. vol. 38 (1964): 1–18; Arthur Kuflik, "Majority Rule Procedure," in *Due Process: Nomos XVIII*, edited by J. Roland Pennock and John W. Chapman (New York: New York University Press, 1977), 296–322; and Elaine Spitz, *Majority Rule* (Chatham, N.J.: Chatham House, 1984), 206.

19. On the potential epistemic downside of political equality, see David Estlund, "Political Quality," *Social Philosophy and Policy* 17 (2000): 127–60.

20. David Estlund, "Opinion Leaders, Independence and Condorcet's Jury Theorem," *Theory and Decision* 36 (1994): 131–62.
21. Christian List and Robert E. Goodin, "Epistemic Democracy: Generalizing the Condorcet Jury Theorem," *Journal of Political Philosophy* 9 (2001): 276–306.
22. The assumption of voter competence can take different forms, depending on the other assumptions used in proving a version of the theorem. In the plurality extension of the theorem in List and Goodin, "Epistemic Democracy," for instance, one of their proofs, for a situation with $k$ options, goes through on the assumption that each individual is better than $1/k$ reliable.
23. As Bernard Manin, *The Principles of Representative Government* (Cambridge, England: Cambridge University Press, 1997), chaps. 3 and 4, shows, this is the classic basis for preferring representative government to selection by lot. For a modern argument based on the expressive theory of voting, see Geoffrey Brennan and Alan Hamlin, *Democratic Devices and Desires* (Cambridge, England: Cambridge University Press, 2000), chap. 9.
24. Estlund is careful to note this point: see Estlund, "Beyond Fairness and Deliberation," 189.
25. I allude to Habermas's endorsement to the "solution" to the problem of the compatibility between majority rule and truth-orientation that originated in the work of the nineteenth-century political philosopher Julius Fröbel. See Jürgen Habermas, *Between Facts and Norms: Contributions to a Discourse Theory of Law and Democracy*, translated by William Rehg (Cambridge: MIT Press, 1996), 613; compare 179.
26. I focus on the case in which the minority has already focused on considerations of the public good and has a different view about what is in the public good than does the majority. This is a different and, in some ways, more difficult case than the one considered in Philip Pettit, "Democracy, Electoral and Contestatory," in *Designing Democratic Institutions*, edited by Ian Shapiro and Stephen Macedo (New York: New York University Press, 2000), 131, in which the minority had voted their narrow self-interest and can be later brought to see the legitimacy of the decision by getting them to consider the matter from the point of view of the public good.
27. For earlier treatments of the position of the losing voters, see Wollheim, "A Paradox in the Theory of Democracy." and David L. Estlund, "The Persistent Puzzle of the Minority Democrat," *American Philosophical Quarterly* 26, no. 2 (April 1989): 143–51.
28. Here, the distinction between justice (or what ought to be done?) and legitimacy in Estlund, "Beyond Fairness and Deliberation," comes into its own.
29. Compare James Bohman, *Public Deliberation: Pluralism, Complexity, and Democracy* (Cambridge: MIT Press, 1996), 184, on "deliberative majority rule."
30. See, e.g., Lani Guinier, *The Tyranny of the Majority* (New York: Free Press, 1994).

## CHAPTER 16

1. This conclusion from chapter 10 is, if anything, strengthened by my deployment in chapter 15 of the Condorcet jury theorem.

2. The idea that democracy involves an epistemic division of labor, which has roots in Aristotle and Dewey, has recently been articulated by, e.g., Elaine Spitz, *Majority Rule* (Chatham, N.J.: Chatham House, 1984); S. L. Hurley, *Natural Reasons: Personality and Polity* (New York: Oxford University Press, 1989), 353; and James Bohman, *Public Deliberation: Pluralism, Complexity, and Democracy* (Cambridge: MIT Press, 1996), 189.

3. For two very different general discussions of this question, see David Epstein and Sharyn O'Halloran, *Delegating Powers: A Transaction Cost Politics Approach to Policy Making under Separate Powers* (Cambridge, England: Cambridge University Press, 1999), and Cass R. Sunstein and Edna Ullmann-Margalit, "Second-Order Decisions," *Ethics* 110 (1999): 5–31.

4. On informal directives, see Martin Shapiro, "Administrative Discretion: The Next Stage," *Yale Law Journal* 92 (1983): 1487–522. On privatization, see Jody Freeman, "The Real Democracy Problem in Administrative Law," in *Recrafting the Rule of Law: The Limits of Legal Order*, edited by David Dyzenhaus (Oxford: Hart, 1999), 336–41. Because I abstract from this diversity of possibilities, my proposals for institutional reform need to be viewed as merely illustrative. One would need to consider, for instance, how weighing the rulemaking process down with a requirement of negotiated rulemaking (discussed in the next section) might lead agencies to employ less formal modes of policy-making in order to evade these burdens.

5. For an illuminating discussion of a range of uses of administrative discretion, discussed with regard to the ethics of individual officials' actions, see Arthur Applbaum, "Democratic Legitimacy and Official Discretion," *Philosophy and Public Affairs* 21 (1992): 240–74.

6. Thus, I accept the criticism of William E. Scheuerman, "Globalization and the Fate of Law," in Dyzenhaus, *Recrafting the Rule of Law*, 245n.: traditional constraints of administrative law need to be supplemented by this rationality constraint and by the newer institutional processes mentioned hereafter, rather than being replaced by them. Further, as I emphasized in chapter 6, background distributive justice remains an independent concern.

7. The importance of these sorts of contestatory constraints are emphasized in Pettit's version of republican theory: See Philip Pettit, *Republicanism: A Theory of Freedom and Government* (Oxford: Oxford University Press, 1997), chaps. 7 and 8. The upshot of my argument in chapter 3 was that the republican ideal of nondomination, or freedom from subjection to nonarbitrary power, demands more than this; ultimately, as I argued (in chapters 4 and 5), it demands an active popular role in a fair process of determining policy.

8. See, e.g., David Dyzenhaus, *Legality and Legitimacy: Carl Schmitt, Hans Kelsen and Hermann Heller in Weimar* (Oxford: Oxford University Press, 1997).

9. My account, here, which draws on Henry S. Richardson, "Administrative Policy-Making: Rule of Law or Bureaucracy?" in Dyzenhaus, *Recrafting the Rule of Law*, 309–10, is an amalgam of William E. Scheuerman, "The Rule of Law and the Welfare State: Toward a New Synthesis," *Politics and Society* 22 (1994): 195–213, and John Rawls, *A Theory of Justice*, rev. ed. (Cambridge: Harvard University Press, 1999), sec. 38.

10. In U.S. constitutional law, the ban on *ex post facto* legislation has, for centuries,

been limited to the criminal law. See, however, Justice Thomas's concurring opinion in *Eastern Enterprises v. Apfel*, 524 U.S. 498 (1998).

11. See chapter 2.

12. For details, see Henry S. Richardson, "Specifying Norms as a Way to Resolve Concrete Ethical Problems," *Philosophy and Public Affairs* 19 (1990): 279–310.

13. Let me emphasize that I am invoking the relation of specification, here, solely as a way of spelling out an ideal rational constraint on the appropriate relation between agency policy-making and enacted legislation. I do not intend it as a theory of the judicial review of agency actions. Accordingly, I do not mean to be providing the kind of "legal test" attributed to me in Freeman, "The Real Democracy Problem in Administrative Law," 332n. My aim in this book is to articulate an understanding of democratic self-rule, a task that unavoidably remains a step or two away from stating standards sufficiently definite to stand up in the courts.

14. There is a body of U.S. constitutional law, based in the due process clause of the Fifth Amendment, which subjects statutes to invalidation for vagueness. This body of constitutional doctrine, however, is somewhat vaguer than its German counterpart, and, unlike article 80 of the German constitution, it is not explicitly addressed to the relation between statutes and the administrative rules that fill them out.

15. The Constitutional Court of the Federal Republic of Germany (Bundesverfassungsgericht) has struck down several laws because they were too vague to allow any regulation written under their authorization to meet these requirements. For a general discussion, see *Entscheidungen des Bundesverfassungsgerichts* [BVerfGE] 1 (1951) 14. Two examples of statutes struck down are the following: a statute establishing a program of compensation for prisoners of war that left unclear whether it was authorizing the issuing of regulations merely setting standards of proof for claims under the act or also establishing who should count as an eligible recipient under the act (BVerfGE 5 [1956] 71); and a statute imposing a value-added tax that left it wholly to the agencies to determine what would be meant by a crucial distinction between "single-stage" and "multiple-stage" enterprises, not even suggesting any criteria in terms of which the appropriateness of a definition could be assessed (BVerfGE 7 [1958] 282, 294; cp. BVerfGE 10 [1959] 251).

16. When a law or other norm is too vague, its satisfaction will not be well enough defined in order to allow the specification relation (which demands that all actions that satisfy the specified norm also satisfy the initial one) to be well defined. For further discussion of this point, see Henry S. Richardson, "Specifying, Balancing, and Interpreting Bioethical Principles," *Journal of Medicine and Philosophy* 25 (2000): 290.

17. This is not to imply that there are no justifiable exceptions to the general requirement of publicity in government decision. Cases of war, espionage, military secrets, and negotiations with foreign powers generate some well-recognized, if debated, exceptions. See, e.g., Amy Gutmann and Dennis Thompson, *Democracy and Disagreement* (Cambridge: Harvard University Press, 1996), chap. 3.

18. See David M. Pritzker and Deborah S. Dalton, eds., *Negotiated Rulemaking Sourcebook* (Administrative Conference of the United States, 1995).

19. On the positive role associations can play in a deliberative democracy, see Mark Warren, *Democracy and Association* (Princeton: Princeton University Press, 2000).

20. Here, I have benefited from discussion with Cass Sunstein.

21. See Jody Freeman, "Collaborative Governance in the Administrative State," *University of California Los Angeles Law Review* 45 (1997): 88, which applauds the "collaborative" aspect of negotiated rulemaking but admits to some nervousness about the voice it gives to interest groups, quoting from a decision by Judge Posner, in *USA Group Loan Services v. Riley*, 82 F.3d 708, 714 (7th Cir. 1996), that held that agencies are not bound to promulgate the rules in the form agreed to by such drafting committees. Taking the agencies so to be bound, writes Posner, would be "an abdication of regulatory authority to the regulated, the full burgeoning of the interest-group state, and the final confirmation of the 'capture' theory of administrative regulation."

22. This quotation from Stephen Macedo's *Liberal Virtues* forms a kind of epigraph to Fred D'Agostino, *Free Public Reason: Making It Up as We Go* (New York: Oxford University Press, 1996), vii.

23. Thus, compare Herbert Simon: "Democratic institutions find their principal justification as a procedure for the validation of value judgments. There is no 'scientific' or 'expert' way of making such judgments, hence expertise of whatever kind is no qualification for the performance of this function." Herbert A. Simon, *Administrative Behavior: A Study of Decision-Making Processes in Administrative Organizations* (New York: Free Press, 1997), 65.

24. John Rawls, "A Study in the Grounds of Ethical Knowledge: Considered with Reference to Judgments on the Moral Worth of Character" (Ph.D. dissertation, Princeton University, 1951), quoted in David Estlund, "Beyond Fairness and Deliberation: The Epistemic Dimension of Democratic Authority," in *Deliberative Democracy: Essays on Reason and Politics*, edited by James F. Bohman and William Rehg (Cambridge: MIT Press, 1997), 184. As Estlund also notes, Rawls takes a similar position with regard specifically to majority rule in *A Theory of Justice*: "Although in given circumstances it is justified that the majority . . . has the constitutional right to make law, this does not imply that the laws enacted are just . . . [W]hile citizens normally submit their conduct to democratic authority, that is, recognize the outcome of a vote as establishing a binding rule, other things equal, they do not submit their judgment to it" (315–6).

25. For a general argument that deference to expertise is not inimical to democracy, see Mark E. Warren, "Deliberative Democracy and Authority," *American Political Science Review* 90 (1996): 1–15.

26. *Washington Post*, April 9, 1997, p. A7. I discuss this example in a somewhat more general context in Henry S. Richardson, "Institutionally Divided Moral Responsibility," *Social Philosophy and Policy* 16 (1999): 246.

27. While it is conceivable that the task of devising policies in pursuit of some end and the task of specifying that end might be assigned to sharply distinct sets of officials, my foregoing discussion in the text of the development of expertise relevant to the latter task, coupled with my discussion in chapter 9 of the continuum of end-means, suggests that this split should not be a radical one. While this may be a reasonable way to divide tasks within an office, the crucial thing

is for those with experience implementing policy in a given area to be able to communicate intensively with those who are charged with specifying the ends to guide policy formation. We need not insist that these two tasks be carried out by one mind, just that they need to be carried out in close conjunction.

28. For discussion of the rationality of trust see, e.g., Russell Hardin, "The Street-Level Epistemology of Trust," *Analyse und Kritik* 14 (1992): 152–76.

29. Alternatively put, our trust in officials must be more like an emotional attitude than a judgment: see Lawrence C. Becker. "Trust as Noncognitive Security about Motives," *Ethics* 107 (1996): 43–61.

30. For a good overview of these complex issues, see Dennis F. Thompson, *Political Ethics and Public Office* (Cambridge: Harvard University Press, 1987).

31. Cynicism is also fed by the assumption, as in the "public choice" analysis of bureaucracies as "rent-seeking," that the relevant officials are self-interestedly motivated rather than being concerned with the public good. Both kinds of motivation must be appealed to in order to explain what actually goes on. Representative Biaggi's case illustrates how the two kinds of motive can blend together.

CHAPTER 17

1. Frank P. Ramsey, "Truth and Probability," in *Decision, Probability, Utility*, edited by Peter Gärdenfors and Nils-Eric Sahlin (Cambridge, England: Cambridge University Press, 1988), 19–47. John Von Neumann and Oskar Morgenstern, *Theory of Games and Economic Behavior*, 3d ed. (1953; reprint, Princeton: Princeton University Press, 1980), chap. 3.

2. I discuss this distinction between two versions of preference theory in chapter 9.

3. I confine myself to defending my overall account's general ability to cope with decision-making involving risk and hence I only scratch the surface of that subject. For an in-depth treatment, also critical of the view I am calling "risk rationalism," see, e.g., K. S. Schrader-Frechette, *Risk and Rationality: Philosophical Foundations for Populist Reforms* (Berkeley: University of California Press, 1991).

4. Stephen Breyer, *Breaking the Vicious Circle: Toward Effective Risk Regulation* (Cambridge: Harvard University Press, 1993).

5. Ibid., 73–4.

6. For a nontechnical discussion of the way reasons may fail to be additively separable, see Shelly Kagan, "The Additive Fallacy," *Ethics* 90 (1988): 5–31.

7. On this issue of individuating outcomes according to the goods and bads involved, see John Broome, *Weighing Goods: Equality, Uncertainty, and Time* (Oxford: Blackwell, 1991), chap. 5.

8. See Breyer, *Breaking the Vicious Circle*, 16–7.

9. Ibid., 24–7; see Cass R. Sunstein, "Cognition and Cost-Benefit Analysis," in *Cost-Benefit Analysis: Legal, Economic, and Philosophical Perspectives*, edited by Matthew D. Adler and Eric A. Posner (Chicago: University of Chicago Press, 2001), 226.

10. Breyer, *Breaking the Vicious Circle*, 11–9.
11. Ibid., 16.

## CHAPTER 18

1. See Martha C. Nussbaum, "Aristotelian Social Democracy," in *Liberalism and the Good*, edited by R. Bruce Douglass, Gerald M. Mara, and Henry S. Richardson (New York: Routledge, 1990), 235.
2. For a fuller development of this contrast, see Henry S. Richardson, *Practical Reasoning about Final Ends* (Cambridge, England: Cambridge University Press, 1994), chap. 8.

# BIBLIOGRAPHY

Ackerman, Bruce. *We the People*. Vol. 1, *Foundations*. Cambridge: Harvard University Press, 1991.

———. *We the People*. Vol. 2, *Transformations*. Cambridge: Harvard University Press, 1998.

Adler, Matthew D., and Eric A. Posner. "Implementing Cost-Benefit Analysis When Preferences Are Distorted." In *Cost-Benefit Analysis: Legal, Economic, and Philosophical Perspectives*, edited by Matthew D. Adler and Eric A. Posner, 269–311. Chicago: University of Chicago Press, 2001.

Anderson, Elizabeth. *Value in Ethics and Economics*. Cambridge: Harvard University Press, 1993.

Applbaum, Arthur. "Democratic Legitimacy and Official Discretion." *Philosophy and Public Affairs* 21 (1992): 240–74.

Aquinas, Thomas. *Summa Theologica*. Translated by Fathers of the English Dominican Province. 5 vols. Westminister, Md.: Christian Classics, 1981.

Aristotle. *Nicomachean Ethics*. Translated by Terence Irwin. Indianapolis: Hackett, 1985.

Arrow, Kenneth J. *Social Choice and Individual Values*. 2d ed. New Haven: Yale University Press, 1963.

———. "Utilities, Attitudes, Choices: A Review Note." In *Individual Choice under Certainty and Uncertainty*. In *Collected Papers of Kenneth J. Arrow*, 55–84. Cambridge: Harvard University Press, 1984.

Audi, Robert, and Nicholas Wolterstorff. *Religion in the Public Sphere: The Place of Religious Convictions in Political Debate*. Lanham, Md.: Rowman and Littlefield, 1997.

Baier, Annette. *The Commons of the Mind*. Chicago: Open Court, 1997.

Barry, Brian. "The Public Interest." *Proceedings of the Aristotelian Society* suppl. vol. 38 (1964): 1–18.

Becker, Lawrence C. "Trust as Noncognitive Security about Motives." *Ethics* 107 (1996): 43–61.

Beer, Samuel. *To Make a Nation: The Rediscovery of American Federalism*. Cambridge: Harvard University Press, 1993.

Beitz, Charles R. *Political Equality: An Essay in Democratic Theory*. Princeton: Princeton University Press, 1989.

Benjamin, Martin. *Splitting the Difference: Compromise and Integrity in Ethics and Politics.* Lawrence: University Press of Kansas, 1990.

Benson, Paul. "Autonomy and Oppressive Socialization." *Social Theory and Practice* 17 (1991): 385–408.

Berlin, Isaiah. *Four Essays on Liberty.* Oxford: Oxford University Press, 1979.

———. "On the Pursuit of the Ideal." *New York Review of Books*, March 17, 1988, 11–8.

Bessette, Joseph M. *The Mild Voice of Reason: Deliberative Democracy and American National Government.* Chicago: University of Chicago Press, 1994.

Black, Duncan. *The Theory of Committees and Elections.* Cambridge, England: Cambridge University Press, 1958.

Bohman, James. *Public Deliberation: Pluralism, Complexity, and Democracy.* Cambridge: MIT Press, 1996.

Bratman, Michael E. "Shared Cooperative Activity." *Philosophical Review* 101 (1992): 327–41.

———. "Shared Intention and Mutual Obligation." In *Faces of Intention: Selected Essays of Intention and Agency*, 130–41. Cambridge, England: Cambridge University Press, 1999.

Breiner, Peter. "Democratic Autonomy, Political Ethics, and Moral Luck." *Political Theory* 17 (1989): 550–74.

Brennan, Geoffrey, and Alan Hamlin. *Democratic Devices and Desires.* Cambridge, England: Cambridge University Press, 2000.

Brennan, Geoffrey, and Loren Lomasky. *Democracy and Decision.* Cambridge, England: Cambridge University Press, 1993.

Breyer, Stephen. *Breaking the Vicious Circle: Toward Effective Risk Regulation.* Cambridge: Harvard University Press, 1993.

Broadie, Sarah W. *Ethics with Aristotle.* New York: Oxford University Press, 1991.

Broome, John. *Weighing Goods: Equality, Uncertainty, and Time.* Oxford: Blackwell, 1991.

———. "Normative Requirements." In *Normativity*, edited by Jonathan Dancy, 78–99. Oxford: Blackwell, 2000.

Buchanan, James M., and Roger D. Congleton. *Politics by Principle, Not Interest.* Cambridge, England: Cambridge University Press, 1998.

Buchanan, James M., and Richard A. Musgrave. *Public Finance and Public Choice: Two Contrasting Visions of the State.* Cambridge: MIT Press, 1999.

Buchanan, James M., and Gordon Tullock. *The Calculus of Consent: Logical Foundations of Constitutional Democracy.* 1962. Reprint, Ann Arbor: University of Michigan Press, 1965.

Buss, Sarah. "Appearing Respectful: The Moral Significance of Manners." *Ethics* 109 (1999): 795–826.

Carson, Lyn, and Brian Martin. *Random Selection in Politics.* Westport, Conn.: Praeger, 1999.

Christiano, Thomas. "Voting and Democracy." *Canadian Journal of Philosophy* 25 (1995): 395–414.

———. *The Rule of the Many: Fundamental Issues in Democratic Theory.* Boulder, Colo. Westview Press, 1996.

———. "Justice and Disagreement at the Foundations of Political Authority." *Ethics* 110 (1999): 165–87.

Christman, John. "Autonomy and Personal History." *Canadian Journal of Philosophy* 21 (1991): 1–24.

Cohen, Joshua. "An Epistemic Conception of Democracy." *Ethics* 97 (October 1986): 26–38.

———. "The Economic Basis of Deliberative Democracy." *Social Philosophy and Policy* 6 (1989): 25–50.

———. "Democracy and Liberty." In *Deliberative Democracy*, edited by Jon Elster, 185–231. Cambridge, England: Cambridge University Press, 1998.

Coleman, Jules, and John Ferejohn. "Democracy and Social Choice." *Ethics* 97 (October 1986): 6–25.

Condorcet, Marie Jean Antoine Nicolas de Caritat, Marquis de. "A Survey of the Principles Underlying the Draft Constitution." Translated and excerpted in *Condorcet: Foundations of Social Choice and Political Theory*, edited by Iain McLean and Fiona Hewitt, 190–227. Aldershot, England: Elgar, 1994.

Crichton, Anne, and Lyn Jongbloed. *Disability and Social Policy in Canada*. North York, Ontario: Captus Press, 1998.

D'Agostino, Fred. *Free Public Reason: Making It Up as We Go*. New York: Oxford University Press, 1996.

Dahl, Robert A. *Democracy and Its Critics*. New Haven: Yale University Press, 1989.

Davidson, Donald. *Inquiries into Truth and Interpretation*, Corrected ed. 1984. Oxford: Oxford University Press, 1986.

Dewey, John. "The Need for Recovery in Philosophy." In *The Middle Works, 1899–1929*, edited by Jo Ann Boydston. 3–48, 1917. Reprint, Carbondale: Southern Illinois University Press, 1980.

———. "Theory of Valuation," 1939. Reprinted in *The Later Works, 1925–1953*, vol. 13, edited by Jo Ann Boydston, 189–251. Carbondale: Southern Illinois University Press, 1988.

———. *The Public and Its Problems*. Athens, Ohio: Ohio University Press, 1991.

Diggins, John Patrick. *The Promise of Pragmatism: Modernism and the Crisis of Knowledge and Authority*. Chicago: University of Chicago Press, 1994.

Dobel, J. Patrick. *Compromise and Political Action: Political Morality in Liberal and Democratic Life*. Savage, Rowman and Littlefield, 1990.

Douglass, R. Bruce, Gerald M. Mara, and Henry S. Richardson, eds. *Liberalism and the Good*. New York: Routledge, 1990.

Dryzek, John. *Discursive Democracy: Politics, Policy, and Political Science*. Cambridge, England: Cambridge University Press, 1990.

———. *Deliberative Democracy and Beyond: Liberals, Critics, Contestations*. Oxford: Oxford University Press, 2000.

Dworkin, Ronald. *Taking Rights Seriously*. Cambridge: Harvard University Press, 1978.

Dyzenhaus, David. *Legality and Legitimacy: Carl Schmitt, Hans Kelsen and Hermann Heller in Weimar*. Oxford: Oxford University Press, 1997.

Elster, Jon. *Sour Grapes: Studies in the Subversion of Rationality*. Cambridge, England: Cambridge University Press, 1983.

———. "The Market and the Forum: Three Varieties of Political Theory." In *Foundations of Social Choice Theory*, edited by Jon Elster and Aanand Hyllund, 103–32. Cambridge, England: Cambridge University Press.

Epstein, David, and Sharyn O'Halloran. *Delegating Powers: A Transaction Cost Politics Approach to Policy Making under Separate Powers*. Cambridge, England: Cambridge University Press, 1999.

Epstein, Richard A. *Forbidden Grounds: The Case against Employment Discrimination Laws*. Cambridge: Harvard University Press, 1992.

Estlund, David M. "The Persistent Puzzle of the Minority Democrat." *American Philosophical Quarterly* 26 (1989): 143–51.

———. "Who's Afraid of Deliberative Democracy? On the Strategic/Deliberative Dichotomy in Recent Constitutional Jurisprudence." *Texas Law Review* 71 (1993): 1437–77.

———. "Opinion Leaders, Independence and Condorcet's Jury Theorem." *Theory and Decision* 36 (1994): 131–62.

———. "Beyond Fairness and Deliberation: The Epistemic Dimension of Democratic Authority." In *Deliberative Democracy: Essays on Reason and Politics*, edited by James F. Bohman and William Rehg, 173–204. Cambridge: MIT Press, 1997.

———. "Jeremy Waldron on Law and Disagreement." *Philosophical Studies* 99 (2000): 111–28.

———. "Political Quality." *Social Philosophy and Policy* 17 (2000): 127–60.

———. "Deliberation Down and Dirty: Must Political Expression Be Civil?" In *The Boundaries of Freedom of Expression and Order in American Democracy*, edited by Thomas R. Hensley 49–67. Kent, Ohio: Kent State University Press, 2001.

Foot, Philippa. "Morality as a System of Hypothetical Imperatives." In *Virtues and Vices and Other Essays in Moral Philosophy*, 157–73. Berkeley: University of California Press, 1978.

Freeman, Jody. "Collaborative Governance in the Administrative State." *University of California Los Angeles Law Review* 45 (1997): 1–98.

———. "The Real Democracy Problem in Administrative Law." In *Recrafting the Rule of Law: The Limits of Legal Order*, edited by David Dyzenhaus, 330–69. Oxford: Hart, 1999.

Galston, William A. *Liberal Purposes: Goods, Virtues, and Diversity in the Liberal State*. Cambridge, England: Cambridge University Press, 1991.

Gambetta, Diego. " 'Claro': An Essay on Discursive Machismo." In *Deliberative Democracy*, edited by Jon Elster, 19–43. Cambridge, England: Cambridge University Press, 1998.

Gaus, Gerald F. *Justificatory Liberalism: An Essay on Epistemology and Political Theory*. New York: Oxford University Press, 1996.

———. "Reason, Justification, and Consensus: Why Democracy Can't Have It All." In *Deliberative Democracy: Essays on Reason and Politics*, edited by James Bohman and William Rehg, 204–42. Cambridge: MIT Press, 1997.

Gilbert, Margaret. *On Social Facts*. Princeton: Princeton University Press, 1989.

Gosepath, Stefan. *Aufgeklärtes Eigeninteresse*. Frankfurt: Suhrkamp, 1992.

Gould, Carol C. *Rethinking Democracy: Freedom and Social Cooperation in Politics, Economy, and Society*. Cambridge, England: Cambridge University Press, 1988.

Guinier, Lani. *The Tyranny of the Majority*. New York: Free Press, 1994.

Gutmann, Amy, and Dennis Thompson. *Democracy and Disagreement*. Cambridge: Harvard University Press, 1996.

Habermas, Jürgen. *The Theory of Communicative Action*. Vol. 1, *Reason and the Rationalization of Society*. Boston: Beacon Press, 1984.

———. *The Structural Transformation of the Public Sphere: An Inquiry into a Category of Bourgeois Society*. Cambridge: MIT Press, 1989.

———. *Moral Consciousness and Communicative Action*. Translated by Christian Lenhardt and Shierry Weber Nicholsen, with an introduction by Thomas McCarthy. Cambridge: MIT Press, 1990.

———. *Between Facts and Norms: Contributions to a Discourse Theory of Law and Democracy*. Translated by William Rehg. Cambridge: MIT Press, 1996.

———. "Three Normative Models of Democracy." In *Inclusion of the Other: Studies in Political Theory*, 239–52. Cambridge: MIT Press, 1998.

Hamilton, Alexander, James Madison, and John Jay. *The Federalist Papers*. Edited by Clinton Rossiter. New York: New American Library, 1961.

Hardin, Russell. "The Street-Level Epistemology of Trust." *Analyse und Kritik* 14 (1992): 152–76.

———. "Trustworthiness." *Ethics* 107 (1996): 26–42.

Hare, R. M. *Moral Thinking: Its Levels, Method, and Point*. Oxford: Oxford University Press, 1981.

Harman, Gilbert, and Judith Jarvis Thomson. *Moral Relativism and Moral Objectivity*. Cambridge: Blackwell, 1996.

Hayek, Friedrich A. *The Constitution of Liberty*. 1960. Chicago: University of Chicago Press, 1971.

Heath, Joseph. "The Structure of Normative Control." *Law and Philosophy* 17 (1998): 419–42.

———. *Communicative Action and Rational Choice*. Cambridge: MIT Press, 2000.

Held, David. *Models of Democracy*. 2d ed. Stanford: Stanford University Press, 1996.

Hill, Thomas E., Jr. *Respect, Pluralism, and Justice*. Oxford: Oxford University Press, 2000.

Hobbes, Thomas, *Leviathan*, edited by Edwin Curley. Indianapolis: Hackett, 1994.

Hohfeld, Wesley N. "Some Fundamental Legal Conceptions as Applied in Judicial Reasoning." *Yale Law Journal* 23 (1913): 16–59.

Holmes, Stephen. *Benjamin Constant and the Making of Modern Liberalism*. New Haven: Yale University Press, 1984.

———. "Gag Rules and the Politics of Omission." In *Constitutionalism and Democracy*, edited by Jon Elster and Rune Slagstad, 19–58, Cambridge, England: Cambridge University Pres, 1988.

Horwitz, Morton. *The Transformation of American Law*. Cambridge: Harvard University Press, 1977.

Hurley, S. L. *Natural Reasons: Personality and Polity*. New York: Oxford University Press, 1989.

*Improving Transport for People with Mobility Handicaps*. Strasbourg, European Conference of Ministers of Transport, 1999.

Kagan, Shelly. "The Additive Fallacy." *Ethics* 90 (1988): 5–31.

Kant, Immanuel. *Groundwork of the Metaphysics of Morals.* Translated by H. J. Paton. New York: Harper and Row, 1964.

———. *Perpetual Peace and Other Essays.* Translated by Ted Humphrey. Indianapolis: Hackett, 1983.

———. "An Answer to the Question: What Is Enlightenment?" In *Practical Philosophy*, translated and edited by Mary J. Gregor, 17–22. Cambridge, England: Cambridge University Press, 1996.

———. *Practical Philosophy.* Translated by Mary J. Gregor. Cambridge, England: Cambridge University Press, 1996.

Katzmann, Robert A. *Institutional Disability: The Saga of Transportation Policy for the Disabled.* Washington, D.C.: Brookings, 1986.

Kenny, Anthony. *Will, Freedom and Power.* Oxford: Blackwell, 1975.

Kolnai, Aurel. "Deliberation Is of Ends." In *Ethics, Value, and Reality: Selected Papers of Aurel Kolnai*, 44–62. Indianapolis: Hackett, 1978.

Korsgaard, Christine M. *The Sources of Normativity*, (Cambridge, England: Cambridge University Press, 1996).

———. "Self-Constitution in the Ethics of Plato and Kant." *Journal of Ethics* 3 (1999): 1–29.

Kuflik, Arthur. "Majority Rule Procedure." In *Due Process: Nomos XVIII*, edited by J. Roland Pennock and John W. Chapman, 296–322. New York: New York University Press, 1977.

———. "Morality and Compromise." In *Compromise in Ethics, Law, and Politics*, edited by J. Roland Pennock and John W. Chapman, 38–65. New York: New York University Press, 1979.

Kutz, Christopher. "Acting Together." *Philosophy and Phenomenological Research* 61 (2000): 1–31.

Kymlicka, Will. *Contemporary Political Philosophy.* New York: Oxford University Press, 1990.

———. *Multicultural Citizenship.* Oxford: Oxford University Press, 1995.

Lijphart, Arend. *Patterns of Democracy: Government Forms and Performance in Thirty-Six Countries.* New Haven: Yale University Press, 1999.

List, Christian, and Robert E. Goodin. "Epistemic Democracy: Generalizing the Condorcet Jury Theorem," *Journal of Political Philosophy* 9 (2001): 276–306.

Locke, John. *Two Treatises of Government.* Edited by Peter Laslett. 1698. Reprint, New York: Mentor, 1965.

Lowi, Theodore J. *The End of Liberalism: Ideology, Policy, and the Crisis of Public Authority.* New York: Norton, 1979.

Luce, R. Duncan, and Howard Raiffa. *Games and Decisions: Introduction and Critical Survey.* New York: Wiley, 1957.

Manin, Bernard. "On Legitimacy and Political Deliberation." Translated by Elly Stein and Jane Mansbridge. *Political Theory* 15 (1987): 338–68.

———. *The Principles of Representative Government.* Cambridge, England: Cambridge University Press, 1997.

Marx, Karl. *The German Ideology.* Part 1. Edited by C. J. Arthur. New York: International, 1970.

Mashaw, Jerry L. *Greed, Chaos, and Governance: Using Public Choice to Improve Public Law.* New Haven: Yale University Press, 1997.

Mansbridge, Jane. "Using Power/Fighting Power: The Polity." In *Democracy and Difference: Contesting the Boundaries of the Political*, edited by Seyla Benhabib, 46–66. Princeton: Princeton University Press, 1996.

McDowell, John. "Are Moral Requirements Hypothetical Imperatives?" In *Mind, Value, and Reality*, 77–94. Cambridge: Harvard University Press, 1998.

———. "Toward Rehabilitating Objectivity." In *Rorty and His Critics*, edited by Robert Brandom, 109–28. Oxford: Blackwell, 2000.

McKelvey, R. "General Conditions for Global Intransitivities in Formal Voting Models." *Econometrica* 47 (1979): 1085–110.

Michelman, Frank I. "The Supreme Court 1985 Term." *Harvard Law Review* 100 (1986): 4–77.

———. "Constitutional Fidelity/Democratic Agency." *Fordham Law Review* 55 (1997): 1537–43.

———. "How Can the People Ever Make the Laws? A Critique of Deliberative Democracy." In *Deliberative Democracy: Essays on Reasons and Politics*, edited by James Bohman and William Rehg, 145–71. Cambridge: MIT Press, 1997.

Millgram, Elijah. *Practical Induction*. Cambridge: Harvard University Press, 1997.

———. "Coherence: The Price of the Ticket." *Journal of Philosophy* 97 (2000): 82–93.

Misak, C. J. *Truth and the End of Inquiry: A Peircean Account of Truth*. Oxford: Oxford University Press, 1991.

Morris, Christopher W. "The Very Idea of Popular Sovereignty." In *Democracy*, edited by Ellen Frankel Paul, Fred D. Miller, and Jeffrey Paul. 1–26. Cambridge, England: Cambridge University Press, 2000.

Mouffe, Chantal. *The Democratic Paradox*. London: Verso, 2000.

Murphy, Mark. "The Conscience Principle." *Journal of Philosophical Research* 22 (1997): 387–407.

Neustadt, Richard. *Presidential Power: The Politics of Leadership*. New York: Wiley Press, 1960.

Ng, Yew-Kwang. *Welfare Economics: Introduction and Development of Basic Concepts*. London: MacMillan, 1983.

Nozick, Robert. *Anarchy, State, and Utopia*. New York: Basic Books, 1974.

Nussbaum, Martha C. *The Fragility of Goodness: Luck and Ethics in Greek Tragedy and Philosophy*. Cambridge, England: Cambridge University Press, 1986.

———. "Aristotelian Social Democracy." In *Liberalism and the Good*, edited by R. Bruce Douglass, Gerald M. Mara, and Henry S. Richardson, 203–52. New York: Routledge, 1990.

———. *Love's Knowledge: Essays on Philosophy and Literature*. New York: Oxford University Press, 1990.

———. "Skepticism about Practical Reason in Literature and the Law." *Harvard Law Review* 107 (1994): 714–44.

———. *Women and Human Development: The Capabilities Approach*. Cambridge, England: Cambridge University Press, 2000.

———. *Upheavals of Thought: The Intelligence of Emotions*. Cambridge, England: Cambridge University Press, 2001.

Oelbaum, Peter. "Munich's Electronic Timetable Information System." In *Transport for People with Mobility Handicaps: Information and Communication*, 83–90. Strasbourg, European Conference of Ministers of Transport, 1991.

Pettit, Philip. *Republicanism: A Theory of Freedom and Government*. Oxford: Oxford University Press, 1997.

———. "Democracy, Electoral and Contestatory." In *Designing Democratic Institutions*, edited by Ian Shapiro and Stephen Macedo, 105–44. New York: New York University Press, 2000.

Phillips, Anne. *The Politics of Presence*. Oxford: Oxford University Press, 1995.

Pitkin, Hanna Fenichel. *The Concept of Representation*. Berkeley: University of California Press, 1971.

Popper, Karl R. *The Logic of Scientific Discovery*. Rev. ed. New York: Harper and Row, 1968.

Posner, Richard A. *The Economics of Justice*. Cambridge: Harvard University Press, 1981.

———. "Cost-Benefit Analysis: Definition, Justification, and Comment on Conference Papers." In *Cost-Benefit Analysis: Legal, Economic, and Philosophical Perspectives*, edited by Matthew D. Adler and Eric A. Posner, 317–41. Chicago: University of Chicago Press, 2001.

Pritzger, David M., and Deborah S. Dalton, eds. *Negotiated Rulemaking Sourcebook*. Washington, D.C.: Administrative Conference of the United States, 1995.

Putnam, Hilary. *Reason, Truth and History*. Cambridge, England: Cambridge University Press, 1981.

Putnam, Robert. "Bowling Alone: America's Declining Social Capital." *Journal of Democracy* 6 (1995): 65–78.

Rae, Douglas W. "Decision-Rules and Individual Values in Constitutional Choice." *American Political Science Review* 63 (1969): 40–56.

Ramsey, Frank P. "Truth and Probability." In *Decision, Probability, Utility*, edited by Peter Gärdenfors and Nils-Eric Sahlin, 19–47. Cambridge, England: Cambridge University Press, 1988.

Rawls, John. "A Study in the Grounds of Ethical Knowledge: Considered with Reference to Judgments on the Moral Worth of Character." Ph.D. dissertation. Princeton University, 1951.

———. "Kantian Constructivism in Moral Theory: The Dewey Lectures 1980." *Journal of Philosophy* 77 (1980): 515–72.

———. *Political Liberalism*. Rev. ed. New York: Columbia University Press, 1996.

———. *The Law of Peoples*. Cambridge: Harvard University Press, 1999.

———. *A Theory of Justice*. Rev. ed. Cambridge: Harvard University Press, 1999.

Raz, Joseph. *The Morality of Freedom*. Oxford: Oxford University Press, 1986.

Reich, Robert B. "Policy Making in a Democracy." In *The Power of Public Ideas*, edited by Robert B. Reich, 123–56. Cambridge: Ballinger, 1988.

Richardson, Henry S. "The Problem of Liberalism and the Good." In *Liberalism and the Good*, edited by R. Bruce Douglass, Gerald M. Mara, and Henry S. Richardson, 1–28, New York: Routledge, 1990.

———. "Specifying Norms as a Way to Resolve Concrete Ethical Problems." *Philosophy and Public Affairs* 19 (fall 1990): 279–310.

———. *Practical Reasoning about Final Ends*. Cambridge, England: Cambridge University Press, 1994.

———. "Beyond Good and Right: Toward a Constructive Ethical Pragmatism." *Philosophy and Public Affairs* 24 (1995): 108–41.

———. "Democratic Intentions." In *Deliberative Democracy: Essays on Reason and Politics*, edited by James Bohman and William Rehg, 349–82. Cambridge: MIT Press, 1997.

———. "Administrative Policy-Making: Rule of Law or Bureaucracy?" In *Recrafting the Rule of Law: The Limits of Legal Order*, edited by David Dyzenhaus. 309–30. Oxford: Hart Press, 1999.

———. "Institutionally Divided Moral Responsibility." *Social Philosophy and Policy* 16 (1999): 218–49.

———. "Some Limitations of Nussbaum's Capabilities." *Quinnipiac Law Review* 19 (2000): 309–32.

———. "Specifying, Balancing, and Interpreting Bioethical Principles." *Journal of Medicine and Philosophy* 25 (2000): 285–307.

———. "The Stupidity of the Cost-Benefit Standard." *Journal of Legal Studies* 29 (2000): 971–1003.

———. "Truth and Ends in Dewey's Pragmatism." In *Pragmatism*, ed. Cheryl Misak, 109–47. Calgary, Alberta: University of Calgary Press, 2000.

———. "Autonomy's Many Normative Presuppositions." *American Philosophical Quarterly* 38 (2001): 287–303.

———. "Commensurability." In *Encyclopedia of Ethics*, edited by Lawrence Becker, 258–62 New York, 2001.

Riker, William H. *Liberalism against Populism: A Confrontation between the Theory of Democracy and the Theory of Social Choice*. Prospect Heights, Ill.: Waveland Press, 1988. Reprint.

Riley, Jon. *Liberal Utilitarianism: Social Choice Theory and J. S. Mill's Philosophy*. Cambridge, England: Cambridge University Press, 1988.

Risse, Mathias. "Arrow's Theorem, Indeterminacy, and Multiplicity Reconsidered." *Ethics* 111 (2001): 706–34.

Rorty, Richard. "Pragmatism, Davidson, and Truth." In *Objectivity, Relativism, and Truth*, 126–50. Cambridge, England: Cambridge University Press, 1991.

Rousseau, Jean-Jacques. *The Social Contract and Discourses*. Translated by G.D.H. Cole New York: Dutton, 1973.

Sandel, Michael J. *Liberalism and the Limits of Justice*. Cambridge, England: Cambridge University Press, 1982.

———. *Democracy's Discontent: America in Search of a Public Philosophy*. Cambridge: Harvard University Press, 1996.

Scanlon, T. M. "Promises and Practices." *Philosophy and Public Affairs* 19 (1990): 199–226.

Scheuerman, William E. "The Rule of Law and the Welfare State: Toward a New Synthesis." *Politics and Society* 22 (1994): 195–213.

———. "Globalization and the Fate of Law." In *Recrafting the Rule of Law: The Limits of Legal Order*, edited by David Dyzenhaus, 243–66. Oxford: Hart, 1999.

Schoenbrod, David. *Power without Responsibility: How Congress Abuses the People through Delegation*. New Haven: Yale University Press, 1993.

Schrader-Frechette, K. S. *Risk and Rationality: Philosophical Foundations for Populist Reforms*. Berkeley: University of California Press, 1991.

Sen, Amartya K. *Choice, Welfare, and Measurement.* Cambridge: MIT Press, 1982.
———. "Rational Fools." In *Choice, Welfare, and Measurement,* 84–106. Cambridge: MIT Press, 1982.
———. *Collective Choice and Social Welfare.* Amsterdam: North-Holland, 1984.
Shapiro, Martin. "Administrative Discretion: The Next Stage." *Yale Law Journal* 92 (1983): 1487–522.
Sheeran, Michael J. *Beyond Majority Rule: Voteless Decisions in the Religious Society of Friends.* 2d ed. Philadelphia: Philadelphia Yearly Meeting of the Religious Society of Friends, 1996.
Silvers, Anita. "(In)Equality, (Ab)Normality, and the Americans with Disabilities Act." *Journal of Medicine and Philosophy* 21 (1996): 209–24.
Simon, Herbert A. *Administrative Behavior: A Study of Decision-Making Processes in Administrative Organizations.* New York: Free Press, 1997.
Spencer, Herbert, *Political Writings.* Edited by J. Offer. Cambridge, England: Cambridge University Press, 1994.
Spitz, Elaine Mates. "Majority Rule: The Virtue of Numbers." Ethics 89 (1978): 111–4.
———. *Majority Rule.* Chatham, N.J.: Chatham House, 1984.
Spragens, Thomas. *Reason and Democracy.* Durham, N.C.: Duke University Press, 1990.
Sreenivasan, Gopal. "What Is the General Will?" *Philosophical Review* 109 (2000): 545–81.
———. "A Proliferation of Liberties." *Philosophy and Phenomenological Research* 63 (2001): 229–37.
———. "Understanding Alien Morals." *Philosophy and Phenomenological Research* 62 (2001): 1–32.
Ståhl, Agneta, and Per Gunnar Andersson. "Solutions in Sweden." In *Transport for People with Mobility Handicaps: Information and Communication,* 91–99. Strasbourg, European Conference of Ministers of Transport, 1991.
Stewart, Richard B. "The Reformation of American Administrative Law." *Harvard Law Review* 88 (1975): 1669–813.
Stocker, Michael. "Desiring the Bad: An Essay in Moral Psychology." *Journal of Philosophy* 76 (1979): 738–53.
———. "Emotional Thoughts." *American Philosophical Quarterly* 24 (1987): 59–69.
Sunstein, Cass R. "Preferences and Politics." *Philosophy and Public Affairs* 20 (1991): 3–34.
———. *The Partial Constitution.* Cambridge: Harvard University Press, 1993.
———. *Legal Reasoning and Political Conflict.* New York: Oxford University Press, 1996.
———. "Cognition and Cost-Benefit Analysis." In *Cost-Benefit Analysis: Legal, Economic, and Philosophical Perspectives,* edited by Matthew D. Adler and Eric A. Posner, 223–67. Chicago: University of Chicago Press, 2001.
Sunstein, Cass R., and Edna Ullmann-Margalit. "Second-Order Decisions." *Ethics* 110 (1999): 5–31.
Thompson, Dennis F. *Political Ethics and Public Office.* Cambridge: Harvard University Press, 1987.

Tuomela, Raimo. "We Will Do It: An Analysis of Group-Intentions." *Philosophy and Phenomenological Research* 51 (1991): 249–77.

———. *Cooperation: A Philosophical Study.* Dordrecht: Kluwer, 2000.

Ullmann-Margalit, Edna, and Sidney Morgenbesser. "Picking and Choosing." *Social Research* 44 (1977): 757–85.

Velleman, J. David. "The Guise of the Good." *Nous* 26 (1992): 3–26.

Von Neumann, John, and Oskar Morgenstern. *Theory of Games and Economic Behavior.* 3d ed. 1953. Reprint, Princeton: Princeton University Press, 1980.

von Wright, G. H. *The Logic of Preference.* Edinburgh: Edinburgh University Press, 1963.

Waldron, Jeremy. *The Dignity of Legislation.* Cambridge, England: Cambridge University Press, 1999.

Walzer, Michael. "Political Action: The Problem of Dirty Hands." *Philosophy and Public Affairs* 2 (1973): 160–80.

Warren, Mark E. "Deliberative Democracy and Authority." *American Political Science Review* 90 (1996): 1–15.

———, ed. *Democracy and Trust.* Cambridge, England: Cambridge University Press, 1999.

———. *Democracy and Association.* Princeton: Princeton University Press, 2000.

Weber, Max. *Economy and Society: An Outline of Interpretive Sociology.* Translated by G. Roth and C. Wittich. Berkeley: University of California Press, 1968.

———. *From Max Weber.* Edited by H. H. Gerth and C. Wright Mills. New York: Oxford University Press, 1974.

Wicksell, Knut. *Finanztheoretische Untersuchungen.* Jena: Fischer, 1896.

Wiggins, David. "Deliberation and Practical Reason." In *Essays on Aristotle's Ethics,* edited by Amélie Oksenberg Rorty, 241–66. 1975–76. Reprint, Berkeley: University of California Press, 1980.

Wollheim, Richard. "A Paradox in the Theory of Democracy." In *Philosophy, Politics, and Society, Second Series,* edited by Peter Laslett and W. G. Runciman, 71–87. Oxford: Blackwell, 1969.

Young, Iris Marion. "Communication and the Other: Beyond Deliberative Democracy." In *Democracy and Difference: Contesting the Boundaries of the Political,* edited by Seyla Benhabib, 120–35. Princeton: Princeton University Press, 1996.

———. *Inclusion and Democracy.* Oxford: Oxford University Press, 2000.

———. "Review of Nussbaum, *Sex and Social Justice.*" *Ethics* 111 (2001): 819–23.

# INDEX

acceptance
  of compromises, 276n.10
  hypothetical, 52
  of a proposal, by voting, 167–8, 279n.8
  public, 69, 72, 183–4, 188–90, 192, 250,
    278n.27
  reflective, 276n.11
Ackerman, B., 68–70
Adams, J., 197
additive separability, 236
Adler, Matthew, 224n
Administrative Procedures Act of 1946, 5, 6,
  219
agency instrumentalism, 99, 119, 120–1, 129,
  142, 270n.2
  naiveté of, 114, 118–9
agenda-setting, 49–50, 61, 80, 92, 108, 168–9,
  195, 204, 214, 236, 259n.26
aims. See ends
American Smelting and Refining Company
  (Asarco) case, 75, 106
Anderson, Elizabeth, 268n.16
appointment of agency personnel, 229
Aquinas, Thomas, 25
arbitrariness, 7, 27, 37–8, 204, 236, 284n.1.
  See also nonarbitrariness
Aristotle, 61, 77, 103, 117, 261n.13
Arrow, Kenneth, 48–50, 65, 125
Arrow's impossibility theorem, 48
associations and groups, 179, 188, 195,
  221–2, 240, 245, 251
  marginalized, 202
assurance, as giving rise to obligation,
  170–1
authority, 10–11, 16, 26, 34, 54, 87, 115, 129,
  142, 206, 215, 222–3, 253n.2, 274n.17.

  *See also* delegation of power and
    authority; separation of powers
  epistemic, 228
  ramification of, 235
autonomy, 18, 59, 137, 159–60, 213
  as a basis for populism, 67–8, 79
  collective, 57, 71
  democratic, 18, 57, 59, 71–2, 84, 129, 189,
    201, 251, 255n.32
  development of, 78
  engagement of, 70
  individual, 62–3, 69, 83, 276n.11
  as reasoned self-rule, 18, 62–3, 84
  requires more than reflective revision, 71
  respect for, 65, 67, 72, 78–81, 82, 90, 158,
    179, 195, 207, 245
  value of, 56, 63, 82

background justice. See justice, background
bargaining, 150, 155, 204, 222
  falsely contrasted with deliberation, 145
bargaining theory, 145–6, 150
basic structure of society, 31
Benjamin, Martin, 276n.9
Berlin, Isaiah, 29, 34, 151
Biaggi, Mario, 98, 109–10, 194, 290n.31. *See
  also* transportation for the disabled
Blackstone, William, 36
Bohman, James, 86–7, 277n.19
bootstrapping of decisions into reasons, not
  generally licit, 60, 138
Bratman, Michael, 279n.11, 12
Breiner, Peter, 255n.32
Brennan, Geoffrey, 15, 198–9
Breyer, Stephen, 233–4, 237
Broome, John, 265n.21

Buchanan, James, 12, 13–5, 19, 43, 45–6, 257n.15, 258n.13, 259n.20
Bush, George W., 62, 91, 189

campaign financing, 92
candidates, political, 89, 91, 166, 201–2
    qualifications of, 194
    range of, 202
    selection of, 200
    voters' acceptance of, 167
Christiano, Thomas, 85, 87, 115, 264n.7, 283n.12
citizens, 13. *See also* participation; representation; self-originating sources of claims, individuals as; virtue, civic; will of the people, the
    autonomy of, 63–6, 69–70, 72, 79, 82–3
    differential benefit to, 46
    due equal concern and respect, 268n.17
    duties of, 25–6
    equal freedoms of, 88
    equality before the law of, 88
    as free and equal, 37–9, 47, 50–2, 53, 56, 64, 72, 180, 195, 210
    good of each, in relation to the public good, 40
    imposition of duties on, 26, 37, 179, 217, 247
    mutual concern among, 159
    political positions of, 50, 197, 198–9
    in relation to "the people", 205
    set of, 52, 67, 183
        not equivalent to the public, 182
    support for the deliberative capacity of each, 89
    views of, 196
citizenship, 167
civil rights. *See* rights
civil servants
    professionalism of, 227
    protected tenure of, 229
civility not a requirement of democratic debate, 143
coalition-building, 91, 171, 176
Cohen, Joshua, 261n.12, 262n.21, 263n.1
coherence. *See also* reflection; truth, the concept of
    as aspect of the idea of truth, 133–4
    as a basis for reasoning about ends, 108, 110, 112, 150, 160, 239
    reminder of holism rather than criterion, 111
Coleman, Jules, 261n.12

commensurability of values. *See* incommensurability of values
compromise
    bare, 146, 207
    as called for by remedial social virtues, 44
    deep, 144–5, 164, 170, 176, 200, 215, 251
        as an alternative to collaboration and bargaining, 222
        benefits of, 150, 152
        as a condition of joint deliberation about ends, 148–9
        defined, 147
        and emotions, 190–2
        examples, 147–51, 207
        in legislatures, 196, 199, 201–2, 204, 246
        motivations of, 152, 155–6, 159–60, 208, 249
        and open-mindedness, 187
        and openness, 190
        and participation, 216, 220–1
        rationality of, 150–2, 160
        and truth-orientation, 208
        willingness to engage in, 90
Condorcet. *See* jury theorem (Condorcet's)
Congleton, Roger, 46–7, 258n.13, 259n.20
consent. *See* acceptance
consistency across government programs. *See* coherence; risk, rationalism about
constitution. *See also* freedoms, fundamental; judicial review; justice, background
    defined, 11
    and majority rule, 169
    necessity of, 16, 137, 185, 188, 195, 213, 224
    and populism, 67–70
contractarianism, 53–4
Convisser, Martin, 108, 214, 218, 250
cooperation
    disposition for, 155–6
    ideal of fair, 39, 47, 50
coordination of subplans, 174–5
corporations, 210
correspondence. *See* truth, the concept of
critical theory tradition, 74. *See also* Habermas, Jürgen
Crosson, Nicholas, 210n
cynicism about democracy
    countered, 75
    diagnosed, 229, 290n.31
    initial description of, 3

D'Agostino, Fred, 262n.19
Dahl, Robert, 205

decision theory. *See* rational choice theory
deep compromise. *See* compromise, deep
delegation of power and authority, 4, 25, 129, 222–3, 246
  against wholesale and permanent, 63
  constraints on, 215
  and truth-orientation, 129
  unavoidability of, 4, 7
deliberation, 39, 61, 73, 76, 90–1, 100, 112, 131. *See also* division of deliberative labor; questions, practical, distinguished; reasoning; specification
  agency, 127–31, 214, 218–9, 223, 230, 246, 250
  contexts for, 100
  delegated, 141
  democratic, 38–39, 44, 51, 114, 117, 136, 143–5, 153, 160, 164–5, 187, 198, 213, 222, 291, 245, 247, 249–51
    capacity of individuals to enter, 246
    four stages of, 165–8
    general requisites of, 90
    and the informal public sphere, 169
    normative fruitfulness of, 169–73, 211
    public good as object of, 51, 61
    publicity constraints of, 165, 185
    quality of, 91–2
    rational tools of, 175
    and self-government, 195
    taking the place of consent, 189
    as yielding joint intentions, 165, 169
  epistemic benefits of, 77
  glossed, 73, 76
  intelligent, 122, 128, 142, 164, 246
  joint, 112–3, 144–5, 148–9, 155, 159, 162
  normatively fruitful, 139–40
  as reshaping motivation, 154
  structure of, 122
  truth-oriented, 131, 137–9, 141, 158–9, 246, 248–9
    democratic and, 140–1
    and majority rule, 206–8, 210–2
  wrongly contrasted with bargaining, 145
  as yielding intentions, 164
deliberative democracy
  ideals of, 99, 164–5
  meaning of, 73, 76, 83
  theories of, 20, 52, 73–5, 143, 166
deliberative equality 85–8, 92–2, 204, 243–4
  indirect account of, 89–90
deliberative, requirement that democracy be strongly, 73

democracy as democratic autonomy
  as favored interpretation of democracy, 18
  institutionalization of, 179
  label explained, 18
  need not be accepted by citizenry, 160
  as uniting republican, liberal, populist, and rationalist strands, 17–8, 84
Dewey, John, 100, 121–2, 181, 183, 281n.8
dilemma of truth and deference, 131
  merely apparent, 132
disagreement. *See* pluralism
discretion, administrative, 3–5, 7–8, 10, 12, 16–7, 65, 114–5, 129–30, 175, 214–6, 218, 222, 229, 250
discursiveness, potential, as a mark of reasoning, 76
dispersal of powers. *See* separation of powers
division of concern, 226, 246
division of deliberative labor, 113–5, 118, 130, 132, 180–81, 223, 215, 224, 228, 235, 244, 246
  as a division of responsibility, 227
  substantive, 223
Dobel, J. Patrick, 275n.8
domination 3, 35, 84, 143. *See also* arbitrariness; freedom, as nondomination
  bureaucratic, 4, 7–9, 11, 16, 17–20, 23, 56, 65, 84, 104, 235, 242, 244, 247
    conditions for avoiding, 214, 217, 229–30, 248, 250–1
  and instrumental rationality, 74
  models for curbing, 99, 113
  a common concern, 27
  concept of, 29, 32–5
  by ideal guardians, 63–3
  majoritarian, 12–4, 46–7, 51, 56, 58
  private, 44, 244
dualism. *See* will of the people, the
Dukakis, Michael, 191
duties, purported imposition of new, 23–8, 34, 69, 179, 184, 217, 243
  by administrative agencies, 247
  as an aspect of domination, 34
  requirement of good reasons, 59

economic power
  inequality of, 92, 243–4
  tendency to concentrate 88–9, 209
elections, 36, 70, 89, 192–4, 196–7, 202, 211, 221, 244. *See also* parties, political
Elster, Jon, 276n.11

embodiment of reflection, 190–2, 249–50.
    *See also* reflection
emotions, role in deliberation of, 78, 190–2.
    *See also* reflection; rhetoric
end-means reasoning. *See* reasoning, end-
    means
ends. *See also* reasoning; specification
    of an agency, 238
    final, defined, 102
    hierarchy of, 111
    "in view", 100, 121
    incompossible, 33
    intermediate, 173
    often left vague by legislatures, 116
    at play in deep compromise, 147, 221
    of policy, 239
    and preferences, 121
    promotion of means to, 110
    public, 189, 201, 214, 218, 222–3, 231–3,
        235, 237–9
    and the public good, 40
    revision of, 121–2, 130–1, 215
    shared, 19, 26, 112, 145, 173–6, 189, 207
    subject to compromise, 151, 155–6
    superordinate, 218
    ultimate, 102–3
equality. *See also* citizens; inequalities of
        power
    elemental, 27–8, 51, 54–5, 63–4, 157, 159,
        207, 210, 213
    political, 200, 243–4
        qualitative, 85–93, 168, 204, 243
        quantitative, 85, 243
    of the public, 184, 186–8
    and republicanism, 35
Estlund, David, 210–1, 255n.37, 262n.17,
    265n.24, 272n.12
expected-value calculation, 232
expertise, agency. *See also* division of
        deliberative labor
    as a de facto source of power, 4, 222
    justification of reliance on, 215
    substantive, 180, 223, 241
    about values, 231, 235, 237
        defended, 223–5, 226–7
        denied by some, 115
        mandate for, 225
        trust in, 227
expertise, legislative, 195, 199

faction, 12–3, 45, 77, 171, 179, 199, 205, 207
fallibility of democratic procedures, 211–2,
    223–4. *See also* truth, the concept of

fallibility, recognition of
    an aspect of truth-orientation, 133–5, 137,
        139, 207
    a mark of rationality, 62
Federalists, the, 12
Ferejohn, John, 26n.12
fidelity to the law, 7, 215–19. *See also* rule
    of law, the
fora for deliberation, 92–3, 168, 184, 241
Franklin, Benjamin, 106
freedom. *See also* arbitrariness; citizens;
        domination
    and the basic case for democracy, 27–8,
        158
    elemental, 23–7, 51, 59, 63–4, 243
    as nondomination, 9, 29, 32–7, 40–1, 44,
        59, 210, 244, 256n.7
        and populism, 57
        requires a liberal interpretation, 48, 52
    as noninterference, 28, 32, 209, 237
    as obedience, no part of a sensible
        populism, 58–9, 61, 72
    three layers of the idea of, 243
    vs. license, 36, 209
freedoms. *See also* rights
    constitutional protection of, 9, 184–5, 188
    fair value of the political, 89
    fundamental, 16, 24, 26, 47, 50–3, 56, 62,
        68, 79, 82, 84, 86, 88, 250
    of the press, 185–7
    and the rule of law, 217
    of speech and association, 92–3, 186–7,
        194, 196
Freeman, Jody, 288n.13
friendship, civic, 153
Fujimori, Alberto, 89
fundamentalists, reasoning with, 82, 157, 160

game theory, 162, 277n.14
Gaus, Gerald F., 255n.37, 277n.23
gay marriage (illustrating deep compromise),
    148–9
general will (Rousseau), 14, 45, 58
    alleged infallibility of, 57–8
generality
    as a constraint on political decision, 14–6,
        42, 45–7
    of laws, 216–7
    of public reasons, 187
German Constitution of 1948, 5, 218, 251
Gilbert, Margaret, 170
global democracy, conditions for, 188
Gore, Al, 91

Grand Canyon National Park, 237–40
Greece, ancient, 12, 181, 194
groups. *See* associations and groups
guardians, hypothetical, 41, 51, 62–3
Gutmann, Amy, 82, 186–7, 255n.37, 260n.39, 281n.17

Habermas, Jürgen, 49, 86, 90, 114, 258n.14, 264n.5
Hamlin, Alan, 198–9
handing off of premises, 141, 214
Harman, Gilbert, 273n.5
Hawkins County, Tenn. *See* fundamentalists
Hayek, Friedrich, 14, 45
Held, David, 255n.32
Henry, Patrick, 73
Hobbes, Thomas, 209
Hume, David, 154–5

identity
    and deep compromise, 146–8, 155, 159
    practical, 156
ignorance, 199
imperatives, hypothetical vs. categorical, 136–7
incommensurability of values, 246
    distinguished from comparability, 106
    as not precluding shared democratic values, 159–60
    as obtaining, 106, 127
    role of emotions in addressing, 192
    viewed by some as a bar to rational choice, 106
incommensurable conceptions, 156
    not precluding thin agreement, 160–1, 245
incomplete thinking. *See* preferences, incompletely thought-through
individualism, 15, 19, 27–8, 46, 49–51, 61, 153–4, 162, 206, 209, 249. *See also* intentions; organicism
    in the philosophy of mind, 163, 169, 183
    romantic vs. pessimistic, 153–6
inequalities of power, 85–6
input, public, 75, 92, 179, 185, 241. *See also* participation
    in administrative agencies, 180, 214, 219, 237
    and emotion, 191
instrumentalism about practical reason, 136. *See also* reasoning, end-means
    as limiting the scope for collective reasoning, 19
integrity, virtue of. *See* virtue, civic

intelligence, practical, 99, 111, 120, 175, 201, 215. *See also* deliberation
    in agency reasoning, 131–2
    applied to risk, 237, 239
    blocked by using a cost-benefit standard, 122–9
    characterized, 121–2
    in deep compromise, 149
    and the formation of intention, 164
    three modes of, 123
intention
    collective, 66
    conditional, 166, 169, 197
    general structure of, 164
    joint, 162–76, 182–3, 187
        cooperative agreement account of, 165–6, 169
    refinement of political, 218, 227
interests
    alleged fixity of, 153–4
    citizens', 7, 54
        not the focus of representation, 198–9
    conflicting, 143, 153, 245
    Habermas's standards of equal promotion of, 44
    of individuals, and the public good, 181
    public, 181
    special, 3, 8, 13, 77, 221–2
    vs. preference satisfaction, 154

Johnson, Lyndon, 157
joint deliberation about ends. *See* deliberation, joint
joint intentions. *See* intentions, joint
judicial independence, 217
judicial review, 8, 16–7, 66, 216, 223
jurisdiction of a democracy
    to be clarified in a constitution, 67
    and a public, 182
    scope of, left open, 10–11
jury theorem (Condorcet's), 79–80, 210–2
justice, background, 88–92, 244
justification of democracy as democratic autonomy
    direct and reconstructive, distinguished, 18
    direct or value-based, 64
    reconstructive, 48, 62, 64
justification, order of, vs. order of finality, 110
justification, practical 111. *See also* reasoning, public

Kafka, Franz, 4–5
Kamm, Linda, 108, 214
Kant, Immanuel, 62, 136–7, 182, 280n.7
Katzmann, Robert A., 97
Kettner, Matthias, 279n.12
Kuflik, Arthur, 276n.9

law, interpretation of, 72. *See also* fidelity to
    law; legislation; rule of law; statutes,
    interpretation of
law-making as focus of normative concern,
    10, 15, 28, 57–8, 67–70, 72, 179, 195,
    203, 244, 246–7. *See also* rulemaking
legislation 24, 45. *See also* fidelity to law;
    judicial review; publicity, requirement
    of
  agency deference to, 130–2, 142
  authorizing agency discretion, 5
  backward-looking requirements on, 218
  constraining agency discretion, 219
  drafting of, 195
  periodic review of, 244
  setting ends for policy, 115, 174
  vagueness in, 116, 228
    unavoidable, 118
  voting on, 180, 204, 211
legislative intent, 66
legislators
  compromises among, 204, 207–8
  distinction of, 194, 197
  duty to listen to citizens of, 196
  equality among, 204
  expertise of, 195, 199
  independence of judgment of, 194, 199
  influence of the public on, 196
  mutual respect among, 207, 210, 246
  seniority of, 284n.2
  truth-orientation of some, 207, 208, 211
legislatures
  as arenas of public deliberation about
    ends, 112
  natural primacy of, 179
  not the privileged mouthpieces of the
    popular will, 70
  oversight function of, 17, 180
  role in democratic deliberation, three
    models of, 99
  as site of basic compromises, 201
legitimacy, burden of, carried by actions
    impinging on freedom, 23, 26, 175
liberalism
  built into democracy, 48

characterized, 62, 68
entering via interpretation of
    nonarbitrariness, 37–8, 47–8
and entrenched power, 209
Kantian, 182
nonneutralist, 39, 209
as one of four strands of democratic
    autonomy, 17, 74, 84, 242, 245
proceduralism of, defended, 48, 51
as reconciling objectivism with
    individualism, 51
as supporting populism, 84
liberty, negative and positive, 29–32, 34,
    256n.7. *See also* freedom; freedoms
licentiousness, contrasted with liberty, 31,
    36, 209
Lijphart, Arend, 280n.1
Lincoln, Abraham, 68, 72
listening, value of, in democratic
    deliberation, 92, 191–2, 196, 245. *See
    also* legislators
Locke, John 9, 36, 38, 52
Lomasky, Loren, 15, 46
lot, selection by, 181, 194–5, 197, 319n.16

Madison, James, 11–15, 68, 77
magnanimity, virtues of civic. *See* virtue,
    civic
majoritarianism 8, 14, 49
  rejected, 11
majority rule, 14. *See also* jury theorem
    (Condorcet's); minorities
  as central to democracy, 51
  as a closure device, 143, 167–9, 203–13,
    244
  compatibility with populism, 203–4
  criticism of, 43, 45–6
  and deep conflicts, 82
  manipulability of, 49, 65, 204
  and minorities, 89–90, 209, 212–3
  reliability of, 80, 210–11, 261n.12
  and truth-orientation, 206–12
  variety of fora for, 168
  as a vehicle for rule by the people, 213
mandates
  as basis for agency discretion, 224–6, 229,
    235, 239, 246
  as devices limiting legislators, 194, 196
Manin, Bernard, 193
market institutions, 30–31. *See also*
    preferences
Marx, Karl, 47n.77

McCarthy era, 78
McDowell, John, 273n.9
means, pursuit of something as a, 100–1. *See also* instrumentalism; reasoning, end-means
  broad sense, 102
  narrow sense, 103
median voter theorem, 197
Michelman, Frank I., 52, 67, 263n.23, 285n.10
Millgram, Elijah, 112n., 270n.37
minorities. *See also* domination, majoritarian; majoritarianism; majority rule
  permanent, 209, 213
  perspectives of, 241
  voice for, 89–90, 200
monism. *See* will of the people, the
Morris, Christopher W., 260n.1
motivation. *See also* compromise, deep; voting behavior
  to cooperate in democracies, 154–6
  malleability of, 154
Mouffe, Chantal, 258n.15
Murphy, Mark, 268n.13
Musgrave, Richard A., 159n
mutual concern. *See* solidarity
mutual openness to persuasion, 90–1, 247, 249. *See also* open-mindedness; virtue, civic
mutual support of considerations. *See* coherence

nation-state. *See* jurisdiction of a democracy
natural-law position in jurisprudence, 25
negotiated rulemaking, 220–2
Negotiated Rulemaking Act of 1990, 220
Neurath's boat, 263n.33
Neustadt, Richard, 254n.17
Nixon, Richard, 189
nonarbitrariness. *See also* arbitrariness
  and contractualism, 54
  liberal (preferred) interpretation of, 47–8
  minimal interpretation, 37
  objectivist interpretation of, 39–40
  Pettit's interpretation of, 52, 360n.40
  welfarist interpretation of, 48
normative fruitfulness, 140–2, 165, 212, 214. *See also* procedures
  defined, 139
  of joint deliberation, 169–73
Nozick, Robert, 267n.19
Nussbaum, Martha C., 268n.17, 282n.21

objectivity. *See* nonarbitrariness
open-mindedness, 90–1, 187. *See also* mutual openness to persuasion; virtue, civic
openness of the political process, 185–6, 188, 190, 229. *See also* publicity, requirement of
  impact of past, 71
  rationalization of, 57
organicism about the polity, 182, 249. *See also* individualism

Paine, Tom, 38–9
Pareto, Vilfredo, 48
participation, 88, 169, 180, 189, 206, 244, 246–7, 251. *See also* input, public
  in agency decisions, 215–6, 220–2, 227, 247–8, 250
  and autonomy, 62–3
  fair chance for, 50, 89
  and populism, 57–8, 66, 72, 179, 193, 204, 247
parties, political, 150, 197, 201. *See also* coalition-building; elections
  inequality among, 92
  the need for several, 213
  platforms of, 112, 164, 200
perspectives of citizens, 77
  danger of confusion in, 77–8
  listening to, 92
  to be represented, 201–2, 228, 243
Peru, 4, 8, 12, 89, 215
perversion of values, 101
Pettit, Philip, 29–31, 33–6, 38–9, 52, 57, 70–1, 244, 260n.40
picking, as distinct from choosing, 136
Pitkin, Hanna Fenichel, 197
Plato, 90, 266n.14
pluralism, conditions of, 81, 87
  and consensus procedures, 205
  and overlapping consensus, 173
  and the possibility of deep compromise, 156–61
popular sovereignty, individualized, 139
populism 17, 63, 83. *See also* will of the people, the
  defined, 57
  and actual publicity, 182
  at the agency level, 222–4
  and autonomy, 63–4, 78–80, 83
  defense of a qualified, 56–72
  and elections, 192
  feasibility of, 67–72

populism (*continued*)
  limits of, 132
  as one of four strands of democracy as
      democratic autonomy, 17–8, 84, 162,
      165, 242, 247–8
  rationalist, 114–5, 119, 132, 144, 180
  reconciled to majority rule, 203–6, 212
  and representative government, 193
  republican, 216
  separated from Rousseau, 57–61
positivism, legal, 25
Posner, Richard A., 271n.4
power, governmental, 9–10
  decentralization of, 16
  and freedoms, 181
  normative account of, 33–4
  among other sorts of power, 31–2, 35
predictability of law, 9–10, 216–7. *See also*
      rule of law
preferences, 42, 48–51, 81, 126, 145, 150,
      249
  as basis of cost-benefit analysis, 120–1,
      127–8, 132
  change of, 73–4
  formation of, 123–4
  idealized, 125
  and incommensurability, 106–7, 119
  incompletely thought-through, 124–6, 236,
      241
  as insufficient basis of representation,
      198–9
  intrinsic, 126
  not useful in deliberation, 100
  relative poverty of the notion of, 100, 248
  revealed, 121–2, 124–6, 237
  and risk, 231–6
  satisfaction of vs. welfare, 154
  unlimited domain of, rejected, 50
Price, Richard, 33
Priestley, Joseph, 33
proceduralism, 37, 74–5
  liberal, 74–6
procedures, 37, 50–51, 219. *See also*
      standards, process-independent
  fair, 38, 43, 47, 50–2, 54–5, 64–5, 74, 195,
      200, 202–4, 247–8
  liberal, 50–2
  normatively fruitful, not pure or impure,
      139
  and the public good, 39
  pure vs. impure, 139
promotion of ends. *See* ends

proportional representation. *See*
      representation, proportional
proposals, role of in democratic deliberation,
      80–1, 165–7, 192, 199. *See also*
      acceptance
public. *See also* will of the people, the
  the idea of, 180–1
  agreement within, 183–4
  egalitarian aspect of, 184
  existence of, 183–8, 245
  freedoms of, 184–5, 243
  mutual awareness of, 182–3
  reflective role of, 189, 247–8
public choice theory, 12–5, 19, 43, 46, 49,
      73
public feast analogy (Aristotle), 77
public good, the, 12. *See also*
      nonarbitrariness
  actual vs. apparent, 40
  citizens' conceptions of, 15
  combining objectivist, welfarist, and
      liberal understandings of, 51
  concern for, 33
  democratic conceptions of, 158–9, 161,
      198
  idea of a conception of, 40
  and individual claims, 181
  liberal conception of, 47–8, 51, 55
  Madison's conception of, 13
  meaning of the term, 39–40
  need not be agencies' focus, 226
  noncognitivist conceptions of, 13
  objectivist, welfarist, and liberal
      conceptions of, 38–40
  open to deliberative revision, 167
  progressive specification of, 228
  republican conceptions of, 38
  skepticism about, rebutted, 50–1
  and the will of the people, 61
public sphere, the, 89, 112, 168–9
  equality in, 243
  informal, 70, 179
publicity, requirement of, 63, 165, 219
  actual, not just hypothetical, 165, 182
  constitutional guarantee of, 185
  as an element of the rule of law, 216
  and the existence of a public, 185–6, 190

questions, practical, distinguished, 136

ramification. *See* specification, as ramifying
      across agencies

Ramscy, Frank P., 231
rational choice theory, 99, 231, 234, 248–9
rationalism, one of four strands of
    democracy as democratic autonomy,
    17–8, 73–84, 114, 136, 180, 203,
    224, 245. *See also* risk, rationalism
    about
rationalist populism. *See* populism,
    rationalist
rationality. *See also* intelligence, practical;
    reasoning
  and the rule of law, 217
  three models of agency, 99
Rawls, John, 16, 31, 43, 53, 89, 139, 167,
    257n.4, 258n.14, 277n.24, 280n.5
Raz, Joseph, 256n.1, 274n.17
reasoning. *See also* deliberation; division of
    deliberative labor; intelligence,
    practical; rationality
  agency, 76, 114, 119, 137–8, 175, 250–1
    continuity with legislative, 132, 141–2
    extends to ends, 130–1
    three models of, 98–9
  by balancing pros and cons, 105–7
  capabilities for, 85
  collective, 18–20, 149
  communicative, 74
  democratic, 17, 19–20, 75, 78, 162, 166,
    189–90, 242, 246, 248
    final characterization of, 248–9
    with one another, 78, 83–4, 98, 112,
    195, 245
    should extend to ends, 112
    truth-orientation of, 136
  end-means, 74, 99–100
    cannot be formalized, 123–4
    at the core of agency instrumentalism,
    116
    ill modeled by cost-benefit analysis,
    120–1
    narrow vs. broad, 103–4, 113
    and specification, 104–5
    squeezed out by "complete thinking",
    125–6
    from vague ends, 116–7
  about ends, 107–11, 115, 231, 247
  and coherence, 150
  general nature of, 75–6
  practical
    can shift motivations, 154
    issues in intentions, 163
    as paradigm deliberation, 73

    resists formalization, 103–4
    three types, distinguisheed, 98–9
  public, 182–3
  and reflection, 183, 189, 191–2
  truth-orientation of, 76, 90–1, 135
reasons
  acceptable to all, 52, 82, 260n.39
    notion queried, 53
    rejection of the standard of, 82
  new, 274n.17
  requirement that government action be
    based on, 28, 60
recall of representatives, 194, 196
reflection, 110–2, 123, 239. *See also*
    embodiment of reflection; emotions,
    role in deliberation of
  and compromise, 150–1, 160
  public, 141, 180–3, 185, 188–90, 245, 248–
    50, 280n.2
regularity, legal, 9, 217. *See also* rule of law
reliance, as giving rise to obligation, 170–2
representation
  of marginalized groups, 202, 243
  proportional, preferred, 199–200
  what is to be represented, 196–98,
    201–2
representative government, 193–202. *See also*
    legislators
  the best form of government, 198
  concept of, 193
republicanism. *See also* domination;
    Federalists, the; Madison, James;
    nonarbitrariness; Pettit, Philip
  as distinguishing liberty and license, 31,
    209
  as emphasizing contestation, 38, 71, 115,
    179
  as in favor of dispersing power, 14, 143,
    216
  gives a role to the public good, 38
  its ideal of a nondominating government,
    35–7
  and judicial review, 9, 11
  liberal, 52–3
  leads to liberalism, 48, 52
  as one of four strands of democracy as
    democratic autonomy, 17–8, 84, 242,
    244
  as opposing domination, 12, 16, 27, 29, 32–
    6, 142
  reconciled with populism, 59–60
respect for persons, 63, 65–6, 84

respect for persons (*continued*)
  mutual, as a ground for democratic
    reasoning, 78–83, 159, 198, 245
  and positive duties, 30
revision, reflective, 70–1, 141–2
rhetoric, political, 78
  and public emotions, 190–2, 250
  as a tool of democratic reasoning, 90–2
Richardson, Benjamin Challinor, 264n.3
rights. *See also* freedoms
  civil, 157
  to a decent minimum, 89
  voting, 184, 243
Riker, William H., 49, 56–7, 61, 65, 204
risk
  democratic regulation of, 237–41
  noninstrumentalist approaches to, 237
  rationalism about, 231–7
Risse, Matthias, 262n.20
Roman Empire, 181
Rousseau, Jean-Jacques, 14. *See also* general
    will (Rousseau)
  on citizenship, 167
  committed to generality test, 42–5
  dangerous claims of, 58, 212
  his version of populism set aside, 59–
    60
  as inspiring populism, 57–8
  not a democrat, 13
  some views of accepted, 261n.5
  tendency to organicism of, 65, 114
Ruckelshaus, William, 75
rule by the people. *See* will of the people
rule of law, the, 5. *See also* constitution
  and a constitution, 11
  defined in terms of three constraints,
    216–8
  formal constraints of, 215–6
  ideal of, 10, 45
  implications of for legislation, 218–9
  as insufficient to curb bureaucratic
    domination, 6, 276
  part of the needed constraint on agencies,
    179, 216
  publicity as generally required by, 185
rulemaking. *See also* law-making as focus of
    normative concern
  administrative, 5, 7–8, 75, 90, 116, 179,
    215
  democratic, 218–20, 247–8
  negotiated, 220–2, 229, 239, 248, 251

scale. *See* size
Scanlon, T. M., 279n.12
Scheuerman, William E., 287n.6
Schoenbrod, David, 270n.6
secret ballot, 198
self-originating sources of claims,
    individuals as, 63, 81, 138, 140,
    151, 181
Sen, Amartya, 124
separation of powers, 12–6, 244. *See also*
    republicanism
Shapiro, Scott J., 275n.4
Simon, Herbert, 115, 270n.2
Sincerity, 91–2, 166, 207
  of the losers, 212
  as a political virtue, 187
single-member districts, 199–200. *See also*
    representation, proportional
size
  of a democracy, 10, 13, 15–6
  of a legislative assembly, 199
social choice theory, 48–50, 56, 73, 125, 162,
    164, 204
social contract views. *See* contractarianism
solidarity or mutual concern
  pluralism as not fully blocking, 278n.29
  pluralism as threatening, 157
  some needed for democratic deliberation,
    208–9, 245
  supported by well-functioning
    democracies, 155, 208
sour grapes, 150
specialization by officials. *See* expertise;
    specification, ramifying
specification. *See also* public good
  as crucial constraint of agency reasoning,
    218–9
  defined, 104
  of elements of well-being, 154
  of ends, 104, 214, 246
  important to practical intelligence, 127
  as a mode of resolving conflicts, 108
  as potentially yielding new ends, 110
  as ramifying across agencies, 227, 234–5,
    237–9
  skill in generating a, 225
  and the transfer of motivation, 154–5
speech, freedom of. *See* freedoms, of speech
    and association
Spencer, Herbert, 30
Sreenivasan, Gopal, 31n., 256n.7, 278n.29

standards, process-independent, 50, 139, 140–41, 144, 213, 223–4
status quo bias, 43–4, 205, 244. *See also* unanimity
statutes, interpretation of, 10, 175. *See also* law, interpretation of; legislation
stem-cell research (illustrating deep compromise), 151–2, 190, 206, 208
Sunstein, Cass, 52, 289n.20
Supplemental Security Income (SSI) program, 6, 118, 235

Thompson, Dennis, 82, 186–7, 255n.37, 260n.39, 281n.17
trade-offs. *See* incommensurability of values; preferences
tragic choices, 106, 151. *See also* incommensurability of values
transportation for the disabled, 7, 80, 97–8, 100, 103–5, 107–10, 116, 120, 126, 130–2, 141, 144, 149, 174, 189–90, 201, 204, 214, 235, 250
trust
    in agency evaluative expertise, 224, 227–30
    in experts, generally, 199
    in government, 32
    mutual, 209–10
    in others' judgment, 171
truth, the concept of
    coherence aspect of, 134
    correspondence aspect of, 133
    fallibility aspect of, 134, 137, 139. *See also* fallibility, recognition of
    three aspects of the idea of, 133, 135
truth-orientation
    of agency reasoning, 131, 140–1, 214, 227
    and commitment, 135, 37
    in deep compromise, 159–60
    of democratic deliberation, 76–7, 131, 138–9, 140–1, 161, 176, 189, 245–6, 248–9
    idea explained, 133, 135
    implications of, for social choice theory, 259n.29
    not incompatible with persuasive rhetoric, 90–1
    of reasoning in general, 76–7, 135
    reconciled to majority rule, 206–8
    within processes of deep compromise, 158
Tuomela, Raimo, 278n.5
tyranny. *See* domination

unanimity, 14. *See also* status quo bias
    as an interpretation of nondomination, 43–4
    less fair than majority rule, 244
    as a seeming demand of rationalism, 203
    and welfarism, 42
Urban Mass Transit Act of 1970, 98
utilitarianism. *See also* welfarism
    avoided by public choice theory, 14
    as a basis of impersonal rule, 63
    as failing to ground nondomination, 43, 47
    here considered as a type of welfarism, 42

vagueness
    of ends, 104–5, 108, 116, 127
        no bar to instrumental reasoning, 117
    in legislation, 7, 98, 121, 240
        inevitable, yet to be minimized, 116–7, 217, 219, 250
    of the shared conception of the public good, 161
Velleman, J. David, 268n.15
virtue, civic. *See also* open-mindedness
    in general, 184, 209
    integrity and magnanimity, 186–8, 249
    public reasonableness, 81–3
voting behavior. *See also* secret ballot
    expressive theory of, 15, 46, 198
    manipulation of, 49, 204
    strategic, 168, 205, 211
voting paradox, the, 49, 61

Warren, Earl, 9
Weber, Max, 9, 16, 115, 151, 270n.4
welfarism
    and interpretations of nonarbitrary power, 38, 41–9
    normative individualism of, 49–51
Wicksell, Knut, 43, 258n.9
will of the people, the, 7–8. *See also* general will (Rousseau)
    affirmed by populism, 56–8
    cannot constitute a fundamental reason, 60
    distributed, 70, 72, 179
    dualism about, 68–9
    existence of, 67
    framed in part by legislators, 202

will of the people (*continued*)
  and the minority voter, 212
  monism about, 68, 70, 193
  normative significance of, 60–1, 65–6
  not an object of discovery, 61, 206, 212
  not definable in terms of a social choice
      function, 49
  the notion defended, 65
  partially articulated by agencies, 215

  procedural account of, 65–6, 69–70, 72,
      206, 217, 247
  radical conception of, 67
  reflective formation of, 180
  skepticism about, 56–7
Wolf, Susan, 275n.5

Young, Iris Marion, 192, 201, 265n.25,
      267n.15, 282n.22